CHANGING TIMES: CHALLENGES TO IDENTITY

To my family, for their love and support.

Changing Times: Challenges to Identity

12 year-olds in Belfast 1981 and 1992

JEAN WHYTE
Senior Lecturer in Psychology
Faculty of Health Sciences
Trinity College, Dublin

Avebury

Aldershot • Brookfield USA • Hong Kong • Singapore • Sydney

Published by
Avebury
Ashgate Publishing Limited
Gower House
Croft Road
Aldershot
Hants GU11 3HR
England

Ashgate Publishing Company
Old Post Road
Brookfield
Vermont 05036
USA

British Library Cataloguing in Publication Data

Whyte, Jean
  Changing Times: Challenges to Identity –
  12 Year-olds in Belfast 1981 and 1992
  I. Title
  305.235094167
ISBN 1 85972 212 1

Library of Congress Catalog Card Number: 95-81136

Printed and bound by Athenaeum Press, Ltd.,
Gateshead, Tyne & Wear.

Contents

Figures and tables   vi

Acknowledgements   ix

Introduction   1

1   Identity and its challenges   14

2   Changes in Northern Ireland   29

3   12 year-olds in Belfast, Dublin and London   50

4   Leisure for 12 year-olds 1981 and 1992   72

5   Parental salience and the children's autonomy   99

6   Reaching out beyond the family   118

7   Access to information   144

8   Knowledge about the present   168

9   Hopes for the future   191

10   Conclusions: Changing times: challenges to identity?   214

Questionnaire   241

References   252

Index   273

Figures and tables

Table	0.1	The sample	11
Figure	3.1	Ownership of household goods by group 1981 and 1992	56
Figure	3.2	Opportunities to earn money by group 1981 and 1992	57
Figure	3.3	Percentage of girls who had earned money by group 1981 and 1992	58
Figure	3.4	Percentage of boys who had earned money by group 1981 and 1992	58
Figure	3.5	Amounts of weekly pocket money given by location 1981 and 1992	60
Figure	3.6	Relative distribution of weekly pocket money by group 1981 and 1992	61
Figure	3.7	Mean amounts of pocket money for girls and boys	62
Figure	3.8	Relative amounts of pocket money received by girls and boys 1981 and 1992	62
Figure	3.9	Mean amount earned for jobs by group 1981 and 1992	63
Figure	3.10	Amounts of money earned for jobs by group 1981 and 1992	64
Figure	3.11	Mean amounts earned by girls and boys for jobs	64
Figure	3.12	Relative mean amounts earned by girls and boys 1981 and 1992	65
Figure	3.13	Basic household possessions plus availability of disposable income by group 1981 and 1992	66
Table	3.1	How they spent their money in 1981	68
Table	3.2	How they spent their money in 1992	68
Table	3.3	Differences between the sexes overall in patterns of expenditure 1981 and 1992	68
Figure	4.1	Girls' afternoon activities 1981 and 1992	75
Table	4.1	Girls' afternoon activities ranked: 1981	76
Table	4.2	Girls' afternoon activities ranked: 1992	76
Figure	4.2	Boys' afternoon activities 1981 and 1992	77
Table	4.3	Boys' afternoon activities ranked: 1981	77
Table	4.4	Boys' afternoon activities ranked: 1992	78
Figure	4.3	Girls' evening activities 1981 and 1992	79
Figure	4.4	Boys' evening activities 1981 and 1992	79

Figure	4.5	Girls' Saturday activities 1981 and 1992	80
Figure	4.6	Boys' Saturday activities 1981 and 1992	80
Figure	4.7	Girls' Sunday activities 1981 and 1992	82
Figure	4.8	Boys' Sunday activities 1981 and 1992	82
Figure	4.9	Girls' book preferences 1981 and 1992	85
Figure	4.10	Boys' book preferences 1981 and 1992	85
Figure	4.11	Girls' preferred television programmes 1981 and 1992	87
Figure	4.12	Boys' preferred television programmes 1981 and 1992	87
Figure	4.13	Games enjoyed by girls 1981 and 1992	89
Figure	4.14	Games enjoyed by boys 1981 and 1992	89
Figure	4.15	Girls who participated in team sports 1981 and 1992	91
Figure	4.16	Boys who participated in team sports 1981 and 1992	91
Figure	4.17	Girls' leisure activities 1981	92
Figure	4.18	Girls' leisure activities 1992	92
Figure	4.19	Boys' leisure activities 1981	93
Figure	4.20	Boys' leisure activities 1992	93
Table	4.6	Leisure activities of boys and girls 1981/1992	95
Figure	5.1	Nurturance of girls 1981 and 1992	107
Figure	5.2	Nurturance of boys 1981 and 1992	107
Figure	5.4	Salience of Mum 1981 and 1992	112
Figure	5.5	Salience of Dad 1981 and 1992	112
Figure	5.5	Salience of parents 1981 and 1992	112
Figure	5.6	Scores on Independence by group 1981 and 1992	113
Figure	5.7	Scores on Independence by sex 1981 and 1992	114
Figure	6.1	Household chores done by girls 1981 and 1992	126
Figure	6.2	Household chores done by boys 1981 and 1992	126
Figure	6.3	Mean scores on Commitment 1981 and 1992	130
Figure	6.4	Jobs done to earn money by location 1981 and 1992	132
Figure	6.5	Girls: jobs done to earn money 1981 and 1992	133
Figure	6.5	Boys: jobs done to earn money 1981 and 1992	133
Figure	6.7	Club membership by location 1981 and 1992	134
Figure	6.8	Attendance at clubs twice a week or more by location 1981 and 1992	134
Figure	6.9	Travels: mean scores by group 1981 and 1992	138
Figure	6.10	High scorers on 'Travels' by group 1981 and 1992	138
Figure	7.1	Types of newspaper read by groups in the sample 1981 and 1992	147
Figure	7.2	Percentage who watched television news by location 1981 and 1992	149
Figure	7.3	TV news: percentage who watched within 24 hours 1981 and 1992	149
Figure	7.4	Radio news: percentages who listened regularly by group 1981 and 1992	150
Figure	7. 5	'News': scores by group 1981 and 1992	151
Table	7.1	Rank order of items recalled from newspapers 1981	154
Table	7.2	Rank order of items recalled from television news 1981	156
Figure	7.6	Current events recalled from television and/or newapaper 1981 and 1992	157

Figure	7.7	Newspapers: percentages who recalled current affairs items by group 1981 and 1992	158
Table	7.3	Rank order of items recalled from newspapers 1992	158
Figure	7.8	Newspapers: items of current affairs recalled by group 1981 and 1992	159
Figure	7.9	Television: percentages who recalled current affairs items by group 1981 and 1992	161
Table	7.4	Items recalled from television news 1992	162
Figure	7.10	Television: items of current affairs recalled by group 1981 and 1992	162
Figure	8.1	Mean scores on politics questions 1981	176
Figure	8.2	Naming the Prime Minister or equivalent by group 1981	177
Figure	8.3	Political parties named by groups 1981	178
Figure	8.4	Politics questions: scores in 1981 and 1992	180
Figure	8.5	Naming Prime Minister or equivalent 1981 and 1992	181
Figure	8.6	Political parties named by groups 1981 and 1992	181
Figure	8.7	International items: percentages who gave correct responses 1981 and 1992	182
Figure	8.8	Knowledge of sports: mean scores by group 1981 and 1992	184
Figure	8.9	Sports knowledge: percentages who scored more than 8 by group 1981 and 1992	185
Figure	9.1	School as a means to a job by group 1981 and 1992	199
Figure	9.2	School as a means to qualifications 1981 and 1992	199
Figure	9.3	Wishes by group 1981 and 1992.	205
Figure	9.4	Ideal employment aspirations by group 1981 and 1992	207
Figure	9.6	Definitions of 'Happy people' by group 1981 and 1992	209
Figure	9.8	Generative views of the future by group 1981 and 1992	211

Acknowledgements

Any study which spans more than a decade and investigates context and its relationship to experience and to the development of personal identity and to future orientation will rely heavily on resources - mostly human in this case. This project was begun when I was Honorary Fellow in the Department of Psychology in Queen's University Belfast in 1981-82 and I am grateful to Ken Brown who made me feel welcome and offered access to resources for preparing the questionnaires in 1981. It probably would not have happened at all, however, but for the support and encouragement of Irené Turner, in that Department, who maintained a lively interest in the project and provided a sage sounding board until her most untimely death in 1994.

The participating schools are greatly in my debt and I wish to thank the principals, teachers and children for their cooperation. They have been given a summary of the findings relevant to their own groups. I am especially grateful to those who were able to participate for a second time in 1992. This added immensely to the value of the study.

With a move to Trinity College Dublin in 1985, the original data remained practically untouched because of other commitments in spite of the urgings of my husband John, who sensed its value. It was not until some time after his unexpected and premature death in 1990 that I was able to consider the final shape of the study and subsequently undertake the second stage of data collection and analysis.

I was helped at various stages in these tasks in a spirit of cross-border cooperation by Sarah Traynor, Amanda Gallagher and Tríona O hÉalaigh, undergraduate students from the School of Psychology in the University of Ulster To them my thanks. They provided a great stimulus. Trinity College was also supportive in providing me with a means of accommodating them, of producing the questionnaire for 1992 and of analyzing the findings by computer.

When the time came to get it together on paper, I was fortunate to be granted a Fulbright Fellowship and an invitation to be Visiting Fellow at the University of North Carolina, Chapel Hill, North Carolina for the academic year 1994-95. There I benefitted from having time and space and the availability of resources in the Department of Psychology and at the Center for Developmental Science where I was very hospitably received. My thanks to the Fulbright Foundation and especially to Jaan Valsiner and Bob Cairns whose support and friendship I appreciated enormously.

Drafts of the book were read and commented on by a number of people at different stages. Some were 'outsiders' in the USA to whom Northern Ireland was unfamiliar territory - like Glen Elder, Jaan Valsiner, Bob Cairns, Beverly Cairns, Martha Cox and Gilbert Gottlieb and I hope that I have taken account of their comments sufficiently to make it accessible to a non-Northern Ireland readership; I appreciate very much their generosity in sharing their views. The 'insider' readers who have seen it all happening in Northern Ireland were also extremely helpful. They included Ed Cairns, Jeremy Harbison, Joan Harbison, Karen Trew and Brian Turner. The final version is an amalgam of some of their suggestions and some of my own, but I alone bear the responsibility for any limitations.

Finally I thank my family, Nicholas, William, Caroline and Nicholas's wife Anne who accepted the notion of their mother taking off for a year alone in a strange unknown place with marvellous equanimity and continued to support and encourage me; and I am particularly grateful for the practical skills of my sister Nora who was especially helpful in the final stages of frantic proof-reading and checking. I hope that the results are worthy of all the effort.

Jean Whyte
Trinity College, Dublin
September 1995

Introduction

Introduction

The project described in this book began in 1981 with a survey of everyday family life as experienced by 12 year-olds at that time in Belfast, Northern Ireland. By 1981 the 'Troubles' or occurrences of violent civil unrest which had been dormant for some decades and had resurfaced in 1969, had been a constant feature of daily life in Northern Ireland for 12 years. The children in the study were just about born when the 'Troubles' started and had lived all their lives in the shadow and tension of street disturbances, bombings, riots, barricades, sectarian massacres and assassinations on the one hand and on the other with the presence of armed police and other security forces on the streets as they endeavoured to contain the problem. Both 'sides' brought their own kinds of stress to the 'ordinary' population. Concerns were continuously expressed about the effects of the situation on children. It was feared that, for example in the long term, many would be socialized into accepting as normal a higher level of violence and aggression in everyday life than had hitherto been the case, that the social cognition of children exposed to the violence on the streets and on television, would be deficient or deviant and that there would be other psychologically maladaptive outcomes.

Several lines of research arising from these concerns have been developed since the early 1970s by psychologists based both inside and outside Northern Ireland, (reviewed by Cairns, 1987, Cairns and Toner, 1993, Cairns, 1994, Toner, 1994, Cairns, Wilson, Trew and Gallagher, 1995, Cairns and Cairns, 1995). Among them are attempts to understand the impact of the political conflict on the mental health of children and adults, studies directed at understanding the dynamics of the conflict especially through social identity theory and reports evaluating methods of reconciliation especially through education. On the whole the results found on the 'effects' of the 'Troubles' have not borne out the prophets of doom and gloom as will be seen when the findings from some of these studies are summarized later in this Introduction. And while identity has been pinpointed by some researchers as an important construct which could help explain the dynamics of the conflict, it looks as if the centrality of the self-concept for the development of identity within the individual has not been fully taken into account by studies to date. However, they will provide a background for the study described in this book which differed from

1

them in its aims and in the framework adopted for the interpretation of the data.

The development of this project: from 'social address' to 'life course'

The initial model used in the present study was the 'social address' framework which enables a comparison of developmental outcomes for children or adults living in contrasting environments as defined by geography, or by social background. The aim was to look at children and their families who appeared to be coping, who had not been referred for psychological or psychiatric help as far as was known and to try to establish what everyday family life was like for them in 'Troubles'-torn Belfast. This contrasts with the more usual focus of psychological research, which tends to be deficit-oriented and which tends to investigate 'ecologies of family disorganization and developmental disarray' (Bronfenbrenner, 1986). By comparing children in disadvantaged areas of (Catholic) West Belfast and (Protestant) East Belfast with children of similar socio-economic level, living in similar suburban environments and of similar general educational standing in Dublin and London it was hoped that we might find differences in socialization practices which contribute to self-concept and identity formation and which might explain the apparent 'resilience' of Northern Ireland children (McWhirter, 1983b). A questionnaire was drawn up and data collected in the period November 1981–January 1982.

Time passed, life events intervened, and while the initial analysis of the 1981 data gave rise to a number of papers and publications (Whyte, Jean, 1983a, 1983b, 1984, 1986, 1988, 1989a, 1992a, 1993a), the shortcomings of the social address framework as a basis for a satisfactory investigation of the variable of interest gradually became apparent. Although, like a surveyor's grid, this paradigm provides a useful way of describing at least the surface of events, researchers generally want to go a little beyond that in looking for explanations and since the 1980s there has been a shift to models which make time, context and process more salient dimensions of theory and analysis and which offer the means of considering intervening structures or processes through which the environment might affect the course of development. The life course model (Elder, 1994) and the ecological model (Bronfenbrenner, 1986) are almost like two sides of the same coin. The life course model favours a framing statement which views the sociocultural background as a point of departure and a developmental study guided by such a frame would investigate the process whereby this environment makes a difference to children's lives and behaviour. Research in the tradition of an ecology of human development would focus on characteristics of the individual or organism and identify relevant ecological influences.

The opportunity to repeat the initial study in 1992, in the same schools, in the same cities, with a new generation of 12 year-olds, led to a reappraisal of the underlying model of analysis, though not of the method - exactly the same questionnaire was used. The adoption of a life course paradigm seemed appropriate in an investigation of the influence of context on development and vice versa. This approach takes into account the impact of social forces over time and enables one to evaluate their developmental consequences. In the present study, the added factors of historical time events and structural social changes in Northern Ireland in the interval between timepoints when data were collected could, by using the life course paradigm, be accorded recognition of their relevance for the socialization processes and ultimately the formation of the self-concept and identity of the children

2

involved. This was the framework within which the data from both timepoints were eventually analyzed.

Studies of environment-development interaction

Previous research in Northern Ireland relating environmental factors to aspects of individual development has been mostly confined on the one hand to the direct effects of the violence arising from the 'Troubles', and on the other to the effects of segregated education. Some of this research with children and adults has investigated the psychological sequelae of specific incidents (Wilson and Cairns, 1994), of upward and downward trends in the incidence of violence (Fee, 1983), and of the high or low intensity of violence in particular locations at particular points in time (Cairns and Wilson, 1989). Studies which investigate the psychological consequences for individuals of changes over time in Northern Ireland in the socio-historical environment, beyond, though including, trends in the violence - along the lines of Elder's (1974) *Children of the Great Depression* - could contribute a great deal to our understanding of the situation. It would be interesting too to be able to say whether individuals whose self-concepts had been formed by socialization practices and attitudes specific to Northern Ireland had in their turn been responsible for developing particular socio-environmental conditions. But studies of how personalities have influenced the environmental context are even rarer, and not just in Northern Ireland (Runyan, 1988, Turner, 1988).

The dearth of even descriptive studies of the interface between social and family conditions and personality development is true not only for Northern Ireland - about which it has been written that, in proportion to its size, it is possibly the most heavily researched place on earth, but also for other countries. Indeed, the literature resounds with cries pleading the desirability of such studies. (Magnusson, 1981, Montemayor and Flannery, 1990, Kreppner and Lerner, 1989, Damon, 1989, Van Hasselt and Hersen, 1987, Goodnow, 1986; Elder, Modell and Parke, 1994, Silbereisen, Eyferth and Rudinger, 1986). There is by now, however, a substantial literature, providing models of the life course approach applied to a number of countries on a microlevel, which deals with the intersection of biography and history with social structure and with the dynamics of multiple interdependent pathways (Baltes and Schaie, 1973, Harevan, 1982, Modell, 1989, Moen, Dempster-McClain and Williams, 1992, Clausen, 1993). The present study is therefore very timely.

Using the life-course approach

The selection of the self concept as the central focus of the study and of the life course framework for analyzing the data had consequences for the composition of this book and made it necessary to expand it beyond a simple report of the findings. The study took account of recent advances in theory which place the self firmly in a socio-historical context and some account of these advances will follow in Chapter One. Three points from that literature stood out:

- A recognition that the self is dynamic,
- the proposal that construals of self can be very divergent between cultures (Markus and Kitayama, 1991), and
- the idea that 'possible selves' or those elements of the self-concept that represent the individual's goals, fears and anxieties reflect the extent to which the self is socially determined and constrained and will be quite responsive to change in the environment (Markus and Nurius, 1986).

These points and their application to the study described in this book will be discussed in Chapter One.

It was realized that for the reader to make sense of the data within the life course framework, more background information on the situation in the country which constitutes the main focus of interest, Northern Ireland, would have to be included than is customary in books written by psychologists about child development in context. Accordingly, in Chapter Two a thread of salient events is spun for the period leading up to the first data collection in 1981 and between then and the second data collection in 1992. This gives an indication of both positive and negative changes over time in the political and economic environment and in the kinds of social structures supporting the development of the children and their 'possible selves' to which data in the following chapters may be related. The effects of some of those changes will have been mediated through the children's interactions with significant adults in their lives and an attempt is made in that chapter to indicate the 'psychological climate' within the groups at the times of data collection.

The scene is set in this Introduction for those two 'background' chapters by a summary of relevant research since 1969 by psychologists and others on Northern Ireland. This is followed by an extended outline of the aims and methods of the present study.

Psychological research on the 'Troubles'

A number of areas have been explored by psychologists in trying to understand the causes and consequences of the conflict and these have been reviewed most recently by Cairns, Wilson, Trew and Gallagher (1995), by Cairns and Cairns (1995) and earlier most comprehensively by Cairns (1987). Those of concern for the present summary, since they investigate areas relevant to self-concept and identity, include research on:

- the impact of segregated vs. integrated education on attitudes
- awareness of ethnic identity
- effects on mental health

The educational context

The school system in which over 90 per cent of Catholics and Protestants are educated separately in Northern Ireland is an obvious candidate for the role of differential values reinforcer. The main issue of concern for psychologists has been the effect segregation in schools might be having on the attitudes of each community towards the other and on the value systems they are developing. It is a complex issue, compounded by the fact that segregation also exists in other areas of life to varying extents in different areas of the country and within different sectors of the population. There may be increased integration in some areas of life for some people, but not in housing where segregation in housing has been increasing at a fast rate through the 70s and 80s as people moved out of previously 'mixed' areas to be with 'their own'. By 1991, about half of the people in Northern Ireland lived in areas that are more than 90 per cent Catholic or 90 per cent Protestant and only about 7 per cent live in areas with roughly equal numbers of Catholics and Protestants.

Studies on schools have been reported by researchers from different disciplines, and have been reviewed by Darby, Murray, Batts, Dunn, Farren and Harris (1977), Cairns (1987) and Darby and Dunn (1987). But they use different kinds of samples, at different timepoints, starting from different baselines and asking slightly different questions. The results cannot really be readily agglomerated. For example there has been evidence that stereotyping and prejudice may be promoted by a segregated system (Murray, 1985) and that the political values which are part of the hidden curriculum informally communicated to pupils may be instrumental in instituting and reinforcing values which are divisive. On the other hand it has been found that education in an integrated setting does not inevitably result in more open-mindedness (Rose, 1971, Trew, 1986). These findings should be seen as bounded by time and place and by the unidimemensional focus used as a basis for explanation.

There has been evidence that in the past, the school systems differed in aspects of the curriculum, apart from the expected one of religious instruction (Barritt and Carter, 1962; Robinson, 1971) and in terms of preparation of life after school, this could have had an effect on the self-concept. Catholic schools in the past gave less weight to science and maths (Osborne and Cormack, 1989). Perceptions of nationality and local history presented in schools of different traditions have been found to be at variance. This could be important in determining an individual's view of his or her place in the world and the contribution he or she could make to it. There were also what could be deemed 'structural' problems - differences in the funding available to different types of schools and in the provision of grammar school places for Catholics which could have had an impact on people's perceptions about their role in society.

But there have been changes in recent years, although the impact of the changes will be difficult to assess when so many other things have changed and knowledge of baselines is patchy. Corken (1989) found that the numbers of schools teaching Irish history in 1989 had greatly increased over what had been reported in earlier years. Since 1992 additional funding: has been made available to Catholic schools and extra grammar school places provided (Moffat, 1992). The introduction of the programme 'Education for Mutual Understanding' which provides systematic curriculum-based opportunities for children from schools of different denominations to work together is being viewed as an effective vehicle for change (Smith, 1995) and is being taken up by many schools.

In addition a number of integrated schools have been founded since 1980 (17 elementary and four second-level) and although they only cater for around 4 per cent of the school going population so far, their supporters are very enthusiastic about the possibilities they present for progress. Some studies have compared these with 'unplanned' integrated schools and segregated schools *inter alia* on their effects on attitudes and values (Cairns, Dunn and Giles, 1992). But as Gallagher (1992) has pointed out, the integrated schools are still so few in number and differ along so many dimensions from other schools that valid comparisons are practically impossible. Yet, Irwin (1993) in a submission to the Opsahl Commission based on interviews with children in Lagan College, the first of these planned integrated schools, found that the children themselves were convinced that integrated education offered a way forward and Cairns, Dunn, Morgan and McClenaghan (1992) reported that children in both planned and unplanned integrated schools were making friends on a cross-community basis.

A hope that change in attitudes over time is possible appears to underlie these initiatives. The present study contributes to the debate since its design explicitly addresses the question of change in the environment and its possible effects on the self-concept. The children in this study were attending 'segregated' schools and living in areas which were more than 90 per cent segregated with regard to housing and it is possible that both of these factors were having an influence on their self-concept and their future orientation. Although we did not address the question explicitly of their attitudes towards the other community it will be interesting in the context of the general changes affecting schools to see whether there were changes over time in their view of themselves.

Ethnic identity studies

Using Tajfel's social identity theory as a starting point (Tajfel and Turner, 1979), some researchers have looked for the causes and social consequences of social division in individuals' awareness of ethnic identity (Cairns, 1982, Cairns, 1989). This theory is based on the linked concepts of social categorization, social identity and social comparison, on which some more detail will be given in Chapter One. It has been found that social categorization plays an important role in Northern Ireland and that children have acquired the skills necessary to carry it out by age 10 or 11 (Cairns, 1980, Houston, Crozier and Walker, 1990). The relationship of ethnic identity to the self-concept, which is the central concern of the present study will be discussed further in Chapter One.

Up to now studies based on this approach have failed to yield clear-cut findings according to Cairns, Wilson, Trew and Gallagher (1995). Most of the evidence suggests that young people are not in any way obsessed with their identity and these authors say further that the findings indicate the importance of taking into account the multiplicity of identities that can be subsumed under category labels and that it may also be pointing to the problems inherent in studying a complex social issue from a single theoretical perspective. This had been suggested also by Gough, Robinson, Kremer and Mitchell (1992) and by Trew (1992). And it has been pointed out that this approach assumes that the problems between the groups arise from misperceptions held by one about the other which could be amenable to correction because they are the result of simple lack of knowledge through lack of contact due to segregated housing and segregated schooling.

If we take the view however that the self-concept underlying identity rather than identity *per se* is paramount and that the self-concept may be subject to the totality of influences within the environment, a number of consequences follow. Educational and housing segregation, although important, are seen not to be the only factors exerting influence on the development of self-concept and identity, but

6

space is made for the role of societal structures and their outcomes for the individual's view of him or herself (self-concept) and of him or herself in relation to the other group (identity). Factors within the societal structures must be examined (as will be seen in Chapter Two) in order to establish whether for example there might have been social injustice, either sporadically or as an endemic feature of society before the 'Troubles' (O'Callaghan, 1989), the effects of which might underlie attitudes and feelings expressed towards the self and others. And this more widely based approach leaves open the possibility of change in self-concept, not in identity but in the meanings associated with identity, which could happen in conjunction with changes in environmental conditions (Deaux, 1991).

Effects on mental health

Research looking for evidence of psychopathology in samples of Northern Ireland children who had not been referred for diagnosis or treatment, has not been conclusive. McWhirter (1983a) compared children in Belfast and Manchester using standardized measures and her results indicated that children in Northern Ireland did not appear to be any more neurotic/anxious than their English or North American counterparts, although their 'psychoticism' scores were higher, especially if they were from more violence-prone areas. Whyte and Montgomery (1984) found higher than normal neuroticism scores at age 11 and at age 14 on the JEPI in a group of Belfast boys, when they were compared to a pre-1969 Northern Ireland sample and to the mostly English standardization sample. McGrath and Wilson (1985) and Fee (1980, 1983) presented results suggesting that children in Northern Ireland had a somewhat higher Rutter scale (Rutter, Cox, Tupling, Berger and Yule, 1975) score than children in other parts of the world and that this was linked to direct or indirect experiences of 'Troubles'-related violence.

In addition, there has been some work on clinical groups. Blease (1983) and McAuley and Troy (1983) reported research on maladjusted school children in a Belfast centre and on the impact of urban conflict and violence on children referred to a child psychiatry clinic. Research on the association between political conflict and the mental health of adults has also been reported from clinical case studies (Lyons, 1974, Hadden, Rutherford and Merrett, 1978, Loughrey, Bell, Kee, Roddy and Curran, 1988) and shows that many people who have been innocently caught up in the violence have suffered adverse psychological reactions. A higher rate of psychiatric admission has been found for Northern Ireland in 1981 than for Scotland or England (Orbell, Trew and McWhirter, 1990) and surveys using the General Health Questionnaire (Goldberg, 1978) in 1983 and 1984 found that perceptions of the level of political violence significantly influenced psychiatric morbidity after the effects of other variables - employment status, marital status and family size were controlled (Cairns and Wilson, 1985).

Research reported in Harbison and Harbison (1980), and in Harbison (1983, 1989a) however, yielded contradictory views on whether the effects of the violence had been as negative as had been feared and it was suggested that economic factors and social disadvantage are substantial confounding issues in any assessment of outcome (Harbison, 1989b). The confounding effects of economic disadvantage have been pointed out by many other writers also. However, Cairns and Wilson (1989a) concluded that there was no evidence of widespread mental disorder as a result of the 'Troubles', although they acknowledge that referral and reporting systems were far

7

from attaining from what would be considered even a minimum level of reliability in other countries such as the USA over the period studied although there was a noticeable incremental improvement in services during that time.

The children in the present study lived in areas of Belfast which would have been classified as socially disadvantaged and 'high in street violence' in 1981 and although this was not asked about directly, the responses to the 'free time' items suggested that some at least had had some contact with it, perhaps more than would admit it to an outsider. In 1992, however, the nature of the violence had changed from general disturbances to more specific incidents, such as sectarian assassinations, in more random locations. This meant that the risk of personal injury or worse was still there with the associated tension, but that the likelihood of personal active involvement in the perpetration of violence was considerably less for these children. The 'free time' activities did not hint at any such involvement.

Child development in context

Since children's psychological development is a complex texture woven from genetic, familial and environmental threads, differences between the self-concepts of children living in different places and at the same or different times are likely to be related to some more deeply-rooted elements, or values and attitudes within the culture which have impacted on their personalities (Hettema, 1989) through the process of socialization. The period around age 12 is generally recognized as being very significant for the development of personal identity and it has been reported that while important changes in the organization of the self-concept (an aspect of identity) have been noted in early adolescence (Livesley and Bromley, 1973) there is factorial stability after that age (Dusek and Flaherty, 1981) if conditions in society are reasonably constant. Our questions were:

- whether the experiences of socialization in Belfast, Dublin and London differed in some essential aspects for the children in the sample
- whether there was any association between socialization processes and aspects of the self-concept expressed by the children in 1981
- whether there were any associations between socialization practices and environmental conditions in 1981 and 1992
- whether there were changes in the children over time which could be linked to changes in socialization and in societal structures over the period 1981-1992.

Answering the questions

Socialization experiences were investigated by determining how their daily lives compared with those of young people of similar age, socioeconomic background and general educational standing in other big cities - Dublin and London. In looking at the young people in the present study we asked whether among the socialization experiences in Belfast there could be some that might have contributed to aspects of their self-concept such as the 'resilience' of the children. If differences were found between the children in access to opportunities for developing their personal resources such as experiences of self-efficacy, which would have an effect on their self-concept, as well as familial and social resources, we might have part of an

8

explanation for the apparent lack of detrimental effects: as evidenced by Cairns and Wilson (1989a). The extent to which children - and indeed adults - can call on such protective factors is generally felt to be critical in determining their level of resilience to physical and psychological challenges (Kobasa and Puccetti, 1983).

The link between socialization practices and outcomes in terms of other aspects of self-concept and personal identity was made by asking about the children's orientation towards the future, their 'possible selves', their attitude towards education and their social intelligence as shown by their level of 'declarative knowledge'. Such an association should, of course, be made only with extreme caution but if we found differences between 12 year-olds who had been brought up in Catholic and Protestant communities respectively, we could probably assume that such differences also existed between the adults in those communities in 1981. If it were found that some of these elements underlying personal identity were differentially developed in children from the Catholic and Protestant communities, we might have part of an explanation for the continuation of the problem situation and the extreme difficulties encountered by those attempting to promote constructive communication between the two communities in Northern Ireland.

The analysis of the effects of societal conditions is based on research which has found associations between societal structures and personality development in other cultures. These are extrapolated to the Northern Ireland situation. Chapter Two will be important in setting the context for such relationships.

The possibility of change was investigated by adopting a model which collected data at two timepoints from the same environments and similar groups based on the same instrument. As early as 1980 Heskin (1980) pointed out that studies relating to the conflict in Northern Ireland and in particular to its effects on children, frequently assume that nothing has changed since 1969. In fact, the truth is more complicated. In the first place, there is more to the context of development than episodes of violence though these tend to get media attention. For example there have been structural changes in the way in which the affairs of the country and its citizens are conducted (Bardon 1992, Wichert, 1991, Livingstone and Morison, 1995), and shifts in the stances taken by the chief protagonists playing the political field (Bew, Gibbon and Patterson, 1995). People have learnt to deal with new and different institutions, there has been an increase in the number of community development associations and groups which have involved local people and people from different traditions working together and more detail will be given on these changes in Chapter Two. In addition, as Cairns and Toner (1993) have pointed out, the violence has varied in intensity, in quality and by geographical location from year to year.

It is clear therefore that the events which provide a context for children's development have been far from constant. Undoubtedly, it takes some time for the psychological implications of such changes to make an impact even on adults - but perhaps such an impact is evidenced by the apparently determined, although snail-like, movement towards negotiation for a peaceful solution which began in the summer of 1993. If we accept the assumption behind any theory of socialization (Hurrelmann, 1988) - i.e. that socially conveyed influences on the development of personality actually exist and that a human being can become a subject who is capable of social action only through assimilation into and active dealing with the social and material environment, we would expect to find that changes in the wider social context would influence the beliefs and expectations of individuals. And we would expect to see some effects of the changes in the societal structures of Northern Ireland reflected in the values expressed by the children in our sample in 1992.

In the present instance, the replication of the 1981 study in 1992 provided evidence to support an informed view about the effects of background events on the lives of children and families over that period.

Rationale

It was felt that this book could be useful at several levels:
* Firstly, in terms of the data reported, it could provide baseline information about socialization practices and other indices of familial context, hitherto unrecorded in Northern Ireland, which would enable comparisons to be made with the situation in other locations (Dublin and London in the present instance) and with the 1981 and 1992 situations at a later date.
* Secondly, by involving the kinds of families and children normally treated as control groups (and not clinical groups, or families who had come to the attention of the authorities for some reason) we could get some idea of the ecologies that 'sustain and strengthen the constructive processes in society, the family and the self' (Bronfenbrenner, 1986)
* Thirdly, in terms of the research model adopted, differences between the socialization experiences of children in Belfast, Dublin and London and between those of the two communities in Belfast could be related to outcomes in terms of aspects of identity as expressed by the children.
* Fourthly, in terms of the time span of the study, it was possible to determine whether there were changes over time in the socialization practices and identity outcomes.
* Finally, the framework provided by the life course model permitted an investigation of the possibility that changes within the family, as reflected in aspects of identity as expressed by the children, were linked to changes in the wider society.

How the study was carried out

The participants in the study from (Catholic) West Belfast, (Protestant) East Belfast, Dublin and London were selected from neighbourhoods which appeared to be comparable in terms of socio-economic level of participants. They were all situated in suburban housing developments, a mixture of public authority and private housing, which had initially been built in the 1960s to accommodate families rehoused from inner city areas. Families lived in one-family units, which consisted of terraced or semi-detached houses mostly with small gardens and some lived in apartments. The neighbourhoods served by the schools in Belfast and Dublin were stable, with very little movement of population in and out (as measured by children joining and leaving the schools at times other than the end of the school year); the London neighbourhoods had been stable in 1981, but turned out to be less stable when we went back there in 1992. All four neighbourhoods could be characterized as being representative of .social disadvantage; in their own cities in terms of the percentage of unemployed heads of household (50-70 per cent in West Belfast; 20-25 per cent in East Belfast, 40 per cent in London, 30 per cent in Dublin as estimated by the schools).

The schools approached were second level comprehensive, mixed ability schools serving areas in West Belfast, East Belfast, Dublin and London with parental employment mainly at the skilled manual or unskilled level. The schools in Dublin were coeducational, those in Belfast and London were all single sex in 1981, but in 1992, one of the East Belfast schools had become coeducational and since this had consequences for the number of boys and girls who could be included, an additional coeducational school in the same area was approached and agreed to invite its pupils to participate. One of the West Belfast schools had closed by 1992 and the school which had taken over its catchment area agreed to approach its pupils who consented to participate. The London schools were ethnically more mixed than the Belfast or Dublin schools - about 40 per cent non-Caucasian children in the girls' school and 55 per cent in the boys' school in 1981. The less stable nature of their neighbourhoods is reflected in the increase in non-Caucasian pupils in the schools over the time period of the study (to 50 per cent in the girls' school and 65 per cent in the boys' school). All the schools which participated in the study were broadly similar in academic performance and were non-selective.

The children were distributed as seen in Table 0.1. Two complete class groups of 12 year-olds in the first year of secondary education were selected from the middle range of ability in each school. The total number of participants was 404 in 1981 and 476 in 1992. Each participant was given an individual copy of the 18 page questionnaire and completed it in writing during one class period of about 50 minutes without consultation with the researcher, who supervised, or with peers. Previous research has established that this is a reliable method of obtaining information from this age group (Bill, 1977). They were assured of confidentiality and that spelling was not being tested and no assistance was offered; this resulted in some very ingeniously constructed, though still comprehensible, responses.

Table 0.1
The sample

Year	West Belfast Girls	West Belfast Boys	East Belfast Girls	East Belfast Boys	Dublin Girls	Dublin Boys	London Girls	London Boys
1981	41	34	49	47	51	56	60	66
1992	64	56	52	78	44	71	51	60

Format of the questionnaire

Questions were a mixture of structured yes / no and multiple choice together with open-ended items some of which required a single word answer and some of which were of the sentence completion type. Individual questions, with some exceptions, were not grouped in the questionnaire under the topic headings as they will be presented here but were differently ordered. Details are given throughout the text as the findings are discussed. The questionnaire is reproduced after Chapter Ten.

11

The responses were analyzed firstly by individual question - the percentages giving each kind of answer were calculated and compared across groups and timepoints. Composite variables were created by summing, for example, affirmative responses to a range of items within particular categories and a score was awarded for each item counted. Differences between groups on these scores within timepoints were tested for significance using Chi Sq for numbers of children and ANOVAs for scores. But statistical tests were not used to compare groups across time as it was felt that the numbers were too small, there were too many uncontrollable variables and we were content to try to define trends.

Outline of the book

Chapter 1 sets the study in the context of research on early adolescence with specific reference to the elements and processes involved in self-concept and identity formation; research on evidence for differences in identity among the communities in Northern Ireland is reviewed .

Chapter 2 provides some background on events in Northern Ireland in the period leading up to and during the children's lifetime.

Chapter 3 gives information about the sample - their standard of living, disposable income, expenditure patterns..

Chapters 4, 5, 6 and 7 present the first set of findings. These relate to the context and experiences of socialization in the daily lives of the children, including leisure activities. The composite variables described in these chapters have been designated 'grounding variables' since they constitute variables arising from the environment and contributing to the context in which the children live. They include variables made up of measures of child autonomy/independence and parental salience, of outreach to the community outside the family for leisure and work activities and of measures of access to information. It is suggested that the grounding variables would have contributed to aspects of their personal identity such as their sense of personal efficacy and self- esteem (part of 'resilience'), their declarative and procedural knowledge (part of 'social intelligence'), their awareness of their own location within the social system which would in turn have influenced their perception of options and possible selves, their interest in societal action and their own aspirations and future orientation. The description of these variables also provides a baseline, lacking up to now, to which the findings of future investigations may be compared.

Chapters 8 and 9 present the second set of findings. These relate to a key element of the children's identity formation, their orientation towards the future, which gives us a clue about the range of 'possible selves' they envisaged for themselves. This aspect was selected as it would seem to be important in the context of any society, and in particular a society such as that in Northern Ireland, to know how its younger citizens feel about the future. The composite variables contributing to this orientation are designated 'outcome variables' and an aim of the study was to investigate to what extent they could be deemed to be outcomes of the 'grounding variables'. The 'outcome variables' are derived from measures of their declarative knowledge or knowledge about the world, which contributes to their social intelligence, their attitudes towards education, and their wishes and aspirations for the future.

Chapter 10 addresses the issue of whether the differences in 'outcome variables', which were found between the children in the locations under study, could be seen as being related to differences in the 'grounding variables'. Differences found between girls and boys which are masked by but also contribute to the overall picture are discussed as are possible reasons for the changes which were observed over the time period involved in both grounding and outcome variables in some of the locations. We then set the findings in the broader societal context and suggest that these changes reflect underlying developments in the communities in which these children lived and that there are implications for social and educational policy-makers.

1 Identity and its challenges

Introduction

Our 12 year-olds were at the stage of early adolescence and the chief task of early adolescence is said to be identity formation (Erickson, 1968). Since, as we have seen, it is possible that aspects of self-concept and personal identity could be contributing to the conflict in Northern Ireland it would seem important to clarify what exactly we are talking about with regard to identity.

Current theories propose that identity formation is an interactive process involving factors intrinsic to the adolescent, to his or her family as a whole and in its parts, and factors intrinsic to the social and cultural environment made up of peers and adults other than parents as well as the general structures and ecology of the society in which the development is taking place (Magnusson and Törestad, 1993). Opportunities to develop autonomy in moving through the social environment, to develop rôles within societal structures and to gain recognition for those rôles will contribute to the strength and stability of one's personal identity (Hurrelmann, 1988, p. 51). This could be deemed 'scaffolding' in the Vygotskyan sense. And the relationship between the self and social behaviour is not unidirectional; behavioural strategies that an individual adopts will affect his or her self-concept (Banaji and Prentice, 1994).

It follows that a person's identity will be influenced by the kind of scaffolding available at periods crucial for identity formation, that communities may differ in the kinds of scaffolding they offer, and that this can vary also with historical time with implications for the personal identity formation of their members. Once established, the identity of the individual will be sustained by the social and personal scaffolding mentioned above. Researchers in cultural psychology believe that the constituted self is variable across temporal and spatial regions of the world and that it is possible to characterize that variation theoretically in terms of independent vs. interdependent, egocentric vs. sociocentric and other contrasts. (Schweder and Sullivan, 1993). It would not be surprising therefore if differences were found between Protestants and Catholics in Northern Ireland given the history of events there (see Chapter Two).

Some researchers have suggested that there is evidence of differences between groups in Northern Ireland, starting with a biological basis proposed first by Fraser

14

(1973), who contended that community inbreeding in Northern Ireland had exaggerated unique characteristics which resulted in two races which contrast emotionally, ideologically and physically. Burton (1978) found himself becoming aware of cues - name, face, dress, demeanour, residence, education, language and iconography which those 'in the know' use to distinguish one community from the other. Other researchers have proposed that specific personality differences can be discerned between Catholics and Protestants and have presented findings in support of this.

But research evidence on differences between the groups has not all pointed in the same direction. On the one hand some findings have given Catholics credit for being more liberal-minded - for example, Catholics were found to have a more charitable attitude towards Protestants (Jahoda and Harrison, 1975), Protestants to show more social distance towards Catholics than vice versa (Fairleigh, 1975); Catholics revealed more general and religious tolerance (Salters, 1970) a greater understanding of (Doob and Foltz, 1973) and more openness towards Protestants than the other way around (Greer, 1985, Arthur, 1974, Russell, 1974). But on the other hand, researchers who looked at samples in different locations and at different times from those already cited, found evidence that Catholics were more hostile and prejudiced towards Protestants than vice versa (O'Donnell, 1977, Kremer, Barry and McNally, 1986) and Trew (1980) was unable to replicate the findings of Fairleigh or of Jahoda and Harrison, albeit at a different time and in a different place.

On the question of how far the communities differ, John Whyte (1990) provides illustrations of the spectrum of opinion in the literature. On the one extreme are those who imply that differences in attitudes towards almost all subjects and differences in the rates of participation in certain activities are almost total (Beattie, 1979, p. 250), and antagonism between the communities is very bitter (Burton, 1978, Jenkins, 1982, 1983, Nelson, 1984), and on the other we find authors who stress the common bonds between communities (Glassie, 1982, p. 645, Buckley, 1988, p. 54, Larsen, 1982, p. 135). Rose (1971), in an attitude survey carried out before the onset of the 'Troubles' found striking similarities between the attitudes of Catholics and Protestants on many issues with differences confined mostly to the spheres of politics and ecumenism. Lorenc and Branthwaite (1986) found no differences between groups of 10-11 year-old Catholic and Protestant children in Northern Ireland in their evaluation of political violence. And in one of the few studies which compared children in Northern Ireland, the Republic of Ireland and England (O'Kane and Cairns, 1988), and identified groups by culture while controlling for religion (they were all attending Catholic schools), the Northern Irish children were not found to be more or less conservative than those in the other locations.

On the whole these studies have categorized the groups by their reference group orientation, the 'social' or 'group' label, since religious affiliation and political allegiance are usually part of it. This is obviously an important factor differentiating the communities and the term 'identity' has been used in this way by a number of writers who have made valuable contributions to our understanding of the situation in Northern Ireland (see for example Murphy, 1978, Fennell, 1989, Belfrage, 1987, Stewart, 1977, Rea, 1982, Townshend, 1988, New Ireland Forum Report, 1984, O'Connor, 1993, Trew, 1994, Kinahan, 1995, Dunlop, 1995). But the general variety of the findings based on categorizing the groups by social, group or ethnic identity and the inescapable conclusion that they do not give clearcut and consistent pointers to differences between the groups as labeled and yet the fact that it is generally agreed that the communities are distinct from one another suggests that there must be sources of differences which go deeper than that of social, group or ethnic identity. This would tie in with the conclusion reached by Cairns, Wilson, Trew and Gallagher (1995) and reported above in the Introduction that ethnic identity was not an important issue for the young people in the studies they reviewed.

Deaux (1991, p. 77) remarked that 'identity is an intellectually seductive concept, capable of drawing on a number of diverse literatures'. We draw on some of those literatures in the remainder of this chapter to justify our contention that environment is important for identity development and in order to provide a rationale for the main purpose of this book - a report of the 'scaffolding' which underlies aspects of the development of personal identity in young people in Belfast, Dublin and London. Relevant issues include:

- facets of identity, including the self-concept
- the formation of identity and self-concept
- elements underlying the self-concept
- self-concept development in adolescence
- the role of socialization
- the relevance of the reference group for identity
- stability and change in self-concept and identity.

Facets of identity

It would seem that we need to 'unpack' the concept of identity a little more. We need to distinguish, for example, between reference group orientation and personal identity, both of which underlie the self-concept according to self-categorization theory (Turner and Oakes, 1989).

Reference group orientation involves ethnic attitudes, group identity, ethnic preference or racial image for the group; reference group orientation results in social identity which refers to the social categorization of the self based on interpersonal similarities derived from group membership (Banaji and Prentice, 1994). It can also include the characteristics of self that emerge in interaction with others, for example popularity, attractiveness (Cheek, 1989). Ethnic identity is sometimes understood as the ethnic component of social identity and is defined by Phinney (1990) as an aspect of acculturation with the focus being on individuals and how they relate to their own group as a subgroup of the larger society. Another aspect of acculturation deals with how minority groups relate to the dominant or host society.

Personal identity, on the other hand involves the individual's self-esteem, self-confidence, perceived competence and personality. It refers to one's self-knowledge and self-evaluation. Studies which failed to make the distinction between reference group orientation and personal identity in the American context led in the past to the erroneous conclusion that African-Americans personally suffered from low self-esteem and self-hatred. More recent studies find that positive self-esteem at a personal level can exist in the face of potentially negative attitudes towards the group of which the individual is a member (Harter, 1993). And presumably, the contrary is also true - that low self-esteem and self-confidence can also exist in individual members of social groups who are in the dominant position in a community. Self-esteem will have an impact on one's working self-concept since this is derived from a range of self-conceptions that are presently active in thought and memory - a continually shifting array of available self-knowledge - and will therefore affect one's current state and future self-relevant thinking.

Researchers frequently obtain measures of self-efficacy, self-confidence and self-esteem in individuals by asking them to give an estimate or a rating about themselves. In the present study we took to heart the remark made by Neisser that 'there is a remarkable variety in what people believe about themselves and not all of it is true' (1988). Instead of such 'soft' data we substituted another kind of slightly less 'soft' data, in line with our interest in context, by asking for factual information about opportunities available to the children which we thought would be conducive to the development of self-efficacy, self-confidence and self-esteem. While acknowledging that other factors, both internal and external to the children, including reference group orientation, would come into the equation, it was anticipated that this information would give us a basis for comparison between the groups and enable us to make some estimate about the possible levels of self-confidence and self-esteem underlying their self-concept and personal identity.

Identity formation

Is identity an essential part of the individual's make-up, are there separate distinguishable elements; is there an age or stage at which important developments are said to occur and how stable is it?

Identity has been defined as a 'sense' an 'attitude' a 'resolution' - an internal self-constructed dynamic organization of drives, abilities, beliefs and individual history. (Marcia, 1980). It is what keeps us going. It can be said to include a life-historical component - the experience of an unchanging self in the course of passing through different phases of life, developmental tasks and life events. It can represent widely accepted social categories,- wife, husband, student, banker, housewife, plumber, roadworker, Protestant, Catholic, - but the meaning associated with acceptance of categorical membership is constructed by the individual (Deaux, 1991). It includes ethnic identity, sometimes seen as the ethnic component of social identity (Phinney, 1990) which has as its focus the relationship of individuals to their own group as a subgroup of a larger society. It includes, in a very general sense, the self-concept, definition, or image of the self.

Elements underlying self concept and identity

The self-concept is the internal conception of the entirety of motives, attitudes and properties and action competencies, and it incorporates self esteem - the evaluation of them that a person gains when looking at his or her own activities. Further elements of the self-concept that are very relevant for the present study are those representing a range of 'possible selves' (Markus and Nurius, 1986), which provide the link between self-concept and motivation and represent enduring goals, aspirations, motives, fears and threats and are susceptible to changes in the environment. We need to look at factors which contribute to these possible selves in more detail, as they may ultimately explain differences between groups which

17

inhibit effective communication, and they may also help us understand whether changes in the self-concept are possible. The following have been identified as important by different theorists and were selected for further investigation in the present study:

- a sense of competence, personal efficacy and self-esteem (Bandura, 1977, 1995),
- the degree to which the individual has developed social intelligence by assimilating declarative and procedural knowledge (Cantor and Kihlstrom, 1987),
- the way in which the individual interprets reality and the awareness of the location of the self within the social system (Tallman, Marotz-Baden and Pindas, 1983),
- the perception of options in the environment and of their relative costs, (Goodnow, 1986),
- the extent to which the individual is interested in societal action (van der Linden, 1988)
- and is concerned to understand and develop socially responsible behaviour (Havighurst, 1948, 1972, Jackson and Rodriguez-Tomé, 1993).

One could posit that these factors result from developmental tasks such as those outlined first by Havighurst (1948, 1972), but found to be equally relevant more recently (Oerter, 1985). Such tasks could arise from different sources, namely physical maturation, cultural pressures or societal expectations and individual aspirations or values and that they, and hence it might be proposed that the outcomes could vary from culture to culture and even from one social stratum to another (Kirchler, Palomari and Pombeni, 1993). The contribution of these factors to the self-concept and personal identity will be elaborated later in this Chapter after a general look at how identity is believed to develop in adolescence and the kinds of influences that can affect it.

Adolescence and identity formation

The period of adolescence is generally regarded as an important phase. It is a period in which the child is undergoing changes in physical social and cognitive status and experiences changes also in the social contexts in which they occur (Worell and Danner, 1989). Theories trying to explain the underlying dynamics of development in adolescents have emphasized different factors, which can be loosely grouped as biological, psychoanalytic, psychosocial and socio-cultural and they may be placed along a continuum which moves from an emphasis on internal biological factors to an emphasis on external environmental influences although all are concerned with emotional-social-personality facets of adolescence (Miller, 1989). They differ primarily in respect of the aspect of adolescence they choose to emphasize - (e.g. thinking versus feeling) and in terms of the types of influences they select as being important (e.g. biological versus environmental). Theorists recently have begun to differ also in the basic assumptions they make about issues like continuity/discontinuity, and storm and stress as an inevitable characteristic of the adolescent, and in how they characterize the emotional disengagement which seems necessary between parents and offspring at this time.

Continuity / discontinuity

Theorists have been preoccupied by questions such as whether adolescence is a universal inevitable unique stage of life, or a creation of the recent history of the Western world (Modell and Goodman, 1993). The idea that because so many changes in the young person manifest themselves during this time, adolescence constitutes an altogether separate, discontinuous developmental stage (first proposed by Hall, 1904) led to a research focus in the past on the differences between adolescents and themselves at younger ages and on disparities in values and conflicts between adolescents and parents. Current wisdom has it that there is no discontinuity involved, that the groundwork for transition in adolescence must have been laid in childhood and that adjustments and relationships are not occurring *de novo*. It is also accepted now that changes are multi-faceted and that the dynamics of the situation mean that the influences of the various elements - child, parents, environment - are reciprocal and incorporate a time element.

Early adolescence is an appropriate timepoint at which to investigate the existence or otherwise of behaviours conducive to the development of what is normally considered to be a sane and healthy personality. In the present study we compared the groups on their movement towards independence/autonomy and we also looked at behavioural precursors to Marcia's (1967) notion of 'commitment' in terms of the opportunities offered to the children to undertake socially responsible activities.

Storm and stress

The disturbance model, often called 'storm and stress' (Olbrich, 1990) postulated that all young people experience major dysfunction during adolescence. Few take this notion of 'storm and stress' seriously now, although it is still informing some research agendas. The result of its popularity however has been that we know more about differences and conflicts between adolescents and significant others in their lives, than about harmony and intergenerational similarities within families. Another result has been the perpetuation of the 'negative stereotype' of the adolescent which has led to the anticipatory socialization of parents whose children are nearing that age, sometimes quite unnecessarily raising their anxieties about potential problems. There has been a shift in recent research towards an emphasis more on determining the skills and strategies which have been found to assist young people in the adjustments needed during adolescence (e.g. Seiffke Krenke, 1992, Seiffke-Krenke and Shulman, 1992). These include opportunities to develop self-efficacy, self-confidence and self-esteem and in the present study these were investigated by means of the items about survival skills, making choices and opportunities for travel - which made up the composite variables 'survival', 'choice' and 'travels'.

The psychoanalytic notion of disengagement - the severing during adolescence of emotional ties established at an earlier time - seemed to be soundly based on powerful evidence (Blos, 1979). Adolescents are becoming adults in their own right and are trying to distance themselves from their parents, sometimes by challenging them. Clashes occur; the adolescent turns to people outside the immediate family for support and develops new relationships. However, empirical evidence has not provided support for the notion that generational conflict was related, for example, to student activism in the 60s - student activists were typically offspring of parents with similar beliefs (Bengston and Laufer, 1974). But it is now acknowledged that while relationships with parents may alter, they are not broken off altogether and while there may be gender differences, strong ties will continue to exist and to be supportive. Attachment and detachment are no longer seen as mutually exclusive (Rice, 1990).

In the present study we concentrated on determining the actual salience of parents for their 12 year-olds through an enumeration of everyday practical interaction situations which could be objectively assessed rather than attempting to enter the labyrinth of subjective reactions which are transient and can be unreliable indicators of characteristics of both parents and children. We also were able to investigate whether there is any relationship between the salience of individual parents and of parents jointly to outcomes such as attitudes towards education and future orientation.

Socio-cultural factors

Erickson's (1959) psychosocial theory, unlike the biological and basic psychoanalytic theories, recognized the importance of cultural, sociohistorical and interpersonal factors in helping the adolescent resolve the turmoil resulting from new biological and social pressures. The developmental task of achieving an identity was what he saw as central for the adolescent. Identity meant for him a sense of continuity between what one has been and what one will become, but also the maintenance of an inner solidarity with a group's ideals and identity. A further set of theories, known as socio-cultural theories, puts even more stress on social influences and has its origin in the anthropological work of researchers such as Margaret Mead which resulted in a playing down of the role of biological influences.

The process by which behaviours are acquired interested the proponents of social learning theory and they showed how the environment can exert an influence by responding in different ways to the actions of the adolescent. They claimed that behaviours are reinforced or extinguished depending on the situational determinants. The present study investigated the opportunities available to the children to develop certain behaviours through leisure activities and through the range of items collected under 'Reaching out' in Chapter Six. It also investigated the opportunities available to them to develop cognitive skills by examining the extent to which they had access to information (Chapter Seven) and the kinds of information to which they had frequent access. Many studies have supported social learning as an explanation of how behaviours, both prosocial and aggressive, are acquired in adolescence and throughout the lifespan. More recent accounts of the theory have been becoming more cognitive than earlier versions (Bandura, 1977) and have recognized the role of cognitive and personality variables in learning.

Cognitive theories

Cognitive theories focus on the adolescent's developing abilities to solve problems which result from a combination of the neurological changes in early adolescence and exposure to the new experiences possible for the individual. The combination, according to Piaget (1947) is driven by the force of equilibration and results in the development of 'formal operations' or the ability to manipulate abstract symbols and to use propositional logic. Elkind (1967), and Elkind and Bowen, (1979) related cognitive structures in early adolescence to a type of egocentric perception of the self, the assumption that everyone is as preoccupied with them as they are themselves and the 'personal fable' or the belief that the self is unique, special, indestructible and immortal. The link between the development of cognitive processes and social activity was made by Selman (1980). The increasing ability of the individual to move through levels of perspective-taking was seen by him as being stimulated by social interaction experiences. He was in effect saying that socialization experiences shape the way we think. It follows that if socialization experiences are different for different groups, they will probably differ in the ways in which they think.

This was taken into account in the present study by finding out about the opportunities available to the children in the different locations to interact with people outside the family home and to what extent they had experience of different environments up to age 12.

Ecopsychological approaches

Criticism of these focused theories has often been based on the relative lack of consideration given by them to environmental factors as an element in the experiences contributing to development and on the absence of recognition in general by these theories of the reciprocal effects operating between the individual and the environment at every stage. The ecopsychological approach, initiated by Lewin (1948, 1951) with his concept of 'lifespace' and developed by Bronfenbrenner (1977a, 1977b, 1979, 1986) and others (e.g. Valsiner, 1987) integrates socialization theory, interactionism and social ecology. It assumes synergy in the interaction between the individual and the environment and brings out in detail both the environmental conditions and the mental system influenced by them. The focus of research using this model is 'the progressive mutual accommodation between an active growing human being and the changing properties of the immediate settings in which the developing person lives, as this process is affected by relations between these settings and by the larger contexts in which the settings are embedded' (Bronfenbrenner, 1979). It is based on a much broader view of the meaning of socialization.

The present study fits into this framework in recognizing the relevance of happenings in the social environment for the development of the individual's personal identity and by having as one of its aims an investigation of the possible association between changes in societal structures and changes in the self-concept of developing individuals.

21

The role of socialization

Socialization is defined by Hurrelmann (1988) as the process of the emergence, formation and development of the human personality in dependence on and in interaction with the human organism on the one hand and the social and ecological living conditions that exist at a given time within the historical development of a society on the other. Many writers agree that the primary source of socialization is the family as it prepares the individual to cope with the outside world, mediating between society and individuals, reflecting and interpreting society to family members, enabling them to learn attitudes and skills which help them to function effectively in social groups.

Researchers studying adolescent development within the context of the family share the basic premise that development is influenced by the quality of the adolescent-parent relationship. But researchers are influenced by a variety of theoretical perspectives including family systems theory, family therapy, psychoanalytic theory and cognitive development theory and have used numerous assessment techniques in their research. This makes it difficult to compare data across studies, but in general there is at least tentative support for the proposition that family context influences adolescent psychological development and that progressive growth is underpinned by increased psychological differentiation and integration which in turn are affected by social differentiation and social integration. Some of what has been found is relevant for the present study and will be referred to *passim*.

Parents and children

It is generally accepted that parents play an important role in the socialization of their children (Goodnow and Collins, 1990). Smith (1983) presents four kinds of evidence supporting the idea that parents may be regarded as the primary socializing agents. These include the relationship of the adolescent's patterns of personality and behaviour to patterns of parental child-rearing practices; adolescents' reports of the extent to which they rely on and are influenced by their parents; the relationship between the adolescents' orientations and their perception of orientations preferred by their parents (see also Adelson, 1980) and the relationships between adolescents' orientations and their parents actual (independently reported) orientations (see also Silbereisen, Eyferth and Rudinger, 1986). Feather (1980) asserts that 'a lot of evidence now exists to show that children will resemble their parents in some of their social and political orientations and behaviours'. In addition it has been noted that most young people continue to turn to their parents for advice and support, that parental influences continue to play a very important part in a wide range of areas of social behaviours and that there is, in general, support for the proposition that family context influences adolescent psychological development (Jackson and Rodriguez-Tomé, 1983).

Quicke (1991) found that parents were still principal agents in maintaining 18-year-old subjects' sense of self and identity and that self-perceptions were derived from a social world in the UK where the family experience of social mobility and class identity was a significant theme. A 1987 study by Owen and Dennis of levels and origins of political tolerance in 10-17 year-olds (N = 366) found that there were small but significant parent and child correspondences and concluded that familial interpersonal communication patterns had an influence on the development of tolerance in children. Avery (1989) reviews studies which suggest that adolescence and preadolescence may be a critical period for the development of tolerance and draws attention to the importance of level of cognitive moral reasoning for the endorsement and application of abstract democratic principles in concrete situations. It has been claimed that these behaviours provide a basis for identification with parents and, it may be added, ultimately with the group with whom the parents in their turn, identify.

Liebes, Katz and Ribak (1991) report a study of 400 Jewish families about the conditions under which parents reproduce ideologies in their adolescent children (aged 12-18 years) which found that parents *did* succeed in reproducing their political outlook, that there was a greater likelihood that 'hawkish' parents would have like-minded children than 'dovish' parents and that whereas the reproduction of 'doves' was dependent on higher education, 'hawks' reproduced regardless of their educational level. The dovish position was seen to be relatively complex. The process by which this occurs is not clear. It is suggested that the 'training' involved in socialization is usually unconscious and indirect (Tallman, Marotz-Baden and Pindas, 1983), partly accounted for by social learning theories, but partly also simply by virtue of being part of a group and sharing that group's experiences and fate.

In the present study we did not ask parents directly about their views and attitudes, but research such as that described led us to expect that they were probably close to those of the children in the sample.

Social intelligence

Children learn through observation, identification and personal experience within the family context. They may or may not have direct access to sources of information such as books, newspapers, television, radio, and they may or may not be encouraged to acquire information, think critically and voice opinions about current issues. In this way they acquire a degree of social intelligence made up of two basic kinds of knowledge:

i) 'declarative knowledge' or the individual's static knowledge about other people, social situations and themselves which help them to make sense of social events, and

ii) 'procedural knowledge' which involves dynamic processes such as forming impressions of people, making attributions about the causes of events and predicting the likely events in a social situation (Cantor and Kihlstrom, 1987).

They learn about the status of their family within society, the location of power, and how family members relate to social institutions. They learn about attitudes to authority, the consequences of other people's diverse behaviours and whether they can influence decisions. These learning experiences lead to individual differences in cognition, which in turn guide behaviour, and to the acquisition of values which will influence the choices they make in relation to their own future and the range of possible selves that they generate. An example is provided by the series of studies reported by Chaffee and others (Stone and Chaffee, 1970, Steinkopf, 1973, Chaffee, McLeod and Wackman, 1973, Jackskon-Beeck and Chaffee, 1975 and Chaffee,

1977) which examined the effects of four different kinds of family communication patterns on children's political socialization. The patterns of communication identified were:

- Laissez-faire (homes offering no directives for political socialization)
- Protective (homes stressing obedience and social harmony)
- Consensual (homes encouraging openness but discouraging family disputes)
- Pluralistic (emphasizing free communication and discussion).

It was found that teenagers from consensual and pluralistic families were 'prepared to encounter more civic responsibility than were those from protective or laissez faire home environments' (Chaffee, 1977, p. 245) and that in addition, children from pluralistic households made the best showing on measures of political knowledge and those from protective families performed the worst even when controls for IQ were applied. Earlier studies by Pinner (1965) and Renshon (1974) supported these findings in relation to the effects of overprotectiveness in the home. In a study of Belgian adolescents, Pinner (1965) concluded that those who came from overprotective families were more suspicious of government than those who were not so carefully shielded. Renshon (1974) found that with college students, lack of autonomy within the home was associated with external locus of control which in turn was correlated with political distrust.

Tallman, Marotz-Baden and Pindas, (1983) predicted that families who have access to diverse kinds of information and a broader range of rôle choices would provide a context for development in which a free flow of information, tolerance for the conflict of ideas and for ambiguity and the communication of abstract ideas would be more likely than in families living in relatively simple community social structures. The research by Zellman and Sears (1971) extended this into the area of self-esteem and found that adolescents with the highest self-esteem levels were also most tolerant of dissent. Familism, or devotion to the family as found in relatively simple community structures, has been found to result in a nonmaterialistic orientation, but it may also have the effect of preventing the participants from improving their material lot because reliance on older family members results in an unwillingness to take risks or to favour innovations (Rogers, 1969).

In the present study the social intelligence of the groups was investigated by means of the questions on declarative knowledge - questions on current affairs - politics and sport. We were able to determine whether there was any relationship between this and parental salience and group membership as well as looking at relationships between social intelligence and independence/autonomy. We were also able to examine possible associations between social intelligence and differential access to media news as well as to differential opportunities for experiences and interactions outside the home and family environment.

Identity and group membership

The relationships between parents and children are part of larger more complex networks of social relationships which, according to Tallman, Marotz-Baden and Pindas (1983) are characterized by a division of labour in which specified tasks are attached to particular positions and also by the feature that not all positions in a

24

network are linked to all other positions. This means that everyone does not have the same opportunities for obtaining desired goods or services. Through the processes of identification and interaction we learn about our relative positions within a network, we can identify with a group defined as different from other groups, and claim a particular rôle, status and life style. This gives us a base from which we can interact with peers and people in other social positions and an incentive to adopt and maintain a particular identity. The extent to which the social structures permit self-direction, whether in paid employment or in the home or school environment will also influence the value systems developed by the individual (Kohn and Slomczynski, 1990). Through the process, the individual becomes aware of differences in life chances and how these may be linked to social identity. The social structure therefore may be seen as shaping the possibilities for interaction which will ultimately influence the social and personal identity of the individual and the ways of thinking which he or she adopts (Berger, 1977). A consideration of where a person is located in the social structure and what influences and socio-economic realities within that location shape his or her development and control the behavioural options that are available would therefore seem essential in any discussion of identity formation.

The account given of the background to the 'Troubles' in Chapter Two will give an indication of how the various groups in Northern Ireland saw their place in society and how socio-historical events during the years leading up to 1968 and following that date may have resulted in changes for the adults which percolated through to the children's range of possible selves (described in Chapter Nine).

Being part of a group can be seen as contributing to the individual's self-esteem and self-concept. These will be influenced also by the relationship of the group to other groups which impinge on day-to-day life, whether, for example the group is dominant or not. Minorities feel threatened; threatened groups are liable to be hypersensitive. In Northern Ireland both groups, if broadly defined as Catholic and Protestant, display these characteristics. The situation is more complicated for Protestants since that grouping encompasses those of all faiths other than Roman Catholic; it is a much less homogeneous grouping than that of the Roman Catholics and many of them constitute minorities within it. Many writers have espoused this 'double-minority' model as an interpretation of the cause of the problems in Northern Ireland (Palley, 1972, Stewart, 1977, Fields, 1977, O'Malley, 1983, Singleton, 1985).

A development of the double-minority model suggested by some authors (Douglas and Boal, 1982, Moxon-Browne, 1983, M. A. Poole, 1983, Kennedy 1988) is the triple-minority situation. Northern Protestants are not just a minority in Ireland but a minority in the UK as well. They thus feel vulnerable twice over, because while they may consider the majority in the island of Ireland hostile, they are also not too sure about the reliability of their support from the British majority. If this view is valid one would expect Protestants to show the psychological characteristics of a minority even more sharply than Catholics do. Research has not specifically addressed this issue, but it has been found that Protestants have greater problems defining their identity; they feel more secure with a religious label ('Protestant') than a political one (Bruce, 1986). Some of the behaviour of some members of the dominant Protestant unionist group in Northern Ireland, such as in-group favouritism as will be seen in Chapter Two, links in with studies which have found such behaviour to be stronger when group membership status is ambiguous

25

(Brown and Wade, 1987) and when there are doubts about the legitimacy of one's claim to a particular social identity (Breakwell, 1986). This suggests too that they may have a more negative self-concept as studies have shown a positive self-concept to be related to the process of identity formation (Phinney, 1989, Phinney and Alipuria, 1990, Parham and Helms, 1985a, Parham and Helms, 1985b) and subjects with an achieved ethnic identity are predicted to have higher self-esteem (Marcia, 1980). But the importance of context is stressed by these researchers and not enough is known about that to make any definitive statements.

These models suggest however that particular characteristics of the identity of individuals have developed as a result of the status of the group. Does this mean that if the status of a group or other environmental conditions have occasion to change, these characteristics will also change? And are there other factors which could bring about change in aspects of a person's felt or self-perceived identity?

Stability and change in identity

The self-concept is an important part of identity, as mentioned above, apart from reference group orientation, and it has been found that there are important changes in the organization of self-concepts during early adolescence. It has to be presumed that social structures and relationships for those individuals were stable over the time periods covered by the studies of Livesley and Bromley (1973) and Dusek and Flaherty (1983) who found high levels of stability in the years between 12 and 18, for socio-ecological theory would have it that identity structure is dynamic, not static and that characteristics which manifest themselves at this stage, may be mitigated through subsequent experience, especially people's beliefs about their 'possible selves' or their future orientation. These are open to changes in society and to changes in relationships and, according to Marcia (1980), there will be numerous reorganizations of identity contents throughout a person's life.

Krosnik and Alwin (1989) tested two hypotheses about the relation between age and susceptibility to change in a study of political attitudes, an element of the self-concept which can motivate the individual to action and may be seen as comparable to the notion of 'future orientation' or 'possible selves' which can also motivate to action. The 'impressionable years' hypothesis proposes that individuals are highly susceptible to attitude change during late adolescence and early adulthood and that susceptibility drops precipitously immediately thereafter and remains low throughout the life cycle. The 'increasing persistence' hypothesis proposes that people become gradually more resistant to change throughout their lives. The results supported the 'impressionable years' hypothesis and disconfirmed the 'increasing persistence' hypothesis.

What kinds of circumstances might have the effect of bringing about change? While value systems develop from past experiences as organized and relatively stable products of information processing and are formed as a person copes with the influx of information from both the social and physical environments, they can change as new and discrepant information is encountered that cannot readily be interpreted in terms of existing schemata (Feather, 1980, p. 249). In a study of political learning in children and adolescents aged 12–17 using the Piagetian model, Torney-Purta (1989) reported that experiences could lead to the restructuring of both spatial and event representations of political knowledge. Looking at simple community structures in poverty-stricken rural areas, Tallman, Marotz-Baden and Pindas (1983) found that the desire for a better life is pervasive and if new information is introduced, with clearly beneficial consequences, it will gradually become incorporated into people's thought processes. As structures become more complex, people adapt their thought processes to deal with and integrate the new information and they become more adept at dealing with ambiguity and at recognizing that existing rules do not always apply. It follows that in communities with more complex social structures, families will in general be less authoritarian, more tolerant of ambiguity and of conflicts over ideas, more ready to negotiate (Hurrelmann and Engel, 1989).

The research of Yankelovich (1973, 1974) illustrates well how closely adolescent values are intertwined with the forces and fabric of society and the forces of history. His findings indicated that new values emerged on American college campuses during the 1960s, a period when many dramatic events occurred - the Kennedy presidency and the assassinations, Vietnam, the rise of the Civil Rights movement and, interestingly, that these values diffused at differential rates through other segments of the population. A longitudinal study reported by Bachman and van Duinen (1971) showed how changes in adolescent attitudes towards the Vietnam War kept pace with changes in adult opinion. In 1966, before public opinion had turned against the conflict, only about 7 per cent of the sample expressed much concern. But by 1970, when public dissatisfaction was beginning to peak, the percentage of adolescents who were worried about Vietnam had jumped to 70 per cent. Sigel and Hoskin (1977) report similar reflections of adult attitudes in adolescents at the time of Watergate in 1974 when high-school students registered only lukewarm sentiments about many aspects of government which, traditionally, they would have been expected to hold in high regard.

In the case of Northern Ireland, stability in the social structures between 1921 and the mid 1960's (as will be seen in Chapter Two) would have meant, in terms of socio-ecological theory, that any differences in elements of identity between the communities would have remained fairly stable in the form of consistent and unchanging features within groups. It is generally agreed however (MacFarlane, 1989) that in Northern Ireland there has been a period of intensive political and social change over the past 20 years or so. Changes in society which make the structures with which people have to interact more complex may result in changes in the ways in which people process information. It will depend partly on the extent to which they are actively engaged in dealing with societal structures and institutions. This in turn may result in changes in some of the elements that make up their identity - the ways in which they perceive themselves and their role and their options and the meaning of their identity for them. On the basis of reported research we would expect adolescents to reflect the values of the adults around them and any changes over time.

Can any more be said on identity and self-concept?

While this study focused in particular on children in Belfast, and to a lesser extent in Dublin and London, and some of its basic concerns are specific to the children of Northern Ireland, some of its value must also be derived from its contribution to the study of early adolescence in general. The theoretical perspectives underlying research in the area of early adolescence are constantly being revised especially since the 1970s and many methodological issues remain unresolved. Indeed it has been said that studying identity in adolescence is not a task for the methodologically hypersensitive (Marcia 1980)! And in the context of research in Northern Ireland, Beloff (1980), recognizing the difficulties of the situation and the problems of ethics, diplomacy and even physical danger, still encouraged researchers to forge ahead, even if 'data are likely to be a bit rough and ready [and] compromises with objectivity and the niceties of measurement are likely to have to be made'. While every possible effort has been made to ensure that the present study is as unassailable as possible on methodological grounds, these possible justifications for weaknesses should be borne in mind.

This project looked at how 12 year-olds from different groups expressed aspects of their identity - their social intelligence, their orientation towards the future, at two points in time in Northern Ireland, 1981 and 1992. Their views, representing the way in which their self-concept had developed, are seen as the outcome of socio-historical conditions and the process of socialization. This was a period of violent civil conflict and of great changes in societal structures the main events of which will be outlined in Chapter Two in order to set the stage for the findings of the project itself.

2 Changes in Northern Ireland

Introduction

Context-related research on the psychological development of children in Northern Ireland since 1968 has centred mainly on the effects of two aspects of their socio-cultural environment. The first of these is the climate of unrest and civil disturbances, those aspects of life which were so vividly characterized by McWhirter (1984) as 'abnormality which has become normality' and its effects on mental health and social cognition. The second major focus has been the education system which together with family socialization processes would normally be expected to have some effect on identity formation (Adelson, 1986, Hill, 1983, Kohn and Slomczynski, 1990, Simmons and Blyth, 1987, Hurrelmann and Engel, 1989, Emler, 1993). A summary of the major findings in these areas was given in the Introduction. Missing to date has been any attempt to take into account the psychological impact of the changes in political, economic and societal structures generally which have been happening in Northern Ireland since the early 1960s, but especially since 1968.

We saw in Chapter One that many researchers propose that self-concept and identity are influenced in their formation by socio-environmental factors in addition to family, school and situation specific events such as street violence. Since the existence of groups with different 'identities' in Northern Ireland has been recognized by many writers and these differences are thought by some to constitute part of the problem which has resulted in conflict, it would seem appropriate to present here some outline of the background events which provided the context for the development of self-concept and identity in our samples of 1981 and 1992. For the children, the impact of societal changes would have been mediated by the reactions of the adults in their lives, especially the adults in their families, to changing circumstances and challenges, and, as research has shown, 12 year-olds would be expected to reflect the attitudes of their parents. (Hurrelmann and Engel, 1989, Jackson and Rodriguez-Tomé, 1993, Thomas, Gecas, Weigart and Rooney, 1974, Smith, 1983). By looking at what the children say, we may get some idea of the feelings of the adults in the communities as well.

Pursuing the question of the possible influence of societal structures on self-concept and identity formation we look first at the period from the foundation of the state of Northern Ireland to events leading up to the outbreak of the 'Troubles' in 1968, drawing on a range of published material, but especially on the work of John Whyte (1990), Sabine Wichert (1991), Jonathan Bardon (1992), Paul Bew, Peter Gibbon and Henry Patterson, (1995), Séamus Dunn (1995) and the periodical *Fortnight*. Following the summary of events leading up to 1968 we survey briefly the areas of formalized change to the system introduced after that date, the economic situation, political developments and social policy initiatives during the period of the 'Troubles' preceding the first questionnaire which was completed by 12 year-olds in 1981. We then look at the period 1981-1992 to try and establish whether there were any events during that period which might have presented a challenge to the personal identity of the adults and which might have affected the socialization of their children and hence the self-concept including the future orientation of the children who were 12 in 1992.

What follows is necessarily a very abbreviated outline of the events felt to be relevant to the topic of this book, selected from what is a most complex situation in Northern Ireland. Since our main focus of interest was the children in East and West Belfast and their environment presented the most challenge, and is possibly the least well known of those of the groups in this study in spite of all the research published on it, we decided to attempt a broad and simplified (though we hope not simplistic) sweep of the background to life in Belfast in the early 80s and 90s. Although there were undoubtedly ups and downs in economic circumstances for the children in Dublin and London, the other sectors of life described here - political, social policy, community development, street conditions - were essentially stable and will not be gone into in detail for those groups.

In this chapter we:

• outline events thought to have contributed to the establishment and maintenance of the differences leading up to the conflict which began in 1968
• describe the environment in which children in Northern Ireland were growing up between 1968 and 1981 and between 1981 and 1992
• determine which might be the relevant elements within that environment for this aspect of their development,
• review what research has discovered about the impact of such factors and see where the present study might contribute to further understanding.

Life before the 'Troubles'

The island of Ireland has been divided into two states since 1921. The Republic of Ireland with about 3.5 million people is an independent state with jurisdiction over 26 of the 32 counties and Northern Ireland, with about 1.5 million, is in the north-eastern corner of the island with six counties. There are historical reasons for the existence of communities with differing loyalties and identities in Northern Ireland, as in so many other countries. The partition of the island in 1921 took account of the fact that the origin of the population in the North-East happened to be different from that in the rest of the country. Many of the people there were descended from English and Scottish settlers or planters who had moved in when the English colonized the island in the 17th century. These people had settled in the North in bigger numbers than in other parts of the country. They were of Protestant denominations and the people they dispossessed were Roman Catholic, like the majority in the rest of the island. Differences between the two communities can be traced back further (Adamson, 1974, 1981, Hall, 1986, Darby, 1995) but it seems that only since 1798 have some, at least, of the Protestants been so keen on the British link - both Presbyterians and Catholics took part in the 1798 rebellion (John Whyte, 1990, p. 123) against the English. The Act of Union in 1801 formally sealed the union of Ireland with Britain under one parliament.

In the late 19th and early 20th century the issue of whether Ireland would have a devolved form of government, also known as 'home rule', became one of the central issues of British politics. The question of whether some or all of Ireland should remain within the United Kingdom became more urgent after the suppression of the Easter Rising of 1916 in Dublin when it was clear than many in the south would prefer an independent Ireland, but many in the north wished to stay within the union with Britain. In the end, with the Government of Ireland Act (1920) which established the Irish Free State in the southern part of the island, the London government gave in to unionist pressure and set up a devolved parliament, known as 'Stormont' from its location in Belfast, in six of the nine counties of the province of Ulster in the north-eastern part of the island where the majority were Protestant, and 'unionist', and most of them felt themselves to be British.

There was quite a big minority however - about 40% of the population - in what became known as Northern Ireland, who were Catholic and nationalist. Many of them did not feel that they were British. They felt aggrieved that their wish to be part of a united Ireland had not been satisfied and their reluctance to accept the legitimacy of the Northern Ireland state, and their tendency to look rather towards the Free State, later the Republic of Ireland, for inspiration and moral support, led to an attitude of active and passive resistance towards the Stormont government, sometimes reinforced through intimidation by extremists, and this of course contributed to their 'out-group' status in the eyes of the unionists. At a very early stage, they refused, for example, to take part in the Lynn Committee in 1921 which met to consider plans for the education system. Their opposition did not take physical form in any major organized way over the period 1921-1969 but there were intermittent episodes of fierce rioting between the groups in almost every decade, in Belfast and Derry, caused usually by what Murray (1995) has called the 'associations and appendages' that accompany the manifestation of the differing cultures, often in the form of parades.

Devolved power in Northern Ireland 1922-72

It has been said that from 1922 to 1973 Northern Ireland had arguably the greatest degree of popular control in the United Kingdom - its own parliament governed 1.5 million people compared to Westminster where similar legislation was enacted for over 50 million (Livingstone and Morison, 1995). But it was not a situation of political equality. One community in effect ruled over the other; one party controlled parliament and executive throughout the period and extended its influence into local government and quango (quasi-autononmous non-governmental organization) appointments. The unionist party's control tended to exclude those who were not unionist, and especially those whose politics were nationalist (i.e. the Catholics) from public office; nationalists were looked on by a very sizable proportion of loyalists as traitors who could not be entrusted with political influence and little if any effort was made to draw them into fuller participation in the public affairs of the region. The nationalists refused to become an official opposition and the Northern Ireland parliament had no official opposition until 1958 when that role was taken on by the Northern Ireland Labour Party. But, as reported by Bardon (1992), Viscount Brookeborough, the then Prime Minister of Northern Ireland refused to accord this opposition privileges normally given at Westminster. The nationalists finally became part of the official opposition in 1965 and tended in John Hume's words (1964) to fall back on flags and slogans rather than trying to make constructive proposals and for this both they and the system are generally held to share the responsibility.

The parliament at Stormont was subject in theory to the parliament at Westminster, and Northern Ireland elected thirteen members of that body, but in practice Stormont functioned with a significant degree of autonomy. Even in financial matters the Belfast government achieved a measure of self-determination. Although it was originally envisaged that there would be an 'Imperial Contribution' from excess revenues raised in Northern Ireland, in practice, because of principle of parity and the step-by-step approach or ensuring that services in Northern Ireland were kept on a level with those in the rest of the UK, Westminster diverted money annually from central funds as a subvention to Northern Ireland. And there has always been a higher level of economic disadvantage in Northern Ireland than in the rest of the UK (Wichert, 1991, Harbison, 1989b, Bardon, 1992).

Drawbacks of the system

The dominance of the unionists and lack of interest from London had unfortunate consequences. Buckland (1981) writes that while the régime was neither as vindictive nor as oppressive as régimes elsewhere in the world with problems of irredentist minorities, the fact remains that owing to local conditions the power of government was used in the interests of unionists and Protestants with scant regard for the interests of the region as a whole or for the claims and susceptibilities of the substantial minority. Abuses of power were documented, but no action was taken by Westminster ostensibly because of the convention that Northern Ireland matters within the province of Stormont would not be debated there. Evidence emerged, for example, that the siting of some constituency boundaries was gerrymandered, that the housing requirements of sectors of the population were neglected; local government franchise was limited to property-owners and this limited the voice of nationalists even more, since more of them proportionately were in rented housing. Non-unionists found it difficult to gain entry to public employment and even more difficult to rise on promotion. There were cases of new industries, and even a university, offering employment to substantial numbers, being located in areas with Protestant unionist majorities, without similar advantages being offered to Catholic nationalist areas.

Stirrings for change in the 60s

Jonathan Bardon (1992) gives the Northern Ireland Labour Party the credit for the opening salvo of the civil rights movement in 1962. It drew attention to the very poor standards of public housing and local government in Northern Ireland and called for an end to discrimination on religious or political grounds. Unfortunately it did not do well in the Westminster elections and although it drew considerable cross-community support, it could not make any progress at parliamentary level.

Some members of the British Labour Party were stimulated by Gerry Fitt, Republican Labour MP for a Belfast constituency, into launching the Campaign for Democracy in Ulster in June, 1965. This aimed to investigate electoral law and electoral boundaries, and to set up a Royal Commission to inquire into the administration of government in Northern Ireland with particular reference to allegations of discrimination. But the convention that Westminster MPs would not debate matters related to Northern Ireland was not breached and no progress was made on that front at that time. However, alarm bells had started ringing.

Beginnings of reappraisal

The reappraisal of the situation from the Protestant point of view was possibly set in train initially by the overtures of Captain Terence O'Neill who became Prime Minister in 1963. According to Bew, Gibbon and Patterson (1995), he realized that reforms were necessary to stave off a feared British intervention that would end autonomy and re-open vistas of more fundamental constitutional change. He was aware of intercommunal tensions and aimed to build bridges and bring the benefits of modernization to all sectors of the population. He took the initiative in inviting the Irish Taoiseach (Prime Minister), Seán Lemass, to Stormont in 1965 as a gesture of reconciliation between the communities north and south

The reappraisal of their political stance by the nationalists may have begun before that time. The nationalists' aspiration for a united Ireland had provided unionists with an excuse not to share power and nationalists with an excuse not to try to participate. But nationalists had felt sure of the support of politicians in the Republic - their aspiration to a united Ireland was written into the Irish Constitution and it was proclaimed regularly, almost mantra-like, by certain politicians in the Republic, even though it had become clear over the years that the Republic's economy could not afford the kinds of subsidies being paid by Westminster to sustain Northern Ireland. It was not until 1958 that a shift in Catholic middle-class opinion was apparent (Bardon, 1992, p. 610) when Gerard Newe, later to become the first Catholic in the Stormont cabinet, condemned the futility of depending on the republic's claim to be the *de jure* government of the six north-eastern counties and declared that Catholics had a duty to 'co-operate with the *de facto* authority that controls ......life and welfare'.

This challenge was taken up by the Campaign for Social Justice, formed in 1964 by Conn and Patricia McCluskey following on from their activity in founding the Homeless Citizens' League in 1963 based in Dungannon, Co. Tyrone. The Homeless Citizens' League had collected evidence of inequality and discrimination especially in the housing sector. It advocated direct action, drawing inspiration from the Civil Rights movement in the United States and based its approach on the rights of the population to the ordinary rights of British citizens. The Campaign for Social Justice went further and planned to oppose policies of discrimination, collect comprehensive and accurate data on all injustices '.....and seek equality for all'. The Northern Ireland Civil Rights Association was formed in 1967 as an umbrella group for those seeking reform within the region (for a comparison with the Civil Rights movement in the United States see Wright, 1987). These moves reflected a greater confidence at this time that action was possible than had previously been the case in the Catholic population and they were spearheaded by the first generation to have benefitted from free secondary and higher level education following the Education Act of 1947.

In the early 1960s then, it looked as though the nationalists were becoming more articulate about injustices, consciousness was being raised about the causes underlying the situation which were perceived to be structural within society, suggestions were being made for reform and there was a Prime Minister apparently willing to make a start. But he failed to bring the majority of Protestants with him and faced opposition from within the cabinet - to the extent, for example, that he had not informed them in advance of the visit of Seán Lemass fearing that it would be vetoed. He raised the expectations of Catholics in promising reforms but was unable in the end to follow through for a number of reasons including lack of support from his own party and opposition at grass-roots level.

The rise of paramilitary organizations

In 1966 tensions mounted in Northern Ireland as the nationalist community prepared to celebrate the 50th anniversary of the Dublin Easter Rising. Militant Protestants thought they saw the hand of the IRA behind the celebrations, but although this has not been documented, the rhetoric of the occasion would probably support that impression. The IRA had been banned in the Republic since 1936 and although they had mounted a 'campaign' in the period 1942–45 in border areas and in Belfast, action by the Dublin government ('unwavering repression' in Bardon's words [1992, p. 583]) as well as by the Stormont government had meant that Northern Ireland was entirely free of IRA activity by the end of World War II. There had been a resurgence of activity in the 1950s, but again in Bardon's words, the high points of the campaign to drive British troops out of Ireland were usually 'glorious failures' (Bardon, p. 606). Once more, measures taken by both the Dublin and Stormont governments meant that most of the leading activists were either interned or dead by the end of 1958, Northern Catholics had mostly withheld their support, and in 1962 the campaign was officially called off. In 1966 however, it was agreed within the IRA to support any groups seeking reform within Northern Ireland (Bardon, 1992, p. 651) and it is likely that they infiltrated the Civil Rights movement from that time. Indeed Bardon (1992) states that militants (People's Democracy and republicans) had gained control of the movement in March 1969, leading to the resignation of people who did not share their views.

So the Protestants did not feel secure. A mark of this insecurity was the formation in early 1966 by extremist Protestant loyalists of the Ulster Volunteer Force with the aims of toppling Prime Minister O'Neill and combating the IRA. Its gruesome activities were such that it was proscribed by O'Neill in September of that year, but it had already done much to foment trouble and exacerbate tensions between the communities. And it continued to be active, together with fraternal organizations during the period of the 'Troubles'.

Adopting a proactive stance

The beginning of the on-street campaign for civil rights which resulted in the 'Troubles' is usually dated to June 1968 when a council house in Caledon Co. Tyrone was allocated to an unmarried 19 year-old Protestant girl with political

34

connections at a time and in a place when many Catholic families were in dire need of housing. Protest meetings were organized about this particular incident and the catalogue of grievances rapidly became more comprehensive. Meetings and marches became frequent (for a chronology of events see the journal *Fortnight* for the period of interest). Many Protestants identified civil rights with republican and nationalist politics and this renewed their fear of being swallowed by a united Ireland (Wichert, p. 111) even though the consensus in the literature reported by John Whyte (1990) is that Southern Protestants are not a downtrodden group and, with typical caution, he adds that 'all in all, the evidence does not suggest that Protestants feel the country is one in which they are unable to thrive' (p. 153).

Some of the unionists resented the demands of the civil rights movement, denied that there was any problem and started counter marches or demonstrations. The local parliament in Stormont was slow in making an effective response. The marchers and counter-marchers clashed. There were riots, street barricades were erected, the police could not keep order; television news reports showed the world that they were clearly making life much more difficult for nationalist and pro-civil rights marchers than for unionist counter-demonstrators. People's houses were burnt down, thousands were made homeless and many were intimidated out of their homes (O'Connor, p. 160) and a mass movement of population began which affected both 'sides' and continued on a large scale in the early 1970s. Between 30,000 and 60,000 people were forced to leave their homes between August 1969 and February 1973 and it has been estimated that 80 per cent of these were Catholic. This movement has continued on a lesser scale since then to the point where the majority of urban working class people now live in neighbourhoods which are predominantly of their own tradition (Melaugh, 1995) - as did the groups in the present study.

The IRA emerged from the shadows, in the autumn of 1969, to 'defend' the Catholics. They were ill-prepared at first and gradually acquired arms (Bardon, 1992, p. 675); they had another agenda - a united Ireland - and they thrived on the discontent and fear of Catholics who felt that they needed protection against the local police force (the Royal Ulster Constabulary, RUC) and the locally raised militia (then called the B Specials), both groups being overwhelmingly Protestant and manifesting sectarianism in their reactions. The Ulster Volunteer Force was already in place on the unionist side to 'defend' the Protestants. It should be noted though, that the paramilitaries on both sides emerged after rather than before the initiation of the 'Troubles' (see also Guelke, 1995), although their basic organizations were in existence before that. There were subsequently splits on both sides and more paramilitary groupings developed with a lessening of control over the 'wild men' from the centre. The violence got worse and worse.

Arrival of the British Army

Finally in August 1969 the Stormont parliament asked Westminster to send the British army to restore order. They came, and were seen by both sides as coming, to rescue the Catholics from Protestant and RUC violence (John Whyte, 1990, p. 121) and initially they were welcomed. However, the army was operating in support of the civil power, which was still in Protestant unionist hands and it gradually slid during 1970-72 into operating openly on behalf of the unionist regime. Matters went steadily downhill especially after the introduction of internment in August 1971 and came to a head in early 1972. After a number of horrific events - 'Bloody

Sunday' in Derry, the Aldershot army canteen bomb, the Abercorn restaurant bomb, a bomb in Donegall St. in central Belfast, all of which resulted in the deaths of civilians and terrible injuries, Edward Heath, the British Prime Minister decided to take control of security back from Stormont and the Stormont government, outraged at this move, resigned in protest. A secretary of state, William Whitelaw, was appointed and it was envisaged that this would be a temporary solution.

The prorogation of Stormont was a bitter pill for the unionists and an encouraging sign that reforms were possible for those advocating change in the structures. But it did not prevent the continuation of the violence and permanent acceptable changes have not yet been agreed 23 years later.

Events 1972-92

We now turn to events in the period 1972 - 1992 in an attempt to see whether at the times of our 'windows' in 1991-2 and 1992-3 there were distinguishing features which could have affected people's perceptions of themselves differentially. We will first remind ourselves of what was meant by the 'climate of violence', then look at what happened to the impetus for reforms within Northern Ireland, and following that, at economic developments, political developments and developments at community level.

The climate of violence

It has been pointed out by Cairns and Toner (1993) that the 'Troubles', as they came to be colloquially known, varied along a number of dimensions over the period. These they label as follows:

a) intensity - the number of deaths, the extent of personal injuries and the amount of physical destruction which varied from year to year with a generally acknowledged peak during the early 1970s and smaller peaks in the '80s.
b) quality - the type of violence varied; there were different trends in different years rarely all at once or continuously.
c) location - the geographical locus of the violence varied. Some areas saw many incidents - parts of West Belfast and of the city of Derry; some saw only one which hit the headlines - Claudy; some saw none at all.

The kinds of events which made up the 'Troubles' included explosions caused by massive bombs placed in streets, public buildings, restaurants, public houses, shops and cars, often with a warning received and understood too late to be of use; sometimes without any warning at all; ambushes of groups of innocent civilians by outlawed paramilitary groups and attacks on and by the security forces resulting in deaths and injuries; individual assassinations of people in all walks of life, including MPs and clergymen, and tit-for-tat sectarian killings; intimidation, relocation, riots and barricade building in residential areas; armed patrols of soldiers with blackened faces dodging along residential streets and into gardens and alleyways, searching homes, sometimes apparently at random, in the early hours of the morning, stopping and questioning individuals at road blocks, and standing on platforms at the rear of army jeeps facing following traffic with rifles cocked; routine body-searches at the entrance to shopping areas; frequent closures of shops, offices and neighbourhoods and restrictions of public transport due to bombscares and explosions, necessitating detours to collect children from school, go shopping or to the hospital or visit the doctor or one's relations or to get home safely - these were part of daily living conditions in some parts of Northern Ireland which curtailed normal everyday life from 1968 to 1994.

In a random sample of 522 children from all over Northern Ireland it was found that almost 20 per cent had been in or near a bomb explosion, another 20 per cent said that they had had a friend or relative killed or injured and 12 per cent felt that their area was not safe to live in (McGrath and Wilson, 1985). While it has been said that by international standards the death rate in Northern Ireland could be seen as modest (a total of 3,028 died between 1968 and 1992 and almost 30,000 were recorded as having been injured), survey evidence suggests that one in ten of the population has had a relative killed and one in two knew someone who died as a result of the violence (Smith, 1987). And yet, the average uninvolved individual was ten times more likely to be killed by a car than by a bomb or bullet and if he or she lived outside the Catholic ghettos of Belfast or Derry or the rural border areas, the chances were overwhelmingly better than that (Bardon, 1992, p. 819). Still, because of the unpredictable and somewhat random nature of the violence, it is probable that everyone was at some degree of uncontrollable risk (Cairns, Wilson, Trew and Gallagher, 1995).

At the end of 1981, when the first groups in this study completed their questionnaire, there was no end in sight to the 'Troubles' and Provisional Sinn Féin, the political wing of the Provisional IRA had endorsed a new strategy to contest elections while continuing the campaign of violence which was now to be targeted more carefully at their political enemies and at members of the security forces with less destruction of commercial premises. The Official Unionist MP for South Belfast, Rev. Robert Bradford, was shot dead outside his constituency office in November and extremist unionists were calling for strong measures to suppress republican violence.

In the period from 1969 to the end of 1981 there had been 2,172 deaths directly attributable to the 'Troubles', 101 of them in 1981; of those in 1981, 57 had been of civilians, 69 of them murders attributed to republican paramilitaraiaes and 12 to loyalists; further figures for 1981 show that there had been 1,142 shooting incidents, and 398 explosions. The same sources report 131 bombs defused, over 536 malicious fires, 689 armed robberies and £854,929 had been stolen. and that 357 firearms, 3.4 tons of explosives and 47,127 rounds of ammunition were found in searches and 4,104 house searches were carried out (Flackes and Elliott, 1994).

In 1992 there had been a de-escalation. Between 1982 and the end of 1992, there were 856 deaths due to the 'Troubles', 85 of them in 1992 and 76 of these were civilians, 36 of them attributed to republican paramilitaries and 39 to loyalists. There were 506 shooting incidents logged and 222 explosions. The number of bombs defused was 149; there were 419 malicious fires, and 738 armed robberies got away with £1,665,863. In addition, 194 firearms, 2.1 tons of explosives and 29,131 rounds of ammunition were found; 3,415 house searches were carried out (Flackes and Elliott, 1994).

Against this background, made up of individual episodes which dominated the media, other events were taking place within societal structures which could have influenced the lives of our groups and the formation of their self-concept and personal identity. For events in some categories - for example the administrative reforms - one would expect the effects to be positive and cumulative and not to find much of a contrast between the situation in 1981 and 1992, except perhaps of degree; the economic scene, on the other hand, was different in 1992 from what it had been in 1981 and affected Catholics and Protestants differentially; the political scene changed substantially after 1981 when the hunger strikes which resulted in the deaths of 10 republican prisoners left matters at an all-time low; some government social policies became more interventionist in the late 80s than in the 70s; organizations offering opportunities to 'ordinary' people for participation in decision-making began to develop higher profiles and these developments made the period before 1992 different from the period before 1981 especially in politics and the social arena as will be seen below.

The reforms

The main complaints voiced by Civil Rights activists had been in relation to housing and local government. In August 1969, the Westminster and Stormont governments agreed to remove control of public housing from local councils and transfer it to a regional authority, the Northern Ireland Housing Executive, which was established in 1971. Livingstone and Morison (1995) comment that no findings of discrimination have been made against this body in contrast to its predecessors. Although it took some time - almost 20 years - before the impact of its work was really effective, its establishment meant that one of the worst abuses of the previous system was being addressed - the standards and allocation of public housing. The second major demand of the Civil Rights people was universal suffrage in local council elections. Prime Minister O'Neill was forced to implement this by the Westminster government in April 1969, although members of his own party opposed it.

Soon afterwards, a review body was set up, headed by Sir Patrick Macrory, to produce a plan for local government reform. This reported in 1970 and its proposals were implemented in 1973. The new elected district councils had very limited responsibilities - 'bogs (i.e. sanitation), bins and burials' plus the administration of community and leisure centres - this latter responsibility did however leave a way for possible continued discrimination against particular sectors of the population as the allocation of funding was discretionary (Rolston, 1981, Abbott and Frazer, 1985). It has also been argued that reducing the range of functions of local government limited its responsiveness and lowered the quality of representation (John, 1993).

By the end of that year all responsibility for housing (as seen above), education, personal social services and policing had been transferred to appointed bodies ('quangoes') and elected local authorities had no rôle to play. The Northern Ireland Office appointed the majority of members to these boards thus ensuring that there was balanced representation from both communities and preventing local services from being controlled entirely by and for members of one community. Livingstone and Morison (1995) report that there are now over 100 'quangoes' functioning in Northern Ireland with the main ones being in the service delivery sector (health and social services, education, policing), in economic development (Industrial Development Board, Local Enterprise Development Unit), in the regulation of the social and economic sphere (Fair Employment Commission, Equal Opportunities Commission) plus a category comprising quangoes established by government to provide independent advice (Northern Ireland Economic Council, Standing Advisory Commission on Human Rights). We have mentioned only the more prominent in each category.

The main arguments against quangoes seem to be their undemocratic nature and their lack of accountability to the electorate. Although they may be composed of the best people for the job and they are accountable financially and to the law, there have been fears expressed that they are too subservient either to their professional staff or to the Government departments which fund them. On the other hand, the arguments put forward for their existence in Northern Ireland are undeniably forceful - control of their functions by representative authorities in the past either produced the tyranny of the majority over the minority, or a paralysis of decision making due to irreconcilable differences over what decision should be taken.

The advance of the quangoes was well under way by 1981 and psychologically, it could be suggested that while their existence lessened the danger of discriminatory decisions, there are disadvantages too. Their remoteness from the person in the street could be having the effect of distancing ordinary people from taking an interest in affairs which would, and should, normally be of concern to them. When people have no say in what is being proposed and decided, and they have no say in choosing the best person for the job, they naturally enough do not feel any responsibility for policies being implemented. They feel less part of the process and may become alienated from the institutions of state.

The economic scene

Economically, Northern Ireland had been on a 'high' during the 60s. Commentators have observed, in retrospect, that it was unfortunate that opportunities to mend fences and advance reconciliation between the communities were not pushed with more vigour at that time, when economic circumstances were favourable.

But the fortunes of Northern Ireland suffered as a result of the oil crisis in 1973. Between 1973 and 1979 Northern Ireland's manufacturing output declined by 5% annually. It was estimated that over 30,000 industrial jobs had been lost due to the violence (Bardon, 1992). Many other causes contributed to the situation, including the world slump, the dependence of the Northern Ireland economy on exports to Britain which had a sluggish economy, the configuration of the industrial structure in Northern Ireland with its over-dependence on 'problem' industries and the fact that many of the larger employers in Northern Ireland were subsidiaries of multinationals which made them particularly vulnerable to contraction when there was pressure on the parent company. Between 1979 and the autumn of 1981 no fewer than 110 substantial manufacturing firms in the region closed down. The lowest numbers for years were employed in services and in the construction industry. The shipbuilding industry, the Province's major employer, nearly went to the wall and eventually had to be subsidized by the government. Short Brothers, a major aviation company, was more successful but was also dependent on subventions from the Exchequer. Unemployment was up to 21.1 per cent by July 1982 so that the period of 1981-82 was one of severe economic hardship for many Northern Ireland families. Male unemployment for Catholics was 30 per cent in 1981 and it was 12 per cent for Protestants.

The imbalance between rates of employment and occupational levels for Catholics and Protestants which was and still is a feature of the economy has been well documented, most recently by Melaugh (1995), and there is plenty of evidence of more widespread and acute poverty among the Catholic population (John Whyte, [1990, pp. 51-66] reviews the literature). And the social deprivation of certain neighbourhoods and efforts made to alleviate it have been described in many publications (Burton, 1978, Conroy, 1988, Rolston and Tomlinson, 1988, Blackman, Evason, Melaugh and Woods, 1989, Jenkins, 1982, 1983, Darby, 1986, Teague, 1987). Writers such as Belfrage (1987) and Parker (1993) have described vividly the street atmosphere in local neighbourhoods in Belfast at various times during the 1970s and 1980s when they were riven by violence, patrolled by the army and 'protected' by 'hoods' or paramilitaries.

Up to about 1980 (Canning, Moore and Rhodes, 1987) the jobs created in the public sector practically made up what was being lost; but after 1980 the curves flattened out, indicating that differential employment growth had ceased in that sector. An interesting observation is that female employment rose while male employment fell against a background of roughly constant total employment during that period. Matters continued to go downhill during the 1980s with jobs in traditional industries formerly the preserve of Protestant families disappearing with rationalization and cutbacks. (Wichert, 1991, p. 93). This put Protestants on the line, many of them for the first time.

The economic situation in 1992 was not much better than in 1981; although there was a slight improvement in Catholic employment figures, there was a slight decrease in employment figures for Protestants. Male unemployment for Catholics was 28 per cent in 1991 and 13 per cent for Protestants. Psychologically, the economic recession over the period of the later 1970s and 1980s would probably not have made such an impact on Catholics as on Protestants. Unemployment and hardship were not new for them. But for Protestants, who had previously found it relatively easy to find and hold jobs, often through family networking in businesses which were traditionally owned and run by Protestants, the changes must have been devastating. Many faced a real decline in their standard of living. As well as job losses to breadwinners, it was more difficult to find a job in the first place. A new code of practice recommending an end to preferential employment policies was issued by the government in 1987. Although adoption of the code was voluntary, the Government pledged to refuse to do business with those who did not comply and was seen to follow up on this promise.

Bardon (1992) comments that by the beginning of the 1990s, Northern Ireland had all but ceased to be a manufacturing region, with the majority of jobs heavily dependent on public subsidy. The British subvention had increased from less than £100 million in 1970 to £1.6 billion in 1988-9 - apart altogether from expenditure on the British army and on European grants. In 1989 The Economic Council reported that public expenditure in NI (excluding social security) had grown by about 1.3 per cent per annum in real terms over the past five years. This compared with an average decrease nationally of about 0.5 per cent As part of the United Kingdom and one poor in natural resources, with larger families, fewer single parent and retired households, and much lower average incomes than in the rest of the UK, this may be seen as what was only fair and due to the Province, but it makes it one of the most dependent economies in the world (Bardon, 1992, p. 789). There were hopes in the early 1990s however that measures such as Fair Employment legislation and the perceptible diminution of violence would create a more welcoming climate for investment.

Political developments

In the meantime on the political front, successive Secretaries of State had been trying to suggest alternatives and to seek a 'political solution'. This means a constitutional compromise that will end the alienation of the minority, marginalise the terrorists and establish a fair and democratic system of government. Livingstone and Morison (1995) detail the various attempts that have been made and point out that they all incorporate to varying degrees four main agenda items - that Northern Ireland remain part of the UK, that there be an all-Ireland dimension to any settlement, that there should be devolved government and that there should be a cross-community aspect to the solution.

Four attempts got as far as the election of a locally elected regional assembly. The first, in 1973, based on the Sunningdale Agreement, with William Whitelaw as broker, resulted in a power-sharing executive and was opposed tooth and nail by loyalists largely because of the inclusion of what has since become known as an 'Irish dimension' in the form of a Council of Ireland. The power-sharing executive was forced to resign after five months as a result of a massive strike organized by the (extremist Protestant) Ulster Workers Council.

Direct rule was extended indefinitely and legislation was passed in Westminster establishing an elected Constitutional Convention which was to consider future arrangements which would be acceptable throughout the community. Merlyn Rees was Secretary of State for Northern Ireland at this time. The majority unionists made proposals which advocated the return of majority rule and did not include power-sharing to a level acceptable by Westminster and the Convention was dissolved in 1976. The unionists did not seem to have taken into account the evidence before them that such a strategy would not work.

The third attempt was the round-table conference called by Humphrey Atkins, the Secretary of State in 1979, to discuss six models of government for the region, but he ruled out of order any discussion on Irish unity or the constitutional status of Northern Ireland. This time it was the nationalists who refused to participate initially, since there was to be no consideration of an Irish dimension; the unionists also rejected the White Paper, since all the options would have involved power-sharing and the initiative was admitted to be a failure in November 1980.

In 1981, things looked very bleak after the hunger strikes; the Catholic community was split into more moderate anti-violence supporters of the Social Democratic and Labour Party (SDLP) and more extremist militant pro-violence supporters of Sinn Féin. There were fears that Sinn Féin would take over the Catholic electorate and it appeared to be preparing to try by making itself more attractive - fewer robberies, more visibility, more involvement with the community at local level.

The fourth attempt was the 'rolling devolution' proposed by James Prior in 1982 with an elected assembly which had only an advisory and consultative role with the anticipation that executive power would be transferred in stages depending on cross-community support. This was boycotted by the nationalists and its demise was brought about in 1986 by the activities of Protestant unionist members in opposition to the Anglo-Irish Agreement of 1985.

The Anglo-Irish Agreement (the Hillsborough Agreement) represented an advance along a different front on the parts of the London and Dublin governments in an attempt to keep things moving in the face of the apparent impossibility of getting Northern Ireland politicians to make any progress towards a settlement by themselves.

Bardon (1992) places the origins of the initiative which led to the Agreement at a meeting in Dublin between the British Prime Minister, Margaret Thatcher and the Irish Taoiseach, Charles Haughey in December 1980, just after the failure of the Atkins proposals. It was the first visit by a British premier to Dublin since partition and appeared to open promising possibilities. Initial consultations focused on cross-border security and cooperation between the RUC and the Gárda Siochána. Relationships deteriorated because of the hunger strikes by republican prisoners, protesting about conditions from March to October 1981 during which 10 prisoners died. After every death, riots erupted and eventually resulted in the deaths through violence of 61 people. The disapproval by the Irish government of the Falklands War in 1982 also contributed to this deterioration so that although the Anglo-Irish Inter-Governmental Council had been set up in November 1981 providing a structure for discussions which were supposed to take place twice yearly, not much progress was made until November 1983. After that time it started to meet more frequently with informal and then more formal talks taking place between the secretary to the British cabinet and the Irish Government from March 1984 onwards. The process was not diverted by the Brighton bombing of October 1984 nor by the insistence by Margaret Thatcher that none of the three solutions suggested by the New Ireland Forum (see below) was acceptable

Intervening events which appear to have influenced this development included the elections of 1982 for the Northern Ireland assembly in which Provisional Sinn Fein gained 10.1 per cent of first preference votes, largely at the expense of the SDLP and the Westminster election of June 1983 in which 13.4 per cent voted for Sinn Fein as against 17.9 per cent for the SDLP. These results concentrated minds at Westminster and were also perceived as a threat to the stability of the Irish state. On the Dublin side, the election of a new government in early 1983, headed by Garrett FitzGerald offered an opportunity for a new start and the process was no doubt informed in the background by the deliberations of the New Ireland Forum, held in Dublin Castle 1983-4. Wichert (1991) gives the SDLP credit for persuading the Irish Government to set up this Forum, intended to rally all Irish political opinion against the IRA. It turned out to be very educative especially for politicians and people in the Republic (See *Report of Proceedings 1-13, 1983-84, Report,* 1984).

The Anglo Irish Agreement was a carefully crafted document of twelve clauses. Those which have attracted most attention were firstly the one which confirmed that any change in the status of Northern Ireland would only come about with the consent of the majority of the people in Northern Ireland (which did not fully reassure the unionists because of demographic trends) and secondly that an Intergovernmental conference would be set up, headed by the Secretary of State and the Irish foreign minister which would meet regularly to promote cross-border cooperation and deal with security, legal and political matters. A permanent secretariat would be serviced by northern and southern civil servants.

Loyalist reaction Protests against it by loyalists, who were outraged that the Republic should have any say in the affairs of Northern Ireland, were firmly countered by the police and indeed the fact that the police were largely Protestant like the protesters led to a dilemma on the part of the leaders of the protesters; passive resistance in the form of non-cooperation by unionists in quangoes and other institutions of state made no difference to their functioning; the economic situation was so bad that workers were unwilling to strike, unlike in 1974 when the Ulster Workers' Strike had brought down the power-sharing executive. A twelve-point plan of civil disobedience was in most respects a 'miserable failure' (Bardon, p. 764). As a result of street violence instigated by them, the image of loyalists suffered a severe blow. New public order regulations proved highly effective in controlling parades and paramilitary displays and a hefty fine imposed on Belfast City Council by the High Court for refusing to strike a rate eventually punctured the unionists campaign of non-cooperation in local government. The elections in January 1986 resulting from the resignation of Unionist MPs in protest from Westminster showed support rather than a repudiation of the Agreement from both sides of the electorate. But there was a notable increase in loyalist (extremist Protestant) paramilitary activity in the late 80s and early 90s.

The Anglo-Irish Agreement could be said also to signal another watershed for the unionists and perhaps even a turning point. For the first time, they were having to face the fact that the British government to whom they had pledged unwavering loyalty, and whom they felt they had served unflinchingly over the years, especially in the two World Wars, accepted a role for the Irish government in their affairs. They felt betrayed and bewildered by the firmness with which their protests were ignored. Their previous demonstrations against change had been successful - dating way back to 1921 when they had secured their own parliament. The position of having change imposed was a new and uncomfortable one for them, especially when the implications were (probably deliberately) not spelled out and the first reaction was undoubtedly the old reliable one of 'not an inch'. Bew, Gibbon and Patterson (1995) note the fundamental unpopularity of the Anglo-Irish Agreement with Protestants, but they also find signs of a 'growing awareness that it was a more-or-less permanent fixture in the governance of Northern Ireland' (p. 218).

Nationalist reaction The Agreement also gave rise to difficulties for militant republicans. The January 1986 Westminster elections showed a fall in their share of the vote by 5 per cent in Northern Ireland. The British general election in June 1987 showed a further decrease in their share of the vote. And following a decision in November 1986 that Provisional Sinn Fein candidates should, if elected, take their seats in the Dáil in Dublin, the party did not succeed in capturing even one seat, with 27 candidates contesting 24 constituencies, in the February 1987 election in the Republic. They received a mere 1.85 per cent of the total votes cast. The Dáil in Dublin passed laws to expedite the extradition of terrorists and they gradually were implemented. In desperation the IRA continued with its campaign of violence now directed mainly towards members of the security forces and anyone who worked for them. This threat to civilians, many of them Catholics in building and catering occupations, who depended on such work for their livelihood, served to alienate the militants from their supporters but the catalogue of horrors continued unrelentingly.

These are detailed in other sources but those which probably made the most impact were the Enniskillen Remembrance Day bomb, the shooting of three apparently unarmed IRA members by the SAS in Gibraltar with its sequels of the murders of mourners in Milltown cemetery by a loyalist and of two British army corporals in West Belfast by mourners at the funeral of one of those killed in Milltown. The Agreement and its aftermath may have helped consolidate the policies already in process of germination by militant republicans since the period after the hunger strikes with a view to finding another route. They seemed readier to allow even more time for the realization of their ultimate aspirations; but they probably felt that their aspirations were at least being recognized and this was a boost. Even so, there was little evidence of any reduction in the violence from their side until the late 80s and early 90s.

By 1992, although there was still no sign of permanent peace, there were some signs of accommodation on both sides to the notion that the future would be different from what either 'side' had been envisaging. This was being supported by strategic initiatives in social policies to which we must now turn.

Social policy

The Anglo Irish Agreement also marked changes in other spheres. Livingstone and Morison (1995) note that whereas the large increases in public expenditure in NI during the 1970s seemed to be aimed at reducing the sense of deprivation, essentially by ignoring differences and rendering irrelevant the religious and ethnic divisions, it had become clear that this was not achieving all that was intended. Perhaps this was because of fuzziness in the guidelines, or the discretion still allowed, for example, to local councils in allocating funding for community-type development in a situation where, as Gallagher (1995) puts it there was considerable 'dynamic tension' not to mention 'conceptual confusion' and in addition, it must be admitted, resources were very stretched and competing needs were great .

In the late 80s a second type of approach became apparent. This gave recognition to the existence of different traditions; it made it officially acceptable to be different. Tentative steps were taken towards recognizing aspects of the nationalist tradition - support for Irish language schools, presentations of Gaelic culture. The necessity to give 'parity of esteem' was signaled and was marked by, for example, the introduction and eventual strengthening of anti-discrimination laws with effective monitoring mechanisms on the recommendation of SACHR and the development of guidelines relating to policy appraisal and fair treatment (PAFT). Programmes such as Targeting Social Need recognized that resources should be channeled to the areas of greatest need regardless of religious affiliation. And the Making Belfast Work initiative which had as its objective to deal with the social and economic problems of Belfast's most disadvantaged areas included a new element - a commitment to partnership between government and the community sector. This led to a revitalization of Belfast in the late 1980s.

In addition, agencies were established such as the Central Community Relations Unit in 1987 to ensure that all statutory bodies promoted greater understanding between the two sides of the community in Northern Ireland in their policies and programmes and the Cultural Traditions Unit came on stream the following year to encourage a more general public awareness of and sensitivity to local cultural diversity. The Community Relations Council; (CRC), formed in 1990, aimed to

44

encourage greater understanding between the two sides of the Northern Ireland community and to build trust and reduce prejudice. Like the Fair Employment Commission, the CRC was empowered to actively promote change and social activity in a whole range of areas beyond the traditional remit of public law; in 1989, for example, it invited district councils to submit proposals for action to improve community relations; in their areas; by 1993 all 26 councils were involved (see McCartney, 1993, Gallagher, 1995, for an assessment of progress in government-supported initiatives promoting community relations). A programme called Education for Mutual Understanding was introduced in schools in 1989 and incorporated into the educational reform order of 1990.

Implications of social policy strategies

The publicity and publications and some of the activities associated with these initiatives in the late 80s reached into most of the homes in the Province and it is possible that gradually their psychological impact was being felt as strenuous efforts were and are being made by the agencies concerned to explore myths, encourage people on both sides of the 'cultural divide' to take possession and enjoy ownership of their joint cultural heritage and feel that they are gaining rather than losing by broadening the basis of their personal identity. It is the Protestants who would appear to have the most ground to cover psychologically. Having disowned the Gaelic and Celtic cultural tradition as 'foreign' and 'alien' in the past, they are now being asked to sit back and enjoy and feel that it is theirs too and to accept that the future will be different, but that they can contribute also, for both 'sides' will be equally valued. They are being asked not to give up but to reinterpret their identity and give it an expanded meaning.

While the Catholic minority continue to harbour deep misgivings about security policies and the administration of justice (Committee on the Administration of Justice, 1995), it has been acknowledged that much more is being done to tackle disadvantage in employment and education, to give nationalist cultural interests their rightful place and to promote better community relations. There have, in fact, been some signs of change, albeit unevenly, throughout Northern Ireland. The members of Dungannon District Council agreed to a form of powersharing in 1988 and their example was subsequently followed by a number of other district councils. Members of Belfast City Council, on the other hand have found it much more difficult to move from their entrenched positions (see McDowell, 1993, Knox and Hughes, 1995).

Will the changes of attitude which appear to be surfacing through the behaviour of adults in their communities be reflected in the responses of the 12 year olds about their attitudes towards the future and their possible selves? Are there any other elements in the social structures which might be helping bring about and sustain and reinforce the changes?

Participatory politics / community development

The people of Northern Ireland were faced during all this period with the spectacle of their politicians continually in disagreement, refusing to compromise and showing themselves unable to interact positively. In addition their MPs had little or no influence at Westminster, compared to MPs in the rest of the UK or TDs in

Dublin. Now, while the average person in the streets of Dublin or London may not be inclined to scrutinize the events in Parliament, it is certain that he or she has more opportunities and options to do so than the average person in Belfast. Major legislation affecting the people of Northern Ireland was and is being passed at Westminster using mechanisms designed for secondary legislation and with little opportunity for scrutiny, debate, or amendment (Livingstone and Morison, 1995, p 12). It would not be surprising then, if the electorate took its responsibilities less seriously in Northern Ireland and even refused to become involved.

However it would seem that there is an innate need for people to try and find a way to have some say in decisions. A further development in Northern Ireland society relates to new means by which people have sought to render government power accountable. Since the areas of public power over which political parties have direct influence have declined it is perhaps not surprising, according to Livingstone and Morison (1995) that the search for means to render such power accountable has also moved away from traditional political forums. Stimulation for action and resistance to government influence is seen in the form of associations and interest groups focused on particular issues or policies and not 'politically-minded' in the party-political sense.

Initiative '92 was an example in Northern Ireland of the model first adopted by the New Ireland Forum, but in expanded form. Set up by a group in Northern Ireland in 1992, and chaired by an eminent Norwegian, Torkel Opsahl, it invited submissions from individuals and groups and traveled around Northern Ireland targeting people whose voices are not normally heard - women, rural dwellers, activists, prisoners and ex-prisoners and young people. Public hearings were held, with attendant publicity, to hear people's ideas of how the future of Northern Ireland should be shaped. A report was subsequently published on the findings (Pollak, 1993).

Most of the opportunities for people in the street to become involved in community action and decision have been on a smaller, more local scale. By far the majority have been in the area of what has come to be known as community development or community work, although there are also many groups which are motivated by the desire to improve community relations, to bring about 'reconciliation'. These come in a number of guises with varying aims and philosophies and some have been more long-lived than others, some have been wide ranging, others more narrowly focused. We will look briefly first at the 'community development' type of group and then at those involved specifically in bringing together people from different traditions in an attempt to determine whether they might have a role in bringing about changes in attitudes, self-concept and identity.

The period to 1981

Deane (1981) says that four elements are necessary for community work although the degrees to which they are present may vary widely:
• the work is self-help in nature
• it is located in an area of social and economic deprivation
• it demands some collective activity
• it is concerned in some way with an extension of democracy

Among the first of such action groups were probably the Homeless Citizens' League in Dungannon, alluded to above, and the Derry Unemployed Action Committee which was formed in January 1965 (Bardon, p. 648). These were really not totally new ventures but a further development of cooperative movements like Credit Unions and Housing Associations which had been established in Northern Ireland in the 1950s and '60s. Deane (1981) claims that in 1968 (after the Caledon housing episode and what ensued) there was abroad a feeling that change was not only desirable, but possible. In his view, the feeling of wanting to take control over the decision-making in their own lives was almost exclusively a Catholic and nationalist one, while Protestants/loyalists were locked into an attitude of entrenched imperialism and fear of change. Both views, in the turbulent times of the late 1960s and early 70s led to the formation of self-help groups - but now taking a more proactive stance - with titles like Tenants' and Welfare Rights Groups, and Defence Associations. Some of these groups were set up to meet immediate needs like summer play schemes for children, others to protest at local conditions (Save the Shankill). Hundreds of individuals became involved.

The movement was encouraged officially as it was felt in some quarters that community action could be one way of breaking the paralysis of the formal sectarian political system by heightening awareness of communal needs and stimulating groups across the sectarian divide to jointly address common social problems (Gafikin and Morrissey, 1987). Frazer wrote of the

> tremendous growth in community activity and new dynamic and progressive forms of voluntary effort in Northern Ireland...over the past decade (Frazer, 1981).

At a later stage it seemed that there were fears that voluntary-led initiatives might become dominant and there was a backing off by statutory agencies. However, considerable statutory funding was made available initially through the Community Relations Commission. After 1976, the funding function was handed over to local authorities. Rolston (1981) expressed grave misgivings at this move and felt that decisions on funding local community initiatives from then on were in many cases affected by sectionalism and sectarianism.

In relation to the 1981-82 window of this book, the overall note in the publication *Community Work in a Divided Society* (Frazer, 1981) is one of profound discouragement from the point of view of professional workers in the field. And as far as the influence of such groups is concerned, Deane (1981) noted that in the second part of the decade (1970s) opportunities to influence change in the decision-making process narrowed rather than broadened because of competition for resources and the emphasis in developing a neighbourhood identity, and he was sceptical about their effects on intergroup harmony.

The period to 1992

Figures from the following decade, leading up to our next window, 1992-93, tell a different story about the effectiveness of such groups for involving 'ordinary' people and going some way towards meeting their needs for participation in the development of their communities. Oliver (1995) reported that there has been an explosion in the volume and range of non-governmental / non-profit / thirdsector / independent sector / community-based / charitable / philanthropic / voluntary sector activity between 1981 and 1992.

The reasons adduced for this growth are that

some arose out of the Hunger Strike period, others responded to increasing social deprivation, and yet more to the nascent support given by groups such as the 'Community Development in Protestant Areas' group in the late '80s. We guesstimate that there at least 5000 such groups working across Northern Ireland (Oliver, 1995)

This marks a significant increase from the figure of 300 such groups cited for the mid 1970s (Livingstone and Morison, 1995). And if there were 'hundreds' of people participating in those 300 groups in the 70s, there must have been tens of thousands involved in the 5,000 groups in the early 90s (even two people per group, would have added up to 10,000 people). In relation to the locations involved in the present study it is of interest to note that the *Index of Community Groups in Northern Ireland* (NICVA, 1989) lists 32 such groups in (Protestant) East Belfast and 51 in (Catholic) West Belfast.

Some measure of what could be gained from participation in such groups may be found in *Women and Community Work in Northern Ireland* (Abbott and Frazer, 1985) especially in the article by Kelly (1985), although we must bear in mind Rowlands' point that it is a very slow process (1985). The outcomes probably apply to men also, but no research has been reported. They include:

- the formation of networks sometimes crossing the sectarian divide
- increases in declarative knowledge - information about matters affecting their lives,
- increases in procedural knowledge - how things work, including committees meetings, delegations and protests,
- increases in organizational skills,
- increases in self-confidence and self-esteem.
- enhanced ability to cope with stress

No formal measures have been carried out - it would make an interesting study - but it would seem likely that for participants in these organizations their ways of processing information have probably been changed as they tried to integrate new knowledge which was obviously beneficial to them; they will have developed different ways of thinking and perhaps become more flexible, more able to deal with ambiguity and to realize that the normal rules don't always apply. Would this be reflected in the self-concept and future orientation of our sample?

Reconciliation groups

A recent account of the development of 'institutions for conciliation and mediation' is provided by Wilson and Tyrrell (1995). They refer also to Gallagher and Worall (1982) and Bowman and Shivers (1984), in placing the time of the first emergence of such groups in 1964 and their 'mushrooming' in the post-1969 period. They provide some anecdotal evidence to illustrate the ways in people developed greater cognitive and emotional understanding through participating in such groups. A first step, they say, was frequently learning to deal with members of their own community who reacted harshly to the whole notion of groups and discussions of this kind. They also learned about different understandings of history, differing attitudes to the role of the police; but also on a practical level, they had to come to terms with different procedures accepted as 'normal' for discussion and decision-making but which differed for the two traditions and frequently reflected their roles in the wider society. Wilson and Tyrrell categorize the range of reconciliation groups as a) intentional groups of reconciliation; b) local groups formed in the midst of hostility; c) groups formed out of the experience of violent bereavement and d) children's community relations holidays. Over 70 such groups are now listed in *A Guide to Peace and Reconciliation Groups* (NICRC, 1993). Again, we wondered if any effects of this kind of participation by adults might have percolated through to the children in our sample.

Trends over time

On balance it would seem that a number of factors underlying societal structures in Northern Ireland could have been working to bring about challenges to self-concept and personal identity during the late 1980s. Events in the period up to 1981 would lead us to expect somewhat pessimistic views of the future, if our sample of children reflects the views of the adults in their environment. Some things were changing by 1992 - not much on the economic front and there was increased segregation in e.g. housing, but a slow diminution of violence, and on the other hand there were positive attempts to lessen the putative effects of segregation in schools, new political developments slowly evolving with openings for dialogue, the development of opportunities to participate in a meaningful way at local level and an increase in those who wished to do so and thereby showed themselves open to change.

This outline of events has described some of the historical, political, economic, social and community factors which could have had an influence on the ways people in Northern saw themselves, their possible selves, their place in society and their future there. We now turn to the results of the questionnaires in 1981 and 1992 to see whether these factors are reflected in the responses of 12 year-olds in Catholic West Belfast and Protestant East Belfast and how their attitudes compare with those of matched groups in Dublin and London.

3   12 year-olds in Belfast, Dublin and London

Introduction

The social environment in some working class areas of Northern Ireland and the extent to which it is 'disadvantaged' has been well documented for the period in which this study took place. The economic backdrop to the 'Troubles' is generally acknowledged to have been a contributory factor. Even now, in 1995, Government statistics (Jardine, 1995) show that gross domestic product per head is significantly lower in Northern Ireland than the UK average (82 per cent of the UK level and 79 per cent of the EU average) reflecting in part higher unemployment, (16.5 per cent for males, 6.6 per cent for females in December 1994 compared to 8.5 per cent for the rest of the UK), but also lower economic activity and a younger population. For people in work, average earnings tend to be lower than in the rest of the UK for both men and women in manual and non-manual occupations. NI average earnings for men in manual occupations are 86 per cent of those in the rest of the UK and average household income form all sources is also significantly lower in Northern Ireland. However while the overall average picture may be different in Belfast, there are undoubtedly areas in Dublin and London where employment, housing and general standards of living are similar to those in areas of Belfast as there would be in any large city. Our samples were drawn from such areas.

Socio-economic level has been found in many studies to be important for children's development and for their life chances (Essen and Wedge, 1982, Feldman and Elliott, 1993, Modell and Siegler, 1994, Cairns and Cairns, 1994). Children from families in receipt of social welfare payments been found to be less likely to stay at school and to have less pocket money; fewer of them had part-time jobs while at school and they were vaguer about post-school plans (Essen and Ghodsian, 1977). It would be expected that their standard of living would have a bearing on aspects of the children's identity formation in that it might influence the availability of opportunities for the development of a sense of competence, personal efficacy and self-esteem; it could also influence the development of social intelligence through the extent of accessibility to declarative knowledge and procedural knowledge; it would undoubtedly give the individual a sense of where he or she was located within the social system and thus affect his or perception of future orientation options and possible selves; and this in turn would possibly

50

guide decisions about participation in socially responsible behaviour and societal action.

In this chapter we try to form a picture of the standard of living of participants in the study in 1981 and in 1992. This investigation was designed so that socio-economic variables would be reasonably constant across the four locations since the interest in the study was in determining whether there would be cultural variability in the aspects of identity under consideration and whether these could be related to other factors in the socio-ecological environment.

Information was obtained on a range of elements relating to standard of living, not all of them conventional ones, in an effort to establish the comparability of the material circumstances of the home environments of the children in the different locations. The elements selected included

- ownership of household possessions
- whether or not the subject children had ever earned money earned by doing a job.
- the amount of weekly pocket money they received
- the amount they had earned, and
- how they spent their money

Selection of socio-economic indicators

Usually studies of this kind can present statistics on a range of social and economic factors which have been found to be related to particular aspects of children's academic, social and personality development. These include type of housing, size and composition of family, material possessions such as ownership of television sets, washing machines and other household appliances, the occupation and employment status of parents and household income and expenditure - factors also usually taken into account in assessing standards of living.

But, as will be explained below, it was not within the scope of the present project to obtain details of the types usually ascertained to confirm economic status. However, it was obviously necessary to have some grounding anchors to which relationships with outcomes could be investigated and possibly associated. A range of additional indicators was therefore devised to provide information to support the impressionistic one of the neighbourhoods and schools. These additional indicators were selected because they were likely to impinge actively on children's everyday lives and, it was felt that they could be regarded as socio-ecologically valid on a micro-level. The reasons for taking this course stemmed from the objectives of this part of the study (the delineation of contexts of development), and the nature and age of the respondents who were the sole sources of data (12 year-olds).

A first consideration in deciding on the indicators was related to the aims of the study and to the quality or texture of the information which it was thought would fulfill those aims. Since one of the aims of the study was directed towards establishing the relationship of particular elements of context with specific outcomes in terms of development, the selection of the elements to be studied had

51

to be made from the thousands of small details and daily interactions which constitute dynamic contributions to the holistic development of the individual.

The dearth of data in this area has been pointed out by many researchers. Magnusson (1981) writes of 'the dire need for systematic knowledge in appropriate terms about the environment and situations'; Silbereisen, Noack and Eyferth (1986) state that 'research on adolescents in their environment is fairly rare'. Elder, Modell and Parke (1994) say that '[while] the social environment - social relations and values- conditions the child's practices of everyday life....we know relatively little about the social environments of children'.

The second consideration was related to the sources of data available to the study. This was a small-scale project and without direct funding. Information was obtained only from the respondents to the questionnaire and access to school or other records was not provided for, although some general statistics on enrolments were made available to the researcher. Since the children in the present study were therefore the main sources of data, this had implications for the kinds of information which could be sought. It was necessary to choose indicators on which the children would be likely to be able to give reliable information and to focus on elements which would be meaningful and accessible to them.

A further limiting consideration in deciding on the information to be sought was a professional and ethical one - the need not to offend sensibilities and to maintain access for researchers. McWhirter (1984) mentions that because of the objections of some school principals, she had to remove certain questions from a study she was undertaking, which measured children's experience of 'Troubles' - related events. And it has been known for parents in Northern Ireland to protest against questions being asked by researchers of their children in school and to demand that researchers be excluded, even when such questions appeared quite innocuous and non-threatening to the children and were professionally and ethically quite legitimate. At least one episode has also been reported in which social science researchers were asked to leave particular housing areas in Northern Ireland because of objections to their line of questioning. In hard-line areas, researchers may be an object of suspicion and there have been cases of researchers being driven out and even shot (Taylor, 1988, pp. 136-39).

In the present case it was decided that although there could well be merit in uncovering and analyzing issues of a sensitive nature in an investigation of contextual variables related to families and child development in Northern Ireland, the interests of science and professionalism could also be well served by an investigation of non-contentious issues.

Staying with the basic categories of factors usually considered to contribute to standard of living/lifestyle - housing, occupational level, income and expenditure, an attempt was made to select elements within those categories on which the children in the study would be able to provide information.

Elements contributing to standard of living

i) Housing factors / material possessions

While standards and type of housing and whether it was rented or owned would be considered in large-scale studies to be a useful indicator of a particular socio-economic level, it was likely in the first place that this variable would not differentiate adequately within or between the groups of children in the present study, since the majority in all the locations under study were living in areas where most people were in rented public authority housing. Secondly, it was considered unlikely that the 12 year-olds who were the subjects of this study would reliably know, when asked for an instant response, whether their families rented or owned their homes. Thirdly, while they would probably be able to give details about the size and type of accommodation this information would need qualification by reference to the number of people resident in the family home, their ages, relationships, occupations and so on if it were to be useful. The costs of collecting and analyzing such information were felt to outweigh possible benefits in the present study and it was felt that the energies of researcher and respondents could be more usefully channeled.

Instead of information on a macro-level about housing accommodation therefore, respondents were asked about specific material possessions which have been found in other studies to be related to socio-economic level. The questions asked at different points in the Questionnaire were:

• *Have you got a telephone in your house?*	*No*	*Yes*
• *Have you got any books of your own?:*	*No*	*Yes*
• *Do you ride a bicycle*	*No*	*Yes*
Have you got one of your own?	*No*	*Yes*
• *Has you family got a car at the moment*	*No*	*Yes*

ii) Occupational level and employment status

It was known that there was a certain degree of unemployment among parents of all the groups in the study and they were claiming unemployment benefits. The psychological outcomes of unemployment for adults in Northern Ireland have been researched (Gallagher, 1991, Evason, 1985, Trew and Kilpatrick, 1984) and the relationship of unemployment to the incidence of marital strain and domestic violence (Rolston and Tomlinson, 1988) but the only mention of children in these studies has been in terms of what they were deprived of because of lack of family finance (Evason, 1985). Some evidence that patterns of behaviour may differ between families where parents have been unemployed while a particular child is aged 11 - 16 and families where parents have been employed during that time was found by Whyte (1992b) in Belfast. The findings suggested that these patterns of behaviour may have had an effect on the post-school outcomes for the children concerned.

In the present study it was not thought feasible to ask directly about the occupations or employment status of parents. The reliability of such information, whether parents were actually employed or not, was felt to be suspect for a number of reasons. It is an acknowledged fact in both the United Kingdom (including Northern Ireland) and the Republic of Ireland that some of those adults who claim unemployment benefit (i.e. are 'on the dole') operate in the black economy and earn considerable sums (SACHR, 1987, Howe, 1989a, 1989b). Children of such parents would be warned to be wary of disclosing parental occupations in case the welfare authorities came to hear of it.

In addition, among those parents who were employed in Belfast, there might have been the possibility of breaching confidentiality, and worse, of putting lives at risk. Children in Northern Ireland whose parents work in the security forces (the British army or the locally recruited Ulster Defence Regiment as it was then, later the Royal Irish Rangers), or in the prison service or in the police force (Royal Ulster Constabulary) are instructed not to reveal this fact to anyone. The identification of an individual with an occupation in those categories could put them or their families in danger. In fact many individual members of the security forces have been killed since 1969 simply on the grounds of their occupation and in some cases their families were also physically attacked.

So in order to get some kind of a handle on family employment status, as it affected twelve-year-olds, respondents were asked:

•*Have you ever done a job for money*	*No*	*Yes*
If so, what did you do?		

iii) Income

It was felt that 12 year olds were unlikely to know about the weekly, monthly or annual income of the household. But they were asked:

• *Does anyone give you pocket money?*	*No*	*Yes*
• *[If yes], about how much do you get each week altogether?*		
• *How much did you earn* (if they had done a job for money)?		
• *Do you save any of your money?*	*Yes*	*No*

iv) Expenditure

While it was not expected that the respondents would know the amount spent weekly on groceries and other items by their families, it was thought that they should be able to provide some information on their own spending patterns. They were asked to indicate items on a checklist on which they spent their own money (with the possibility of adding additional items).

•*What do you usually spend your money on?*

sweets	books magazines
cokes/drinks	youth club
crisps	space invaders
comics	clothes
charity	records

•*Please say what else.*

How the findings were added together

A composite variable 'Goods' was calculated on the basis of one point awarded for each of the items relating to household possessions - ownership of books, bicycle, car and telephone. The totals were used to give a rough approximation of overall standard of living which could be used to compare groups and to relate with other variables.

A further composite variable 'Goods Plus' was composed of a point for each of the material possessions - books, phone, car, bicycle, receiving pocket money, having done a job for money and savings. Some respondents had said that they received pocket money or that they had earned money without giving the actual amounts, so this procedure gave credit to probably a greater number of respondents than if simply amounts received or earned had been taken into account.

A third composite variable 'Goods plus Money' was made up of the items included in the 'Goods' variable plus a weighted score for pocket money and for money earned.

In the next sections of this chapter the findings on these individual questions and on the composite variables will be presented for the groups in West and East Belfast, Dublin and London, for girls and boys separately and for the samples at both time points of the study, 1981 and 1992.

Findings on household goods

i) Books Between 81 per cent and 99 per cent of the children in each location said that they owned books in 1981 and between 93 per cent and 96 per cent in 1992 - an increase overall. There were no statistically significant differences between groups or between boys and girls. The percentages of children who owned books increased slightly but did not differ substantially between 1981 and 1992 and ownership of books appeared to be a stable feature for the vast majority of children in the samples in all four locations.

ii) Bicycle Between 65 per cent (London) and 84 per cent (East Belfast) of the respondents owned a bicycle in 1981 and there were statistically significant differences between locations. The East Belfast (84 per cent) and Dublin (74 per cent) children were more likely to have a bicycle than the West Belfast (70 per cent) or London children. By 1992, perhaps a mark of increased prosperity, the West Belfast children had caught up with the others with an ownership rate of 86 per cent (compared to 84 per cent, still, in East Belfast, 74 per cent in Dublin and 65 per cent in London). Like owning books this appeared to be a fairly stable feature of life for children once a certain standard of living has been reached.

iii) Family car Around 75 per cent of the East Belfast and London families had cars at both time points. The West Belfast children had the lowest percentage (56 per cent) of car owners in 1981, but they increased to 64 per cent in 1992. Car ownership in the Dublin sample decreased between 1981 (68 per cent) and 1992 (54 per cent) and remained level in London and East Belfast (74 per cent).

iv) Household telephone There were significant differences between locations in 1981 with Dublin (41 per cent) and West Belfast (60 per cent) being well below the others in the percentage of households with telephones (75 per cent in East Belfast; 91 per cent in London). By 1992, there was a big increase in telephone ownership in both the Dublin and West Belfast groups to around 76 per cent and there was a slight fall in London to 86 per cent, so that the differences between locations at that time were not significant.

Composite variable: 'Goods'

The composite variable 'Goods' was made up of a 'score' awarded depending on the number of the above items in the household. The scores are depicted in Figure 3.1.

Analysis of variance showed significant differences between groups in both 1981 and 1992 (F = 12.098, P<.001 in 1981; F = 4.511; p<.006 in 1992) although the differences appeared to be less in 1992. The overall score of the London children had declined in line with other indices, for example the number of free school dinners in the schools involved had doubled in the time period; the 'scores' of all the other groups had increased. West Belfast had a low score in 1981, but had a score equal to that of East Belfast in 1992 - both at 4.3 - and this was higher than the London or Dublin groups. This suggests an increase in standard of living for the West Belfast children greater than for any of the other groups over the period of the study, and it seems to have served to bring them up to the level of those in East Belfast, to a certain extent.

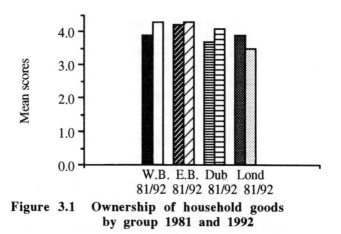

**Figure 3.1   Ownership of household goods
by group 1981 and 1992**

It will be interesting to see how these findings are related to the aspects of self-concept and identity investigated in this project; whether, for example, those with the lowest score in terms of material possessions were also inclined to have a more materialistic outlook and a shorter-term view of gratification needs, whether there were differences between the groups in the way in which this variable related to other variables and whether there were changes over time.

Differences between girls and boys

There was a statistically significant difference between the sexes overall with regard to mean score on 'Goods' in 1981. This was undoubtedly due to the differences between the percentages of girls (64 per cent) and boys (83 per cent) overall with bicycles in 1981 (P<.001). When the findings for girls and boys were examined separately at location level this difference appeared to be due mainly to the London children, for although there was a slight trend for more boys to have bicycles in every location the differences were not significant in Belfast or Dublin.

The significant differences had vanished overall in 1992 however, due perhaps mainly to an increase in the number of West Belfast girls and, to a lesser extent, London girls with bicycles (increase from 67 percent to 86 percent in West Belfast and from 46 percent to 57 percent in London) - a sign perhaps of greater independence being allowed to girls.

Had the respondents ever worked for payment themselves?

More than two thirds of the children in Dublin (74 per cent) and in Belfast (72 per cent, WB; 66 per cent, EB) had done a job to earn money in 1981 (Figure 3.2). A lower percentage of London children (44 per cent) than of children from the other locations had earned some money from doing a job in 1981. And, as shown in Figure 3.2 they also had fewer job opportunities in 1992 compared to 1981 whereas slightly higher percentages in all the other locations had worked for money in 1992 (36 per cent, London; 74 per cent, East and West Belfast; 76 per cent, Dublin).

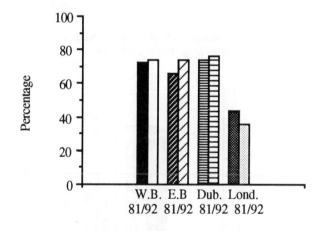

Figure 3.2 Opportunities to earn money by group 1981 and 1992

The finding that the London children had least opportunities in this area was stable over the time period. Taken in conjunction with the decline in level of material household possessions for the London sample as described above, it suggests that the dynamics of their developmental context were different from those, for example of the West Belfast children who seemed to be on an upward slope. Perhaps the neighbourhoods where the London children lived were less stable in terms of population giving rise also to fewer providers of jobs on a regular basis and less of a neighbourhood support system. Perhaps also, the area where the London children lived had suffered from the effects of the recession to a greater extent than those in Dublin or Belfast, resulting in less money being available to pay for small jobs; perhaps the families in London did not wish to encourage their children to take on jobs to earn money at that age.

Girls and boys

When we look at the findings separately for girls and boys (Figures 3.3, 3.4), we can see slightly different trends in some areas.

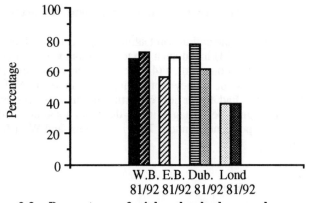

Figure 3.3   Percentage of girls who had earned money by group 1981 and 1992

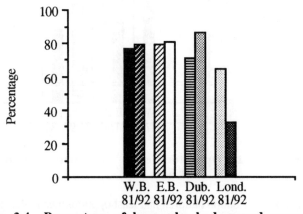

Figure 3.4   Percentage of boys who had earned money by group 1981 and 1992

There were significant differences between the sexes at both time points with more boys overall (68 per cent in 1981; 70 per cent in 1992) having had jobs for money compared to the girls (60 per cent in 1981; 62 per cent in 1992). The biggest gaps between the percentages of girls and boys were in London - which had the least opportunities for money-earning - and East Belfast - which had less part-time casual job opportunities for this age group than West Belfast in 1981. The gap between girls' and boys' job opportunities had narrowed on the whole in 1992. This is another indicator of changes happening for girls - along with increased possession of a bicycle which may be seen as a symbol of independence. It looks as though opportunities for activities outside the family were also increasing for them over this period.

The London girls fared better than the London boys over the time period - they did not lose any ground as the same percentage of them had worked in 1992 as in 1981, whereas there was a substantial decrease in the percentage of London boys who had earned money over the period. The trend was upwards for the Belfast girls and the Dublin girls lost ground - but then a higher percentage of them than of the others had had opportunities to earn money in 1981 and the decrease brought them closer into line with the Belfast children, still higher than the London girls.

A higher percentage of boys than of girls in every location except Dublin had earned money in 1981 (Figure 3.4). The opportunities increased at a similar rate to those for the girls in Belfast; in London they decreased sharply and in Dublin, they increased at the same rate as those for girls decreased.

The actual work done to earn money will be discussed in conjunction with other extra-familial experiences in Chapter Six.

Pocket money - how many were given a weekly allowance?

There were no statistically significant differences between the groups in 1981 in the percentages of children who actually received pocket money with between 89 per cent (Dublin) and 99 per cent (West Belfast) getting a weekly allowance. While differences between the groups were not significant, the trend was for fewer of the Dublin children, whose group also scored lowest for possession of household goods, to be given pocket money; but among the West Belfast children whose level of household possessions was very close to that of the Dublin children, a much higher percentage were given a weekly allowance. We seem to be getting a hint of different sets of values in the different locations from these findings, and the possibility of differences therefore in developmental context.

What about the actual amounts involved?

However, receiving pocket money is only part of the story. The actual amount can be important. Figure 3.5 shows the mean amounts received. One might have expected the difference in material possessions to be reflected in variable amounts of pocket money given to the children in the different locations. But when the mean amounts were compared across groups, it was found that the differences were not statistically significant in 1981 or in 1992 (Figure 3.6). However, it would seem that the distribution was not normal in that the median was in every case lower than the mean. A few children in each location were probably pushing up the average.

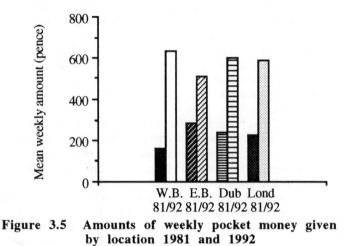

Figure 3.5   Amounts of weekly pocket money given by location 1981 and 1992

The amounts given as pocket money, ranged from a mean of £1.60 (WB) to £2.81 (EB) in 1981. The trend was partly in line with material possessions in that, in 1981, the East Belfast children, who had the highest score on 'Goods', received the highest amounts of pocket money; but the Dublin children, with the lowest 'score' for material possessions did not receive the lowest amounts. Instead it was the London children whose position on the material possessions scale in 1981 had been in the middle. One obviously cannot assume that ownership of household goods is the only criterion for deciding on amount of pocket money.

There was an increase in the mean amounts of pocket money in every location in 1992 when they ranged from £5.08 (EB) to £6.31 (WB). In line with the increase in material possessions already noted, the West Belfast children had the greatest increase in pocket money, whereas the East Belfast children had the least increase of all and in 1992 were no longer at the top of the scale for this variable; in fact they were at the bottom, although not by very much. This may reflect the greater economic challenges faced by this community in the late '80s and early '90's - increasing unemployment among parents, a situation where they were being financially squeezed. The Dublin and London children maintained their positions vis-à-vis each other. This finding provides more evidence for the idea that the developmental contexts within their families and their communities for these children were different - more stability possibly in the Dublin situation, more change happening in Belfast, both East and West, with hints of more prosperity in West Belfast and possibly less in East Belfast. This could obviously have implications for other aspects of their psychological development.

But statistics can obscure reality. The mean amounts only tell part of the story. When the findings are looked at in terms of the way in which the amounts were distributed we get a better idea of the disposable income available to the children in each group and the way in which it differed between locations and changed over the time period (Figure 3.6).

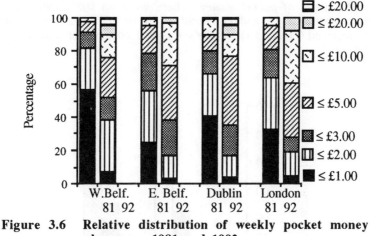

Figure 3.6   Relative distribution of weekly pocket money by group 1981 and 1992

Going beyond 'average' earnings

The figure (3.6) shows that in 1981 around half of the children in the sample from East Belfast were given £3.00 or more per week and this was the case for under 20 per cent of West Belfast children. A higher percentage of children from West Belfast than from anywhere else in the study were given £1.00 or less. This shows a bigger difference between the children in our samples in West and East Belfast, than between the children in Dublin and London. The London and Dublin children were quite similar in the distribution of amounts in both 1981 and 1992.

Over time, the percentage getting larger amounts increased everywhere. The percentage increase over the 1981 amounts ranged from 296 per cent (WB), 159 per cent (London) 148 per cent (Dublin) to 81 per cent (EB). The sizable increase in West Belfast is consistent with the other data on improvements in possession of material goods and the lower rate of increase for the East Belfast children, who had, of course, started from a higher baseline, may, as previously noted, reflect a decline in economic well-being in that community over the period.

But there was still a big differential between the children in West and East Belfast, with 62 per cent of those in East Belfast getting amounts of £3.00 or more and 44 per cent of those in West Belfast getting that amount. It may also be noted that more children in London and East Belfast than in the other two locations tended to get amounts of over £10.00.

Differences between girls and boys

Pocket money There were no statistically significant differences between the sexes with 93 percent of the girls and 93 percent of the boys receiving pocket money in 1981. There was a slight decrease in the percentages in 1992, but they were still similar across locations and between the sexes.

Average amount of pocket money There were no statistically significant differences between girls and boys in either 1981 or 1992 in the amounts of pocket money received (Figure 3.7), but the sums involved were not equally distributed (Figure 3.8)

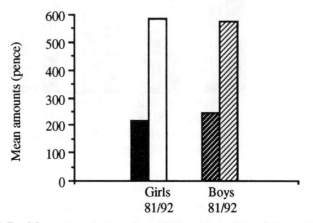

Figure 3.7   Mean amounts of pocket money for girls and boys

Relative distribution of pocket money When we break down the distribution by amount and examine the sums given to girls and boys separately (Figure 3.8), we see that girls were disadvantaged to a considerable extent, although the mean amounts of pocket money received only differed slightly from those of the boys.

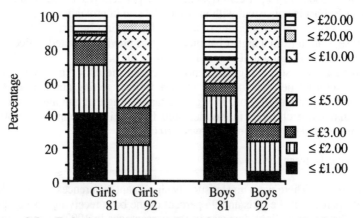

Figure 3.8   Relative amounts of pocket money received by girls and boys 1981 and 1992

Girls (£2.15) got slightly less on average than boys (£2.46) in 1981, and slightly more in 1992 (girls, £5.83; boys, £5.74), when mean amounts are considered. But looking at the actual sums involved, more girls were getting lower amounts at both time points. Over 80 percent of girls received amounts of £3.00 or less in 1981 compared to the 60 percent of boys. In 1992, amounts had increased for both girls and boys, and similar percentages received amounts of more than £5.00. The main difference in 1992 was that more boys than girls received amounts of between £3.00 and £5.00. However, it should be noted that the mean increase for girls was higher than that for boys in that it was 171 percent for girls and 133 percent for boys. This suggests that things may correct themselves with time.

Doing a job for money

As stated above, fewer London children had had a job for money in 1981 compared to the other groups.While the percentage of those having worked for money was similar for the Dublin and Belfast groups, there were differences in the mean amounts they earned in 1981 which almost reached significance (F= 2.633; P<.051) (Figure 3.9). The Dublin children appeared to earn higher amounts.

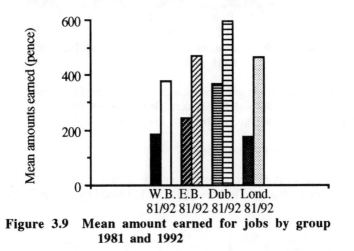

Figure 3.9   Mean amount earned for jobs by group 1981 and 1992

The mean amounts earned ranged from £1.73 (London), through £1.84 (WB), £2.41 (EB), to £3.66 (Dublin). Figure 3.9 shows the mean amounts earned for a random job for each group in 1981 and 1992. The difference between the East and West Belfast children may reflect the differential incomes of the communities.

By 1992, the differences were not significant between groups and the mean earnings had increased to £4.64 (London), £3.77 (WB), £4.69 (EB) and £5.92 (Dublin). Dublin children were still, however, the highest earners; some of the London children (fewer of whom had worked) obviously were on to a good thing as their earnings were quite high and the East Belfast children still earned more than those in West Belfast, as was the case with their parents.

When the amounts earned are analyzed according to the sums involved, we get a slightly different picture (Figure 3.10). The distribution of amounts earned was very similar for West and East Belfast children although the mean amounts had been different and by 1992, the London children resemble the Belfast children also. The Dublin children however have a different profile as regards earnings with a higher percentage of them earning higher amounts than in any other group at both time points.

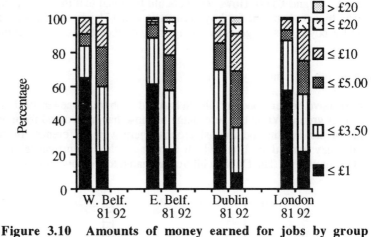

Figure 3.10   Amounts of money earned for jobs by group 1981 and 1992

The mean amount earned increased in every group. The increases ranged from 168 per cent (London), 104 per cent (WB), 94 per cent (EB) to 61 per cent (Dublin), but they were greater for boys (91 per cent) than for girls (67 per cent).

Differences between girls and boys

It is clear that in 1981 boys earned more than girls (Figure 3.11). The difference was not statistically significant in 1981 (£2.15 earned by girls and £2.46 by boys),

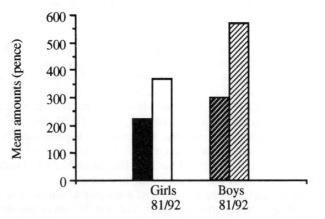

Figure 3.11   Mean amounts earned by girls and boys for jobs

but it was statistically significant in 1992 (F= 9.133; P<.003), with girls earning £3.69 and boys on average £5.71 for a job done by them.

There was also a 2-way interaction by sex and group in 1992. Girls in Dublin appeared to earn considerably more than their sisters in Belfast and London. Those in East Belfast earned least in 1992.

Relative earnings of girls and boys

The disadvantage of being a girl looking for part-time work to earn money is further seen when we look at the distribution of the amounts earned (Figure 3.12). Only 6 per cent of the girls earned more than £5.00 for a job in 1981, in comparison with 14 per cent of the boys; at the other end of the scale, 86 per cent of the girls earned less than £3.50 compared to 76 per cent of the boys. In 1992 the increases ranged from 168 per cent (London), 104 per cent (WB), 94 per cent (EB), to 61 per cent (Dublin), but they were greater for boys (91 per cent) than for girls (67 per cent) so that the pattern is similar, with more girls earning lower amounts and more boys earning higher amounts. It could be a question of the kinds of jobs they do, but it must also be a factor of the value attached to them.

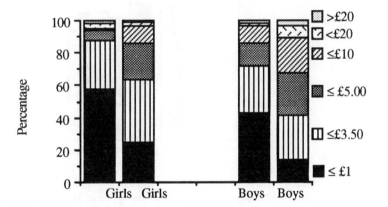

Figure 3.12   Relative mean amounts earned by girls and boys 1981 and 1992

Savings

There were significant differences between the locations in the percentages of the groups who said that they saved some of their money. Across locations those most likely to have had savings in 1981 were the Dublin children (91 per cent) and those least likely were the West Belfast children (73 per cent). In 1992, however, the West Belfast children had improved their performance to 87 per cent and the Dublin children had fallen off considerably to 78 per cent while the East Belfast and London groups had 86-90 per cent savers among them. This made the groups more congruent in 1992.

Girls and boys

There were no statistically significant differences between girls and boys overall, nor in any location with 86 per cent of girls and 84 per cent of boys overall putting some money into savings in 1981 and 87 per cent of the girls and 84 per cent of the boys in 1992. The percentages were very close in every location.

Composite variables 'Goods Plus', 'Goods plus Money'

This was composed of a point for each of the material possessions - books, phone, car, bicycle, and the three variables based on availability of income - receiving pocket money, having done a job for money and savings. Some respondents had said that they received pocket money or that they had earned money without giving the actual amounts, so this procedure gave credit to probably a greater number of respondents than if simply amounts received or earned had been taken into account.

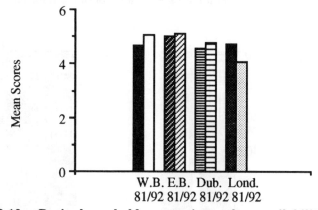

Figure 3.13   Basic household possessions plus availability of disposable income by group 1981 and 1992

In 1981 the East Belfast children had the highest scores on this variable and the Dublin children were the lowest (Figure 3.13). But in 1992, the West Belfast children had caught up with the East Belfast children; the Dublin children had also increased their scores and the London children registered a decrease.

Goods plus money

This variable was composed of the items included in the 'Goods' variable plus a weighted score for pocket money and for money earned.

Analysis of variance showed significant differences by sex and by group for both 1981 and 1992, but no interactive effects. The Belfast and Dublin children had similar scores to each other in both 1981 and 1992, when amounts of money available to them were taken into account and the London children had lower composite mean scores on this variable than the other three groups at both time points. Boys had higher scores than girls at both time points.

Relationship between goods owned and money?

Correlation coefficients were calculated between the scores for 'Goods' and the amounts of pocket money and money earned. No significant relationship was found for any group or for either sex. This meant that children in families which had all four of the household amenities - phone, car, books, bike, were as likely as children in families which lacked any or all of these - to receive higher or lower amounts of pocket money and to earn high or lower sums for work done.

What did they spend their money on?

A list of 8 items was provided and respondents were invited to check items which they liked to spend their money on. The results are presented in Tables 3.1 and 3.2. Apart from the daring few who wrote in alcohol and cigarettes (2 per cent overall), no additional items were added.

The most interesting finding may be the different rank accorded to Youth Club activities - highest for West Belfast, but higher for both the Belfast groups than for the Dublin or London groups at both timepoints. Records/tapes were higher for the East Belfast and Dublin groups than for the others and clothes were higher for the Dublin group than for the others. Apart from the daring few who wrote in alcohol and cigarettes (2 per cent overall), no additional items were added.

Differences between girls and boys

The main differences between the sexes may be seen to lie in the greater interest of girls in clothes, especially in 1981, and also in the greater interest of boys in space invaders and similar slot-machine activities. By 1992, boys were becoming more interested in clothes (Table 3.3).

Both girls and boys had lost interest in comics or picture papers in 1992 compared to 1981, but whereas fewer boys than girls were buying them in 1981, and the percentages of both girls and boys declined, the percentage of girls declined by more than that of boys so that more boys than girls were buying them in 1992.

The percentages spending money on books remained stable over the period, but the difference between girls and boys remained the same with considerably more girls than boys buying books. There was also quite a stable percentage who gave some money to charity - again more girls than boys. The percentage spending money on records and tapes went down over the period, as did the percentage spending money on sweets.

Tables 3.1, 3.2 and 3.3 give details of how they spent their money by location and by sex in 1981 and 1992.

Table 3.1
How they spent their money in 1981

W. Belfast	E. Belfast	Dublin	London
Sweets	Sweets	Sweets	Sweets
Comics	Records,tapes	Clothes	Comics
Youth club	Clothes	Records,tapes	Books/mag.
Clothes	Comics	Comics	Clothes
Books/mag.	Books/mag.	Books/mag.	Records,tapes
Records,tapes	Youth Club	Space Invaders	Space Invaders
Space Invaders	Space Invaders	Youth Club	Youth Club
Charity	Charity	Charity	Charity
Cig./alcohol	Cig./alcohol		Cig./alcohol

Table 3.2
How they spent their money in 1992

W. Belfast	E. Belfast	Dublin	London
Sweets etc.	Sweets etc.	Sweets etc.	Sweets etc.
Youth Club	Clothes	Clothes	Books/mag.
Clothes	Books/mag.	Books/mag.	Clothes
Books/mag.	Comics	Space Invaders	Comics
Charity	Youth Club	Records,tapes	Records,tapes
Space Invaders	Records,tapes	Comics	Space invaders
Comics	Space Invaders	Youth club	Charity
Records,tapes	Charity	Charity	Youth club
Cigs./Alcohol			

Table 3.3
Differences between the sexes overall
in patterns of expenditure 1981/1992

Girls 1981	Boys 1981	Girls 1992	Boys 1992
Sweets 74%	Sweets 73%	Sweets 71%	Sweets 61%
Clothes 51%	Comics 35%	Clothes 47%	Clothes 33%
Comics 38%	Space invaders 33%	Books 40%	Space invaders 30%
Books 37%	Records/tapes 24%	Youth Club 20%	Comics 27%
Records/tapes 36%	Books 22%	Records/tapes 20%	Books 24%
Youth Club 26%	Youth Club 20%	Comics 18%	Youth Club 21%
Charity 17%	Clothes 19%	charity 16%	Records/tapes 16%
Space invaders 9%	Charity 17%	Space invaders 9%	Charity 13%

Summary

Goods and pocket money

- When basic household possessions only were taken into account, the East Belfast children were best off at both time points and the Dublin children least well off. The same was true, but only in 1981 and not in 1992, when the simple fact of receiving pocket money, earning money and saving i.e. having some available disposable income, were entered into the calculation.
- When amounts received as pocket money and earned as job money were taken into account, there were no differences between the Belfast and Dublin children; money compensated for lack of material possessions in the Dublin children, particularly money earned. The London children were the most disadvantaged.
- There was an increase in material possessions over time for all groups except the London group. Pocket-money increased by up to 296 per cent and money earned by up to 168 per cent.

Earnings and savings

- Dublin children were more likely to have earned money and London children were the least likely to have done so at both time points.
- Dublin children earned on average more money than any other group at both time points.
- There was an increase in the percentage of those doing jobs for money in every location over the time period, except London.
- A higher percentage of Dublin children said that they saved money in 1981 and a higher percentage of West Belfast children than of the others said so in 1992.

Girls and boys

- Boys were financially better off than girls - more of them received higher amounts of pocket money although the mean amount was similar - and the mean amount earned per job was significantly higher for boys.
- More girls received and earned lower amounts.
- Boys had more opportunities to earn money than girls.
- There were no differences between the sexes with regard to savings
- There were no differences over time - similar findings in 1992 as in 1981
- Having household possessions was not significantly related to amount of pocket money nor money earned for any group or for girls or boys.

Trends over time

The groups in the four locations seemed to be quite well matched in terms of socio-economic level in 1981 with slight differences in some items favouring the East Belfast children at that time. The West and East Belfast children and the Dublin children appeared to have experienced an increase in material prosperity over the period 1981 to 1992 and this was especially true for the children in West

Belfast. The increase for the East Belfast children had been somewhat less than for the others, but in 1992 the Dublin and Belfast groups were fairly equally endowed with material possessions and income. The population from which London children were drawn seemed to have undergone a reversal of fortunes and in 1992 their position was well below that of the other three groups on most of the variables investigated here.

Previous research would suggest that in terms of developmental life paths, the (Protestant) East Belfast children could be assumed to be enjoying a better start, as they appeared to be slightly less materially disadvantaged and they would be expected to have a better chance in educational terms of achieving their ambitions. On this index, the Catholic West Belfast children's prospects changed quite substantially for the better over the time period, so we would expect them to have lower expectations in 1981 and perhaps higher expectations in 1992. Research on 'possible selves' to date does not indicate what we should expect, but time will tell.

When the actual amounts of money available to the children as pocket money or as money earned from jobs were added into the equation, the differences between the Belfast and Dublin children were not statistically significant. If this is an important underlying factor, one would expect them to have similar ideas about their stake in the future. The London children were considerably more disadvantaged, and their material standards appeared to decline over the period of the study so that they would, on this basis, be expected to have different ideas about themselves and their future.

However, it should be noted that while the composite 'scores' of the Dublin and Belfast children were similar for lifestyle as defined in this way, it is clear that the elements which made up the composite score were differently weighted. The elements which made up the balance were the amounts of money at the disposition of the children, in particular the money they earned and over which they had some control. In a way, although they were living in similar surroundings, household possessions were a 'given' in which the children had no say, but they had choices about whether or not to look for part-time work, presumably with the support of their parents, which would enable them to earn variable amounts of money. The Dublin children may have had opportunities in this regard which were not available to the children in the other locations perhaps due to the 'Troubles' in Belfast and to the 'big city' environment in London. This factor could constitute an element of difference between them and the Belfast children in the contextual composition of their lifestyle which could have an effect on their life paths.

The differences between girls and boys, particularly in 1981 are worth noting, and they were similar in all locations. The trends towards increased equality of opportunity in terms of pocket money, bicycles, and job possibilities, though not earnings, which denote greater freedom of choice, the opening out of more options for girls, particularly in West Belfast and East Belfast may be significant in terms of the outcome variables being investigated in this study. It is possible that these changes, rooted in historical time and linked with social and economic forces will have implications for other aspects of the children's development, such as their orientation towards the future.

We ask next whether the differences in aspects of standards of living found in this chapter for the groups in 1981 actually made any difference to their lifestyle - the way they spent their free time, the opportunities they had to develop friendships with peers, try out activities, develop social competencies and interests, - behaviours which contribute also to identity formation. Given the contrast between girls and boys in certain areas of their lives, we wondered whether this would carry through to leisure activities and interests - would differences be more salient by location or by sex? We also wondered if any differences found in 1981 would level out over time as appeared to be happening for standards of living between the Belfast children (especially the Catholic West Belfast children) and the others.

4 Leisure for 12 year-olds 1981 and 1992

Introduction

Leisure activities are becoming an increasingly important part of culture and for adolescents they represent one of the areas in their lives in which they can often make real choices and be independent, even if within certain limits. Fine, Mortimer and Roberts (1993) point out that adolescents spend a significant portion of their time engaged in leisure activities, including those that involve the mass media. Socializing with others, engaging in hobbies or sports, listening to music and watching television have been found to account for 15 per cent of young people's time at school, 47 per cent of their time at home and 58 per cent of their time with peers (Csikszentmihalyi and Larson, 1984).

The kinds of leisure activity in which adolescents engage has been found in some cases to be influenced by social class, as well as by race and ethnicity (Engstrom, 1974, Flegle, 1972, Goldstein, 1979) although the evidence here is mixed (Gras, 1976, M. E. Poole, 1983). There is evidence too that teenage boys and girls have different leisure preferences in countries as diverse as Nigeria (Amuchie, 1982), Sweden (Engstrom, 1974), Australia, (Garton and Pratt, 1987), Great Britain (Carrington, Chivers and Williams, 1987), the United States (Colley, 1984) and among Israeli Jews and Arabs (Florian and Har-Even, 1984). The strong tendency for boys to prefer sports, especially team sports and vigorous activities, would appear to be mediated by the relatively greater social support they get for such participation. Public leisure scenes such as pinball arcades, slot machine games and so on have also been found to be dominated by boys (Kestenbaum and Weinstein, 1983, Manning and Campbell, 1973, Ng and June, 1985). Girls' leisure activities have been less well studied, perhaps because they frequently occur in private settings rather than in public (McRobbie and Garber, 1976, Eder, 1985, Wulff, 1988).

In relation to the process of personal identity formation, it is likely that spare time activities are very influential. They offer opportunities to meet with peers, and to initiate relationships which will influence their self-esteem and self-concept, and which will enable them to develop and try out values which perhaps differ from those of their parents. In their leisure time, young people may participate in activities which add to their declarative knowledge and procedural knowledge particularly if their leisure activities include reading and watching television and this will in turn enhance their feelings of self-efficacy

This chapter will focus on issues related to leisure. We asked whether the children in West Belfast, East Belfast, Dublin and London had similar opportunities with regard to leisure activities, whether they enjoyed similar pastimes and whether there were changes over time. We describe in the following pages:

- how the children spent their spare time
- what kinds of books they read,
- what kinds of television programmes they enjoyed.
- what kinds of games and team sports they played
- what other activities they participated in.

We wondered if differences between the locations existed; whether, for example, the 'Troubles' might have resulted in a restriction of activities for the Belfast children and whether any differences might contribute to an explanation for differential identity formation.

Finding out about leisure activities

Questions were grouped in different parts of the questionnaire as follows:

•What did you yesterday afternoon after school?
•What did you do the day before that in the afternoon?
•What else do you sometimes do after school?
•What did you do yesterday after your evening meal/
•What did you do in the evening the day before yesterday?
•What else do you sometimes do in the evenings?
•What do you usually do on Saturdays?
•What do you usually do on Sundays?

and, at another point,

•Do you ever read books outside school?
•Do you belong to a library?
•Do you ever read comics or magazines?
  - name one you have read lately
•Name three books you have read in the past month

and, in a different section:

•Name the three [TV] programmes which you have enjoyed most
  during the past week

In addition a list was provided of sports, team games and general activities and the children were invited to place a checkmark against any of them in which they had participated during the last month.

Questions about games and activities

•What games and activities do you enjoy outside school hours?
(tick any you have enjoyed during the last month)

Group A

Athletics	Gymnastics
Badminton	Riding
Bowling	Swimming
Boxing	Table-tennis
Dancing	Tennis

Do you play for a club?　　Yes　　No

Group B

Basketball/Netball
Football
Handball
Hockey/Camogie

Do you play for a team?　　Yes　　No

Group C

Art	Handicrafts
Birdwatching	Knitting
Chess	Model-making
Cooking	Music lessons
Drama/Speech	Night classes
Reading	Sewing/embroidery

Anything else?　Please name it

We start with a picture of the how the children's free time was spent in general - in the afternoons and evenings and on Saturdays and Sundays. Reading and watching television will be seen to be significant pastimes in terms of the number of children who gave these as responses and so we then go on to look in more detail at their favourite books and at their viewing preferences. The final section of the chapter gives an account of the sports, games and other general leisure activities in which they participated on a regular basis.

As noted above the children were asked to name three things they normally did in the afternoons after school. Very few actually named three different activities and it could be concluded that there was quite a routine to most children's lives and that they usually did the same things every day after school.

74

The kinds of activities mentioned in response to the questions on how spare time was spent were listed and were found to cover over 30 different categories. These were then grouped as follows

1   Homework: quiet activities such as homework, reading writing, music, computers.
2   Friends: playing in the street, visiting friends, chatting, biking with friends.
3   Clubs: youth clubs, discos, snooker
4   Sports - i.e. participation in sports, including sports at school, informal street football, hurling, other sports.
5   Housework:
6   TV: which included television and video watching.
7   Visit relations:
8   Bored: response 'bored' plus responses indicating activities such as sleeping, eating, 'messing' at home .
9   Shopping:
10   Church:
11   Other: voluntary work, job, girlfriend/boyfriend; being in a riot (mentioned by under 3 per cent of Belfast children in 1981 only) ; alcohol, smoking, slot machines.

Afternoon activities

Figures 4.1 and 4.2 show the percentages of girls and boys who named each kind of activity first in response to the question about how they spent their afternoons after school at each time point.

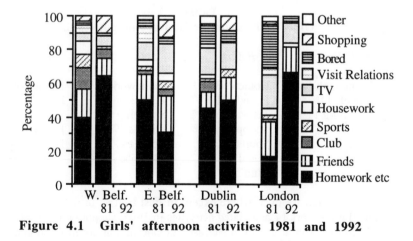

Figure 4.1   Girls' afternoon activities 1981 and 1992

The findings are presented separately for girls and boys since the percentages giving each type of response differed considerably by sex and that it was felt that amalgamating the responses would give an unreal picture.

The top ranked activities are possibly the most interesting as it was in these that there were some differences between locations and some changes over time. These are presented for girls in Table 4.1.

Table 4.1
Girls' afternoon activities ranked: 1981

W. Belfast	E. Belfast	Dublin	London
Homework 40%	Homework 50%	Homework 45%	Bored etc. 26%
Friends 16%	Friends 15%	Television 16%	Television 20%
Club 13%	Television 11%	Bored etc. 12%	Friends 20%
Sports 8%	Visiting 9%	Friends 10%	Homework 17%
Housework 8%	Housework 4%	Club 6%	Housework 4%
Television 5%	Bored etc. 4%		Visiting 4%

Homework was obviously more of a preoccupation for the Belfast and Dublin girls than for those in London. Meeting with friends was fairly equally important for all groups, but the more of the London and Dublin girls appeared to watch television in the afternoons than of the girls in Belfast. Sports activities were mentioned only by the West Belfast girls and this may be linked to their higher rate of attendance at clubs (see below, Chapter Six) where they may have participated in sports. It looks as though the 'Troubles' were not confining the girls in Belfast to their homes to a greater extent than their peers in Dublin and London.

In 1992, there were some changes as shown in Table 4.2.

Table 4.2
Girls' afternoon activities ranked: 1992

W. Belfast	E. Belfast	Dublin	London
Homework 64%	Homework 31%	Homework 50%	Homework 67%
Friends 11%	Friends 21%	Television 16%	Friends 15%
Shopping 11%	Television 17%	Shopping 9%	TV 11%
TV 6%	Shopping 10%	Friends 8%	Bored etc. 4%
Club 5%	Sports 5%	Bored etc. 7%	Housework 2%
	Bored etc. 5%	Club 5%	
	Club 5%		

There was an increase everywhere except in East Belfast in the percentages who mentioned homework or associated activities in 1992; shopping as an activity was creeping in to a similar extent in Belfast and Dublin, but not in London and there was a decrease in those who said that they did housework everywhere. The percentage who mentioned television viewing as an afternoon activity remained practically unchanged with a slight increase only in East Belfast where there was also a slight increase in the mention of friends, perhaps an indication of more freedom to move around and be out of the family home. Fewer girls in West Belfast than in the other locations mentioned television at either timepoint and club and sports activities were mentioned by very few.

Boys' afternoon activities

Boys' afternoon activities are shown in Figure 4.2.

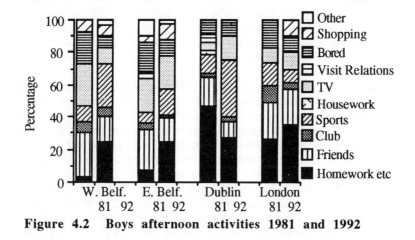

Figure 4.2   Boys afternoon activities 1981 and 1992

The ranked order of activities mentioned by boys in 1981 and 1992 is given in Table 4.3 and Table 4.4.

Table 4.3
Boys' afternoon activities ranked: 1981

W. Belfast	E. Belfast	Dublin	London
Television 27%	Friends 25%	Homework 47%	Homework 26%
Friends 27%	Television 21%	Friends 18%	Friends 23%
Bored etc. 20%	Bored etc. 18%	Sports 12%	Bored 17%
Sports 8%	Sports 7%	Bored 8%	Sports 14%
Shopping 7%	Homework 7%	Television 5%	Club 11%
Club 6%			

In 1981, homework was less important for the boys in Belfast than for those in London and to an even greater extent, in Dublin. Indeed it did not figure among the priorities of the boys in Belfast at all in 1981. Television was more important for the Belfast boys than for the Dublin or London boys - in 1981, as will be seen they watched the news more than other groups - and spending time with friends was of fairly similar importance in all four locations. Sports participation was mentioned by a similar percentage in West and East Belfast and by slightly higher percentages in Dublin and London.

Table 4.4
Boys' afternoon activities ranked: 1992

W. Belfast	E. Belfast	Dublin	London
Sports 27%	Homework 25%	Sports 35%	Homework 35%
Homework 25%	Television 20%	Homework 27%	Friends 12%
Friends 15%	Sports 16%	Television 15%	Shopping 10%
Television 10%	Friends 14%	Friends 10%	Television 10%
Bored etc. 8%	Shopping 10%	Bored 7%	Bored 10%
	Bored 10%		

There were some changes in 1992 (Table 4.4). Homework was more important for the Belfast boys in 1992 than in 1981 and the Dublin and Belfast boys also registered an increase in sports activities over 1981, perhaps an indication of improved facilities and more money to spend on enjoying them. Sports appeared to be less important for the London boys than in 1981. This could be related to the already noted decline in their socio-economic standing. A lower percentage in every location, except London, said that they spent time simply with friends in the afternoons. There was a decrease in television viewing for the West Belfast boys (perhaps because more of them were involved in sports), an increase for the Dublin boys (fewer of whom mentioned homework and related activities) and little change in the percentage naming this activity among the East Belfast boys, the highest among the groups in 1992.

Trends over time for afternoon activities

In 1992, both boys and girls seemed to have more organized activities in the afternoons than in 1981 - more homework, more sports, especially for boys. There was a slight decrease overall in television viewing, although it varied from place to place. Fewer children in 1992 gave a response suggesting boredom, or just sleeping/ eating/existing in the afternoons. Fewer boys spent time with friends, but there was little change in the pattern for girls, except that they did more homework and less housework.

Evening activities

There were slight differences between groups for the girls in both 1981 and 1992 - more London girls watched television, for example - but in general the percentages naming each activity were remarkably similar (Figure 4.3). The trends over time for girls showed less attendance at clubs, less housework (except in East Belfast), more television and video viewing for all groups and the introduction of evening shopping for the Belfast children. There was also a slight decrease in all locations except London in the percentage who spent time with friends in the evenings.

Television and sports were less important for girls than for boys in the evenings, friends were of equal importance. More girls than boys attended clubs.

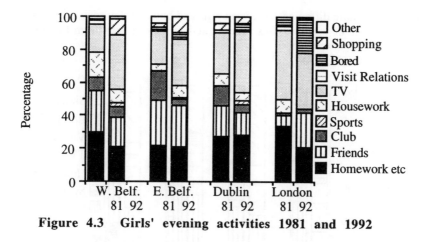

Figure 4.3 Girls' evening activities 1981 and 1992

Boys

The boys' groups were very similar across locations and also in the trends over time (Figure 4.4).

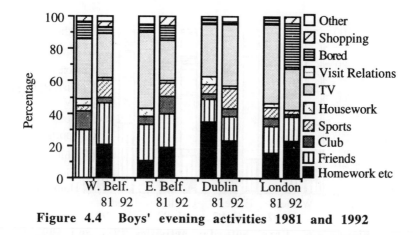

Figure 4.4 Boys' evening activities 1981 and 1992

An increase in the percentages doing homework and similar activities was noted for every group except the Dublin boys, who nevertheless still registered the highest percentage for this item. More of the West Belfast and Dublin boys watched television than in 1981. In East Belfast there was a slight increase in club attendance and in London more boys said that they did nothing or were bored. Participation in sports increased slightly everywhere except in London. Housework declined.

Saturday activities

There were more differences between girls and boys for Saturday activities than for any other one of the time slots investigated as may be seen from Figures 4.5 and 4.6.

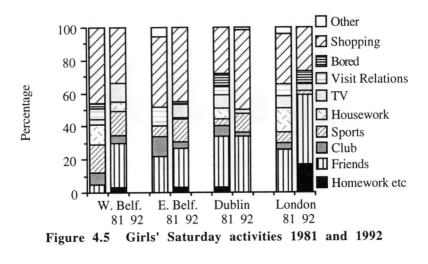

Figure 4.5   Girls' Saturday activities 1981 and 1992

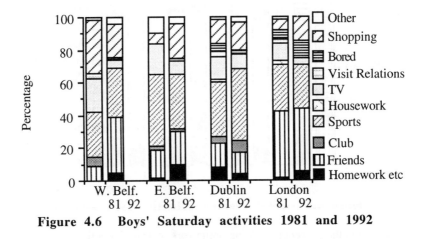

Figure 4.6   Boys' Saturday activities 1981 and 1992

Going into town to look at the shops, or do shopping and meeting with friends were the top priorities for girls at both time points. Over time there was an increase in those participating in sports on Saturdays in East Belfast and Dublin and, yet again, a decrease in those doing household chores in every location. In 1981 a proportion had spent time visiting relations, but this decreased to near zero in 1992 as did the percentage attending clubs.

Playing in sports and meeting friends were the most important activities for boys (Figure 4.6). There was a decrease in television viewing for them over time in every location and more of them went into town, or to do shopping in 1992 than in 1981, except in West Belfast, where time spent on sports and with friends increased markedly, perhaps an indication of greater freedom to move around in the streets compared to 1981.

Sunday activities: girls and boys

The children had been asked to respond to the question:

• *What do you usually do on Sundays ?*

and while there was space beneath for up to three responses, there were no indications that more than one response was required (no numbered lines for example, unlike for other items) and most children give just one response. The results may be seen in Figures 4.7 and 4.8.

In 1981 in all locations the highest percentage of activities stated related to religious practice. In London, the percentage of those giving religious activity as their Sunday occupation was the lowest of all the groups and this activity was jointly ranked in London with friends (22 per cent). The other three locations had similar percentages giving the religious response (WB, 45 per cent; EB, 44 per cent; Dublin 39 per cent). Church-going was more salient for girls than for boys in every location (42 per cent girls, 32 per cent boys overall).

Trends over time

The most notable change in 1992, which affected all locations and both sexes was that no child mentioned attendance at religious services as what they usually did on a Sunday. This does not necessarily mean that none of them attended church services, but it would seem to indicate that it did not spring to mind as readily when asked about Sunday activities as it had in 1981 even for those who did attend services. The experiences reported by one of O'Connor's (1992) West Belfast respondents supports this finding. Neither he nor his friends had been to Mass, he said, since their mothers had last been able to make them go at twelve or thirteen (p. 331). Elsewhere O'Connor offers further confirmation when she states (p. 328) that Sunday Mass attendances.....have slipped badly in the biggest urban areas, although she believes that commitment and devotion to Catholicism are still very strong and very important to a wide variety of people.

There was an increase in the percentages who spent time with friends everywhere - particularly for the East Belfast girls - and a decrease in visiting relations. Otherwise no particular activity appeared to have taken the place of church-going and there was a huge increase in the percentages everywhere who said that they did nothing or were bored and there was also an increase in the percentages who said that they watched television everywhere.

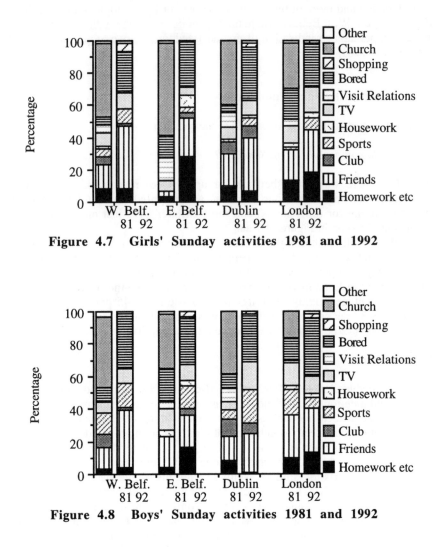

Figure 4.7   Girls' Sunday activities 1981 and 1992

Figure 4.8   Boys' Sunday activities 1981 and 1992

General trends for free time

The data collected with these questions were very non-specific - simply the first activity that came to mind when the subjects were asked what they had done at specific times of the day. We do not know how much time they usually spent on that activity, although we can be reasonably sure that it was part of their routine every day. All we have are the percentages of children who, in an open response format, named each type of activity spontaneously. However they provide some indication of how free time was spent in 1981 and 1992 by our samples. Looking at each kind of activity in turn will give us a general picture of trends in each of the locataions and by sex.

Sports activities

The finding in previous research that more boys than girls tend to spend time in sporting activities is supported here. This time probably also served the purpose for boys of developing social skills with peers since in many instances, the sports recorded were of an informal nature. But it is interesting that the boys' social activities seem to be centred on more formal situations than those of the girls. Participation in sports, both formal and informal, actually increased for all the children in the sample over the period, both for girls and boys.

Church-going and visiting relations

The decline in church-going as a salient activity has been noted by other writers (O'Connor, 1993), and supported by data on church attendances in Ireland, but the decline in visiting relatives which was also noted here could be interpreted as indicating a certain loosening of family ties, with less effort being made to keep in contact. However, a range of explanations is possible for this finding and it might not necessarily be a sign of the disintegration of the wider family network. It could be that previously the relatives visited were grandparents or aunts or uncles who were living separately, but within visiting distance and it is possible that in 1992, such relatives were living further away, or were perhaps in employment, and not at home to be visited, or that they actually had moved in with the families concerned.

Housework

The decrease in the percentages of girls in most locations who said that they did housework might be taken as a sign of a move towards equality of the sexes , but it was not balanced by an increase on the part of the boys. With more mothers in general being employed (although we do not know the figures for this sample), it is possible that they do not have the time or energy to supervise 12 year-olds doing housework and prefer to do it themselves; perhaps more fathers are involved, or perhaps less housework is being done. But it would seem that fewer children are expected to give a hand.

Reading and television

One trend over time common to both girls and boys was that more of them in the locations studied here were spending time on homework and associated quiet activities - including reading and computers in 1992 than in 1981. This was supported by the rise in children asking parents for help with homework (see Chapter Five) - a sign of increased pressure at school perhaps compared to 1981. We did not ask how much time was spent on watching television, but the data did not show a substantial increase in the percentage of the sample in 1992 in any location who mentioned it is their main activity at any of the timeslots investigated. There was a slight increase for some groups on, for example Sundays, but decreases at other times, for example, Saturdays and weekday afternoons. We now turn to the findings on the kinds of books they read and the television programmes they enjoyed

Books, library, comics

A high percentage of all groups (91 per cent - 93 per cent in 1981 ; 84 per cent - 90 per cent in 1992) claimed to read books outside school. Between 70 per cent (East Belfast) and 87 per cent (London) belonged to the public library in 1981. In 1992 there was an increase in the Belfast children who belonged to a library and slight decreases in Dublin and London. Very similar percentages in all groups said that they read comics or magazines in 1981 and the figures hardly changed in 1992 (overall, 88 per cent of girls, 83 per cent of boys in 1981; 86 per cent of girls, 83 per cent of boys in 1992); there were no differences between the sexes on the item on reading books outside school or comics / magazines.

These figures are much higher than those reported by Fine, Mortimer and Roberts (1993) for children of similar age in the USA. They found that just over a third of high school juniors and seniors claimed daily magazine reading and over 20 per cent claimed daily reading of nonschool books. They also found that comic reading declined steadily from age 10 to 18. In the present study, expenditure on comics decreased markedly over the period of the study for 12 year-olds (Chapter Three), but the item on reading comics in the present section was confounded because magazines were also included and it is possible that fewer 12 year-olds were reading comics in 1992 and more of them were reading other types of magazines. This would be more in line with the patterns of expenditure.

What kinds of books did they read?

Responses were categorized into the following types and are shown in Figures 4.9 and 4.10:
- classics
- tv/film spin-offs
- popular fiction, non-fiction
- adult
- teen romance
- comics / magazines.

It was found that differences between locations were less than differences between the sexes and that differences between locations diminished over time. Figures 4.9 and 4.10 show the percentages of girls and boys in 1981 and in 1992 who gave responses in the different categories.

The most striking findings in 1981 are the higher percentage of girls than of boys in every location (except in London) who read popular fiction and the higher percentage of boys everywhere claiming to have read non-fiction and (except in London) comics/magazines. Similar percentages gave the names of books usually aimed at the adult market: detective stories, war stories, crime fiction and thrillers. Similar percentages of girls in West and East Belfast read TV and film spinoffs and while more of the London girls than of those in the other locations read comics, fewer of them read popular fiction.

The boys in Belfast and Dublin read more comics in 1981 than those in London - the opposite of what was found for girls; those in West Belfast were less interested in TV and film spinoffs and the Dublin boys appeared to read less popular fiction; but percentages were similar in all four locations for non-fiction.

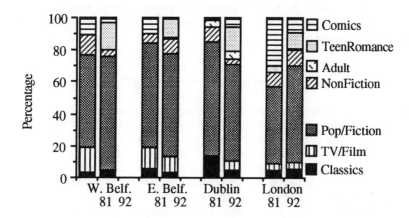

Figure 4.9   Girls' book preferences 1981 and 1992

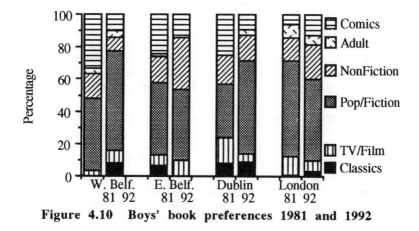

Figure 4.10   Boys' book preferences 1981 and 1992

Changes in 1992

The most remarkable finding is the increase in the percentages of girls who are reading teenage romances - a genre which was hardly named at all in 1981 and which does not seem to attract the boys in the slightest. Even the London girls had taken to popular fiction and teenage romance and their reading of comics and magazines had declined. The findings suggest a leveling out of interests as far as reading is concerned between the locations in this study for girls.

There was an increase in nearly every location for both girls and boys in the percentages who read popular fiction and it was still the case in 1992 that more girls than boys were reading that category of book and that more boys than girls were reading non-fiction and comics. The percentage of both girls and boys reading comics had however declined as might be expected from the expenditure data.

The East Belfast boys appeared to be reading more non-fiction, but fewer classics, while West Belfast boys read more popular fiction than the other groups. None of the boys mentioned teenage romance. The trend was towards congruence between locations as with the girls.

What television programmes did they watch?

Estimates of adolescent television viewing range from two to four hours per day with a great deal of variation around the averages (Fine, Mortimer and Roberts, 1993). Viewing is said to peak in early adolescence. It has been found that people can and do learn from media messages - they acquire a wide variety of information, ideas, attitudes and behaviours from the mass media particularly from television. A range of content characteristics and context characteristics are thought to influence the probability of both learning and acting on media messages (Bandura, 1993, Pearl, Bouthilet and Lazar, 1982). In later chapters we look at the association between watching television news and the children's interest in and knowledge of current affairs. In the present chapter our interest is in the other programmes most commonly watched by them

Respondents were asked to name three programmes they had enjoyed during the past week. In 1981, the top favourites were children's programmes everywhere, except for the London children who mentioned chat shows, cartoons and soaps most frequently. In 1992, the top favourite for girls everywhere was soap opera; for boys it varied by location and the different rankings were not so clearcut between soap operas, sports, and serials. The preferences of the boys were more evenly distributed than were those of the girls as may be seen from Figures 4.11 and 4.12.

Differences between girls and boys

Children's programmes were the most frequently mentioned type of programme in 1981 for all groups except those in London. Similar percentages of girls and boys watched children's programmes in 1981, except in Dublin where more boys gave this response. By 1992, the percentages watching children's programmes had declined considerably in every location; but the West Belfast boys named more programmes of this type than did any other group.

Soap operas were watched by more girls than boys in every location in 1981 and by 1992 had become fast favourites with girls, more than doubling the percentage who had been watching in 1981 and making up 61 per cent of their choices. These were the types of programme most frequently mentioned by girls in 1992 everywhere. There was a greater variety of such programmes available in 1992 than in 1981, especially non-UK produced series, and these were particularly popular.

Cartoons More boys than girls everywhere watched cartoons at both time points, but the percentages watching cartoons declined for both girls and boys everywhere except for the London and Dublin boys; More West Belfast girls than girls from the other locations had watched cartoons in 1981, but this was not the case in 1992.

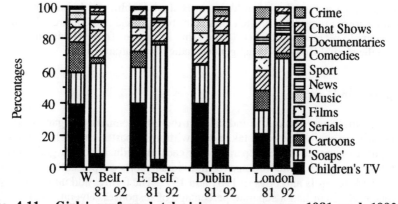

Figure 4.11   Girls' preferred television programmes 1981 and 1992

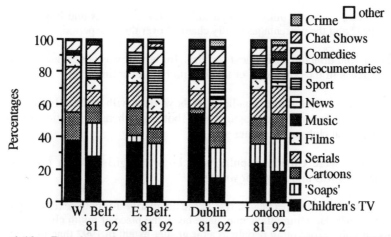

Figure 4.12   Boys' preferred television programmes 1981 and 1992

Films and serials The percentages who watched these remained fairly stable among the girls, but there appeared to be a slight decrease among boys.

News and documentaries were mentioned more often by the boys and higher percentages of boys than of girls also named comedy shows and serials.

Trends over time

Overall the respondents in 1981 in every location named more programmes designed specifically for children than did the respondents in 1992 as well as cartoons and situation comedies with few soap operas. By contrast in 1992, respondents tended to name the types of programmes produced for adults - soap operas, thrillers, drama serials, comedy shows and sports programmes. The finding that this was widespread across the sample points to the leveling effects of television - where the same programmes are available, children in Belfast, Dublin and London will make the same choices regardless of their particular background and culture. The children in the sample seemed to be open to the same influences from television programmes with the main differences being gender- rather than culture-based.

Sports and games

The children were asked to indicate on the questionnaire the games, sports and activities in which they had taken part within the past month. The percentages of responses were calculated separately for each individual sport or game, team sport and other activity. The findings for individual sports are presented in Figures 4.13 and 4.14 for girls and boys in 1981 and 1992. The figures add up to varying totals since each item had a separate percentage of responses. Overall, more girls than boys participated in these kinds of games in all locations.

Swimming was the most popular activity for both girls and boys in both 1981 and 1992 and the percentages hardly changed over the time period.

Tennis and dancing were next for girls; for boys it was table tennis, but there was an increase in the popularity of tennis with boys over time.

Tabletennis was more popular with boys than with girls at both time points although it became less popular with both - perhaps a function of the lower attendance at clubs noted earlier.

Athletics were equally popular with boys and girls at both time points, but gymnastics was more popular with girls.

Bowling showed a spectacular rise in the popularity for both sexes and particularly for the girls. Bowling alleys may have taken the place of youth clubs or provided a meeting place for young people to a far greater extent in 1992 than in 1981.

Were there differences by location and over time?

Swimming The highest percentage indicating swimming as a popular sporting activity was from West Belfast both in 1981 (77 per cent) and 1992 (78 per cent) and the lowest from Dublin (63 per cent; 59 per cent) - possibly a reflection of the facilities available. There was little change over time.

Tennis The percentages were very close for all locations and did not change much over time. They ranged from between 30 per cent (Dublin) and 35 per cent (Belfast) in 1981 and between 31 per cent (London) and 39 per cent (Belfast) in 1992. London decreased slightly.

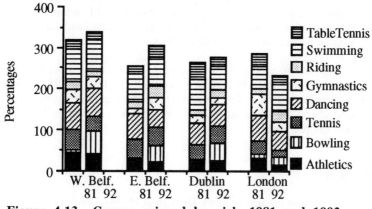

Figure 4.13   Games enjoyed by girls 1981 and 1992

Figure 4.14   Games enjoyed by boys 1981 and 1992

Athletics Very close in 1981 - between 29 per cent (East Belfast) and 38 per cent (West Belfast) but a decline everywhere over time to between 21 per cent (London) and 36 per cent (West Belfast). It seemed most popular in West Belfast at both time points.

Tabletennis This was more popular in East Belfast, Dublin and London (40-45 per cent than in West Belfast (35 per cent) in 1981. It had fallen everywhere in 1992, but to a lesser extent in West Belfast. London still headed the groups in 1992 with this activity with 33 per cent, compared to 17 per cent (Dublin), 27 per cent (East Belfast) and 31 per cent (West Belfast).

Gymnastics It was most popular in London in 1981 (37 per cent) compared to between 14 per cent (Dublin) and 20 per cent (WB) for the others. In 1992 however it had declined in popularity in Dublin (7 per cent) and London (19 per cent) and increased in popularity in Belfast both West (25 per cent) and East (26 per cent) - possibly again a result of facilities or teachers.

Bowling This was more popular in London (15 per cent) in 1981 than in the other locations (4 per cent West Belfast to 8 per cent, Dublin). In 1992 however, there was little change in the London rating (20 per cent) and big increases everywhere else, especially in West Belfast (60 per cent), but also in East Belfast (36 per cent) and Dublin (32 per cent).

Team sports

These were more a feature of boys' lives than of girls' lives in every location in 1981 (Figures 4.15 and 4.16) Twice as many boys (51 per cent) as girls (26 per cent) overall participated in team sports in 1981. There was a decrease everywhere, except for girls in West Belfast, for both girls and boys involved in team sports in 1992. Figures 4.15 and 4.16 are presented on the same page below to make comparisons easier. Twice as many boys (51 per cent) as girls (26 per cent) overall participated in team sports in 1981. There was a decrease everywhere, except for girls in West Belfast, for both girls and boys involved in team sports in 1992.

Other leisure time activities

A list was provided, as indicated earlier in the chapter, and respondents were asked to indicate which of the activities they had enjoyed during the past month.

The results are given in Figures 4.17 and 4.18 for girls in 1981 and 1992 and in Figures 4.19 and 4.20 for boys in 1981 and 1992; girls and boys are compared in Table 4.6. It may be seen that more girls than boys enjoyed the kinds of activities listed at both time points, but that there was a decrease in the percentages of both girls and boys over time, except for the West Belfast boys. The decreases seemed generally to be across the board, although sewing and knitting lost more advocates than cooking or artistic hobbies.

Differences between locations

Reading The percentages giving reading as an interest ranged from 46 per cent
(EB) to 53 per cent (WB) in 1981 and from 32 per cent (Dublin) to 38 per cent
(WB) in 1992 - very close. There was a decrease everywhere, except in London in
the percentages giving this response.

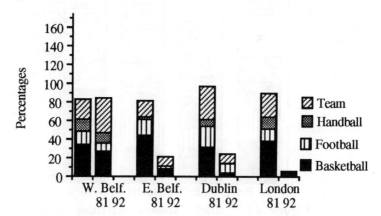

**Figure 4.15   Girls who participated in team sports 1981 and
1992**

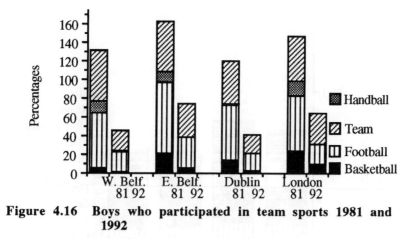

**Figure 4.16   Boys who participated in team sports 1981 and
1992**

Artistic Fewer children in East Belfast gave this response (32 per cent compared to
the other locations in 1981 (39–41 per cent. Fewer children in Dublin gave it in
1992 (30 per cent) than in 1981, but in the other locations the percentages remained
constant.

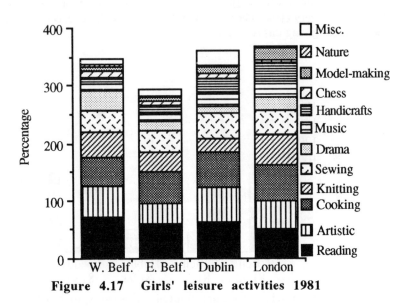

Figure 4.17   Girls' leisure activities 1981

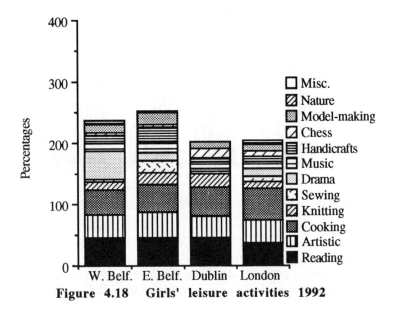

Figure 4.18   Girls' leisure activities 1992

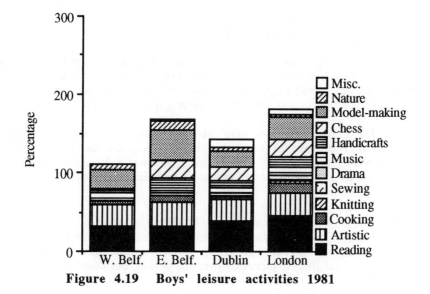

Figure 4.19   Boys' leisure activities 1981

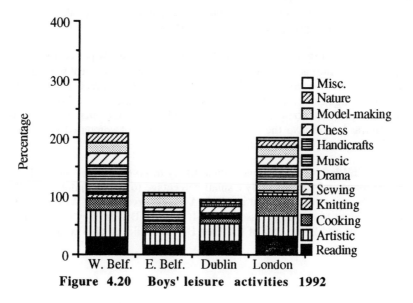

Figure 4.20   Boys' leisure activities 1992

Handicrafts These were more popular in East Belfast (18 per cent), Dublin (16 per cent and London (23 per cent) than in West Belfast (9 per cent) in 1981; in 1992, the percentages overall in East and West Belfast remained stable.

Cooking The percentages were very even across locations at both timepoints - 31 per cent (Dublin and West Belfast) to 37 per cent (London) in 1981 and 24 per cent (Dublin) to 42 per cent (London) in 1992.

Making models This was more a feature of the London and East Belfast children's' lives than of the lives of the Dublin and West Belfast children at both time points. The percentages overall ranged from 15 per cent (WB) to 24 per cent (London) in 1981 and from 7 per cent (Dublin) to 19 per cent (East Belfast) in 1992.

Music The London children were the most likely to participate in musical activities in 1981 with 20 per cent giving this response and the East Belfast children were the least likely (9 per cent). There was a decrease in Dublin and London and in increase in the percentages in both East and West Belfast over the period .

Drama The Dublin children at 6 per cent had less exposure to working in drama than the others. Those in London and West Belfast were best served in this respect with percentages of 20 per cent and 19 per cent respectively. The percentages involved in West Belfast increased over the period, but those everywhere else decreased.

Chess The West Belfast children were less likely to play chess, (5 per cent and children in the other locations had a fairly equal chance (13-14 per cent in 1981); but in 1992, the West Belfast children had caught up with the others (12 per cent and the East Belfast group had fallen behind (6 per cent).

Knitting and sewing were more popular in West Belfast (24 per cent knitting WB; 20 per cent sewing) and London (30 per cent knitting; 22 per cent sewing) in 1981 than in the other locations and far more girls than boys practised them. But the position changed over the ten years and in 1992, East Belfast boasted the most sewers (11 per cent, compared to 7 per cent in London and 3 per cent in Dublin and West Belfast) and also the most knitters (12 per cent compared to 10 per cent, Dublin; 9 per cent WB and 6 per cent London).

Classes Children in London were most likely to go to classes - probably in their own language and culture. Only a small percentage (6 per cent) did so in 1981 and this had decreased to 1 per cent in 1992. A small percentage in West Belfast (1 per cent) also went to evening classes in 1981. In West Belfast they increased slightly to 3 per cent and 2 per cent of the East Belfast children also went to classes in 1992.

Differences between girls and boys

The percentage of girls who named each activity was higher than that of boys and the rank ordering changed differentially over time for girls and boys as may be seen in Table 4.6.

Table 4.6
Leisure activities of girls and boys 1981/1992

Girls 1981	*Girls 1992*	*Boys 1981*	*Boys 1992*
Reading 60%	Cooking 46%	Reading 38%	Artistic 32%
Cooking 58%	Reading 43%	Artistic 28%	Reading 26%
Artistic 50%	Artistic 38%	Models 28%	Cooking 19%
Knitting 39%	Drama 20%	Chess 17%	Models 15%
Sewing 39%	Music 16%	Handicrafts 12%	Music 14%
Handicrafts 22%	Knitting 16%	Music 7%	Chess 13%
Music 20%	Handicrafts 14%	Cooking 7%	Handicrafts 11%
Drama 20%	Models 14%	Drama 7%	Nature 9%
Models 13%	Sewing 10%	Nature 7%	Drama 4%
Chess 8%	Chess 8%	Knitting 2%	Knitting 3%
Nature 3%	Classes 2%	Sewing 1%	Sewing 2%
Classes 2%	Nature 1%	Classes 1%	Classes 1%

The findings suggest that more girls had a wider range of interests among the activities named, than was the case for the boys. Over 14 per cent of the girls indicated that they enjoyed eight of the 12 items presented to them in both 1981 and 1992. But only five of the 12 items were ticked by 14 per cent or more of the boys in 1981. There was a slight improvement in 1992, when seven of the items were ticked by 7 per cent or more boys. They would appear to more limited in their interests than girls.

Sex stereotyping?

Was there stereotyping in the choices made by the subjects? If the popular view is to consider Arts/Humanities subjects like music, drama, artistic subjects to be less attractive to boys than to girls, that would seem to have been the case in 1981 when, although in terms of their ranked order for both sexes they were in similar positions and in a similar order, the percentages of girls opting for each of these was considerably higher than the percentage of boys.

In relation to more practical hobbies like handicrafts, model making, cooking, knitting and sewing in 1981, it may be seen that handicrafts were equally popular with girls and boys and that the traditionally domestically-oriented pursuits of cooking, sewing and knitting were far higher up the ranking for girls than for boys. Model making was more popular for boys than for girls and chess, often associated with males rather than females was also higher for boys.

Any of these findings could simply reflect lack of opportunity or of encouragement to have experience in these areas of activity. Opportunities and encouragement will depend largely on adults in the environment and what they think is appropriate. It was interesting that in 1992, although once again, a higher percentage of girls appeared to be interested in more activities, a number of indications showed that attitudes were changing and that there was somewhat less stereotyping in the responses. This was the case up to a point for the arts/humanities area like artistic hobbies and music in which a higher percentage of boys in 1992 than in 1981 evinced an interest.

In the area of practical hobbies, the great success was cooking which a much higher percentage of boys professed to like and to have done in 1992 than in 1981. Although the girls' interest in model-making had increased somewhat they had not changed their attitudes in relation to chess. Domestically oriented hobbies like sewing and knitting were less popular in 1992 than in 1981 for girls. More boys everywhere were willing to admit enjoying knitting and sewing in 1992 than in 1981 - still not very many, but perhaps an indication of a broadening of attitudes. It is possible that a bigger effort is being made to attract boys to traditional female occupations and interests than vice versa.

Summary

Afternoon activities

- There were only slight differences between locations.
- The relative frequency of afternoon activities mentioned was similar for girls and boys
- Sports activities were more important for boys in 1992 than in 1981.
- More children, but especially girls, claimed to do homework / study in 1992 than in 1981.
- More girls listed going into town as an activity in 1992 than in 1981.
- Fewer girls listed housework or visiting relations in 1992 than in 1981.
- There was no increase in boys doing housework.
- Girls main activities appeared to be homework and meeting friends; boys preferred television and sport.

Evening activities

- More children in Dublin and London than in Belfast did homework.
- Similar percentages watched television.
- More girls than boys did homework in Belfast - more boys watched television.
- Both girls and boys put homework first in Dublin; television was first in London in 1981.
- Children in all locations watched more television in 1992.

Saturdays

- More differences by gender than by location;
- Girls tended to go into town, meet friends and do shopping; boys to participate in or watch sport.

- No differences over time - except that housework and visiting relations were mentioned less in 1992.

Sundays

- Attendance at religious services was the first ranked response for all locations in 1981.
- London children registered the lowest percentage on this response; percentages elsewhere were similar.
- Religious observance was not mentioned by anyone in 1992.
- More children claimed to be bored in 1992; there were slight increases in meeting friends and in sports activities for boys especially in Dublin and in East Belfast.

Books read during the past month

- There were more differences between girls and boys than between locations.
- Over time, book choices within sex groups across location became more alike.
- The biggest change in 1992 was the appearance of teenage romance among girls' preferences and the absence of this genre for boys.

Television programmes enjoyed

- More differences here too between girls and boys than between locations.
- There was a big increase in the viewing of soap operas by girls.
- There was a decrease generally in the viewing of programmes geared to children.

Preferred activities

- Girls appeared to have a wider range of interests in both 1981 and 1992.
- Swimming was the favourite activity for both girls and boys at both time points.
- After that preferences diverged.
- There was an increase in the popularity of bowling and a decrease in athletics and table-tennis.
- More girls than boys enjoyed swimming and tennis in every location.
- More girls enjoyed reading.
- More boys played table-tennis and more boys played team sports.
- There was a decline over time in participation in sports except for girls in West Belfast.

Trends over time

Leisure activities were very similar for all the groups and the greatest differences were between boys and girls. It did not look as though any of the groups was disadvantaged in comparison to the others. All the children seemed to have equal opportunities to participate in interactions which would provide stimulation and socialization possibilities. Trends over time were similar in all locations too. Preferences in books and television programmes became more alike in the different locations between the two timepoints. The fall-off in the recording of religious observance as a significant Sunday activity bears out what has been recorded by other researchers. It was perhaps also remarkable that the East Belfast children registered an increase in sports activities on Sundays, which suggests a broadening out of experiences for them and perhaps a change in attitude on the part of the parents in 1992.

While it may seem in retrospect that this section of the questionnaire has not brought us any further in our quest for socio-ecological factors differentiating the groups in East Belfast, West Belfast, Dublin and London, we can say with some confidence that the experiences detailed in this chapter were fairly closely equivalent for all the children, in spite of the minor differences in socio-economic background uncovererd in Chapter Three. They seemed to be all experiencing the same secular trends. This in itself is a relevant datum. In addition we have got some insight into trends over time and will be able to establish whether these are a feature also of other dimensions of the children's background which will be explored in later chapters.

One of the tendencies seen in this chapter was an apparent increase in independence/autonomy. This is the topic addressed in Chapter 5, where we ask whether this was more apparent in some locations than others and whether it was related only to specific situations and activities.

5 Parental salience and the children's autonomy

Introduction

It has been proposed that resources within family life have contributed to a large extent to the 'resilience' of children in Northern Ireland vis à vis the 'Troubles' (Fraser, 1973). One could speculate that the emotional support, security and structure which are generally associated with family life, though largely undocumented in specific detail, might explain the findings of Trew (1981) and McWhirter (1981) that children's perceptions of themselves or their understanding of their social world appear not to have been affected by the turmoil in the community. Recent figures on the increase of divorce and remarriage in Northern Ireland (Jardine, 1995) which also show the doubling of the percentage of lone parent families (from 11 per cent in 1983 to about 21 per cent in 1995) remind us that changes in family structure may confound future findings and should be taken into account where possible in any study of individual development (Furstenberg, 1993).

The development and maintenance of healthy relationships between parents and children has long been seen as essential for the growth of a mature independent personality, of which an important element is the formation of a personal identity and social identity. (Montemayor and Flannery, 1990, Lerner, 1989). Research on the development of relationships has tended to focus on the subjective feelings of the protagonists. But feelings result from interactions and so will depend partly on the opportunities available within families to develop mutual understanding through the day-to day activities shared by members of the family. The belief that the traditional family unit composed of a parent of each sex plus their joint children provides the optimal environment for development has led to research which tends to be deficit oriented. For example, research on the relative weighting of the contributions of mother and father has been stimulated by situations where one parent is absent and such research is frequently looking for signs of harm to the child which might be associated with that situation. There is, however, little if any research which has established beyond question the basic elements within the family unit, traditional or not, which actually contribute to the ideal context for development, apart from the need to provide for the satisfaction of basic physical, intellectual, social and emotional needs. Many are skeptical that the traditional family - the classical family of Western nostalgia (Goode, 1982), ever existed in the form in which it is portrayed today: a stable harmonious, well-functioning supportive unit, in which children were tenderly and skillfully guided into adulthood. A further challenge comes from the profound changes which have been occurring in the family over the past several decades.

A good deal of research has addressed the question of the realignment and redefinition of family ties and the transformation of relationships during the early part of the second decade of the child's life (Collins, 1990, Steinberg, 1993). There has been an emphasis on adolescent upheaval, based on psychoanalytic models, and some work on individuation or the process by which the adolescent develops a clearer sense of self as psychologically separate from his or her parents (Blos, 1979, Kaplan, 1984). Recent theoretical developments have emphasized the reciprocal nature of parent-child influences, the relevance of family and individual differences and have urged that families be seen as a system of intertwining relationships rather than as a collection of independent dyads (Greenberg, Siegel and Leitch, 1983). Grotevant and Cooper (1986) have looked at individuality and connectedness in family interactions from a family systems perspective and suggest that these features provide an adaptive context for adolescent development. This could be related to the 'parental salience' variable in the present study. Powers, Hauser, Schwartz, Noam, and Jacobson, (1983), using a structural-developmental perspective, emphasized the need for a cognitively stimulating physical and social environment to promote ego development and found that family interaction patterns were valuable predictors of adolescent ego development. One set of researchers have suggested that early attachment relationships help foster working models of working relationships that are carried, albeit in modified form, over the life span. If this view is correct, variations in the security of young people's attachment to their parents prior to adolescence should have an influence on the way in which family relations are transformed during adolescence, and in turn on the management of interpersonal relationships after that time (Kobak and Sceery, 1988).

Research on the family in Northern Ireland

Cairns (1987) has commented that remarkably little is known about contemporary Irish family life; we do not know how the family support systems and socialization processes are operationalized. He hinted that the socio-familial aspect of the environment was possibly a crucial one when he suggested that children in Northern Ireland tend to accept their parents' views more than children in other societies. While studies of social cognition have been reported, there are few if any studies on the actual social behaviour of children in Northern Ireland and their families (McWhirter, 1983b), except that the rate of reported and detected crime is low (Cairns, Wilson, Trew and Gallagher, 1995, Livingstone and Morison, 1995, Jardine, 1995).

Apart from Vannan's (1989) study of 14 year-olds in Northern Ireland which had a different focus and investigated the associations between social conditions, behaviour problems and parenting styles (as perceived by the subjects) there has been no study of the elements of the context in which children develop attitudes and values and ideas about their possible selves through their interactions with family and peers, nor on whether there are elements within that context which might support and reinforce differences in self concept. Vannan's study, which looked at the vulnerability of young people in Northern Ireland to behaviour problems found no significant differences on measures of behaviour between Catholic and Protestant adolescents in Northern Ireland, but she concluded that the relationship between low socio-economic status, large families and adolescent behaviour problems was compounded by both religious and gender differences.

Research on moral development in Northern Ireland and Republic of Ireland children has been reported by Fields (1973) - though somewhat controversially - and by Greer (1980), Breslin (1982), Cairns (1983) and Cairns and Conlin (1985), and, apart from Fields's study, the results indicated essentially that there was nothing to worry about. And the findings of McKernan's (1980) study replicated by McClenaghan, Cairns, Dunn and Morgan (1992) found that there was a consensus of value systems across and between groups, with more differences between girls and boys than between religious groups.

Parental salience in the present study

In the present study we were not looking at family relationships *per se* in adolescence, nor at family systems, but at the interactions which occur in family groupings on a micro-level, since these form the basis for the establishment of relationships, a feeling of security and eventually attitudes and values which are part of personal identity. One aim of the study was to determine whether there was any evidence that children in Belfast might experience higher levels of attachment and security than those in Dublin and London. If so we might have the beginnings of an explanation for their resilience in the face of the 'Troubles'. A second aim was to establish whether there might be any basis in the data on these experiences for the conclusion that either or both of the Belfast groups might have lower levels of self-esteem than the Dublin and London groups.

Parental support has been found to be strongly and consistently related to adolescent self-esteem, but this has not been found to be the case for parental control. The effects of different levels and combinations of parental support and control on children's self-esteem have been reported by Thomas, Gecas, Weigert and Rooney (1974) to vary for secondary school age girls and boys, Protestants and Catholics, in Minneapolis. A negative relationship was found, for example, between self esteem and parental control for Catholic working-class males, whereas a positive relationship was found between those variables for Protestant males. There was no relationship for females. Maternal support was more strongly related to self-esteem than paternal support for the Protestant subjects, but the opposite was found for Catholics. In addition, parental support was significantly related to conformity with the expectations of authoritative others.

In this study of children in West and East Belfast, Dublin and London, the opportunities for developing relationships and the formation of identity through family interactions involving control and support were investigated within a contextual framework as opposed to a hierarchical framework. With a hierarchical model the focus tends to be on the adults who are seen as setting the tone and being to blame if things go wrong. Within the contextual model of development, we must examine not only the roles played by parents in modeling behaviour and directing the development of their children within the family unit, but also the opportunities available to and availed of by children to make choices, take responsibility and contribute to the well-being and functioning of the family unit.

These could constitute a potential source of self-respect and confidence for them, they would give practice in commitment and provide a way into autonomous functioning and thus have long-lasting effects on their life outcomes.

A first step, reported in the present chapter, was to determine the extent of parental control and support by looking at interactions which included some in which normally an adult would be in control and also situations where decisions could equally well have been taken by the child or by an adult. The second step, reported in Chapter Six, gives an account of what we found when we inquired whether a 12 year-old in Belfast, London and Dublin was being offered similar opportunities to contribute to the family's day-to-day functioning and to develop skills which would eventually contribute to his or her autonomy - a vitally important means of feeling valued and respected. This followed Hill's (1983) proposal that behavioural autonomy is often the result of positive socialization for initiative and responsibility.

We were interested in discovering :

- whether one parent was perceived as more salient than the other,
- whether parents were perceived as acting together and having equal salience and whether this was contingent on the situation.
- whether there were any changes over the eleven years between the two surveys.
- whether there were differences in the level of autonomy/independence of the children in the areas investigated
- whether there were changes in autonomy/independence over time.

A composite measure of salience was developed and was used to relate to outcomes on other variables such as socio-economic level, attitudes towards education, interest in current affairs, independence and hopes and wishes for the future, in subsequent chapters.

Parental salience

Eleven items representing examples of control and support situations were included in the parental salience measure. They were selected from the gamut of everyday activities which occur in a family involving joint decision making in families and an element of negotiation between the individuals concerned. For analysis they have been divided into sub-categories of Nurturance/Support and Control. The questions about these eleven topics were dispersed throughout the questionnaire and were open-ended; respondents answered by writing in the name of the person who fulfilled that particular function for them. In some cases, it was the respondent; but in other cases it was father, mother, both parents, siblings, aunts, uncles, grandparents. Responses were analyzed separately by question. Each mention of a specific person was awarded a point and the total number of points per respondent for each category of response was calculated. In this way each respondent had a score for Dad Mum, Parents, Self and Others.

In the present chapter, the discussion is confined to the findings for Dad, Mum, Parents and Self. The findings for Self constitute the independence/autonomy measure. We also report whether there were links between the levels of salience and the variables discussed in Chapter Three - possession of household goods and availability of money. In later chapters the findings on Dad, Mum, Parents and Self are related to other aspects of the children's lives.

Nurturance/support situations

These are situations in which the child is expected to behave in a particular way and is being assisted to that end without necessarily being exposed to an overt model of the desired behaviour. He or she is expected eventually to undertake this particular behaviour unprompted. Some of the behaviours in this category could be seen as socially desirable and contributing to the physical presentation of the individual. - for example decisions related to personal hygiene - when to have a bath, actually preparing the bath, and washing one's hair. On one level they could be seen as elements of the interface between the family and society - where the family or the individual is making choices about how to present him or herself to society and the parents have predetermined ideas about what is expected.

Another set of behaviours in this category is related to the comfort and security and nurturing qualities of the relationship where the adult performs more overtly as a role model. They include being tucked up at night, being called in the morning, having clothes left ready, getting help with homework. These nurturance/support elements are normally withdrawn gradually as children grow up, but it was of interest to know whether the children in the sample were all at the same stage in this process.

Nurturance/support questions:

•*When you are washing your hair, who helps you?*
•*If you have a bath, who runs the water?*
•*Who decides when you are going to have a bath?*
•*Does anyone call you in the mornings?*
•*Are your clothes left ready for you?*
•*Who switches off the light when you are in bed?*
•*If I get stuck with homework I...............*

Controlling behaviours

The second category of situations, taking the family/society interface from another angle, included those where the family made decisions about those aspects of society to which it would allow children to have exposure through the choice of television and radio programmes. Further dimensions of control were explored by asking about who gave the children pocket money and who drove the family car. The questions are given below.

This chapter reports the findings for nurturance/support and for controlling behaviours in the first two sections. The formula adopted for arriving at an indication of the salience of mother, father and both parents is described and the results presented with comparisons by location and over time. We then look at an index of independence/autonomy for the children and compare them across location and by sex and time. The relationship between the salience and independence variables and the variables developed in Chapter Three - goods and money - is discussed.

Control questions:
- *Can you choose what you want to watch on television yourself?*
- *Who decides what you can watch?*
- *Who turns the radio on and off in your house, mostly ?*
- *Who drives {the family car] usually?*
- *Who gives you pocket money?*

How salient are parents?

i) Nurturance/support situations

Who nudges 12 year-olds towards cleanliness? There was agreement across locations that very few fathers anywhere played a part in this process at either timepoint.

Preparing a bath Similar percentages of girls and boys perceived mothers as being actively involved in preparing their bath in 1981 (9 per cent) and again in 1992 (7 –11 per cent). There were no differences across locations or by sex within location and the numbers involved hardly changed at all between 1981 and 1992 - so there is obviously a residual core of mothers out there who insist on doing this for their 12 year olds regardless of what other people may be doing.

Deciding on a bath The decision about taking a bath was another matter. Boys were more aware than girls of mothers making decisions (19 per cent of girls and 33 per cent of boys in 1981 said mother decided when they should have a bath; the percentages for 1992 were 10 per cent and 20 per cent). The difference between girls and boys obtained for all locations to a similar extent. In 1992, in line with other increases in independence, fewer mothers were involved in this and more children made their own decisions with an increase of about 15 per cent in those taking personal responsibility everywhere, although the differential between boys and girls was still there in every location with mothers not so active on behalf of girls as of boys.

Hairwashing But girls were more likely to have help from their mother with hairwashing than boys in 1981 (19 per cent girls; 12 per cent boys overall). Looked at by location, there were differences. In fact the East Belfast (23 per cent) and London (19 per cent) mothers were more likely to do this than the West Belfast (10 per cent) or Dublin mothers (11 per cent). In 1992, the percentages of mothers involved overall had dropped everywhere (to between 5 per cent and 14 per cent for different locations) and the involvement with girls had also dropped everywhere except in West Belfast, and London, with more children taking responsibility for this task themselves.

Getting oneself up Overall more than 55 per cent of the children depended on their mothers to call them in the mornings in 1981. Fathers performed this function for about 7 per cent. There were no significant differences between locations or between sexes in 1981. At the same time there was a tendency for London children to be least likely to be called by their mother in 1981 (50 per cent compared to 64 per cent in East Belfast). The trend was for the Belfast children to be less independent in this regard.

In 1992 the percentage of children who relied on other people to get them up in the morning had declined everywhere. While there were again no significant differences between locations or by sex, the figures suggested less involvement by mothers - a fall of around 10 per cent across the board in their involvement - while the percentage of fathers remained steady. In 1981 there were no significant differences - around 25 per cent of the Dublin and Belfast children got themselves up in the morning and around 39 per cent of the London children. In 1992 there were no significant differences between the groups either; all had become more independent in this respect - no change for London, a big increase for the Dublin children (to 66 per cent) and increases also for the Belfast children (to 43 per cent WB; 53 per cent, EB), so the trend for the Belfast children to be a little slower in being allowed responsibility was to be seen here too.

Preparing for the morning Mothers alone were active in leaving ready the children's clothes and the incidence varied significantly by location (P.<.001) in 1981. Dublin mothers were least likely to leave clothes ready (41 per cent in 1981) whereas 62 per cent of the London mothers and 73 per cent (EB) and 78 per cent (WB) of the Belfast mothers did so. This was not related to the sex of the child - there were no significant differences between the sexes at either time point.

Differences between locations were not significant in 1992, but the same trend of more dependence in the Belfast groups was observed. The Dublin finding for 1981 may be regarded possibly as a 'blip', for in 1992, the percentage of mothers leaving clothes ready there increased to around 60 per cent - in line with the Belfast groups. Although the London mothers' participation in this activity declined to 45 per cent, this did not make a significant difference between the groups. And there were no differences between girls and boys at either time point.

Saying goodnight Approximately three times as many mothers as fathers did this in Belfast. Fathers elsewhere were slightly more active - half as many fathers as mothers did so in London and Dublin. This gives us a picture of more involvement by mothers than by fathers in the lives of the Belfast children - to a greater extent than in the other locations in the sample.

The picture of greater nurturance of the Belfast children is confirmed when we look at how many of them actually switched off their own lights. In 1981 between 48 per cent (West Belfast) and 71 per cent (Dublin) switched off their own lights and in 1992 there was an increase everywhere in children doing this for themselves, but the Dublin (81 per cent) and London (82 per cent) groups were still higher while percentages in Belfast ranged from 70–72 per cent. Differences between the sexes were not significant.

Similar percentages of fathers and of mothers switched off the light for girls as for boys in both 1981 and 1992.

Helping with homework There were differences across location for the item on asking for help with homework. Dublin children were less likely to consult either parent individually and more likely to consult both parents or other people than were children from other locations. More East Belfast children (21 per cent) consulted Dad than did children from other locations and a similar percentage of London and Belfast children (18 per cent–21 per cent) consulted Mum first.

Interestingly whereas parental intervention appeared to decline in many areas of interaction investigated in this study over the time period, this was one area where parental participation actually increased. The percentage of children consulting mothers increased everywhere except West Belfast, where it fell and the numbers consulting both parents increased everywhere in 1992. The percentage consulting fathers decreased slightly everywhere except Dublin and there was less consultation with other people by children in all locations in 1992.

Summary - nurturance/support

An overview of nurturance and support for girls and boys is given in Figures 5.1 and 5.2 showing the percentages who had the support of either or both parents for each item. In the socialization areas of presentation and nurturance, it would seem that mothers are more active and salient than fathers and this did not vary across locations or time points. There was some evidence that mothers in Belfast were more involved than mothers in Dublin and London. There was also evidence that children in Belfast were allowed less responsibility for the kinds of behaviours investigated in this section than were children in London and Dublin. More support, or nurturance, was offered by parents, and in particular by mothers. Between girls and boys within locations there were differences on just one or two of the variables, but the overall picture remains the same.

Over time there was an indication of a loosening of the apron strings for both sexes in all these matters of a domestic nature. However it is interesting that in the one area observed in this study where the initiative has to be taken by children - perception of the need for help with homework - there was an increase in parental intervention in all locations but not of fathers *per se*. While mothers were withdrawing from matters practical, they were still involved in matters intellectual (see Figure 5.4 for a composite view), especially for girls; but while fathers were retaining their admittedly tiny share of practical duties they were being consulted less on matters intellectual. It may be significant to note the lessening participation by fathers in the lives of their children; a composite view of the supporting and controlling salience of Dad is shown in Figure 5.3 .

Nurturance and self-esteem

In terms of possible effects on feelings of security and on resilience, the data suggest that the Belfast children, especially the boys in 1981 were enjoying higher levels of support than the Dublin and London children in the areas investigated here, particularly in 1981 and particularly by mothers. And this could indeed have contributed to their resilience in the face of the 'Troubles'. On the other hand, the London girls were just as nurtured as the Belfast girls. And in 1992, West Belfast girls got slightly more attention than East Belfast girls, but East Belfast boys got more attention than West Belfast boys. If the findings of Thomas, Gecas, Weigert and Rooney (1974) apply also in this case, we would expect self-esteem to be high in both groups, since it was found to be related to parental support and the level of parental support was higher for the Belfast children overall on both occasions than for the Dublin children and similar to that for the London children.

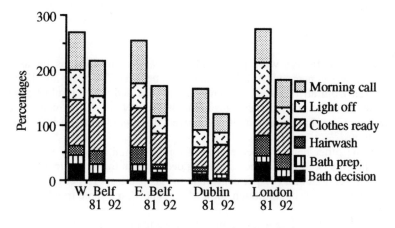

Figure 5.1   Nurturance of girls 1981 and 1992

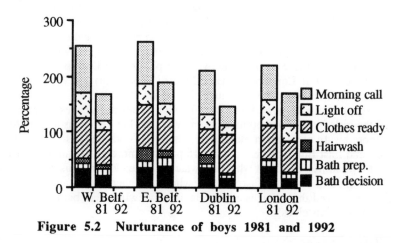

Figure 5.2   Nurturance of boys 1981 and 1992

But maternal support was found by Thomas, Gecas, Weigert and Rooney (1974) to have more positive effects for Protestants than for Catholics; we might therefore expect to find higher self-esteem among the East Belfast children than among the West Belfast children in our sample, if this as a relevant factor, since maternal support was negatively associated with self-esteem for Catholics. However, if this is a relevant factor, we must also ask whether the decline in parental and maternal support over the period could also have led to a decline in self-esteem in the Belfast groups or whether this decline in support was balanced by an increase in, for example, self-efficacy, resulting from increased autonomy which would also have contributed to self-esteem in the children.

Control

i) Television viewing

Mothers and fathers were perceived as equally controlling as far as television viewing was concerned. At both time points, between 7 per cent and 17 per cent of children from all locations said that mother decided what should be watched on television and similar percentages nominated fathers (4–19 per cent). It cannot be said therefore that either parent was universally dominant as an individual for this function.

On the other hand the perception of joint parental authority was stronger- i.e. both parents were perceived as making decisions in this area - in West Belfast (30 per cent) and Dublin (27 per cent) than in East Belfast (12 per cent) or London (8 per cent) in 1981 and although somewhat reduced, the same trend was apparent in 1992.

Over time there was a substantial decrease in decision-making by parents about television viewing. In 1981, 74 per cent of the girls and 78 per cent of the boys responded that someone else decided what they could watch on television. This had fallen to 31 per cent of the girls and 37 per cent of the boys in 1992. The biggest change was in West Belfast, with a decrease from 80 per cent to 31 per cent over the period. In 1981, the places with the highest percentages of independent choice were East Belfast (39 per cent) and London (35 per cent) and the lowest in Dublin and W. Belfast (21 per cent). But in 1992 there was a massive increase in every location giving percentages of between 67 per cent in Dublin - still the lowest - and 80 per cent in London with East Belfast (72 per cent) and West Belfast (72 per cent) similar, but representing a huge change for West Belfast.

Except in one location there were no significant differences between the boys and the girls in their perceptions on this variable, but there was a trend for boys to be more aware of decision-making by others. This was the case especially in both West and East Belfast where at least 15 per cent more girls than boys in 1981 said that they had free choice of what they watched on television. This difference reached significance in West Belfast in 1992 where a higher percentage of boys than of girls perceived that choices about television viewing were being made by people other than themselves.

ii) Radio listening

Decisions about radio listening turned out to be more stable over time than television choices. More mothers than fathers appeared to make decisions in this area (31–37 per cent of mothers in 1981; 15–25 per cent of fathers). Joint parental decisions about radio listening were rarely perceived to be the case. There were no significant differences between the perceptions of boys and girls as to who was in charge - in about 25 per cent of all families, it was the mother in 1981 and again in 1992, while Dad's involvement in 1981 ranged from 15 per cent (Dublin and

London) to 25 per cent (East Belfast) and in 1992 from 7 per cent (Dublin) to 22 per cent (East Belfast).

iii) Pocket money - who gives it?

There were differences between locations. London children were more likely to be given money by Mum (30 per cent) or by both parents (34 per cent) than by Dad (23 per cent) or by others (12 per cent) in 1981 and the percentages were similar in 1992. Dublin children were most likely to get money from Dad in 1981 (41 per cent - twice as many as from Mum) - but in 1992 a higher percentage of them than of children from other locations were given money by both parents (42 per cent); the percentage getting it from Dad alone had fallen to 28 per cent and as many now got it from their Mum.

The percentage of Mums contributing pocket money rose sharply in both West Belfast (from 15 to 29 per cent) and East Belfast (from 21 to 31 per cent) and the percentage of Dads contributing declined (from 32 to 31 per cent in West Belfast and from 32 to 22 percent in East Belfast) and so did the percentage of 'others' as happened also in the other locations. In West Belfast a similar percentage got money from both parents in 1992 as in 1981 (29–30 per cent) and in East Belfast, the percentage receiving it from both parents increased (14–24 per cent).

Girls and boys There were no significant differences between boys and girls in the sources of their pocket money. Around 32 per cent received pocket money from their fathers and 21 per cent from mothers in 1981. Around 23 per cent got money from both parents and 22 per cent from other family members. In 1992 however, Dad's dominance in this area had decreased substantially. Similar percentages of children overall now got money from mothers alone (28 per cent) or from both parents (31 per cent) as from Dads alone (26 per cent). The percentage getting money from other sources declined from 22 per cent to 14 per cent over the period studied.

Mothers or fathers? Overall the trend was for greater contributions by mothers as evidenced by the percentages naming mothers alone or both parents over the period, where Dads were more prominent in 1981. This could reflect a higher participation rate by mothers in the workforce or a lower employment rate for fathers and a lower rate of participation by fathers in family life. It could also reflect father absence in a growing number of families. These data possibly also reflect economic changes in the various locations and how they may have affected positions and relationships within the family. It is clear that the role models for the children in the different locations with regard to the financial support of the family were different and they changed differentially over the time period of the study.

iv) Driving the family car

There were differences between locations in 1981 which had widened by 1992, as there appeared to be fewer car-owning families in the London group in 1992 than in 1981. Fathers were most likely to be car drivers in every location - between 56 per cent (Dublin) and 64 per cent (London) of respondents said that Dad drove in 1981 and between 40 per cent (London) and 59 per cent (East Belfast) said the same in

1992. The percentage saying that Mum drove varied across locations and time (between 15 per cent (EB) and 21 per cent (London) in 1981; between 5 per cent (Dublin) and 15 per cent (London) in 1992). But the percentage saying that both parents drove increased in all locations over time (from 8 per cent overall in 1981 to 23 per cent in 1992) indicating that more women were becoming mobile, though fewer in London than elsewhere. The percentage saying that Dad alone was the driver decreased everywhere except in Dublin where it remained the same. Dublin also had the highest percentage of respondents (24 per cent) naming both parents as drivers in 1981 with little change in 1992 (though in other areas there was an increase).

There were no significant differences overall between girls and boys in their perceptions of who drove the family car.

Summary: controlling behaviours

In the area of exposure to socializing influences, through choice of television viewing, it looks as though children in West Belfast (79 per cent) and Dublin (79 per cent) were more likely to have decisions made for them in 1981 with decisions being made more by both parents than by either parent individually. The children in East Belfast and London had more independence in making decisions about television viewing and they differed from the West Belfast and Dublin children also in that decisions tended to be made as much by one parent or the other rather than by both on a joint basis. One could characterize this as a less controlling approach for East Belfast and London. In general mothers maintained their position of decision-maker and this would seem to suggest a difference in the kinds of family interaction and relationships separating the West Belfast and Dublin children on the one hand from the East Belfast and London children on the other. This could be an important contextual element in terms of their psychological development .

While parents were less likely overall to make decisions on television viewing in 1992, they were still more controlling in Dublin and the children there were still less independent in this regard - 48 per cent had their viewing choices decided for them compared to 31 per cent (WB), 33 per cent (EB) and 26 per cent (London). It is interesting that the West Belfast children had become similar to the East Belfast children over the time period - as in the variables investigated in Chapter Three. It looks as though the groups in Belfast are becoming more congruent and subscribing to similar values in 1992 from a position of difference in 1981.

A similar trend towards greater independence and less control by parents was seen in the choice of radio programmes. Overall, fewer children appeared to listen to the radio than watched television. Once again there were no significant differences between locations at either time point. The percentages making own choices ranged from 5 per cent (West Belfast) to 28 per cent (Dublin) in 1981 and from 27 per cent (Dublin) to 37 per cent (London) in 1992. Similar percentages of girls and of boys were independent in this at both time points and there was a similar increase over time in the percentages saying that they made their own decisions.

Control and self-esteem

In the behaviours explored under socialization/control, - giving pocket money and driving the car - it would appear that mothers are assuming more control and responsibility and the dominance of fathers over these aspects of the family is declining. With higher levels of control we would expect lower levels of self-esteem among Catholic working class males according to Thomas, Gecas, Weigert and Rooney (1974), but we would expect a positive relationship between level of control and self-esteem for Protestant males. In the present case, the levels of control were much lower for Protestants and one might therefore expect a lower level of self-esteem there too. So we are not really helped in determining whether there are different levels of self-esteem and possible causes for it in the East and West Belfast boys by using this approach.

Parental salience overall

An overall view of the salience of individual parents and of both parents together was obtained by summing the number of mentions made over the topics investigated. Analysis of variance of the scores thus obtained by location and sex was carried out and some statistically significant results were found, though because of the nature of the data these should be regarded with caution (Figures 5.4, 5.5, 5.6).

Salience of Mum

Salience of mother differed by location (P<.001) and by sex of child (P<.05) in 1981, but there were no interaction effects. The scores suggested that mothers were most salient in Belfast (score of 2.9 in both East and West Belfast) less so in London (2.6) and least in Dublin (2.0). Mums were more salient for boys than for girls overall, but this did not hold across all locations. It was more evident in East Belfast and Dublin in 1981, but in 1992, while it was still highest in East Belfast, West Belfast had the second highest score on this variable.

Salience of Dad

There were significant differences by location but not by sex for fathers in 1981 (P<.05) as may be seen in Figure 5.2. Fathers appeared to be more salient for the East Belfast children (mean score 2.4) than for any of the other groups (2.2 for London and West Belfast; 2.1 for Dublin). In 1992, there were no significant differences by group or sex for salience of father. This is consistent with the decline of mentions of salience of father in response to the various questions.

Salience of parents

There were significant differences for salience of parents jointly across locations, but not by sex and without interaction effects. Parents were most salient in West Belfast (mean 'score' of 1.9) in both 1981 and 1992 and the other three locations had similar scores of between 0.6 and 0.8 in 1981 and between 0.6 and 1.1 in 1992). The level was low and decreased over time for all groups.

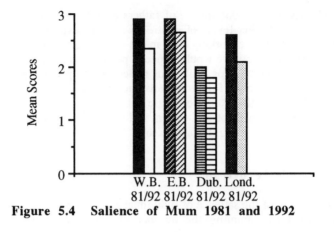

Figure 5.4   Salience of Mum 1981 and 1992

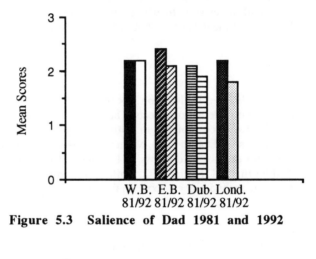

Figure 5.3   Salience of Dad 1981 and 1992

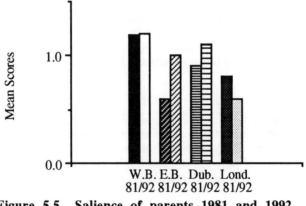

Figure 5.5   Salience of parents 1981 and 1992

The overall findings suggest that parents individually and jointly have more salience in Belfast than in Dublin or London. They interact more with their 12 year olds and figure more extensively in their day to day socialization activities. The down side of this is that those children are in fact given less responsibility and control over their lives than children of the same age in Dublin and London.

Independence/autonomy

The development of independence from parents in various areas of life is obviously an important feature of the social context for 12 year olds and the composite scores for this are discussed next. Two composite variables were developed - Independence and Choice.

Independence

Respondents were awarded a point for each area where they indicated that in fact they had responsibility for decision-making. Scores for the composite variable Independence were derived from the items on nurturance/support. An ANOVA of these scores showed that there were significant differences between the groups in 1981 ($F = 7.311$; df = 3; P<.001) and also in 1992. F= 10.792, df = 3, P< .001).

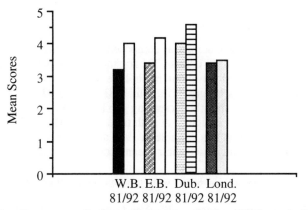

Figure 5.6   Scores on Independence by group 1981 and 1992

Given the nature of the scores these should be viewed as simply denoting a trend. The Dublin children were the most independent on both occasions, with West Belfast least independent in 1981 and London in that position in 1992 (Figure 5.6). All groups increased their mean scores over the time period by similar amounts except the London group which overall had similar mean scores in 1981 and in 1992.

Girls and boys

While differences between boys and girls on independence were not significant overall (Figure 5.7) nor in any location in 1981, there was a bigger gap between them in favour of the girls in Dublin than in any other location By 1992 the gap had closed however, the boys had caught up and the girls had also increased their scores.

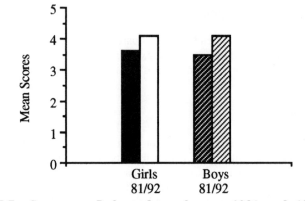

Figure 5.7   Scores on Independence by sex 1981 and 1992

Choice

The composite variable Choice was composed of the items scored for Independence plus a point if they could choose TV for themselves plus another point if they made their own decisions about radio listening. Analysis of variance yielded significant differences by group in both 1981 (F = 7.697, P<.001) and 1992 (F= 4.661, P<.003) with a slightly decreasing gap between the groups.

Dublin children scored highest at both time-points. The children of West Belfast had the lowest score on this variable in 1981 and the London children were lowest in 1992. All groups increased their mean score indicating increasing freedom of choice.

Differences between the sexes were not significant at either time point.

Parental salience, independence, choice and socioeconomic factors

We must now ask whether level of parental salience and other variables were related to any other grounding feature of the children's lives - for example to their socio-economic standing as measured in this study? Did parents tend to be more involved with their children if they were better off or did they tend to be more involved if they were worse off economically in terms of life's comforts? Was more responsibility allowed to children whose parents were better off or if they had more disposable income? Were children given more choices by parents who had more material goods?

Parental salience The children in East Belfast had been the best off in 1981 when household goods alone were taken into account and the Dublin children least well off. In 1981 the London children were similar to the West Belfast children on this

114

measure. Mum was most salient for the Belfast children, both East and West, and least salient for the Dublin children at both time points, as was Dad. Dad was most salient for the East Belfast children and equally so for the London and West Belfast children. Parents were jointly less salient in these two groups than in the other groups in 1981. But in 1992 when the West Belfast children had caught up with those in East Belfast in household goods and the London children had lower scores, parents jointly were still more salient in West Belfast and less salient in London and in East Belfast. Clearly the relationship is not a straightforward one and it depends whether one is looking at the salience of parents individually or together.

Choice Dublin children were highest on Choice in 1981 and had the lowest score on Goods; the West Belfast children had the lowest score on Choice in 1981, and were the second highest on Goods then. In 1992, the Dublin children were again highest on Choice and the London children, who were lowest on Goods at this time were also lowest on Choice. Again, not a straightforward relationship

Independence The Dublin children were highest on Independence, but lowest on 'Goods' in 1981 and the West Belfast children were second highest on Goods and lowest on Independence. The London children, whose score on 'Goods' declined, increased their score on 'Independence over the period. The East Belfast children although highest on 'Goods' were not highest on Independence at either timepoint.

It would seem that factors other than socioeconomic level must be taken into consideration in accounting for differential levels of independence

Summary

Mum

- Mum was more salient than Dad in every location at both time-points, but the scores in Dublin were closer for Mum and Dad than they were in any other location.
- There were significant differences in scores by location in 1981.
- Mothers were most salient in Belfast in 1981 less so in London and least in Dublin.
- There was a decrease in the salience of Mum in every location between 1981 and 1992.
- Salience of Mum differed significantly by sex in 1981.
- Mums were more salient for boys than for girls overall in 1981, but not in 1992, and this did not hold across all locations. It was more evident in East Belfast and Dublin.

Dad

- Dad was marginally less salient than Mum in every location.
- He was more important for the children of East Belfast than for any of the other groups in 1981

- Over the time period there was a decline for salience of Dad in every location except West Belfast.
- And in 1992, there were no significant differences between locations for salience of Dad
- He was least important for London children in 1992 with a bigger decrease in salience score from 1981 than elsewhere.
- In 1981 and again in 1992 there were no significant differences between the sexes for salience of Dad

Parents

- Salience of parents together differed significantly across location in both 1981 and 1992
- Parents were most salient in West Belfast at both time points and the other three locations were similar to each other.
- There were no differences by sex in salience of parents jointly in either 1981 or 1992
- There was a very slight increase in every location except London in the mean score for salience of parents jointly.

Independence of children

- The Dublin children were the most independent on both occasions, with West Belfast least independent in 1981 and London in that position in 1992. The differences were statistically significant. (P<.001)
- The Dublin children also scored highest on Choice at both time points, with West Belfast lowest in 1981 and London lowest in 1992.
- All groups increased their mean scores over the time period by similar amounts except the London group which overall had similar mean scores in 1981 and in 1992 on Independence; they increased their scores on Choice, however.
- Differences between boys and girls were not significant overall or in any location on Independence or Choice at either time-point.
- Scores on Independence increased in every location for both girls and boys over the time-period

Trends over time

This chapter has looked at the salience of parents for the children in the study and discovered differences between the groups which were not related to the socio-economic variables outlined earlier. Parents separately were more salient for the Belfast children than for the Dublin or London groups, especially in 1981; Belfast children were allowed less responsibility and had less independence than the Dublin children. The differences between the groups were greater than those between girls and boys overall or between girls and boys within locations.

This may well be an area of investigation where cultural differences are more important than socio-economic differences. But of course this is a chicken-and-egg situation. It could be that Belfast parents were always more nurturant and that this gave their children a secure base from which to face the Troubles. This could explain the resilience which has been quoted (McWhirter, 1983b) to explain the apparent resistance shown by Northern Ireland to the development of psychopathology and problems of behaviour.

Extra protectiveness could, however, lead to dependence - perhaps overreliance on parents, not just for protection, but for ideas and value systems. As Cairns (1987) said, young people in Northern Ireland seem reluctant to challenge their elders. And it has been found that in social structures centred on the family and kin structure - such as we find in Northern Ireland- reliance on older family members results in an unwillingness to take risks or favour innovations (Rogers, 1969).

But we do not know how children in Dublin or London would have reacted to 'Troubles' in their backyards with their greater independence, so we cannot say with certainty that the greater protectiveness of the Belfast parents, whether or not it predated the Troubles, explains the resilience of the Belfast children. It is possible too that at an earlier period, Belfast parents were just like those in Dublin and London, but that they became more protective because of the Troubles and kept their children more under control because of the physical dangers in the period of the early 80s. As these became less of a threat, they may have become more relaxed.

The trend towards relaxation was happening everywhere, not just in Belfast. Hurrelmann and Engel (1989) characterize it as the trend from the authoritarian to the negotiation family. Tallman, Marotz-Baden and Pindas (1983) link this to the increasing complexity of social structures with which people have to deal. They suggest that in learning to interact with new institutions, people increase their ability to integrate information. They give the example of a health clinic set up in a rural area of a developing country, but in Northern Ireland a more appropriate example might be the establishment of an integrated school presenting an option to parents in a particular area, or the formation of a local community development association. In dealing with these institutions or organizations, people become more aware of the ambiguity of stimuli and they become more able to cope with ambiguity. They become more tolerant of conflicts over ideas. It would follow that gradually their family structures would become less authoritarian.

The trend towards greater independence for children and less salience for parents was happening in Dublin and London too but not at so fast a pace. It is suggested therefore that in Dublin and London, as in Belfast, underlying economic and social trends - employment rates for men and women for example, perhaps the accelerated rate of break-up of nuclear families - could explicate the findings on children's gains in autonomy. Whether the lessening of support and nurturance and the loosening of control meant differences for self-esteem, we cannot really say. It is likely that other factors also enter into the equation such as parental attitudes and changes parents may have undergone, which were not directly measured here or, alternatively, opportunities for the development of self-efficacy in the children .

Moving on

Having looked at interactions within the family setting and found evidence of differences between the Belfast children and the Dublin and London groups, we must now to turn to activities outside the home and determine whether opportunities for developing self-efficacy in the wider community were similar for all our groups.

6 Reaching out beyond the family

Introduction

Did the 'Troubles' in Northern Ireland affect children's opportunities to reach out beyond the family? Parents usually have a concern to prepare children psychologically to move outside the family and to experience interactions with other people in a non-family context. The skills and knowledge which provide structure for these interactions will contribute to the feelings of self-efficacy and the personal identity outcome for the child. It was hypothesized that the development of the skills and knowledge would be contingent on the opportunities provided by parents.

We were interested in the possibilities offered for the development of self-efficacy through opportunities for activities away from the family. Self-efficacy was seen as being important for self concept, personal identity and self-esteem as well as contributing essential elements to the range of 'possible selves' available to the young person and thereby influencing his or her future orientation. As we have already seen, the relevance of socio-environmental factors is widely acknowledged in the formation of personality and identity in addition to those factors endogenous to the individual, and as well as studies of aspects of family context, (reviewed in Feldman and Elliott, 1993), a great deal of research has been reported on the relevance of, for example, macro-systems such as historical time (Runyan, 1988, Elder, Modell and Parke, 1994, Elder, 1994), the economy (Elder, 1974, Conger, Ge, Elder, Lorenz and Simons, 1994), and education (Simmons and Blyth, 1987, Worell and Danner, 1989, Hurrelmann and Engel, 1989, Emler, 1993, Hetherington, Lerner and Perlmutter, 1988, Entwistle, 1993). In this study we looked at what van der Linden (1988) has called the 'ecological periphery' around the 'ecological centre' which is the family, and tried to focus on the context of adolescent living conditions and the existence or otherwise of specific environmental factors, under the control of parents and families, which it was felt might contribute to the process.

In the context of the present study it was of interest to determine whether the situation caused by the 'Troubles' in Belfast was influencing the availability of chances of the young people who lived there were being negatively affected. If the environment offered to Belfast children - and current adults who were children not so long ago - differed substantially from that in Dublin and London it could have resulted in differently developed social interaction skills arising from differing elements underlying the self-concept. Lack of supported practice in the development of these skills could result in additional outcomes which would affect future interactions and might include feeling less competent and having lower self-esteem, leaving the Belfast children less willing to take risks and less prepared to deal on an equal basis with others. We have already seen a possible justification for their feeling like that in the findings of more prolonged dependence on parents and the higher level of protectiveness which they enjoyed compared to the Dublin and London children. An even stronger basis for it would be found if they also lacked the kinds of opportunities the other children had to reach out beyond their family environment.

Characterizing aspects of the peripheral ecology

We looked for normal everyday activities of the kind usually available to 12 year-olds which might contribute to the development of self-confidence, self-esteem and social interaction abilities. We identified three groups of behaviours and classified them as

i)   urban survival
ii)   commitment
iii) outreach

Urban Survival skills

As opportunities for movement outside the family home gradually increase and more freedom is permitted, parents usually ensure that certain 'survival skills' have been acquired. We asked:

•*Have you ever used a public telephone to make a telephone call by yourself?*	*No*	*Yes*
•*Have you ever used a phone book to find a number?*	*No*	*Yes*
•*Do you ever pour tea for yourself or for others?*	*No*	*Yes*
Every day?		
Now and again?		
•*Can you peel apples or potatoes?*	*No*	*Yes*
•*Do you ever travel on a bus or taxi on your own or with friends (apart from a school bus)?*	*No*	*Yes*
•*How much is the fare?*		
•*Where did you last go on a bus or taxi?*		
•*Where else do you usually go on a bus or taxi by yourself or with friends?*		

The last three questions were 'fillers' to encourage greater interest in the project and they were also a means of checking that subjects had actually been in a bus or taxi. Responses to them were not taken into account in scoring. One point was awarded for a 'yes' in each of the other five questions giving a maximum score of five for 'Survival' - familiarity with public phone, phone book, peeling and pouring, and taking a bus or taxi.

Commitment

In addition to the kinds of survival skills outlined above, which relate possibly more to physical survival in the city, but would also contribute to self-esteem through the development of competence, parents often ensure, possibly without articulating it, that their children are prepared by other experiences for the level or perhaps 'register' of interaction and commitment which will eventually be required of them in interacting with people outside the home. As with adults, children's experiences with people outside the family can be of many kinds and are frequently on a more business-like basis than the kinds of interactions described in the chapter on parental salience. In joining a club, for example, one agrees to abide by the rules, to engage in appropriate activities and so on; in taking on a job for money, one has at least an informal contract to fulfill one's obligations and sometimes a more formal one. Parents usually ensure that children are aware of the necessity for commitment and give them practice in developing and maintaining commitment through informal tasks around the house and in the neighbourhood.

In the present study we identified several possibilities under the heading of commitment and investigated the frequency of their occurrence in each group at each time point. These experiences were selected from among those which were thought to be accessible to most if not all children everywhere regardless of socio-economic level or other characteristics of their lives. They were drawn from obligations which can be taken on within the home and are usually taken on in the family context initially under supervision with gradually increasing trust in the child to fulfill the commitment responsibly. They included household chores, looking after pets and doing small errands to the shops at the corner. Questions are given below.

Household chores Subjects were asked to place a checkmark against any jobs they had done at home and were awarded a score corresponding to the number of jobs marked by them. This score became part of the composite variable 'Commitment'.

Pet care This is often the first commitment to another creature that a child willingly takes on. We were interested to see whether the children in the different locations had similar opportunities to develop a sense of responsibility by caring for a pet. One point went towards the composite variable 'Commitment' if they claimed to have looked after a pet.

Shopping It was considered that the act of shopping for small items at the corner shop, could be a useful indicator of the way in which a family functions and the opportunities it gives to the younger members to contribute to the family well-being and to develop self-confidence and feelings of self-efficacy through practice in carrying out the task.

120

Questions: household chores

•Do you ever do any of these jobs at home?
(Tick any you have done during the past week)

Laying the table
clearing the table
washing up
shopping

making the bed
getting in coal or fuel
polishing shoes

•Other jobs around the house - what?

Have you ever done any of these jobs?
(Tick any you have ever done)

cleaning car
cleaning and oiling
bicycle
helping prepare dinner
making tea
washing socks or other
clothes
minding small children
painting doors or windows

cleaning own room
weeding in garden
fixing plug onto flex
planting seeds
mending puncture
fixing shelves
cutting grass or hedges
lighting fire

•Any other jobs you have done around the house?

Questions: pet care

•Does your family have any animals or pets?
•Please circle whatever you have

dog/dogs
cat/cats
pigeons
goldfish
Tropical fish

budgie
parrot
hamster
gerbil
canary

•Other - please name
•Do you help look after it or them?   *No   Yes*
•What did you do the last time you had to
  help with the pet?

Information about shopping habits could also tell us a little more about the socio-economic level of the families. Families who shop from day to day and cater for immediate needs rather than being able to plan ahead probably operate on a different and lower budgetary level than families who can do a weekly shopping trip. The frequency of shopping may also reflect the amenities of the home. The ownership of a freezer or a big refrigerator will mean that less frequent forays are necessary. Similarly ownership of a car may mean that family shopping can be dealt with more summarily because more can be carried at the one time. It was of interest to know whether the families in the different locations in our sample were similar in this respect, as it appeared to provide an indirect indication of socio-economic level. All the areas served by the schools in the sample had small corner shops.

Questions: shopping

•*Do you ever go shopping for your mother?*   *No*   *Yes*
•*What did you buy the last time you went shopping?*
•*When was that?*
•*How many shops do you usually go to?*
•*How often do you go shopping?*

Implications of shopping

As well as giving an indication of the level of economic existence of the families, the experience of shopping was seen as a directly empowering item for the children. Shopping can fulfill a socializing function in that the child usually has to remember what to buy, select a brand and perhaps choose an appropriate size according to any one of a number of criteria including price comparison; he or she must look after the money, bring back the correct change and perhaps use a stated amount for his or her own purposes. In addition the child needs to interact with the shopkeeper and observe social niceties with other customers.

If the child answered yes to the 'Shopping' questions, a score was awarded which was weighted to reflect recency, frequency and complexity (i.e. number of shops visited) of shopping. This score contributed to the overall score for the composite variable 'Commitment'.

Outreach

We asked in addition about opportunities available to the children to reach out beyond the family. Situations were again selected which were thought to be accessible to most, if not all of the children and in which it was judged that the child would be coping alone, physically away from home and separated from at least the adult members of his or her family. They were asked about club membership and attendance, the types of jobs they had done to earn money and holiday travel without the family.

Club Membership

•*Do you belong to any club or organization*
for young people?   *No*   *Yes*
•*Which one?*
•*How often do you go each week altogether?*
•*What do you like doing there?*

What kinds of work did they do to earn money?

This was an open-ended question following the questions already reported in Chapter Three *(Have you ever done a job to earn money?....How much did you earn?)*. The children were asked:

•*What did you do?*

Away without the family

By age 12 many children have been away on overnight 'sleep-overs' with schoolmates, or to stay with grandparents or other relations, or for camping trips with youth organizations. These may be seen as helping them gain confidence in themselves through dealing with new and unfamiliar situations without the immediate support of adult nuclear family members.

•*Have you ever been away without your family?*   No   Yes
•*How many times?*
•*Where have you been to without the family?*
•*How long were you away the last time without the family?*
•*What age were you then?*

The composite variable 'Travels' was made up of scores from the questions on travel, weighted according to the age of the child, time away, distance traveled and number of times away.

Results

i) Survival: separate elements

Using a public phone and consulting a telephone directory Using a public telephone was an experience more common in 1981 for the children in Dublin and Belfast (over 81 per cent) than in London (70 per cent). There were increases everywhere in 1992 except in Dublin. London children were of course more likely to be able to use the phone in their own homes since more of them had household telephones (see Chapter Three) and this might explain also why fewer of the London children had consulted a telephone directory (69 per cent compared to between 85 per cent and 91 per cent elsewhere). With a phone in the home, commonly used numbers may well be noted in a place apart from the directory. It is possible also that the London children were not out often alone and in situations where they would need to use a public telephone. The Dublin and Belfast children (the latter in spite of the 'Troubles') would seem to be have greater opportunities in this respect. Perhaps the dangers in the streets perceived by London parents are greater than those perceived by parents in Dublin and Belfast.

But although the numbers of home phone owners had increased in both West Belfast and Dublin to around a similar level with the other groups in 1992 (78 per cent), the numbers who had consulted a directory remained higher in Dublin and Belfast than in London.

ii) Pouring and peeling The percentages claiming that they poured tea and peeled apples or potatoes were high for all groups in each location at over 93 per cent in 1981.

An interesting trend was the finding of a decrease in every location over time particularly for the peeling job - slightly fewer girls were becoming involved; or perhaps less peeling was being done because more ready-prepared food was available and being used; perhaps more carry-out and shop-cooked food was being consumed. This could also be linked to increased female employment, particularly shift work or part-time work at odd hours, necessitating absence from home of the mother at meal preparation times. But it must also mean higher expenditure on food as ready prepared meals are more expensive than the raw materials and if this is so it must reflect greater spending power.

iii) City travel by bus or taxi More of the Dublin (91 per cent in 1981; 86 per cent in 1992) and West Belfast children (86 per cent in 1981; 85 per cent in 1992) had taken a bus or taxi by themselves compared to 62 per cent (1981) and 68 per cent (1992) in East Belfast and 68 per cent (1981), 71 per cent (1992) in London. This again could reflect differing perceptions of danger and safety which would be understandable in London and, in 1981, in East Belfast; but one would have expected similar if not higher levels of protectiveness to be manifested by the West Belfast parents. On the other hand, as reported in Chapter Three, there could be a more practical explanation. This finding could be due to the fact that more of the East Belfast and London families than of the Dublin and West Belfast families had cars in both 1981 and 1992, and children were taken places by their parents rather than making their own way. There could well have been an element of protectiveness in this behaviour also and if our sample had been a more prosperous middle-class sample, it would probably have been even more prevalent in all groups. But the findings suggest a determination on the part of the families in West Belfast to continue behaving as if there were no extra problems and allow their children to travel alone. A side effect for the East Belfast and London children would have been a reduction in opportunities to develop scripts for independent action.

Survival: composite variable

Analysis of variance on the composite variable 'Survival' showed no significant differences by group in 1981, but there were significant differences by group in 1992 (F = 32.225; P<.001). The London children appeared to have much lower scores than those from the other locations whose scores were all similar. Their mean score decreased over the period, probably leading to the significant difference noted above. The scores in other locations changed very slightly in a positive direction. There were significant differences between girls and boys in both 1981 and 1992 for the composite variable 'Survival'. Girls scored higher than boys in all four locations on both occasions, mainly because of greater experience in the peeling and pouring task.

The skills included in this variable would seem to be stable in the populations under study, except in the London sample - perhaps a more shifting population than in the other locations and this is confirmed by figures provided by the schools about transfers. The findings indicate that similar percentages of families in Dublin and

Belfast offered opportunities to their 12 year-olds to develop these 'survival' skills and the self-confidence resulting from them. The Belfast children, did not appear to be disadvantaged along this dimension, except for the East Belfast children in the element of independent bus or taxi travel

ii) Commitment: separate elements

a) Household chores:

Household chores, narrowly defined to include cleaning, clothes care and food preparation are often seen as offering opportunities only to girls to develop skills. A wider definition was adopted in the present study and care was taken to include tasks in the checklist presented to respondents which would present no problem even to the most chauvinist of boys. The responses were grouped so as to allow viable percentages to accumulate and are presented in Figures 6.1. and 6.2.

Differences by location A brief overview of the findings shows that:

i)   More children in Dublin, both girls and boys, than in the other locations were involved in household tasks in 1981. The next highest percentage, both girls and boys came from West Belfast, then London and then East Belfast.
ii)   In 1992, there were decreases everywhere in the involvement of children in household tasks, except for boys in East Belfast. The greatest decreases were in Dublin and London and this meant that this time overall, the order was different; the West Belfast children were most involved followed by the East Belfast children, and then the Dublin and London children.
iii) The range of chores undertaken was similar in all locations.
iv)   Differences between the groups were in most cases simply because a higher or lower percentage checked the whole range of chores. There seemed to be no particular task or set of tasks which was indicated consistently by one group more than another.

Chores related to food the differences between the groups were not significant in 1981 - with between 89 per cent and 96 per cent of children from each group helping with this kind of task. In 1992, the percentage from each group varied from 52–63 per cent. More girls than boys were involved at each time point and the percentage decrease was similar for both sexes in every location, with a marginally greater decrease in London for boys.

Clothes-related tasks were done by between 32 per cent and 45 per cent in 1981 and 20–27 per cent in 1992. More girls than boys did these tasks in 1981, but in 1992 there was a substantial decrease for girls and a marginal increase for boys (except in London) which meant that percentages of girls and boys were more or less equal everywhere.

Childminding and babysitting chores were much more common in Dublin (83 per cent in 1981) than in the other locations. Similar percentages in East and West Belfast listed this kind of chore, (68 per cent, East Belfast; 69 per cent, West

125

Belfast) and the percentages were lower in London (51 per cent). In 1992, the percentages had dropped for Dublin (62 per cent) and East Belfast (55 per cent) but not in West Belfast and London which remained the same as they had been in 1981. The West Belfast children and the Dublin children seemed to have a more consistently high level of experiences of this kind. Both boys and girls claimed to have done babysitting or childminding. More girls than boys had done so in East Belfast and London in 1981, but in Dublin and West Belfast, percentages were similar.

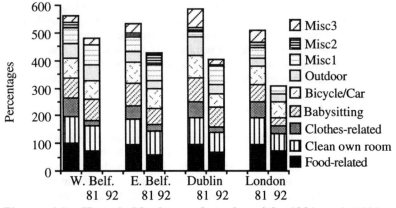

Figure 6.1   Household chores done by girls 1981 and 1992

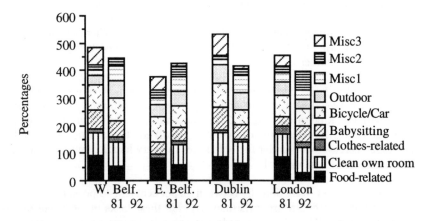

Figure 6.2   Household chores done by boys 1981 and 1992

The percentages increased for boys and decreased for girls in East Belfast and London to a greater extent than elsewhere. This seems to give further support to the possibility that the girls in East Belfast were being allowed more time to themselves and indicates one small area in which boys there were being encouraged to take on more responsibility, though they were still at a lower percentage than the other groups for this variable.

Cleaning tasks were reduced more in Dublin (91 -> 75 per cent) and London (93 -> 76 per cent) than in Belfast. In West Belfast there was only marginal change (92 -> 89 per cent). In East Belfast, where in 1981 they had constituted the lowest percentage, the responses actually increased marginally (82 -> 87 per cent), due to increased participation by boys in this particular activity. But the trend in Dublin and London was for a decrease in participation in activities like this. The decrease in both locations was at a similar rate for girls and boys, whereas for the Belfast children there was not much change - a sign of greater control within the family perhaps.

Bike and car-related tasks had similar percentages everywhere in 1981, (ranging from 76 per cent, London to 87 per cent, Dublin) but they decreased everywhere in 1992 and more in Dublin and London than in Belfast (50 per cent, Dublin; 69 per cent London; 73 per cent West and East Belfast). The Belfast children again, seem to be less subject to change in this area. The findings were similar for girls and boys.

Outdoor tasks increased in West Belfast (45 per cent to 59 per cent), especially for boys, but decreased everywhere else, especially for girls in Dublin and for boys in London; in East Belfast they were up for boys and down for girls. This could indicate greater freedom of movement in West Belfast in 1992 than in 1981 and also perhaps a greater availability of little jobs outside the house - a sign of enhanced standard of living maybe, as reflected also in the percentage who had done jobs for money (Chapter Three).

Overall trends

While the trend overall was a declining one of participation in household tasks in all locations, this was less true for the Belfast children than for those in Dublin and London. This finding could be related to that on independence which found the Belfast children with somewhat less independence and greater parental salience than those in Dublin and London. This could mean that they were somewhat more tied to the home, though perhaps as a result they enjoyed a greater sense of security at an age when than their counterparts in Dublin and London were out of the house more often. It also gave them an opportunity to practise commitment to domestic tasks in a supportive environment at a later stage than the Dublin and London children. This could work both ways - it could benefit them by making them more secure, or it could in fact be counter-productive by being over-protective and result in making them more conformist.

Girls and boys

More girls than boys did household chores in all locations at both time points. Differences between the sexes were significant in 1981. More girls tended to do chores related to food, clothes, babysitting, cleaning and bicycle/car repairs and washing. On average in 1981, about 11 per cent more girls than boys were likely to

127

do particular jobs about the house The differences were not significant for 'outdoor' tasks. In 1992, there was a decrease in the percentage of girls involved in all kinds of household chores. At this time only 3 per cent more girls than boys were involved in household chores and the percentage of boys hardly changed between 1981 and 1992.

This finding suggests the adoption of a different style of household management in these families over time - perhaps less housework is being done, as was shown also by the findings on how spare time was spent in Chapter Four. We saw earlier that in fact they were doing more homework and similar activities and if parents are encouraging this rather than participation in household tasks, we could have a partial explanation for the findings. Perhaps also, girls are being allowed to pursue interests outside the home in their spare time to a greater extent than previously when they were expected to do more around the house. This may be another indication of the trend towards less control by parents over what their children do. And it does not look as though the boys are becoming involved to any greater extent than before, with the exception of the little 'blip' in East Belfast, a finding also supported by those reported in Chapter Four on spare time activities.

b) Pet care

Pet ownership was a stable feature of all locations. There were slight differences by location. East Belfast families were most likely to have a pet (74 per cent in 1981; 73 per cent in 1992). This would give the East Belfast children an advantage possibly, in that more of them had this kind of opportunity for taking on responsibilities. Those in West Belfast were least likely to have a pet, but even here the finding was of 57 per cent in 1981, 53 per cent in 1992. The favourite everywhere was a dog. The next ranked favourites everywhere were cats, fish and budgerigars. The percentages who owned different kinds of pets did not change within locations between 1981 and 1992.

In all locations the percentages of girls and boys who said that they helped with the pet corresponded very closely to the percentages who said that they had pets in the home. There were no differences between the sexes.

c) Shopping

Differences between locations Overall, about 57 per cent of the children went shopping at least twice a week for their mothers in 1981 and this had increased to 81 per cent in 1992, suggesting perhaps the effects of the recession on household budgeting. It could also be an indication of the increased independence being given to children.

There were differences between locations in 1981 and again in 1992. The practice was less common in London (47 per cent in 1981; 74 per cent in 1992) than in the other locations but at both time points it was at a very similar level in West Belfast (63 per cent in 1981; 85 per cent in 1992), Dublin (61 per cent; 81 per cent) and East Belfast (60 per cent; 74 per cent). There were no significant differences between girls and boys, although the trend was for a higher percentage of girls than of boys to go shopping in all locations at both time points.

If we see the need to shop frequently as reflecting a level of socio-economic disadvantage, these data could be interpreted as suggesting that the London children were better off than the groups in the other locations, so that shopping once a week was more likely to be the norm - the London groups also had the highest percentage of car-owners. But it could also have been the case that the children were allowed out less by themselves - it will be remembered that they had the lowest scores on 'Independence' (Chapter 4) - or that their mothers or fathers tended to do all the shopping.

East Belfast, West Belfast and Dublin children did similar amounts of shopping in 1982. There was a greater increase in West Belfast and Dublin in 1992, but in both of these locations there had also been a increase in household goods and in the socio-eonomic level as measured by pocket money and jobmoney. Clearly there may be more to it than the socio-economic explanation.

Shopping frequently may also be part of a family's functioning routine and perhaps more so in Belfast and Dublin than in London. It may transcend other considerations, and may be used consciously as a socializing process. If this were not the case, even with socio-economic deprivation, it is difficult to see how mothers would send children to shop in Belfast where, especially in 1981, dangers beyond the 'normal' urban dangers abounded. If this is the case, one could interpret these findings as indicating that the West Belfast children were being empowered to a greater extent than the children in the other locations especially in 1992 and that the 'Troubles' were not perceived as hindering at least some essential day-to-day activities to any great extent. This attitude could also be a contributory factor in their 'resilience'.

One does not wish to exaggerate the possible contribution of this kind of activity to the overall mentality of the children in West and East Belfast, but that mentality and their attitudes result from the interaction of hundreds of events and experiences. It is difficult if not impossible to tell which of these are of overriding importance, but it would seem that this particular item might give us some insights.

Lösel and Bliesener (1994) emphasize the importance of personal and social resources as protective factors. They point out that these may result from complex nature-nurture interactions and that they may operate directly or indirectly. The balance between stressful life events that heighten children's vulnerability and protective factors in their lives that increase resilience is obviously successfully achieved in cases where the problem situation, or adverse circumstance, does not appear to do lasting damage. A number of the factors previously found to be protective in different research contexts seem to be present for the Belfast children in the context of the item under discussion here. These include the ways in which individuals try to cope actively with problems, which in the present case could mean the determination to continue life as usual, in spite of the 'Troubles', including sending children to the corner shop, and lettng them travel about the city alone. This attitude on the part of the parents was possibly transmitted to the children and may have been one of the elements which together with others had the effect of reducing the psychological impact of the violence. A second factor reported by previous research which helps develop resilience is the availability of experiences of self-efficacy leading to self-confidence and these would have been provided in the present example, *inter alia* for the children by the opportunities to do shopping and travel alone in the city (Cohler, 1987, Garmezy, 1985, Luthar and Zigler, 1991, Masten, 1989, Masten, Best and Garmezy, 1991, Rutter, 1985, 1990, Werner, 1985, 1989).

Results reported by Lösel and Bliesener (1994) showed that children deemed to be at high risk for stress, but who turned out to be resilient were, among other characteristics, more self-efficacious; they undertook more active coping behaviour, were more willing to take on social tasks and they also had a more realistic view of the future. For our sample's views on the future, we must wait until Chapter Nine, but if this is the case as far as the other items are concerned, the West Belfast children would be slightly more resilient than those in East Belfast at both points in time, although over time the groups came closer together on housework if not on shopping; in addition the girls in our sample would be more resilient than the boys - more of them took on social tasks, like housework and shopping, more of them had taken a bus or taxi on their own.

Commitment: composite variable

This was computed from scores awarded for undertaking shopping, helping with pets and for the number of chores each child said that they undertook in the home. Significant differences were found by group and sex (P<.001) in 1981; the West and East Belfast children had similar scores, the Dublin children apparently contributed more in the home at that time with an overall mean score of 6.8, and the London children were lowest with 5.9. Following the discussion of the findings in detail above, it looks as though more of the children in West Belfast did more housework and shopping than those in East Belfast and that the latter's overall score was increased by their higher rate of pet ownership and pet care. The type of 'Commitment' was therefore a bit different, involving differential amounts of interaction with other people. But in 1992, when scores had decreased everywhere, they had decreased less in Belfast, both West and East, than in Dublin and the results showed a marginally smaller decrease for the East Belfast children. The London children had a mean score of 3.2 in 1992 representing a substantial decrease while the other groups were around 4.9–5.0.

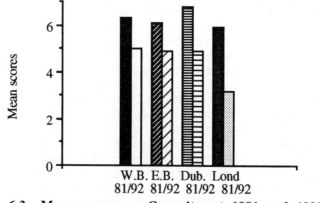

Figure 6.3 Mean scores on Commitment 1981 and 1992

The results suggest that by 1992, the only differences between locations were due to the low scores of the London children - there was a convergence among the

130

other locations. They appeared to offer similar opportunities for commitment to their 12 year-olds. This could of course have been due to the very slight movement towards rebalancing between the sexes in 1992 compared to the 1981 situation when girls had been contributing significantly more in every location with a higher score on the composite variable 'Commitment'. But it was not a situation of give and take in equal measure. In 1992, compared to 1981, girls were contributing less, without boys contributing more.

In terms of how this might contribute to resilience, the composite variable suggests that children in Belfast and Dublin were not very different in terms of the opportunities they had to gain feelings of self-efficacy and self-confidence, as measured here, which might help them withstand stressful events. However, as noted above, more of the children in West Belfast than in East Belfast appeared to be involved in two of the activities investigated, housework and shopping, particularly in 1981 and more of them also were independent travelers around the city. This might have implications for self-esteem and self-concept development.

It was interesting that the gap between them became narrower in 1992, because of a slightly smaller decrease in scores on this composite variable for the children in East Belfast, than for the children elsewhere.

iii) What kinds of work did they do to earn money?

The jury is still out on the benefits or otherwise of young teenagers being employed while they are still at school (Fine, Mortimer and Roberts, 1993) but in the present study we were simply interested in the percentages who had ever undertaken a job for money, not necessarily a steady or regular job, simply from the point of view of establishing the opportunities available to them and the prevalence of earning among them. From the information provided by respondents it was possible to classify the jobs done as those carried out within the home environment, or outside under the supervision of someone else. While both types of jobs obviously had relevance for development, it was felt that the latter might offer more scope for challenge and it was felt important to distinguish between the two and to establish whether children in all locations and of both sexes had similar opportunities in this area.

Differences by location

There were slight differences between locations in the kinds of opportunities available. Opportunities within each location across the two timepoints seemed very stable. There was very little change in the percentages saying that they had done particular kinds of jobs, especially in London (Figure 6.4).

Gardening / carwashing were the types of jobs ranked first in every location at both time points. In 1981, the kind of job done by the second highest percentage of West Belfast children was working in a shop job or café job, whereas in East Belfast and Dublin it was a paper round and in London, housework. In 1992 however there were some changes; gardening / carwashing were not done by such high percentages in Belfast or Dublin and the percentage doing this had increased in London. Housework was more important for the Belfast children than it had been in 1981; this is interesting as it appeared from the findings reported above that fewer of them were actually doing housework. It looks as though housework was being paid for, in Belfast at least, to a greater extent in 1992 than in 1981. The percentages doing housework for remuneration in Dublin and London remained the same in 1992 as in 1981 and more of the children in these locations were doing paper rounds in 1992.

In terms of experiences outside the home, it looks as though the children in West and East Belfast overall were about even, between paper rounds and jobs in shops or cafés and the London children were at about the same level as the Belfast children,

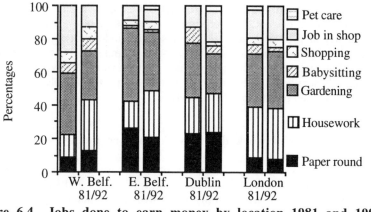

Figure 6.4   Jobs done to earn money by location 1981 and 1992

when the percentages doing these two kinds of jobs are put together. The Dublin children had a slightly higher percentage involved in these jobs outside the home at both timepoints and this could explain their higher earnings.

Girls and boys

As noted in Chapter Three, more boys than girls had had opportunities to earn money. While the same range of jobs emerged for both girls and boys, more boys overall appeared to have had jobs which involved going outside the family home and being paid by someone other than a family member as may be seen in Figures 6.5 and 6.6.

Paper rounds and working in a café or shop were mentioned by 27–28 per cent of the boys in 1981 and 1992, whereas only 15 per cent of the girls overall gave these as jobs they had done at either time point. The findings in this section may depend very much on chance. The fluctuations in the percentages of children who had done the various kinds of jobs in the different locations illustrate this - for example the percentage of girls who had worked in a shop or café increased in West Belfast and London, decreased in East Belfast and stayed about the same in Dublin. Such findings may depend on whether or not the child has a relation or family friend in that kind of business.

There are also 'swings and roundabouts' involved in that the 1981 finding that fewer girls in East Belfast had worked in a shop or café then than in 1992, was

There are also 'swings and roundabouts' involved in that the 1981 finding that fewer girls in East Belfast had worked in a shop or café then than in 1992, was offset by the finding that more girls in East Belfast did paper rounds in 1992 than in 1981.

As noted earlier under 'household chores' less babysitting was recorded in 1992 than in 1981 in every location. More girls than boys did housework in Belfast and London, but in Dublin the percentages for girls and boys were similar at both timepoints.

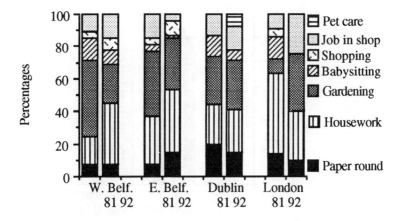

Figure 6.5   Girls: jobs done to earn money 1981 and 1992

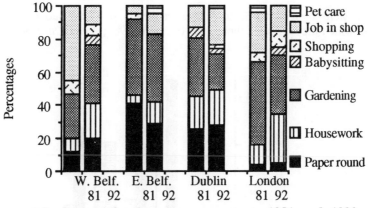

Figure 6.5   Boys: jobs done to earn money 1981 and 1992

iv)   Club membership and club attendance

Between 48 per cent (London) and 68 per cent (East Belfast) of the respondents
belonged to a youth club or group in 1981 (Figure 6.7). East Belfast again had the
highest percentage in 1992 and London the lowest although the percentages had
dropped somewhat (31 per cent in London; 66 per cent in East Belfast). There were
significant differences between locations (P<.05 in 1981; P<.001 in 1992), with
the highest percentages of club members living in Belfast, East and West and the
lowest in London

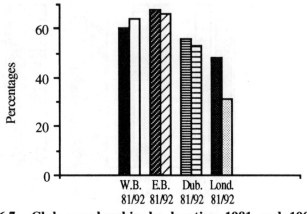

Figure 6.7   Club membership by location 1981 and 1992

Club attendance

There were significant differences between the groups with regard to the frequency
with which they attended their clubs (P<.01 in 1981; P<.001 in 1992).

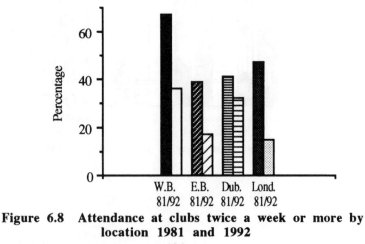

**Figure 6.8   Attendance at clubs twice a week or more by
location 1981 and 1992**

134

There were differences by gender in that a higher percentage of girls than of boys tended to be club members in both East and West Belfast; in Dublin there were no significant differences for membership between girls and boys and in London more boys than girls were members.

Attendance

There was a decrease in every location for attendance in 1992 but a higher percentage of children in West Belfast attended more often in 1981 and also in 1992 than those in the other locations.

Boys overall attended more than girls, but this varied by location. In East Belfast there were no differences between girls and boys for frequency of attendance; in West Belfast more girls appeared to attend more frequently in 1992 but not in 1981, while in Dublin and London, the reverse was the case.

While this could be related to the level of services being provided on a voluntary and statutory level by youth services, schools and parishes in West Belfast as a counter to the 'Troubles', it also showed that where facilities were provided the children were being encouraged by their parents to use them and take advantage of opportunities to participate in activities and interact with people outside the family, even though the 'Troubles' were in full swing.

Club membership as an empowering variable seemed to be more available to the Belfast children than to the others, although the children in West Belfast attended more frequently than those in East Belfast. There was a decrease in membership and in attendance over time in all locations.

v) Travel

Differences by location

How many had been away? In 1981 over 83 per cent of the children from all four locations had been away for one night or longer without their families. More children from East Belfast had been away - the percentage there was 96 per cent in 1981 whereas it was between 83 per cent and 87 per cent for the other groups. In 1992, there were some slight changes - a decrease in the percentages from East Belfast (to 89 per cent) Dublin and London (to 79 per cent). The percentages in West Belfast actually increased slightly (from 87 per cent to 89 per cent). But the figures still show that considerable numbers of children have this experience and that the differences between locations are not remarkable.

Number of occasions While there were few significant differences between groups with regard to whether or not they had been away, there were differences between them with regard to the number of times they had been away at both time points. In 1981, more children from Dublin (30 per cent) and from East Belfast (23 per cent) claimed to have been away more than five times in comparison to children from London (18 per cent) and West Belfast (12 per cent). In 1992, more children from East Belfast (35 per cent) and London (24 per cent) fell into this category (compared with West Belfast 8 per cent; Dublin 14 per cent).

Length of time away With regard to the length of time away, there were also differences between groups at both time points. More of the West Belfast (53 per cent) and Dublin (44 per cent) children had been away for longer periods (i.e. of more than one week) in 1981. In 1992, the West Belfast children were again ahead (40 per cent) and the Dublin children were next (29 per cent) with the London children and East Belfast children on an equal footing (22 per cent). Over the time period studied, the trend was for fewer children everywhere to be away for period of more than one week and conversely for more to be away for a week or less.

Age when away There were differences between the groups at both time points for the percentages who had been away at different ages. Fewer of the Dublin children (13 per cent) had been away at age 10 or younger than of the West Belfast (34 per cent) or London (48 per cent) or East Belfast children (21 per cent) in 1981. In 1992, the trend was similar. Again more of the London children had been away at age 10 or younger (47 per cent) followed by West Belfast (46 per cent), East Belfast (33 per cent and Dublin (17 per cent).

There was an increase in every location in 1992 in the percentages of both girls and boys who claimed that they had been away at a younger age.

Where had they been?

Responses were grouped as:

- Europe plus USA / Canada / Asia
- England, Scotland Wales,
- Republic of Ireland
- Northern Ireland

Travels to Europe and beyond The Belfast children were the most widely traveled - possibly in part due to the community holidays organized in the '70s and '80s and '90s. by charitable organizations and community relations groups both from within Northern Ireland and abroad (Arthur, 1974, Trew, McWhirter, Maguire and Hinds, 1985, Trew, 1989, Toner, 1994). While in 1981, the highest percentage of children who had spent holidays in their own country came from Dublin (45 per cent) and London (80 per cent), a higher percentage of Belfast children both West (45 per cent) and East (48 per cent), had been away in Europe or further than had spent a holiday without their parents in Northern Ireland (30-31 per cent for both groups). The situation was somewhat different in 1992 when the children in Belfast conformed more to the pattern in the other locations and more of them had spent holidays in Northern Ireland (46 per cent WB; 56 per cent EB) than outside the country in more exotic places (35 per cent WB; 15 per cent EB). Children in London seemed to have traveled least in 1992, but the percentage there remained steady (at 20 per cent), of those who had been to Europe or beyond and there was a sharp decline to 8 per cent in the percentage of Dublin children who had been abroad.

Travels within Ireland, England, Wales and Scotland Very few of the Dublin children had been to Northern Ireland (1 per cent in 1981; 6 per cent in 1992) and very few of the East Belfast children had been to the Republic (1 per cent in 1981; 3

per cent in 1992). Similar percentages from both of those groups had been to England, Scotland or Wales (21 per cent from East Belfast in 1981; 23 per cent of the Dublin children; 26 per cent from East Belfast in 1992; 31 per cent of the Dublin children). But 17 per cent of the West Belfast children had been to the Republic in 1981 and 13 per cent in 1992 - more than had been to England, Scotland or Wales (9 per cent; 6 per cent).

Was the situation the same for girls and for boys and did it change over time?

Girls and boys

There appeared to be a move towards greater equality of treatment for girls and boys over time. While there were no differences in relation to whether or not they had been away at all, more boys (28 per cent) than girls (15 per cent) claimed to have been away more than five times in 1981 but in 1992, there was a leveling out and 20 per cent of both girls and boys give this response. On the other hand, while in 1981 more girls (41 per cent girls, 31 per cent boys) appeared to have been away for longer periods (one week or more), there was a leveling out here too and in 1992 the figures were 32 per cent girls, 25 per cent boys. And while there was a tendency for more girls to be away at younger ages (10 years old or less) at both time points, and this increased over time, there was a greater increase in the percentage of boys (22 per cent to 34 per cent) than of girls (34 per cent to 38 per cent) who had been away at that age. The location with the biggest gap between girls and boys in this respect was West Belfast, where about 20 per cent more girls than boys had been away at age 10 or less in 1981. This gap had narrowed to below 10 per cent in 1992. In terms of holiday destinations there were no differences between boys and girls.

Trends over time

Over time, the trend was for slightly fewer children to go away and for fewer of them to go to Europe or beyond. The children from Belfast were perhaps better off than the others in terms of what they were able to avail of especially in 1981 but there was a big decrease in the percentages going far afield between then and 1992. The percentages in London of children going far afield remained the most stable of all locations and that of West Belfast decreased the least.

Composite variable 'Travels'

The composite variable 'Travels' was made up of scores on the questions relating to travel. Enhanced scores were given for more remote locations - designated depending on the location of origin of the group - for length of time away and for travel at a younger age. Mean scores were calculated and then we looked to see how similar the distribution of high scorers was between groups.

When the mean scores for Travels were compared across groups, (Figure 6.9) an interesting picture emerged. In terms of mean scores, in 1981, West Belfast children were highest with 6.6; and the London children very close behind with 6.1. But when the scores were grouped, it was found that more London children in 1981 had higher scores on this variable - 36 per cent had scores over 8, followed by the West under 4. The East Belfast and West Belfast children were similar at between 15 per cent and 18 per cent at this level in 1981. The details are given in Figure 6.10.

In 1992, more of the London children were still scoring higher with 30 per cent having a score of 8 or more, followed by the Belfast children (both groups at 23 per cent with scores of 8 or more) and the Dublin children scored lowest with 11 per cent having high scores. At the other end of the scale, no London children scored at 4 or less, 14 per cent from East Belfast and 20 per cent from West Belfast scored at this level as did 29 per cent of the Dublin children.

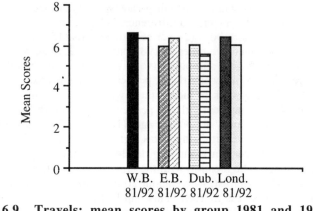

Figure 6.9   Travels: mean scores by group 1981 and 1992

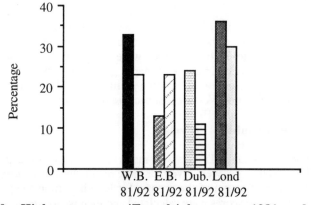

Figure 6.10   High scorers on 'Travels' by group 1981 and 1992

Implications for resilience

If anything these findings suggest that fewer of the East Belfast children than of the West Belfast children were as advantaged in 1981 in terms of the opportunities availed of for travel without their parents and the concomitant benefits for self-confidence, self-efficacy and self-esteem. And in 1992 too, fewer of them had been outside the country. This could result from a view of how to achieve protectiveness and security on the part of the parents of East Belfast which leads them to close in on themselves, thereby actually narrowing their options and their range of possible selves. This is characteristic of a group which feels threatened and on the defensive and could be related to the 'siege' mentality identified by some authors on the part of the Protestants - a fear of opening out to new environments, because of the need to maintain positions within known parameters (Kinahan, 1995, Dunlop 1995).

The parents of West Belfast appeared to have a different attitude towards protectiveness and seemed to be more inclined to encourage their children to develop their own resources. They showed this by apparently being more willing to allow their children to avail of the kinds of opportunities investigated in this study which were geared towards increasing independence, self-confidence, self-efficacy and self-esteem, especially in 1981. This could be seen as helping the development of an internal locus of control to a greater extent than the East Belfast parents.

In 1992, however, in line with the changes noted for variables previously discussed, the East Belfast children were beginning to catch up with the West Belfast children and they were on more of an equal footing. And although more of the East Belfast children still had low 'scores' on this variable, it is noteworthy that they were the only group in which high scorers (and mean scores) increased over the time period..

Relationships between the variables Survival, Commitment, Travels *and* 'Goods', Parental salience and Independence

When the composite scores for survival and commitment were correlated a significant and positive relationship was found for both boys and girls at both timepoints. This confirms what one would intuitively expect - that the children who had more of these 'urban survival skills' and were possibly regarded as more competent, also helped more around the house and scored higher on 'Commitment'.

Travels and Commitment and Survival

The scores on 'Travels' were not related to 'Commitment' or 'Survival' for girls or boys overall, suggesting that survival skills are not necessarily taken into account when children are sent off on holiday without their family - except for the London children overall in 1981 and for London boys in 1992. This suggests that opportunities for travel that arise may be taken advantage of without necessarily taking into account other aspects of the child's development and that the latter might be a consideration for the London children more than for the others. This would make sense in the present context since the London children appeared to be younger when they first traveled and they also went further away.

Survival and 'Goods'

Were families who were better off more likely to encourage survival skills in their children? There was no clearcut answer to this one and it appeared to depend on local circumstances. The 'scores' on Survival did not differ significantly between groups at either timepoint, but in Belfast both West and East, at both timepoints and in London in 1992, but not in 1981, there was a significant positive relationship between the variable 'Goods' (car, phone, bike, books) and the variable 'Survival'. It was not the case in Dublin where the children had, in fact, the lowest score on 'Goods' at both time points. Amount of pocket money or jobmoney was not related to Survival.

Commitment and Independence/Choice

There were no significant correlations between the variable 'Commitment' and the parental salience variables of mum, dad or parents. But in 1981, there was a significant relationship between Commitment and Choice in West Belfast, East Belfast and Dublin, and in 1992, only in London. Children who contributed more around the house also had more independence in making some of the choices considered. Looking at the group means we see that whereas the Dublin children scored highest on Commitment in 1981, they were not as high as the Belfast children on salience of mum or dad and this would confirm the lack of association between these variables.

Commitment and Goods

There was no relationship between Commitment and the basic composite variable 'Goods', so that the children in the better off families were not necessarily contributing more to the household, nor were the less well off children expected to contribute more. The East Belfast children had been highest on 'Goods' but were not highest on Commitment. But when the weighted amounts of pocket money and jobmoney were added in, significant relationships with 'Commitment' were found for some groups. Those who received more pocket money or earned more, tended to score higher on 'Commitment' as well. Giving more help might of course have resulted in having more money and we have seen how more children were, for example being paid for housework in 1992 than in 1981. This was not the case in every location however; it was not true for West Belfast at either timepoint nor for Dublin in 1992. It was true for London and East Belfast at both time points.

This factor could make a difference to the kinds of attitudes being developed in the children towards commitment - with some children being socialized into expecting a monetary reward more frequently as appeared to be the case in East Belfast and London. This could have implications for the development of their value systems.

Summary

Survival

- There were no differences between the groups on 'Survival' in 1981 but in 1992 the London children scored lowest and the other groups had similar scores to each other.
- Scores did not increase or decrease significantly over time on this variable.

140

Commitment

- The Dublin children were highest in 1981.
- West and East Belfast had similar mean scores, although they were composed differently.
- There was a decrease over time for all groups, especially London which was significantly lower on this variable than the other groups in 1992.
- Dublin and Belfast children had similar scores in 1992.

Household chores

- Dublin children did most housework in 1981 and London children the least; in 1992, West Belfast and East Belfast children scored higher than those in Dublin and London.
- The overall trend was towards a decrease in the percentages claiming to have done each chore over time.
- There were only slight differences between the types of jobs done in the different locations and at the two time points.
- Girls were more likely to do household chores.

Shopping

- London children were least likely to go shopping for small items.
- West Belfast children were most likely to go shopping for small items.
- There were no differences between the sexes with regard to doing shopping for the family.
- There was an increase over time everywhere in the percentages who did shopping for the family.

Pets

- There were no statistically significant differences by location or sex in the ownership of pets and amount of care given to pets by the children.

Clubs

- More children in Belfast than elsewhere were members of clubs.
- More children in Belfast attended more frequently (especially West Belfast).
- Membership and attendance fell over time in every location.
- More girls were members, but boys were more frequent attenders in 1981; in 1992 there were no differences overall.

Travels

- Over 83 per cent of all the children had been away without their families at or before age 12 in 1981 and similar percentages in 1992.
- There was no consistent pattern over time in the number of times children from the different groups had been away.

- More West Belfast and Dublin children appeared to have been away for longer at both time points.
- Over the time studied, fewer children went away for longer periods.
- More London children than children from the other locations went away at a younger age.
- Overall, fewer East Belfast children than children from the other locations had higher scores on the composite variable 'Travels' in 1981.
- Boys appeared to have been away more often and girls to have been away for longer and at a younger age in 1981, but in 1992, these differences were leveling out in an upward direction.
- There was a stronger relationship between Commitment and money variables for the East Belfast and London children than for the West Belfast and Dublin children.

Trends over time

This chapter has examined some of the activities which could be said to constitute 'preparation for reaching out' by families for their children in West and East Belfast, London and Dublin. The Belfast and Dublin children were more like each other than they were like the London children at both time points on some of these variables. The London children appeared to have lower scores on Survival and Commitment. The West and East Belfast children were similar on both of these at both time points, although the scores on Survival in 1981, in particular the extent of the experience of traveling alone by bus or taxi and also the scores on Commitment in 1981 which showed that more of the former were involved in housework and shopping seemed to favour greater support for self-efficacy and self-confidence in the West Belfast children than for those in East Belfast. The findings also suggested that commitment was related to monetary reward to a greater extent for the London and East Belfast children than for the Dublin and West Belfast children. The scores on Travels also seemed to suggest that a higher percentage of the West Belfast children than of those from East Belfast had had more extensive opportunities to broaden their experiences though travel. It was suggested that parental attitudes towards protectiveness and preparation for life found different expressions in East and West Belfast at that time. However in 1992, there was a considerable leveling out in scores on all the variables, especially between the West and East Belfast groups. The London groups suffered greater decreases on every side, in line with those found in earlier chapters.

Trends over time also showed a gradual leveling of opportunities available to boys and girls in all these areas. In some, such as Commitment, it was almost a leveling down - fewer girls, but no additional boys scored on this variable; for Clubs there were decreases for both girls and boys; for Travels there was a leveling up - whichever sex had been at a disadvantage in 1981 for any element of this variable, appeared to be catching up with the other, who also enjoyed an increase in 1992. Changes in lifestyle seem to be suggested - less commitment about the house and in the local area to clubs, a greater opening to experiences outside the home locality as reflected in the variable Travels, especially for the Belfast children.

In building up a picture of these 12 year-olds we must next look at their exposure to other influences outside the immediate family, aspects of their environment which will have shaped the development of their thinking - their encounters with the media - through books, newspapers, television and radio. The extent of the exposure of the children in the different locations to these influences and the items which caught their attention are described and analyzed in the next chapter.

7 Access to information

Introduction

As well as family and school, the children in our sample in East and West Belfast, Dublin and London were exposed to a host of other influences which provided them with knowledge, helped define their options and contributed to the formation of their self-concept and identity. This knowledge may be differentiated into declarative knowledge and procedural knowledge and it has been proposed that these combine to form 'social intelligence' (Cantor and Kihlstrom, 1987), which enables the development of expertise for working on the tasks of social life in which social goals are especially salient. Declarative knowledge is interpreted as being the individual's static concepts about other people, social situations and themselves which help them to make sense of social events and procedural knowledge involves dynamic processes such as forming impressions of people, making attributions about causes of events and predicting the likely events in a social situation.

Some of this knowledge comes through the media - newspapers, magazines, books, television, video, radio. Chaffee (1977), found that television and newspapers are both important sources of information about politics for adolescents. Chaffee and Schleuder (1986) reported that attention to media news resulted in an increase in knowledge about public affairs. Correlational studies have shown that teenagers who attend more to news and public affairs media are more knowledgeable of and active in political matters (Chaffee and Yang, 1990). Television news exposure was found to be the strongest predictor variable of political knowledge and behaviour by Garramone and Atkin (1986), with broadcast media better for current events knowledge and newspapers better for specific political knowledge. But Robinson and Davis (1990) reported that those who derive news from television have less comprehension of events and issues than those who obtain information from other sources.

Access to the media may have the effect of broadening one's outlook in a number of ways. (Bandura, 1990, Comstock, Chaffee, Katzman, McCombs and Roberts, 1978, Roberts and Maccoby, 1984). It may simply increase declarative knowledge by providing the means of developing concepts through the content it makes attractively available. And it may influence procedural knowledge by, for example, showing that there are several possibly acceptable solutions to a problem and how they might be applied, or how people deal with complex and ambiguous situations and work towards solutions. But it is not inevitable that access to the media will empower and enable development in this way (McGuire,1986). That will depend on the quality of the material selected for attention and this could equally result in a restriction or inhibition of development. Knowledge or lack of it is the basis for attitudes and studies by Kraus and Davis (1976), and Chaffee, Ward and Tipton (1970) found that teenagers claimed that the media affected their attitudes towards politics. And although it has been found that mass-mediated communication is not significantly related to instilling tolerant values (Owen and Dennis, 1987), access to information will nevertheless contribute to levels of knowledge - reading newspapers and watching television news were found to be significant predictors of the amount of political information adolescents possessed (Torney-Purta, 1985,) and this in turn will have an effect on self esteem, attitudes, motivation for action, and hence on identity.

Given the situation in Northern Ireland where leaders are unwilling to take risks and the level of trust between communities has been very low on the surface until recently at any rate, the question here is - are the children in Northern Ireland subject to opportunities for mind-broadening experiences which differ from those available to children elsewhere? And could their experiences have resulted in their having less declarative knowledge, leading to a lower sense of self-efficacy which would affect their self-confidence and hence their effectiveness in interaction situations, even as adults? A lower sense of self-efficacy could also mean a greater tendency to conform to 'traditional' attitudes and a reluctance to take responsibility for initiating different approaches to old problems. It could be reinforced in adults by the *de facto* dependence on others to take responsibility for economic and political decision-making. In addition a reluctance to take risks will be reinforced by the 'siege' mentality - the feeling that the need for security is paramount and will only be satisfied by staying within well-known territory. The result may be a community who are very conformist, less trusting of other groups than other groups are of them and less willing to take risks by stepping outside the wellworn paths.

The question of access to information is relevant when we consider that people need information in order to be aware of options and make choices (Goodnow, 1986). In addition, if behaviour is seen as the end product of a sequence of cognitive transformations (Hettema, 1989) and the opportunities available to Northern Ireland children to practise such cognitive transformations are limited, because their access to sources of information are restricted, they will be seriously disadvantaged in terms of their abilities to devise strategies, develop plans and predict likely outcomes. Their own awareness of these shortcomings will influence their sense of self-efficacy and self-esteem, and consequently the effectiveness of their communicative interactions.

In this chapter we report the findings related to the children's access to declarative knowledge :

• Did the children have similar access to newspapers, television and radio.?
• What attracted their interest in terms of current events - were they local, national, international?
• Were there differences between the groups and if so how can they be explained?
• Were newspapers and television equally effective in arousing their interest?

Access to newspapers

The following questions were asked:

•*Do you ever look at a newspaper?*	*No*	*Yes*
- on weekdays?	*No*	*Yes*
•*When did you last look at a daily paper?*		
•*Name one paper you have seen lately*		
•*Mention something you read in it*		
•*What else did you look at in it?*		

Television

Respondents answered these questions:

•*Do you ever see the news on television?*	*No*	*Yes*
•*When did you last see a news programme on television?*		
•*Mention something you saw on the news lately*		

Radio

The questions here were:

•*Do you ever hear the news on the radio?*	*No*	*Yes*
•*When did you last hear the news on the radio?*		

Results

Newspapers

a) Did they read newspapers? In 1981, over 95 per cent of children in all the groups said that they looked at a newspaper regularly and there were no significant differences between locations. The percentages overall went down slightly in 1992 - to between 93 per cent and 95 per cent for all except the London children whose percentage decreased by 13 per cent.

b) Recency of reading a paper In 1981 the majority of children in all locations had looked at a daily newspaper that day or the previous day - ranging from 71 per cent (WB) to 80 per cent (London). However the numbers claiming to have seen a newspaper that day or the previous day were substantially lower for all groups in 1992, down to below 50 per cent except for the Dublin children of whom 64 per cent had seen a paper within the past 24 hours. More girls than boys overall had seen a paper within the past 24 hours at both timepoints.

c) Which newspapers did they read? In all three locations - Belfast, London and Dublin, the possibilities included locally produced regional papers, the British popular tabloid press, and quality national papers. Each gives a particular slant to coverage of news and is selective in what is reported. They differ in the space allocated to national versus international and local events. Exposure to different types of newspaper would mean exposure to different kinds of information and could make a difference to the interest generated in local or world events and the possibilities made available for processing information. Figure 7.1 shows the percentages of children in each location who said that they had read the various categories of newspaper

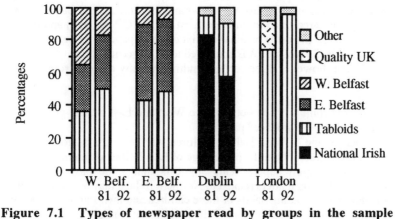

Figure 7.1   Types of newspaper read by groups in the sample 1981 and 1992

National newspapers In 1981, and again in 1992 the findings showed that the majority of each group of children tended to read the newspapers produced in their own location. Belfast children read locally produced papers, Dublin children read Dublin-based papers and London children read London-based popular tabloids. Very few London children read 'national' quality newspapers. Dublin children tended to read national Irish quality newspapers rather than tabloids.

Tabloids London children were the most likely to read the British tabloids and Dublin children were least likely. East Belfast children were slightly more likely to read popular tabloids than West Belfast children, and this would be in line perhaps with the aspirations of their community towards greater identification with British values. However, the percentages everywhere, even in Dublin, who read British tabloids increased between 1981 and 1992.

Local newspapers Locally produced newspapers in Belfast are of a more regional orientation than papers produced in London or Dublin. They tend to concentrate on matters of local interest with less attention to wider national or international affairs. In addition, with a couple of notable exceptions, they tend to be politically oriented either towards the unionists or the nationalists with a corresponding slant to the reporting of news items. Since Dublin and London papers which give wider, and some would say more objective, coverage to national and international matters are easily available in Belfast, people have a choice. Those who choose only regional papers may have their horizons somewhat limited.

We found that a slightly higher percentage of West Belfast than of East Belfast children read papers produced in Belfast in 1981, but in 1992, the percentages reading locally produced papers were lower for both and were similar - largely because of the big increase in tabloid reading, especially in West Belfast. In 1992 similar percentages read tabloids and locally produced papers in both East and West Belfast.

Their choice of local papers differed in the expected direction. More East Belfast children read the unionist *Belfast Newsletter* and the more neutral *Belfast Telegraph* (46 per cent) compared to children from West Belfast (29 per cent) and more West Belfast children (35 per cent) read nationalist oriented papers such as the *Irish News* and *Sunday News* (35 per cent WB compared to 11 per cent EB).

There were however three further findings worthy of note from the data on newspaper reading:

• There was some overlap between the West and East Belfast groups, in their reading of locally produced papers;
• The percentage of West Belfast children who read non-nationalist oriented papers was greater than the percentage of East Belfast children who read non-unionist oriented papers. This suggests that some basis for a broader understanding on matters related to Northern Ireland may be presented through the newspaper reading habits of these children and their families - perhaps to a greater extent than in the East Belfast children; it might go part of the way towards explaining the greater 'openness' and understanding of the 'other side' found among Catholics by some researchers (Doob and Foltzer, 1973, Fairleigh, 1975, Greer, 1985).
• There was a substantial increase in the circulation of the British tabloid press in all four locations which must be resulting in a leveling out of attitudes and perhaps a leveling down of values.

Girls and boys There were differences between girls and boys in some locations but not in others. There was a slight tendency for boys to opt more for tabloids and girls for locally based papers and the increase in tabloid readership overall was reflected more by the boys' than by girls' preferences in 1992, especially in West Belfast.

Television

Did they watch news programmes? In 1981 between 93 per cent and 98 per cent of all groups claimed to watch TV news regularly, with a slightly higher percentage of children in Belfast, especially in East Belfast at both time points doing so (Figure 7.2).

In 1992 there was a very slight decrease for all locations in the percentage claiming to watch the news regularly, but the percentages were still in the 90s for everyone. Significantly more boys (94 per cent) than girls overall (90 per cent) said that they watched the news.

Recency of watching news Between 71 per cent and 81 per cent of those who responded in 1981 had watched the news that day or the previous day (Figure 7.3). The Belfast children tended to be more avid watchers; over 81 per cent of both West Belfast and East Belfast children had watched the news within the past 24 hours whereas the percentage was 71–74 per cent for the Dublin and London children. This may reflect a certain preoccupation with the news in Belfast which was not shared with London and Dublin.

Between 1981 and 1992 there was a substantial decrease for children in all locations who had watched the news that day or the previous day - about 10 per cent less for all groups, although similar percentages still claimed to watch the news regularly (Figure 7.3). But more of the Belfast children had still watched the news more recently than the others (around 75 per cent 'yesterday' or 'this morning' compared to around 61 per cent of the other groups).

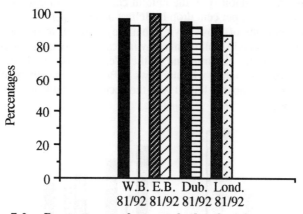

Figure 7.2   Percentage who watched television news: by location 1981 and 1992

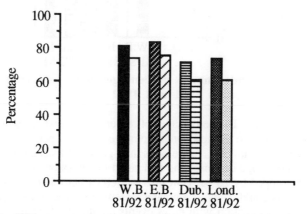

Figure 7.3   TV news: percentage who watched within 24 hours 1981 and 1992

In 1981 there were no significant differences between girls and boys for recency of viewing the news, but in 1992, more boys scored on this item (P<.001). Girls, on the other hand as noted above, were more likely to have looked at a newspaper recently.

Radio news

How many listened regularly to the radio? Between 69 per cent (London) and 91 per cent (West Belfast) listened to the news on the radio in 1981 (Figure 7.4). Here the highest percentage was from West Belfast, followed by East Belfast and could reflect again a greater preoccupation with the news in those groups in 1981. Significantly more girls (83 per cent) than boys (73 per cent) in 1981 said that they listened to radio news (P>.05), but in 1992 the differences were not significant.

In 1992 however, the percentages everywhere had gone down by 14–36 per cent. There was greater stability in the Dublin children - with only a 10 per cent drop, compared to a 30–36 per cent drop in Belfast and a 20 per cent drop in London. The highest percentages of those saying that they listened to the news in 1992 were from West Belfast and Dublin. This may indicate a more enduring interest in current affairs in the Dublin children and in the West Belfast children. It also seems to indicate less preoccupation with the news in Belfast in the 1990s compared with the 1980s, and this is probably linked with the decrease in violence.

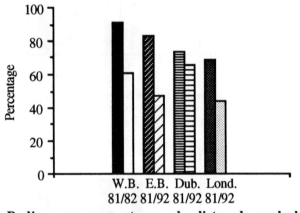

Figure 7.4   Radio news: percentages who listened regularly by group 1981 and 1992

Recency of listening The percentages of respondents who had listened that morning or the previous day to the news on radio ranged from 57 per cent (Dublin) to 75 per cent (East Belfast) in 1981. More boys than girls had listened recently in 1981. In 1992, the percentage of those who had heard the news on radio within the past 24 hours had dropped by 20 per cent in East Belfast but remained stable in the other locations. This could suggest a greater lessening of interest and perhaps a greater decline in preoccupation with news events among the East Belfast children than among the other groups. This could have been due to the decrease in violence in their own area, but also to a 'switching off' from general fatigue at the perpetually

150

bad news. On the other hand maybe it was compensated for by television news which became available in the mornings and was available all through the day in 1992, unlike the situation in 1981.

The composite variable 'News'

The composite variable 'News' was made up of the score awarded to each subject on the six items relating to TV, radio and newspaper access. One point was awarded for each 'yes' answer, if they answered that they had read / looked at / listened to news and one point for recency (today / yesterday) for each item. This gave a possible maximum score of 6 points on this variable. 'News' was correlated at a later stage with other context variables and knowledge variables of interest.

Differences by location

There were significant differences between locations at both time-points. The results suggested that in 1981, the West Belfast and East Belfast children had higher scores than the other groups (Figure 7.5). A higher percentage of the Belfast children gained a score of more than 4 points (90 per cent in WB and EB compared to 83 per cent Dublin and 78 per cent London).
But in 1992, the East Belfast children had dropped behind with only 61 per cent getting more than 4 points and the West Belfast children (69 per cent) were clearly ahead, with higher percentages of them scoring over 4. The percentage of London children scoring over 4 points decreased markedly to 54 per cent.

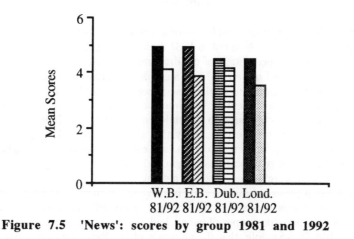

Figure 7.5 **'News': scores by group 1981 and 1992**

This pulls together the individual items reported above and consolidates the finding that the Belfast children had been most interested in news in 1981, but were less so in 1992, with East Belfast trailing a little; the London children's interest had declined substantially. The Dublin children showed less change.

There were no significant differences between boys and girls for their scores on 'News' at either timepoint.

151

We see from these findings that the majority of children appeared to be exposed to news from newspaper, TV and radio in all locations. The Belfast children appeared to have a greater degree of exposure than the others. But over time there was a decrease in the percentages reading, watching and listening to the news in all locations; this was true to a similar degree for all groups in the case of TV news, and to a greater extent for the Belfast and London children than for the Dublin children in the case of newspaper and radio news.

If the amount of exposure reflects interest, there appeared to be less interest overall in 1992 than in 1981. The decrease in the recency and probably the frequency of newspaper reading and the trend towards reading the tabloid press together with the reduction in the recency and probably also the frequency of watching TV news suggests that we may find corresponding downward trends in the level of declarative knowledge in the 1992 generation of 12 year-olds, unless exposure to other sources compensated for it.

However it should also be noted that there was greater stability in the interest of Dublin children in news events reported in newspapers and on television and radio. This may be indicative of the attitudes prevalent in their culture towards involvement and interest in current affairs and this may be relevant for their level of declarative knowledge, their feelings of self-efficacy and their orientation towards the future. This contrasts with the findings for the East Belfast children in particular whose scores on 'News' decreased the most, suggesting a decided lack of interest in 1992 in acquiring information about current events.

Interest in current affairs from both newspapers and television:

Children from all locations displayed an awareness of current events both from the newspapers and on television but in 1981 there were significant differences between the groups. A higher percentage of children in Belfast children, both East and West, than of the Dublin or London children mentioned current events items as what they recalled from television and/or the newspaper. The children in Belfast seemed to have a heightened awareness of and interest in current events as reported in the media in 1981 when compared to the children in Dublin and London. This finding would seem to support the possibility that the children in Belfast were having different experiences with regard to media exposure from those available to the children in the other two locations (Figure 7.6 below).

However this 'score' is composed of a combination of two measures and while it may indicate a gross overall level of interest and it may be telling us something about the general orientation of the children in the different locations, it does not tell us whether particular types of events had more salience for the different groups. It is possible, for example, that the attention of the Belfast children was drawn to current events because they were of concern to themselves and were taking place, so to speak, in their own backyards. It remains to be seen whether the kinds of events they reported were in fact local and whether they also had an interest in and knowledge of wider issues.

Findings will be reported first for 1981 for both newspapers and television in order to determine whether there was a coherent pattern. Findings for 1992 will then be presented together with figures to make comparisons easier.

Interest in items read in newspapers

The children were asked to respond to two open-ended questions:

> •*Mention something you read in the paper*
> •*What else did you look at in it?*

The responses were categorized as

- Items of information on current affairs
- Items related to human interest / entertainment / business / jobs / consumerism

Current affairs news items recalled from newspapers

While many of the children mentioned items like advertisements, comic strips and cartoons, sports, TV programme schedules, horoscopes, crosswords and puzzles, 37 per cent of the children overall mentioned items related to current events in 1981 as being what they remembered from newspapers.

There were differences between the locations. West Belfast children were more likely to mention current events in response to this question than were children from any of the other locations. East Belfast children did so in smaller numbers than Dublin children, though the percentages were close. London children did not display a great interest in current affairs. (Figure 7.7 below). A higher percentage of girls than of boys overall gave responses in this category at both time points.

The responses were categorized as:

- headlines
- events local to Northern Ireland (NI)
- events local to the London children (UK)
- events local to the Dublin children (Ir)
- crime and deaths anywhere, (Cr/Dth)
- international events (Int).

We looked first to see which type of item was recalled more frequently by each group (Table 7.1) and then at the percentages who mentioned each type of item (Figure 7.7 below).

Salience of local items? A clear difference was found between the Belfast children on the one hand and the Dublin and London children on the other in terms of the type of item that first came to mind when asked to recall something they had read in the paper recently. More Belfast children (38 per cent, WB; 53 per cent, EB) tended to mention local NI events before other items; few of the London children mentioned events that could be regarded as 'local' to London or even to the United

153

Kingdom; 13 per cent of the Dublin children gave items related to Irish politics and Irish events in 1981.

Table 7.1
Rank order of items recalled from newspapers 1981

W. Belfast	E. Belfast	Dublin	London
NI	NI	Headlines	Headlines
Cr/Dth	Headlines	Cr/Dth	Int/UK
Headlines	Cr/Dth	Ir	Cr/Dth
Int.	Int.	NI	NI

More Dublin and London children mentioned the more general 'headlines' (47 per cent, Dublin; 46 per cent, London) than events local to themselves. The percentages giving the 'headlines' response in Belfast were around half of those elsewhere (21 per cent, WB; 24 per cent, EB).

It would seem that NI events, i.e. local events, were impacting more on Belfast children and that they attracted their attention more than any other type of item in the newspapers. Children in Dublin and London appeared to have more general interests.

Deaths and Crime The next most frequently mentioned items for every group were those related to deaths and crime. (31 per cent, WB; 16 per cent, EB; 19 per cent, Dublin; 23 per cent, London). These are, of course, locally relevant issues, but are of a different order compared to issues related to politics.

International events The Dublin children were more aware of international events than any of the other groups in 1981. In addition, a higher percentage of them than of the children from Belfast or London gave responses which were not strictly of local interest.

Implications of the findings on news items recalled from newspapers

These findings would seem to indicate a different approach to reading the newspapers on the part of the Belfast children, perhaps a more focused one, in that specific items may have caught their attention and they pursued those rather than generally scanning the pages. This approach could be related to the choice of newspapers available to them to read and to the events which were being given prominence at the time. As we have seen, a much higher percentage of children in Belfast than elsewhere had read locally produced newspapers, which tend to give greater space to local news items and this could explain why they remembered such items rather than others.

If it had been a function of the salience of Northern Ireland events in the news in general one might have expected children in the other locations to have also recalled items related to Northern Ireland, as they would have figured prominently in the national newspapers produced in London and Dublin. But Northern Ireland-related items hardly figured in the responses of the Dublin (4 per cent) and London (4 per cent) children at all. If it had been a function of an inherent interest in local events by virtue of being at a 12 year old stage of development, one would have expected the Dublin and London children to show similar degrees of awareness of events local to themselves. But this was not the case. The overwhelming interest of Belfast children in Northern Ireland- related matters was something special in 1981.

Perhaps this is telling us about the salience of different issues in different locations and the effects it can have on people's awareness of issues in general. Support for this can be found in the higher percentage of West Belfast children than of East Belfast children who mentioned crimes and death. A concern with the incidence of crime was frequently voiced by people in West Belfast during the 1980's and 1990's when there were problems with policing in the area and it looks as if the West Belfast children had a higher level of awareness of these kinds of issues than did the children in the other locations.

For those who responded that they read 'headlines' we could posit an interest in skimming the main news stories of the day. The data suggested that there existed this kind of basis for an awareness of current events in general in almost half of the groups in Dublin and London where about 50 percent of the responses were within this category. However as noted above, just half as many in the two Belfast groups showed this kind of general interest in 1981. Their interest appeared to be more limited perhaps because it was dominated by local events. Perhaps the cognitive effects of this were to limit their ability to deal with different types of knowledge and to acquire information in general. They had reached capacity level with their own local issues. This might have implications in terms of their ability of process information and eventually affect their motivation to play an active role in society.

In addition, the finding that more of the Dublin and London groups than of the Belfast children showed an awareness of non-local events could be interpreted as indicating that these groups had moved beyond a concern with local events to an awareness of the wider stage of world happenings; that they had moved beyond the local arena as the centre of their interest towards the periphery and perhaps how it might ultimately affect the centre. Unlike the Northern Ireland children who read about locally relevant Northern Ireland events, then 'crimes and deaths' and then headlines, more of the Dublin and London children were showing an awareness of and an interest in specific happenings outside their own locality.

But perhaps the Belfast children compensated by absorbing more from television.

What did they remember from television news?

The overall percentages able to recount some item they had seen on the television news in 1981 were far higher than for the comparable newspaper-based question. A higher percentage of East Belfast children than of any other group reported having seen current events on television news - perhaps it was their preferred medium over newspapers - and as may be seen from the figure, the percentages from both Belfast groups were considerably higher than those from Dublin or London (Figure 7.8 below).

How many mentioned current events items?

There were striking differences between locations. Belfast children, both East and West (WB, 73 per cent, 1981; EB, 83 per cent, 1981), were more likely to be able to give an item of current events-related news in response to this question than children in Dublin or London. (59 per cent Dublin, 1981; 61 per cent, London, 1981). This supports the findings from the question regarding newspaper items of a greater awareness of current events among the children in Belfast than among the children in Dublin or London.

What types of current events items were recalled more frequently?

Table 7.2 indicates that more of the children in every location picked up locally related items than recalled other kinds of items. It is interesting to note that the second ranked place in Belfast and London went to international items, whereas for the Dublin children it was Northern Ireland and that the East Belfast children did not apparently notice anything about the Irish Republic. The West Belfast and London groups both had an awareness of Irish affairs in 1981.

Special salience of local items for Belfast children? The percentage of children from Belfast who mentioned local items related to Northern Ireland was greater than the percentages of children elsewhere who mentioned items of local interest to themselves in 1981 (67 per cent for WB; 53 per cent for EB). But children in each location were more likely than children elsewhere to mention items related to their own particular location. And so, while more children from Belfast than from elsewhere mentioned items related to Northern Ireland, UK-related items - crime, politics, strikes, general events - were mentioned by a higher percentage of London children (42 per cent, 1981) than by children from the other locations (all under 20 per cent). In Dublin, the percentage of those noting events of local interest was lower at around 30 per cent, and more of them than of the other children mentioned non-local-related events as was the case for items from the newspapers. In Belfast, on the other hand, more of the children mentioned local items than all the other kinds of items put together. It would seem therefore that local items as reported on television were very salient for the Belfast children - more so than for the children in Dublin and London.

Table 7.2
Rank order of items recalled from television news 1981

W. Belfast	E. Belfast	Dublin	London
NI	NI	Ir	UK
Int	Int	NI	Int
Ir/UK	UK	Int	Ir
Sport	Sport	UK	Sport

The findings of a heightened interest in local affairs could of course simply be a reflection of the kind of items reported on the television screens. Events affecting the children's everyday lives were more likely to come up on NI television news and it is likely therefore that they watched with greater interest. Or it could simply be that because of trouble on the streets which, especially in 1981, sometimes included rioting, barricades, ambushes, they were more confined to the house than children elsewhere with nothing else to do but watch the news.

Were findings different in 1992?

Current events

The percentages who reported current events from television and/or newspapers combined increased everywhere except in London (figure 7.6), but the increase seems to have been largely made up by television.

Items recalled from newspapers

Figure 7.7 shows the percentage from each group who recalled items of current events from newspapers in 1981 and 1992. In terms of what they noticed in the newspaper, the percentages who mentioned current events decreased substantially in both West and East Belfast. bringing them down below the level of the Dublin children and it increased slightly in London. It remains to be seen whether this decrease was in items related to local events and whether these had been replaced by items of wider import.- were they taking more of an interest in other matters?

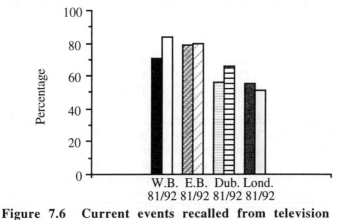

Figure 7.6   Current events recalled from television and/or newspaper 1981 and 1992

In 1992, when the items of current events were broken down by type it showed that the picture had changed somewhat in that the impact of local NI events seemed to have lessened for the NI children. Not only were fewer of them recalling current events, but fewer of the events being recalled were related to local issues. The lessening of the salience of local events did not appear to have been compensated for, however, by an increase in interest in non-local issues (Table 7.3)

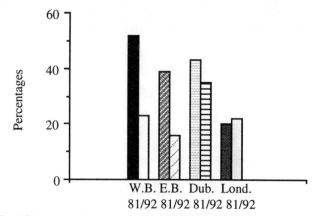

Figure 7.7   Newspapers: percentages who recalled current affairs items by group 1981 and 1992

More of the Belfast children now said that they read 'headlines' than mentioned any other single type of item. London children also still mentioned headlines first but Dublin children were obviously interested by local issues, which at that time included a general election.

Table 7.3
Rank order of items recalled from newspapers 1992

W. Belfast	E. Belfast	Dublin	London
Headlines	Headlines	Ir	Headlines
Cr/Dth	Cr/Dth	Cr/Dth	NI
NI	NI	Headlines	

Figure 7.8 shows that the percentages who said that they had read the headlines had more than doubled in every location (52 per cent, WB; 76 per cent, EB; 92 per cent, London) except Dublin (19 per cent). This could mean that a higher percentage in each location were displaying a general interest, but the corollary is that lower percentages were reading actual reported items in depth or detail.
As before, it is likely that the kinds of items selected for mention and whether they were selected for mention instead of 'headlines' was due to the kinds of items reported in the newspapers.

Salience of local issues in 1992? There was a substantial decrease in the percentage from Belfast mentioning NI-related items (down to 15 per cent WB; 5 per cent, EB). This should be considered in the light of the general finding of a general decrease in the percentages mentioning current affairs reported in the newspapers (from 37 per cent to 24 per cent overall).

On the other hand more Dublin children in 1992 than in 1981 mentioned items of local political interest to them (37 per cent in 1992; 13 per cent in 1981). Again, very few of the London children mentioned specific items.

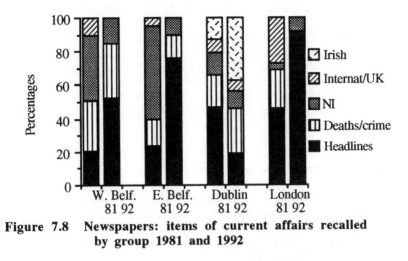

Figure 7.8   Newspapers: items of current affairs recalled by group 1981 and 1992

Differences between girls and boys on interest in current events

More girls than boys in every location except Dublin mentioned current events items in 1981 and again in 1992. It may be significant that in Dublin the schools which participated in the study were coeducational, unlike the schools in West Belfast and most of the schools in the other locations in 1992. In Belfast, both East and West, there was a far higher level of interest among girls than boys at both timepoints with 50% more girls than boys in West Belfast and 100% more girls than boys in East Belfast recalling items of this type. In Dublin and London, the interest levels of girls and boys were more evenly balanced. So perhaps instead of saying that the children of Belfast showed a greater interest in current events in 1992, we should be talking about more girls in West Belfast being interested than girls elsewhere in 1992 and about considerably fewer boys than girls in Belfast, East or West, being interested.

As far as type of item was concerned, girls in Belfast, both East and West, were more interested than Belfast boys in local events, both 'political' and 'deaths and crime' at both timepoints. East Belfast boys did not mention local events at all in 1992. This may have been an artefact of the situation because boys in Dublin and London ranked local political events higher than girls in those locations and deaths and crime were ranked on the same level for Dublin boys and girls.

Boys everywhere were more likely to say that they had read 'Headlines' than girls, suggesting a more general interest on the part of boys and more specific interest for girls. But in Dublin in 1992, girls and boys had very similar rankings for items of current affairs. Since there was a general election in progress, it looks as if situational elements could be important in any data of this kind.

159

Other items

The percentages mentioning crime and death changed very little and this probably indicates a stability in the awareness level and in the reporting level of these kinds of items. Children in all the locations showed an awareness of items in this category, and the differences were very slight. Girls were more aware than boys of this kind of item.

As in 1981, the Dublin children were more aware of non-local and international events than the children in any other location. They actually showed a decrease in the percentages who said that they read the headlines, suggesting that more of them were reading specific items in more depth, and more of them mentioned specific non-local events than mentioned local events, unlike any of the other groups. There was no clearcut pattern differentiating between boys and girls suggesting that situational influences are also important.

Trends over time - explanations?

Several explanations are possible for the shifts in Dublin and Belfast. One is that more of the Belfast children were reading non-local newspapers. As reported above, slightly more of the Northern Ireland children in 1992 than in 1981 were reading London-based tabloids which have a wider and very different baseline of interest from that of local Northern Ireland newspapers. It is possible that fewer items of purely local Northern Ireland interest were reported in these papers. The decline in the awareness shown by Belfast children in NI matters could therefore be due to what they were reading and to the kinds of events being reported. The importance of the kinds of events which were being reported becomes more obvious when we consider the interests of the Dublin children in local matters in 1992.

Perhaps the explanation of the Belfast figures is that less was going on in 1992 than in 1981 and less publicity was being given to NI events in the newspapers in 1981 than in 1992. This would be supported by the figures on deaths and injuries alone resulting from the 'Troubles' which were much lower in 1992 than in 1981 (see Chapter Two). The lessening impact of NI news items might have been expected to encourage an advance in cognitive competence as the children would no longer have been overwhelmed by the flow of incidents being reported on Northern Ireland and would have been freer to take an interest in wider issues. This was perhaps supported by the higher percentage who said that they read 'headlines' thus gaining a broader view of current happenings. And this advance might be reflected in their level of general knowledge about politics. But we would also have expected to see a greater interest in specific international or non-local events to compensate for the reduced awareness of NI events. That was not the case.

Although there was a decline in interest between 1981 and 1992 in both East and West Belfast, it was far more dramatic for East Belfast whose traditions were much more of identification with local issues in the past. The findings here that they were apparently less interested in 1992 could be reflecting a weariness and a letting go on the part of the adults in their lives, an unwillingness to be part of what was happening and a refusal at a subconscious level to be aware of it, perhaps brought about by the feeling that things were being taken out of their hands since the Anglo-Irish Agreement.

The higher percentage in West Belfast expressing interest could, in the same vein, be indicating the beginning of a trend towards becoming more involved on the part of the children in West Belfast, a willingness to notice what was going on and a feeling in the community that perhaps there was a rôle for them to play after all. While in the present study this reaction was found for 12 year-olds, it is possible that it reflects stirrings in the environment supporting them.

The increased awareness of the Dublin children in local events was probably a function of the general election. But it was interesting that more of them at both timepoints were interested in non-local events than was the case for the other groups and that fewer of them just read 'headlines'. A possible explanation along the same lines as that advanced for the Belfast children would suggest that they felt sufficiently at ease with their own situation to be able to take an interest in events outside it and they took an in-depth interest, not simply the more superficial one of skimming the headlines..

Television news in 1992

There were striking differences between locations (Figure 7.9). Belfast children, both East and West, (WB, 87 per cent; EB, 81 per cent), were again more likely to be able to give an item of current events-related news in response to this question than children in Dublin or London (Dublin, 72 per cent; London, 54 per cent)

This suggests again a greater awareness of current events among the children in Belfast than among the children in Dublin or London. There was an increase over time for the West Belfast and Dublin children and a decrease for the London children.

The increase for the Dublin children, as in the case of the newspaper responses, could be explained by the Irish general election; that of the West Belfast children could be partly accounted for in this way, but perhaps also by the explanation advanced above with regard to their higher level of interest in current affairs from newspapers.

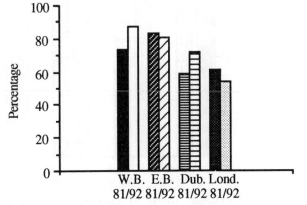

Figure 7.9   Television: percentages who recalled items of current affairs by group 1981 and 1992

As in 1981, the overall percentages able to recount some current affairs item they had seen on the news were far higher than for the comparable newspaper-based question in 1992.

Table 7.4
Items recalled from television news 1992

W. Belfast	E. Belfast	Dublin	London
Int	NI	Ir	UK
NI	Int	Int	Int
UK	UK	UK	NI

In 1992 we can see some changes in Northern Ireland with the West Belfast children more interested in international affairs - a further dimension to the changes already noted in their responses - and the East Belfast, Dublin and London children noticing in the first place items related to their own locality just as in 1981; nobody except the Dublin children noticed items about the Irish Republic.

Items recalled from television news 1992

Although it had declined in 1992, the general picture with regard to the recall of items of local interest showed the same trends with more Belfast children giving locally based items than children from elsewhere. Fewer Belfast children overall mentioned NI items in 1992 than in 1981 reflecting the findings from the newspaper question (Figure 7.10).

An interesting development was a decline in the percentage of West Belfast children who mentioned NI related events in 1992, while the percentage of East Belfast children remained the same.

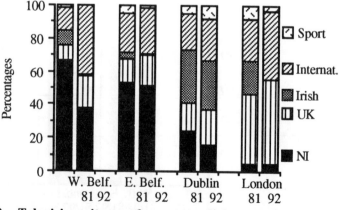

Figure 7.10 **Television: items of current affairs recalled by group 1981 and 1992**

162

This was a shift in a different direction from that found in the responses to the newspaper question where there was a decline for both groups but a far greater decline for the East Belfast children, and more West Belfast children had noted Northern Ireland related events.

But the East Belfast children seemed to get more of their information from television than from newspapers and for the West Belfast children the situation was the reverse. This could have implications in terms of their actual knowledge which, according to Robinson and Davis (1990), would be expected to be less than for those who get their information from newspapers. The percentage of London children giving locally based items increased slightly, while the Dublin children remained stable.

Girls and boys Girls seemed slightly more inclined overall than boys to give local items from television news in 1981, but in 1992, the pattern was different in different locations; the same was true for UK related items. More boys than girls gave international items as a response at both time points.

International events

The Dublin children again had the highest percentage of responses falling into the international category. However, the percentages noting international events increased everywhere between 1981 and 1992, but most notably in West Belfast (from 6 per cent to 41 per cent) and London (from 25 per cent to 39 per cent). In addition, an interesting development was that a percentage of children in all the other locations mentioned items of strictly Irish interest at one or other of the time points as items remembered from television - unlike the responses to the newspaper question.

Trends over time

The hypothesis that West Belfast children were taking more interest in local events than their East Belfast peers, and that East Belfast children might be opting out and not showing an interest in NI related events is not sustained by the evidence from television news viewing. It seems in fact to show that East Belfast children were interested in Northern Ireland events almost to the exclusion of other current affairs events on television, and far from opting out, they were dominated by their immediate circumstances and consistently stable in their awareness of local events.

In the case of the newspaper question there had been changes for both the East and West Belfast children; but for the East Belfast children, unlike those from West Belfast, it did not translate into an awareness of specific non-local events, but rather into the more generic 'headlines'. In the case of the television question there were considerable changes for the West Belfast children on both those fronts but there was no change for the East Belfast children either for local or for internationally -based events - a sign perhaps of greater stability or it could even be called a greater degree of rigidity or less openness to matters not closely related to their own immediate circumstances within the East Belfast community. Their lesser interest in events outside Northern Ireland was illustrated also by the total lack of mention of any item related to the Irish Republic.

The West Belfast children were showing signs of wider interests - considerably more children there reported an international item in 1992 than in 1981 and fewer reported an item of Northern Ireland interest in 1992 than in 1981. These findings may support the idea of changes in orientation towards life in general that may have been happening to a greater extent within the West Belfast community than within the East Belfast community over the period 1981-1992.

Since Northern Ireland items frequently dominate the television news, it is not surprising that the children in Northern Ireland are more aware of them. Such items also appear on the Dublin and London-based channels, but the Dublin children were considerably more aware of Northern Ireland items than were the London children. It is possible that their television screens carried more news of Northern Ireland than did the screens of the London children. But it could be due also to an interest arising from group identity and a feeling that Northern Ireland was closer than the rest of the world. But that would not explain why the Dublin children were just as aware of United Kingdom-related items as the Belfast children and as aware of international-type items as the London children.

Dublin children appeared to have wider interests than those in Belfast or London. There was a medium low percentage (32 per cent, 1981; 30 per cent, 1992), reporting items of strictly Irish interest by them at both time points, and a higher percentage of them than of the other groups reported items of interest from outside their own immediate context. A very high percentage of London children on the other hand responded with items of strictly UK interest and the Northern Ireland children tended to report items concerning their own area.

Impact of television versus newspaper reports

Whereas there had been a decrease overall in the percentages mentioning items read in the newspapers over the time period studied, there was an increase overall for those mentioning current affairs items seen on the television news reflecting the increase in viewing recorded earlier. Television appears to make more of an impact in this respect than newspapers - the number of responses for this question were far higher than for the newspaper question. In addition the responses giving this kind of item were far higher for the television question. In fact, children in all locations in both 1981 and 1992 were more likely to recall items of local interest to themselves than other current affairs items from television news to a greater extent than from newspapers.

The salience of television over the printed media becomes obvious from the finding that more of the Dublin children remembered NI related items in 1981 (24 per cent) and again in 1992 (16 per cent) from television news than had done so from the newspapers (4 per cent; 10 per cent). The same was true of the Belfast children. The decline in mentions over time, however, mirrors that found in the newspapers and supports the possibility that fewer items about Northern Ireland were being reported in 1992 than in 1981. And as we saw in Chapter Two, there was an actual reduction in incidents of 'Troubles'-related violence.

This would suggest however that the children in all locations are taking in a slightly broader sweep of events from television coverage of the news than from what they read in the newspapers, although their actual knowledge base may not be very solid (Robinson and Davis, 1990). But interestingly although a higher percentage of Dublin children than of the other children had mentioned non-Irish, non-local items in response to both the newspaper and the television questions, they gave more Irish politics responses in response to the newspaper question than to the television question, so newspaper reporting seems to have made more of an impact in this area than television for them.

Other categories of items read in the newspaper

Human interest news items which included items about well-known personalities, people known to the respondent, commemorations / celebrations, religious events, road accidents were mentioned by 15 per cent of respondents overall in 1981 and this had dropped to 6 per cent in 1992 with no significant differences between locations. Sporting events were recalled by 23 per cent of the children in 1981 and by 28 per cent in 1992, with a much greater increase for girls than for boys. This increase could not be explained by, for example, the time of year - the questionnaire was administered at a similar time of year (November/December/January) in both 1981 and 1992 - or the kinds of events going on - there appeared to be nothing outstanding at either time-point. So it may represent a real increase in interest in sport, and this would be supported by the findings of greater participation in sport in 1992 reported in Chapter Four.

Over half of the children from all groups and from both sexes reported looking at television schedules in the newspaper in 1981. The percentage decreased over time in East Belfast (50 per cent -> 43 per cent) Dublin (75 per cent -> 51 per cent) and London (51 per cent ->30 per cent) and remained the same in West Belfast (49–50 per cent). Nearly a quarter of the respondents reported looking at comic strips or cartoons in 1981 and this had halved overall in 1992. There was a small percentage, around 3–4 per cent, who said that they looked at the crossword and this did not change over the time period covered. It was similar across locations. Horoscopes were mentioned by 9 per cent in 1981 and by 5 per cent in 1992. Advertisements were mentioned by 6–7 per cent in both 1981 and 1992 as being what they remembered from looking at the newspaper.

Girls and boys

Girls appeared to use the newspaper as a direct means of entertainment more than boys - a higher percentage of them recalled reading comic strips and horoscopes, although the percentages were low for both of these categories. This may be related to girls' documented greater ease with language and also with written language from an earlier age than boys which would enable them to feel more comfortable with and more likely to find recreation through the printed word.

Summary

Access to newspapers

- Over 95 per cent of children in all groups looked at a newspaper regularly; no significant differences were found by sex or location in 1981 or 1992.

- The majority had looked at a paper within 24 hours.
- More Dublin children had seen a paper recently in 1992.

Which papers did they read?

- The majority of the London children read tabloids in 1981, with a minority reading quality national papers; in Belfast around 40 per cent read tabloids in 1981 and most of the others read local or regional papers; in Dublin the majority read national papers, with a minority reading tabloids.
- In 1992 however the readership of tabloids had increased everywhere, even in Dublin with around 33 per cent of Dublin children naming tabloids, 50 per cent in Belfast and over 95 per cent in London.
- Boys were more inclined than girls to read tabloids.

Watching TV news

- A high percentage of all groups - between 93 per cent and 98 per cent - claimed to watch TV news regularly and between 71 per cent and 81 per cent had watched it during the past 24 hours. There was a slight decrease over time on both of these variables.
- Belfast children, both East and West, were more avid watchers at both time points.
- More boys than girls tended to watch television news.

Radio news

- Between 69 per cent (London) and 91 per cent (WB) listened to the news on the radio in 1981.
- Percentages decreased everywhere in 1992.
- In 1981, more children from Belfast than from other locations were listeners to radio news, and in 1992, the highest percentages came from West (but not East) Belfast and Dublin.

Composite variable 'News':

- In 1981 East and West Belfast children scored higher than the others, but in 1992, the West Belfast and Dublin children were higher. There were no differences between girls and boys.

Items read in the paper and remembered from television

- Around 37 per cent overall mentioned items of current affairs in 1981 and this had fallen to 24 per cent in 1992.
- Belfast children tended to mention items of local interest, though less so in 1992.
- There was an increase in the percentage mentioning items of non-local interest, but this was less evident in East Belfast.
- There was no consistent pattern for local versus non-local items between girls and boys.

Our original question in this chapter asked if the children in Northern Ireland were open to opportunities for mind-broadening experiences through the media which differed in range from those available to children elsewhere and which might be having an effect on the development of their ability to process diverse information with implications for their cognitive functioning. Results suggested that their scores on 'News' i.e. access to events reported in the media, was higher than that of children in London and Dublin at both timepoints and that they should therefore have been exposed to even better opportunities for mind-broadening experiences than their peers in Dublin and London. But the kinds of items they were interested in, which were possibly contingent on the quality of the news to which they had access, were much more limited than those mentioned by the children from Dublin and London.

It could be that the kinds of access to information offered to them was closing off options rather than opening up possibilities. It was inevitable probably that locally based media should concentrate on local events, but it looks as though this might have been at the expense of broader issues. The effects appeared to be a narrower range of interests in, and a lesser awareness of events, outside their own immediate environment on the part of the Belfast children. The cognitive consequences of this diminished exposure could have been that the Belfast children had less chance of developing cognitive strategies for processing and integrating more complex information. The open-systems adaptation model sees personality development as a complex of different processes through which the major systems of personality become fixed to situations as a function of experience with those situations (Hettema, 1989) and applying it to the Northern Ireland situation one can see how the findings in this chapter could explain greater rigidity, more conformity, in the Northern Ireland psyche.

The finding of greater openness to events outside Northern Ireland in the West Belfast children was significant and may reflect the percolating through to the children of the effects of the reappraisal of the nationalist stance which had been happening through the 1980's, as noted in Chapter Two. The apparently narrower range of interests of the East Belfast children could in similar fashion be related to their psychological situation at the end of the 80s when their community was very much on the defensive after the Anglo-Irish Agreement and not yet ready to reach out. It is worth noting the greater change in the attitudes of girls than of boys over the period, especially in West Belfast.

Interest in current events would seem intuitively to be a prerequisite for knowledge about underlying institutions. We next look at whether levels of knowledge about current affairs-related institutions, were related in the different groups to the level of awareness and the kinds of interests they had. The level of declarative knowledge may give us clues about the underlying feelings of self-efficacy and self-confidence in the different groups. It may give an indication of their feeling of involvement in their society, and taking it a bit further, their eventual readiness to become involved in societal action, another facet of their identity.

8 Knowledge about the present

Introduction

We have seen in Chapter Seven that the children from Belfast Dublin and London in the sample were certainly interested in current affairs as portrayed by the media. In general however, researchers tell us that social issues and political institutions are not high on the interest agenda of adolescents (Torney-Purta, 1993). Research in the United States on knowledge elements, or the 'facts' that adolescents know about politics and society suggest that they lack many of those elements of knowledge that educators consider important. Multiple-choice questions about political institutions administered to American teenagers in 1971, 1974 and 1987 produced mean scores of 40–60 per cent though it was acknowledged that this may have been a low estimate of existing knowledge since many items were included because they were good discriminators (Torney-Purta, 1993).

It would seem to be desirable that young people should be informed to some extent about how things work and thus able eventually to participate in decision-making processes. Factual knowledge would seem to be a prerequisite for establishing an adult interest in political matters. Indeed, it has been found (Raven and Whelan, 1983) that young people who do not have opinions often also lack factual knowledge. Lack of interest in politics and cynicism about politics and politicians were found in a study by Fife-Schaw and Breakwell (1990) to be the most powerful predictors of unwillingness to vote in elections among 17-18 year-olds. Blumler (1974) suggested that ignorant electors put pressure on governments to adopt ill-conceived and undesirable policies and that a politically ignorant public can be easily manipulated. This could have consequences for the implementation of government policies many of which can be effective only if the public understands the necessity for them.

Factual knowledge of this kind is one of the elements of declarative knowledge which feeds into one's value system and contributes to identity through the motivation it provides for us to be interested and to become involved in society. It may be gleaned from newspaper, television, radio and other sources. In Chapter Seven the findings showed that the sample of children in this study from West and East Belfast, Dublin and London had very high rates of access to newspaper and television news and that they were aware of and therefore probably interested in a range of topics. In the present chapter we look at what the children actually knew about two current-affairs-related types of items: political institutions and organizations and sport; we consider first the kinds of influences that could be important in their acquisition of such knowledge.

The development of political knowledge in children

Studies of political socialization in adolescence were popular in the 1970s and early 1980s, when many of them were triggered by the desire to understand the sources of student political activism; relatively little research has appeared since then. The collection of empirical data about adolescents' political attitudes has declined since that time although a concern has recently been emerging about the development of values in response to the low rate of voting by young people aged 18 to 20 in the USA (Abramson, 1983), and to uneasiness about self-centred values among the current generation (Astin, Green and Korn, 1987). This has led to studies organized around 'agents of socialization' preoccupied with questions such as whether the family or the school is more influential in the development of value systems and to investigations with a focus on determinants rather than correlatives of attitudes.

Media influence on political knowledge

If children are watching more television now than in the past, does this also mean that we should expect them to be more knowledgeable? Studies of political awareness among 10–22 year-olds in England (Furnham and Gunter, 1987) replicating a 1977 survey, found little change across time and few sex, age or class differences in political knowledge when they tested factual knowledge of political leaders, party political policies, parliamentary and local political knowledge and knowledge concerning public services. In the USA, two sets of large-scale national studies on the effectiveness of television as a means of acquiring news information concluded, as mentioned in Chapter Seven, that those who derived news information from television had less comprehension of events and issues reported than had those who obtained information from other sources (Robinson and Davis, 1990). So we might not find high levels of knowledge among our sample; but would there be differences between the groups in line with preferences for television compared to newspapers as sources of news?

Parental, peer and school influence on political knowledge

Some researchers have found that the media are a powerful influence. As noted in Chapter Seven, reading the newspaper and watching television news have been found to be significant predictors of the amount of political information adolescents possess as judged by multiple-choice tests (Chaffee and Yang, 1990, Garramone and Atkin, 1986, Torney-Purta, 1985); but there are influences other than the media which could be important too. Some studies have found significant relationships between parental political interests, attitudes and television viewing patterns and those endorsed by their teenage children (Himmelweit and Swift, 1971; Jennings and Niemi, 1971, Gallatin, 1980). It has been proposed that the influence of the family is mediated by educational level of family and socio-economic level - those who are more highly educated, have reading material in the home and generate family discussions are more likely to produce politically aware teenagers. The absence of such discussions in Mexican American homes has been hypothesized to contribute to these students' lower political awareness (Lamare, 1974). Other studies however, have shown that the association between parental and adolescent levels of political interest is positive but low and have concluded that the direct political impact of parents on children has been overestimated (Stacey, 1978).

Dennis (1986) reported that children in their early teens were quite dependent on their parents for political knowledge. They became more independent as they advanced through the teen years and significant antecedent variables included the parents' independence and education and the preadult's media exposure, attention and trust and interpersonal political information seeking. Glass, Bengston and Dunham (1986) looked at attitude transmission across generations with a sample of 2,044 individuals and found that parental attitudes continued to significantly predict children's orientations after childhood. Possible explanations for this finding may be adduced from a major survey of Swedish high school students by Sidanius, Ekehammar and Brewer (1986). This study found that the sociopolitical attitudes of the subjects seemed firmly embedded within the matrix of socialization experiences investigated. These included parental political ideology, gender effects, parental education, emotional atmosphere in the home, democratic decision making in the home, childrearing practices, daycare experiences and certain interactions among these elements.

A number of researchers have found that students from classrooms where teachers encourage discussion of controversial issues and promote students' expression of their own opinions, even if they disagree with the views of the teacher, perform at a higher level on tests of discrete knowledge (e.g. Torney-Purta, 1989). The influence of peers on political activity and political knowledge was not found to be important by Breakwell, Fife-Schaw and Devereux (1989). Minns and Williams (1989) who tried to establish whether teacher, parent or friend was more influential for the socialization of political beliefs with 10-13 year-olds reported that there was no consistent pattern of agent preference and it seemed to depend on what the agent did rather than on who the agent was.

Socio-historical influences on political knowledge

Knowledge of politics could also be influenced by local conditions. Northern Ireland, Britain and the Republic of Ireland all enjoy democratic forms of government, but local conditions are not similar in terms of the kinds of representation available to the populations at government level, nor in terms of the attitude of the different sectors of the population towards government, nor in terms of the salience to the general public of matters relating to government. Since 1972, as mentioned in Chapter Two, Northern Ireland has been ruled from Westminster in London where it is represented by 17 members of parliament (or approximately one MP per 88,000 population). Events at Westminster relating to Northern Ireland do not get much coverage in the British national press, nor in the local Northern Ireland press or on television. It all seems a bit remote from the average person in the street. Much of the business concerning Northern Ireland, appears to happen late at night, or at odd hours, and the weaknesses of the system as part of the democratic process have been pointed out by a number of commentators (Livingstone and

Morison, 1995). And Cairns and Cairns (1995) concluded that interest in local politics among young people in Northern Ireland is relatively low, although they found evidence that the level of political behaviour represented by voting or intention to vote was similar among young people and adults (Willis and Cairns, 1986, International Youth Bridge, 1985).

In London, issues of government are likely to have more immediacy than in Belfast, since events in the House of Commons and the House of Lords are taking place on the spot and are given publicity on local and national television and in the tabloids and national press to a greater extent than in Northern Ireland.

The Republic of Ireland has an elected parliament (1 member per 21,000 population) in the capital city, Dublin. The scale of events is different from that in the United Kingdom. The business and proceedings of the Oireachtas (Parliament) feature daily in the newspapers and are discussed on television. It was not ever thus, but in recent years there has been an increased openness and something approaching semi-transparency about procedures adopted when issues of principle arise. Committees and tribunals have been set up and have heard evidence and reported to the public; the Supreme Court has been asked to make rulings. The whole population appears to discuss the issues on radio and television, in the newspapers, in the schools and on the streets.

We wondered whether these differences would matter and whether they would have an effect on the kind of profile presented by children in Northern Ireland with regard to knowledge of political matters compared to children in Dublin or London. It was very likely that because of the differences between the systems of government and their location in relation to the children, the amount of direct information readily available to them about government also varied. This could also mean less discussion of these matters in classrooms and in families and among peers. The reduced stimuli available to the Belfast children about the wider political scene might disadvantage them not only in terms of their knowledge base about local and national affairs, but also in relation to gaining information about matters of broader import.

As we have already seen, the Belfast children were more preoccupied with local issues in the media and these were very salient and at times even life-threatening. We wondered whether this meant that their cognitive capacity and resources would be fully utilized by these local events leaving no space or energy for an interest in acquiring knowledge about other matters. It was possible also that even the adults around these children felt alienated by the local situation and did not know very much or try to find out and discuss it much. If any of these factors were operating and had a negative effect on their knowledge of current affairs the outcome would leave them at a disadvantage in terms of declarative knowledge, or basic information, with a reduced sense of self-efficacy and self-confidence and a lower incentive to participate in the democratic process and commit themselves to action in a societal context.

Developmental issues

A further dimension comes from theories of developmental psychology. The centre-periphery progression hypothesis predicts that between age 6–7 years and age 10–11 years children move from an understanding of issues related to the family, or the smallest unit, through locality or city to region or nation and then to a community

171

of nations. By age 12 one would expect children to have moved beyond an interest in, and knowledge of, purely local affairs. We have seen that the interests of the Belfast children - particularly those from East Belfast - were focused on local events more than on events elsewhere. Local events, understandably, seemed to impinge more in the context of 'Troubles'-torn Belfast for them. And research in other countries has also found that local issues are important to adolescents (Sigel and Hoskin, 1981). But we wondered whether this meant that they would also be knowledgeable about the institutions serving their own region and whether they would also, in spite of lack of interest in matters outside their own region, know about more widely based institutions and organizations. The questions about sport were included as a check to see if a similar result would be obtained in terms of locally based versus a broader base of information.

On the other hand, it was possible that 12 year-olds, regardless of interest, would actually be more knowledgeable about locally-related matters than about other matters. If this were the case, London children would be expected to be more interested in and knowledgeable about London-based matters than about international (including Irish) or regional (Northern Ireland) matters; and they would know more about London-based matters than either the Belfast or the Dublin children; similarly, Dublin children would be expected to be more knowledgeable about Dublin-based matters than about London or Belfast-based matters and would know more about Dublin-based matters than the Belfast or London children.

But what about the Belfast children? Would they know more about Belfast based matters than the Dublin or London children? Given the lack of political activity in Northern Ireland, would this affect their knowledge of local affairs?

Reference group orientation and knowledge about politics

These questions gave rise to another which relates the issue of interest in political and sports matters to the question of reference egroup orientation or group identity. You might expect children in Dublin to be more interested in and knowledgeable about Irish matters; but how much would they know about institutions in Northern Ireland? And about sporting heroes from Northern Ireland? Would they be more knowledgeable about such matters in relation to Northern Ireland than in relation to England? Similarly the London children might be expected to show more of an interest in events in their own country. But would they pick up knowledge about Northern Ireland, which is a part of their country, to a greater extent than knowledge about the Republic from watching news programmes or reading newspapers?

In Northern Ireland, it has been generally found that Catholics are more inclined to view themselves as Irish than British and Protestants tend to see themselves as British before they see themselves as Irish (John Whyte, 1990; Trew, 1994). We wondered whether this meant that the Catholics of West Belfast would show more interest than the Protestants of East Belfast in Dublin-based matters, and less interest in London-based matters. Similarly, we wondered whether the Protestants of East Belfast would show more interest in London-based matters than the Catholics of West Belfast and less interest in Irish-based events.

If we accept that socio-political attitudes result from socio-political experiences, it would not be surprising if we found different levels of knowledge and interest in children growing up in different communities such as has been reported by Ianni (1989) and Jankowski, (1986). Research with Mexican-American adolescents (Alva,

1985) found that acculturation played a significant role in mediating affective and cognitive political orientation. The low-acculturated subjects expressed more loyalty to the Mexican political system, they had more knowledge about Mexican political historical events and leaders. Affective experiences (e.g. feelings of political inefficacy) were good predictors of political orientation. The findings challenged the assumption that political socialization follows a normal linear progression along an age continuum irrespective of cultural allegiances, and the author suggests that there is a need to examine the effects of affective symbols on the political socialization process. Abramson too (1977) concluded that there was good empirical support for the view that racial differences in political socialization in the USA resulted from the realities of the political environment and the structure of political opportunities with which the different groups lived. Groups who perceive themselves as being less able to influence politics become aware of ceilings placed on their occupational political and educational achievement and may respond with peer-group-enforced cultural identities that devalue or oppose achievement (Ogbu, 1987).

These kinds of findings might lead us to expect lower levels of political knowledge among the Catholics of West Belfast, since they had traditionally been in a position where they could not influence politics; if they feel allegiance to the Republic of Ireland, identify themselves as 'Irish' and are not 'acculturated' to being part of the United Kingdom, the results should show evidence of more interest in and knowledge of Irish affairs than of UK or Northern Ireland matters. On the other hand, as seen in Chapter One, the Protestants in Northern Ireland do not identify themselves inevitably as 'British', but some prefer 'Ulster' and perhaps they are not 'acculturated' either and will have low scores on knowledge about UK-related matters for this reason.

Socio-emotional factors and knowledge of politics

In addition to the political situation, the level of cognitive development of the children and their sense of identity - all of which could influence the extent and type of their interest in and knowledge of political matters, there could be factors within the child's family environment which are related to the interest the child eventually shows in current affairs. As mentioned above (Chapter One) there has been evidence that over-protectiveness in the family can lead to political cynicism and distrust (Chaffee, 1977). In addition research has found that teenagers with low self-esteem have less concern with public affairs than those with high self-esteem (Rosenberg, 1965) and political cynicism was found to be negatively correlated with personal efficacy during early adolescence by Schwartz (1975). Adolescents with an external locus of control have shown themselves to be less favourably impressed by politics (Renshon, 1974, 1975; Sigel, 1975). In earlier chapters findings were presented which indicated that in 1981 there was some evidence to suggest that the Protestant children were more protected and had slightly fewer opportunities for developing self-efficacy and an internal locus of control. This might lead us to expect a lower score on political knowledge, even though their interest level in local events perceived through the media, especially television, was high.

Previous research on the interest in politics of children in Northern Ireland has been reviewed by Cairns and Cairns (1995). Two of the studies they report are relevant in the present context. In one study (Hosin and Cairns, 1984), when children aged 9, 12 and 15 who lived in Ireland, North and South, in Jordan and in Iraq, were asked to write an essay entitled 'My Country', fewer children in Northern Ireland at every age level mentioned politics and this was interpreted as indicating a lower level of interest for them than for the other groups. In a survey organized by International Youth Bridge (1985) with 940 older young people aged 16–25 in Northern Ireland however, it was found that 17 per cent claimed to be interested in local politics and this suggested a similar level of interest to that found for a European sample in 1982. Whyte (1983b) found that in a sample of 11 and 12-year-old Catholic children in West Belfast, the level of knowledge about non-Northern Ireland politics was higher than that for events directly related to Northern Ireland.

In the present study we have so far found a greater interest level in local happenings for the 12 year-old Belfast children than for the Dublin or London children and we have suggested that this could have been due to the kinds of events happening at the times of the surveys, and also to the quality of media coverage available to the children. In this chapter we ask whether this greater interest translated into knowledge through the responses to two sets of questions which formed part of the questionnaire. We do not have direct measurements of parents' knowledge about current affairs, but we can relate what the children knew to other elements of their environment - the socio-economic variables, the independence variables, the travels and access variables - and investigate whether any of these appeared to be important for the children's knowledge base. We were also able to determine whether there was an increase or decrease in that knowledge base over the period of the study and how the groups compared.

Questions on current affairs

The questions were openended and were set out in two sections, one on sport and one on politics in that order. They are reproduced below.

The issues addressed in this chapter are:

- How did the groups compare on general knowledge about politics?
- How did they compare on general knowledge about sport?
- Was group identity a factor in the kinds of interest expressed - were Catholics and Protestants in Belfast interested in and aware of the same items?
- Were there any elements within the family environment which might have impacted on the level of interest in and awareness of current events shown by the children and were found to be related to the results?
- Were there any trends over time which could have wider implications?

After listing the two sets of questions asked in different parts of the questionnaire, where the sports questions were asked first in order to try to engage the subjects' interest, we give the results for 1981 and then for 1992; first for the political items and then for the sports questions .

174

Questions on political matters/current affairs

1. Who is the President of the United States?
2. What do the letters E.E.C. stand for?
3. Who is the Prime Minister of the United Kingdom?
4. Name any three political parties
   1.
   2.
   3.
5. Who is the Secretary of State for Northern Ireland?
6. What do the letters M. P. stand for?
7. Who is the Russian Prime Minister?
8. What do the letters U. N. O. stand for?
9. At what age can you vote?
10. Who is the Prime Minister of the Republic of Ireland?

Sports Events Questions

1. What team won the last Cup Final?
2. What internationally famous sporting event takes place every four years?
3. Name two well-known boxers.
4. Who won the last All-Ireland Final in hurling or Gaelic football?
6. Name a famous athlete and say what he or she is famous for
7. What kind of sporting event takes place at the White City?
8. Name two famous snooker players.
9. What is meant by the term 'freestyle'?
10. Give the name of a famous horse race that takes place every year.

Knowledge of current affairs

Cross-cultural studies have shown overall similarities between countries in the level of children's interest and knowledge in current affairs with provisos with regard to social background and historical context (International Youth Bureau, 1985). The children in this study were of similar social background, and economic level; all had access to British television channels. The children in Dublin, in addition, had access to the Republic's TV channels. They all read newspapers regularly, they all attended school, were of a similar age and were in the first year of second level education.

Overall score on politics questions 1981

The total scores overall showed that in 1981, the Dublin children were away ahead of the others with a mean score of 8.5; the West Belfast children came next (6.5)

175

and the London and East Belfast children had similar mean scores (5.5 and 5.4). The scores are presented in Figure 8.1.

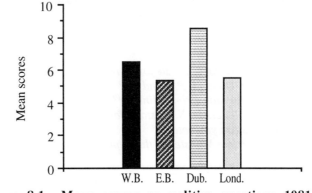

Figure 8.1   Mean scores on politics questions 1981

And yet more of the Belfast children had been able to give items of current events interest that they had seen on TV news and more items of local current events interest from the newspapers? Why did their awareness not translate into knowledge?

Before discussing this question, we must look in more detail at the responses to the individual questions, for the results may reflect the type of questions asked. Perhaps more of them were relevant to the children of the Republic and to West Belfast than to the children of East Belfast or London; perhaps the East Belfast children performed adequately on the more locally-based questions?

Analysis by category of question

The questions were categorized into three types:
i).   *Those requiring very basic general knowledge* - such as the meaning of the initials MP (Member of Parliament; Military Police) knowing the age at which one can vote and being able to name a political party.
ii)   *Those relating to the children's own locality* - the name of the Prime Minister of the United Kingdom, Taoiseach of the Republic of Ireland and Secretary of State for Northern Ireland; the naming of political parties from their own area.
iii).   *Those relating to the wider world* - the meaning of the initials EEC, UNO, the names of the Presidents of the USA and of Russia.

Basic political knowledge

The results showed that a higher percentage of the Dublin children were knowledgeable about the basics like voting age (89 per cent, Dublin; 78 per cent,

176

WB; 71 per cent, London; 69 per cent, EB) in 1981. More of the Dublin children could name one political party and more of them could name three parties.

So the overall findings reflect differences, even at the level of basic knowledge, in favour of the Dublin children.

Local knowledge

i) Naming the Prime Minister or equivalent Results here indicated that as far as the NI Secretary of State and the Taoiseach (Prime Minister of the Republic of Ireland) were concerned, the expectation that 'localness' would be a positive influence on knowledge was correct - more children from their own locations than from the other locations were able to name them. Figure 8.2 gives the results for 1981.

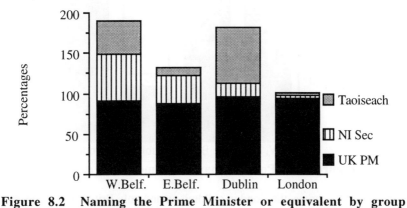

Figure 8.2   Naming the Prime Minister or equivalent by group 1981

It can be seen that more children from Dublin than from elsewhere could name the Irish Prime Minister and more children from Belfast than from elsewhere could name the NI Secretary of State. But the naming of the British Prime Minister was a different matter. As many children from Dublin as from London could name the British Prime Minister. And, in addition, more children from Belfast could name the British Prime Minister than could name either the NI. Secretary of State or the Irish Prime Minister and more children from Dublin could name the British Prime Minister than could name the Irish Prime Minister or the NI Secretary of State. Group identity is obviously not the only factor affecting their knowledge

The personalities involved could possibly be one factor. In 1981, Mrs. Margaret Thatcher, had caught everyone's imagination and between 91 per cent (WB) and 96 per cent (Dublin) of children from all locations named her correctly.

As might be expected fewer children from East than from West Belfast could name the Taoiseach, or Prime Minister of the Irish Republic. The finding that more West Belfast children could do so might suggest a stronger identity for them with the Irish Republic than with Britain.....until one notes that more of them than of the children from East Belfast could also name the NI Secretary of State and the

British Prime Minister. Perhaps it is interest in political matters *per se* that is the deciding factor.

ii) Naming political parties As far as naming political parties was concerned, the prediction was correct for the London and Dublin children - they tended to name parties from their own locations more than from anywhere else. The London children named practically no other parties. The second highest percentage of Dublin children at both time-points named British parties.

But what about the children in Belfast? Would their first inclination be to name local Northern Ireland political parties, or would the Catholics tend to name Republic of Ireland parties and would the Protestants name British parties?

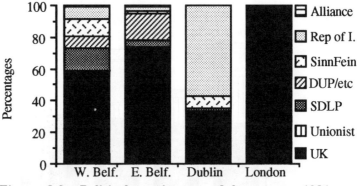

Figure 8.3   Political parties named by groups 1981

As Figure 8.3 shows, the London children named only British 'mainland' parties; a much higher percentage of Belfast children, both Catholic and Protestant, named British political parties than named parties from anywhere else (59 per cent WB; 74 per cent EB, 1981). A small percentage both from West and East Belfast named local parties. As one might expect, more Catholic (WB) children named nationalist (NI) parties, such as the SDLP and Sinn Féin and more Protestant children (EB) named unionist (NI) parties. The mainstream unionist party had an extremely low rating (two per cent). Many more of the children named extremist unionist parties such as the DUP (Democratic Unionist Party).

Small percentages of both West and East Belfast children named Republic of Ireland parties. But the percentages were very small compared to those who named British parties. Interestingly the finding of greater political awareness and maybe interest among the West Belfast children mentioned earlier was supported here by the observation that more of them than of the East Belfast children named a locally based Northern Ireland party of any political persuasion.

So the conclusions from the responses to the questions based on location in 1981 were that children from a particular location are more likely to know the name of the prime minister or his/her equivalent than are children from other locations. But this did not mean that more children from a particular location knew the name of their own prime minister than knew the name of the British Prime Minister. In the case of children from Northern Ireland, Dublin and London, more of them knew the name of the British Prime Minister than of their own local equivalent. The centre-periphery distinction is very blurred here for the Dublin and Belfast children. It is very blurred also for the Belfast children in relation to the political parties that they think of naming. Both East and West Belfast children are more focused on Britain than on their own province. The East Belfast children give a clearer indication of identifying with Britain, with less knowledge of locally based parties. However, the West Belfast children seem to have a slightly different perspective from those of East Belfast, they were more knowledgeable about local parties, and not just of those on the nationalist side.

iii) Knowledge of international events

Children were asked to explain the meaning of the initials EEC and UNO and to give the names of the Presidents of the USA and of Russia. An overall mean percentage of children answering the questions correctly was calculated and this showed that more of the Dublin children than of the others knew the answers to these questions on international affairs in 1981. Figure 8.4 below presents these findings in conjunction with those for 1992.

President of the USA Over 85 per cent (EB and London) and up to 93 per cent (Dublin) knew the name of the American President in 1981, similar to the percentage naming the British Prime Minister, much further away in terms of physical distance but apparently just as meaningful. Once again however the West Belfast children were more knowledgeable than those in East Belfast.

EEC Five times as many Dublin children as of children from Belfast or London could explain what the letters EEC stood for in 1981.

Russian Prime Minister The name of the Russian Prime Minister was known by more Dublin children in 1981 (42 per cent) than children from any other group.

UNO The meaning of the letters UNO was known by more Dublin children in 1981. This could perhaps be explained by the publicity given to the participation by members of the Irish army in UN peacekeeping activities.

Summary of scores on politics questions in 1981

- Dublin and West Belfast children were better informed overall than the London and East Belfast children.
- A higher percentage of children in each of the locations knew the name of the particular prime minister or chief executive for their own location than did children from outside that location; but on the other hand, more from each location outside London knew the name of the British Prime Minister than knew the name of their own chief executive.
- In relation to political parties, more London children named British parties, more Dublin children named Irish parties, but more NI children named British 'mainland' parties than parties based in Northern Ireland.

179

- On the majority of questions, more West Belfast than East Belfast children gave the correct answer.
- A higher percentage of the Dublin children were knowledgeable about the basics like voting age and the names of political parties.

Would the same situation obtain in 1992?

Knowledge of current events: 1992

Scores were lower everywhere in 1992 than in 1981 (Figure 8.4).

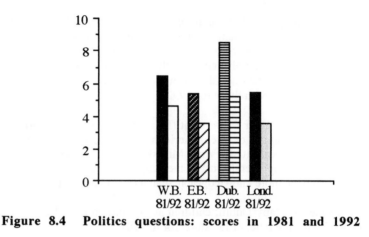

Figure 8.4   Politics questions: scores in 1981 and 1992

But the relative ranking of the groups was similar to 1981 - Dublin children scored highest, then West Belfast children followed by East Belfast and London with a much lower average score.

i) Basic political knowledge

Some of the other groups had come closer to the Dublin children in 1992 in the percentages who could give answers to the questions on basic political knowledge (93 per cent, Dublin; 82 per cent, EB; 80 per cent, WB; 57 per cent, London). Between 1981 and 1992 there was an increase in the percentage who knew about voting age in all locations and an increase in those able to name political parties except in London. More of the East Belfast children in particular, could answer these questions in 1992. But the overall findings again reflect differences, even at the level of basic knowledge, in favour of the Dublin children.

ii) Local knowledge

Naming the Prime Minister or equivalent   As far as naming the NI Secretary of State and the Prime Minister of the Republic were concerned, the prediction was correct as in 1981 - more children from their own locations than from the other locations were able to name them (Figure 8.5)

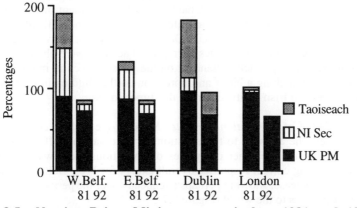

Figure 8.5   Naming Prime Minister or equivalent 1981 and 1992

Where in 1981, between 91 per cent (WB) and 96 per cent (Dublin) of children from all locations named Margaret Thatcher correctly as British Prime Minister, the news was not so good for John Major in 1992. The overall percentages who could name him were much lower. However, the West Belfast children were the best, with the others not far behind. (73 per cent, WB; 69 per cent, EB; 68 per cent, London; 66 per cent, Dublin).

Naming political parties in 1992 (Figure 8.6) A much higher percentage of Belfast

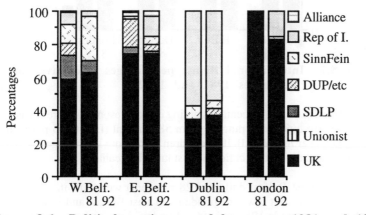

Figure 8.6   Political parties named by groups 1981 and 1992

children, both Catholic and Protestant, named British political parties than named parties from anywhere else just as in 1981 (Figure 8.6) with very little change (59 per cent, WB; 74 per cent EB, 1981; 63 per cent, WB; 74 per cent, EB, 1992).

It is interesting however that while the differences compared to 1981 were marginal, the percentage of West Belfast children who named British ('mainland') parties rose slightly in 1992. Mentions of Sinn Féin (political wing of the IRA) increased substantially in West Belfast - as might be expected given that party's efforts in the early 1990s (see Chapter Two), while mentions of SDLP (Social Democratic and Labour Party, non-militant nationalist) and Official Unionist parties (non-militant) and also of the DUP (Democratic Unionist Party, extremist unionist) or other extremist unionist parties decreased. The latter were obviously making less of an impact. The publicity attendant on the general election in the Irish Republic was obviously making a bit of an impression on the children in East Belfast, some of whom named Irish political parties this time around.

c) Knowledge of international events More of the Dublin children than of the others knew the answers to the questions on international affairs in 1992. In the same way as for the other categories of questions there was a decline in the numbers giving correct responses overall except for West Belfast where there was actually an increase, showing perhaps a tendency over the period, as noted earlier, to greater openness to the world (Figure 8.7).

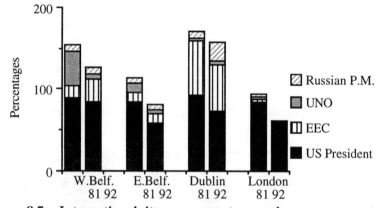

Figure 8.7   International items: percentages who gave correct responses 1981 and 1992

President of the USA The percentages giving correct responses were lower in 1992, but they were still quite high ranging from 58 per cent (EB) to 85 per cent (WB). Once again however the West Belfast children were more knowledgeable than those in East Belfast and the Dublin children most knowledgeable of all.

EEC In 1992, West Belfast children (28 per cent) were still in second place to Dublin (57 per cent), but fewer respondents in East Belfast and London knew the answer (EB 12 per cent in 1981 and 1992; London, 3 per cent in 1981; 5 per cent in 1992).

Russian Prime Minister The biggest increase was for the Dublin children.

182

UNO The meaning of the letters UNO was known by more Dublin children again in 1992.

Differences between boys and girls: knowledge of politics

In spite of the apparently greater interest in news items presented by the media shown by the girls in the study, their scores for knowledge were considerably less than those of the boys and there were differences between the sexes on more questions in 1992 than in 1981. This result is similar to that found in other studies (Torney-Purta, 1993). In the present instance the girls did not even score well on items of greater local relevance. A clue to a possible sexist cause may be found in the finding that the gap between boys and girls in all locations was much less in 1981 for the question relating to the British Prime Minister when that position was filled by Margaret Thatcher than it was in 1992 when John Major was the incumbent. There was some evidence also in the question asking respondents to name three political parties, that there is an underlying potential interest in matters political among the girls. The percentage of girls able to name one political party increased in West Belfast over the period of the study as did the percentage of girls able to name three political parties, unlike the figure for the boys.

Relationships between knowledge of current affairs and other variables

There was no consistent relationship between ownership of goods and knowledge of current events. Level of material well-being did not appear to be associated with interest in politics in these samples. As we noted previously, the East Belfast children had scored highest for possessions of household goods and had been similar to the West Belfast and Dublin children when money was taken into account, but their knowledge of politics was less than that of the other two groups. So the better off were not necessarily more interested in political events, nor were those at the other end of the scale. There was no relationship either with the parental salience/independence variables. But the composite variable 'News' and its subvariables were related to scores for knowledge of politics for all groups at one time point or the other.

Was there a falling off in interest simply in politics and related affairs, or did this lack of interest permeate to other areas such as sport? Did local context have any effect - were responses better where there was a possibility of local interest? We also wondered whether international sporting events had an equally high profile in each of the locations studied.

Knowledge of current events - sport

Ten questions were asked about sports-related matters. Following the line taken with the current affairs questions, the findings will be presented in overall terms by location and over time. The relationship is investigated between scores on this variable and respondents' interest in current affairs in general. Links with other background variables, such as possession of material goods and independence are also explored. Percentages are based on the numbers who actually responded to the questions, as are mean scores. The London response rate was low in 1992 and the percentages probably give an inflated idea of the scores of the London sample as a result. The response rates for the other groups were similar in 1981 and 1992 and similar to each other.

The mean scores on this variable showed small, but statistically significant differences between locations using analysis of variance in 1981 (F = 6.120; P< .001 for df = 3). Mean scores for the groups ranged from 5.92 to 4.52. The Dublin children scored highest, followed by the West Belfast children, just as for the politics questions. The East Belfast and London children had similar scores. The pattern therefore looks similar to that found for the current affairs variable in terms of the rank ordering of the groups (Figure 8.8).

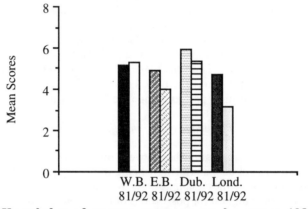

Figure 8.8 Knowledge of sports: mean scores by group 1981 and 1992

The results were however somewhat skewed in that a very low percentage in any group scored 8 or more and a high percentage scored 3 or less. Figure 8.9 shows the percentage in each group who scored 8 or more.

Over time, between 1981 and 1992, there was a decline in the mean number of correct responses, particularly for the London children where the average score dropped by two points. The East Belfast children's average score dropped by one point and that of the Dublin children by somewhat less. The West Belfast mean scores were not very different from 1981. In 1992, the differences between the groups were again statistically significant (F = 30.173; P< .001 for df = 3).

This shows that the percentages scoring 8 or more were highest in Dublin (17 per cent) and West Belfast (10 per cent) at both time-points and decreased to 11 per cent and 8 per cent respectively in 1992. The percentage scoring more than 8 increased in East Belfast only. Figure 8.9 gives a better idea of the range of response levels across locations. At the other end of the scale, the percentages scoring 3 or less were greatest in London (33 per cent) and East Belfast (19 per cent) in 1981 and again in 1992 when they were 61 per cent and 46 per cent respectively.

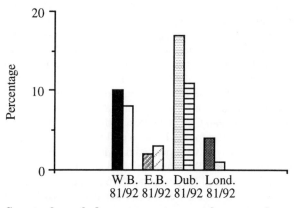

Figure 8.9   Sports knowledge: percentages who scored more than 8 by group 1981 and 1992

Did local salience: sports questions have any effect?

Questions where local context might have had an effect included the following:

- What team won the last Cup Final?
- Give the name of a famous horse race that takes place every year.
- Who won the last All-Ireland final in hurling or in Gaelic football?
- Name two well-known boxers.
- Name two famous snooker players.

What team won the last Cup Final? The specific cup final was not mentioned and if children asked which one was meant they were told to put down whatever one they thought might be correct. The possibilities included the World Cup, the European Cup, the Football Association Cup and indeed any School Cup. Although the Football Association Cup is played in England, it is given wide coverage in Northern Ireland and in the Republic and players who were originally from these locations are frequently involved. At the same time one might expect the FA Cup final to come more readily to mind for respondents in London, where it takes place, than in Belfast or Dublin. If children were really into local affairs, they might name a national, provincial or local school cup.

The pattern of responses in 1981, showed that 75 per cent of the London respondents gave the name of the winners of the FA Cup Final in that year; but the Dublin children were close behind with 73 per cent. The West Belfast children with 60 per cent were next and the East Belfast children were close behind them with 56 per cent.

But in 1992, the picture was different. There was a decrease all round. London was still in the lead with 61 per cent; East Belfast obviously had a hard core of interest, for the percentage of correct responses was almost the same, at 53 per cent; West Belfast was close behind, though with a lower percentage than in 1981, with 50 per cent and there was a considerable decline in Dublin (down to 22 per cent).

The Cup Final is held in early May and the questionnaires were completed each time in November-December-January, so the time of year did not make a difference.

Some children did not reply to this question at all but of those who gave alternative acceptable responses, a higher percentage were from West Belfast at both time-points. In 1981, 18 per cent of the West Belfast responses mentioned the World Cup and 5 per cent the European Cup. This was possibly a purely random finding, for at that time, 24 per cent of the East Belfast children mentioned the European Cup and none of them mentioned the World Cup, although the questionnaires were administered within the same time-span. More Dublin children mentioned the European Cup (10 percent) than the World Cup (6 per cent) in 1981 and the reverse was true for the London children (12 per cent World Cup, 2 per cent European Cup). It may have depended on what was in the news at the time and how close the final was. In 1992, few children in any location mentioned the World Cup. London had the highest percentage (26 per cent) giving the European Cup as a response followed by West Belfast (24 per cent), East Belfast (11 per cent) and Dublin (8 per cent).

Who won the last All-Ireland Final in hurling or in Gaelic football? This was definitely culture-related as an interest. As might be expected, the highest percentage of those giving the correct answer to this question were from Dublin (86 percent in 1981, 31 per cent in 1992). Some of the West Belfast children (55 per cent in 1981; 31 per cent in 1992) produced the right answer for this question too, but very few from East Belfast (15 per cent in 1981; 10 per cent in 1992) and just one or two children from London. Media, and in particular, TV coverage could explain this. GAA (Gaelic Athletic Association which organizes Gaelic football and hurling) news does not get extensive coverage in Northern Ireland but it is possible for aficionados in certain areas, including West Belfast, to tune to RTE (Republic of Ireland's television and radio service). This is obviously enough to inform those who are interested, as may be seen from the West Belfast results. At the same time, just to indicate that the results may not be totally accounted for by cultural background, we should note that three times as many of the West Belfast children knew the FA cup winners as knew the answer to the GAA question, so cultural identity is not the only reason for their higher scores.

Name two well-known boxers This was scored according to the nationality of the boxers mentioned. Exceptionally, more children gave two correct responses to this question in 1992 than in 1981 except in London. The majority in each location named British or American boxers - Mohammed Ali was a favourite in 1981 (with an amazing variety of spelling). This was the question at which the London children did best in 1981 - 73 per cent were able to name two boxers. But there was some evidence of local context being important in that a steady 10-11 per cent of the Dublin children named Irish boxers. In 1981, 4 per cent of the West Belfast children named Irish boxers, but only 1 per cent did so in 1992 - a somewhat surprising finding after the hype of the Olympics when boxers from Belfast and Dublin had brought home medals and had been greeted with civic receptions and a good deal of publicity.

Name two famous snooker players In 1981 there were a number of snooker players on the professional scene who came from Northern Ireland and the Republic. It was

186

not surprising, perhaps, that over 67 per cent of the children in East Belfast and Dublin and over 90 per cent of those in West Belfast named an Irish or Northern Ireland player. It looked as though this 'local interest' might be even responsible for the high level of knowledge in answer to this question in these groups. This seemed to be supported by the lack of interest of the London children, of whom a lower percentage answered this question correctly, though even there 36 per cent of those who responded named an Irish or Northern Ireland player and a similar percentage named players from other countries.

In 1992 however, the scene was different. The competitors at the top of the snooker ladder had changed and no longer included people who had been household names in 1981. There was still a high level of knowledge among respondents although it was somewhat lower everywhere than in 1981. Still, only 5 per cent of respondents from West Belfast and from Dublin, named an Irish or Northern Ireland player. The London children and East Belfast children named only British or other nationals and a higher percentage of them than of the Dublin children did so. The West Belfast children however were just as informed about British snooker players as were the East Belfast children and once again a lower percentage of them than of any other group gave correct responses (41 per cent of London children, 64 per cent from East Belfast, 66 per cent of Dublin children and 72 per cent of those from West Belfast).

This finding suggested that local context or national context was indeed a part of the continuing interest in this particular sport. It is possible of course, that local context had given it a boost in the early '80's and helped the interest to develop initially.

Give the name of a famous horse race that takes place every year There was scope for local context in responses to this question for children especially in Dublin, since there are events in the Irish racing calendar which are famous in Ireland. But they were not so well known to the children in this study as races in Britain - the Grand National, the Derby, the Gold Cup and the 1000 Guineas were the responses given. The Belfast and Dublin children were close on this one (86–89 percent) and the London children were least interested (77 per cent).

This result may be due to greater interest in the media and among the betting fraternity in these particular events and also to the high monetary value of the awards for the winners. The finding may also reflect the varied interests of the people and aspects of the environment in which the children in these four locations lived.

Other questions

Some of the questions were more directly international in flavour:

• *What sport is played for the Davis Cup?*
• *What internationally famous sporting event takes place every four years?*

The responses supported the trend noted in the current affairs section - a higher percentage of the Dublin children gave correct answers about the Davis Cup at both time-points followed by London, West Belfast, East Belfast. For the question about international events which occurred every four years the ranking was: London,

Dublin, then West and East Belfast. Over 50 per cent from each location named the Olympic Games as the internationally famous sporting event in 1981. This had dropped somewhat in 1992 - surprisingly perhaps, as the Olympics had taken place a few months before the questionnaires were completed. It is possible of course, that the months before the Games would have seen more coverage of them in the media than happened in the months following them. By contrast, mention of the World Cup as a four-yearly event increased everywhere except in East Belfast in 1992, perhaps because the preliminary rounds were already starting for 1994.

Few respondents, apart from a handful in London, could name the kind of sporting event that takes place at the White City and few of them could say what was meant by the term 'freestyle' (responses relating it to biking activities were allowed as well as the more conventional one of swimming). These questions seemed more relevant for the London children than for any of the others - more of them were able to answer correctly (67 per cent correct for 'freestyle' in 1981, 43 per cent in 1992; 40 per cent correct for White City in 1981, none in 1992). These particular questions were taken, unchanged, from the Manchester Scales of Social Adaptation (Lunzer, 1966) and it could be suggested that they were more culture and time specific than any of the other questions. On the other hand perhaps, all the other questions were also culture-specific, but of a culture shared both by those on the island of Ireland and the London children.

How did the girls fare?

The questions in this section and indeed the whole questionnaire had originally been drawn up with a sample in mind that was exclusively male since one of its aims was to provide additional information for a group of boys involved in a longitudinal study (Whyte, 1983c, 1989b, 1992a, 1992b, 1993b, Whyte and Montgomery, 1984). When it was decided to broaden the scope of the study, it was too late to make changes as the instrument had already been administered to at least one 'wave' and the somewhat unreconstructed sexist slant of the questions in this section in particular was regretted. Most of the questions relate to sports practised almost exclusively by males or certainly dominated by males, but of course this reflects the situation in real life. This often has the effect of stultifying girls' interests in sports and may explain why they usually are found to score less highly on questions of sporting knowledge.

In the present study, the girls' mean scores were almost a full point and a half below those of the boys in 1981 (4.52; 5.96). However, the climate may have changed somewhat since then for although the mean scores for both girls and boys declined over the time period studied, those of the girls declined by marginally less. Their mean score in 1992 was 3.83 and that of the boys was 5.25. The difference was statistically significant (F =36.880, P<.001 for df = 1 in 1982; F = 24.831, P< .001 for df = 1 in 1992). This supports the finding for 1992 reported in Chapter Four of increased participation by girls in sports in their leisure time and in Chapter Seven of an increased interest by girls in sports events mentioned in the newspaper.

There was also a statistically significantly sex by group interaction at both timepoints which would suggest that socio-cultural and local influences are relevant. Far fewer of the girls than of the boys overall were interested in football or Gaelic games or snooker or racing and in line with their disregard for football, they tended to name the Olympic Games as the four-yearly event rather than the World Cup. But interestingly, they knew about boxing.

There was one question which specifically invited respondents to consider the possibility of naming a female.

• *Name a famous athlete and say what he or she is famous for*

More than four times the percentage of girls (18 per cent) compared to boys (3 per cent) gave the name of a female athlete in response to this question in 1981. The percentages were 15 per cent and 3 per cent respectively in 1992, but the trend was similar. This would suggest that the shortage of role-models and the dominance of media-reported sport by boys and men may have a lot to do with this space in the experience of girls. The failure by boys to recognize that girls and women can perform in sport to international levels is also brought out by these findings. The lack of coverage by the media of female sporting events and the comparatively lower level of sponsorship and support generally are part of the problem.

Summary of findings on general knowledge of current affairs

Politics

• Over the time period of the study overall scores declined everywhere but there was an increase in the percentage who knew about voting age in all locations and an increase in those able to name political parties except in London.
• The biggest reductions *pro-rata* in overall scores for information about current events were in East Belfast and London. The Dublin and West Belfast children also had reduced scores but not by so much.
• Reference group orientation *did* appear to be a factor. More of the children knew about their own country than children elsewhere did; but it was not as simple as it sounds. The Belfast and Dublin children knew about UK and USA related items to a greater extent than some items about their own country.
• There was some evidence that East Belfast children had more restricted knowledge especially in 1981. The West Belfast children had somewhat wider interests especially in 1992.

Sport - overall scores

• The Dublin children had the highest scores for knowledge of sporting events in 1981, followed by West Belfast children.
• Scores decreased over time, but the ranked ordering of the groups remained the same.
• Girls scored significantly less than boys at both time points.

Local knowledge?

- There was some limited evidence for the influence of local participation on knowledge of sports - particularly in sports like boxing and snooker
  However, the 'Cup Final' for the majority meant the FA Cup Final in London and the majority named horse races in England when asked to name a famous race.
- Dublin children were more knowledgeable about international events at both time points.
- Girls took advantage of the opportunity to name female sporting figures when this was offered.

Trends over time

At both timepoints higher percentages of the Dublin children gave correct responses and West Belfast children came next, ahead of East Belfast and London. It is possible that the local situation with all its psychological connotations has been a factor in the poor performance of the East Belfast children and conversely in the better performance shown by the West Belfast children. The East Belfast children were interested in it, and distracted by it, the West Belfast children looked beyond it. The findings indicate a decline in knowledge and therefore probably also in the development of opinions about current events and politics in this age group. The findings for politics were mirrored in those for sport, where however there was some evidence of interest being influenced by locality. Both of these findings must be of concern particularly in Northern Ireland where the future has to be constructed to a greater extent than in Dublin or London. It points to the need for some form of education and consciousness raising among young people about the basic facts of living in a democracy which should be undertaken without delay.

The seriousness of the possible implications of the findings should be considered in conjunction with the percentage decrease in scores on the political questions in each area and the low scores achieved by girls. The biggest reductions *pro-rata* in scores for information about current events were in East Belfast and London. The Dublin and West Belfast children also had reduced scores but not by so much. This could be telling us something about the underlying trends in these communities, the tendencies of parents and other adults to discuss political issues and current affairs in the home with or in front of the children, the general climate of debate in the classroom and attitudes towards the stimulation of interest and involvement in the democratic process and how this has changed over the period of the study in these locations. And it could be telling us something about the quality of information obtained through the media, or about the extent to which the children see political events as relevant to their lives.

These issues will be discussed in Chapter Ten, but first we must examine the question of whether their hopes for the future are reflected by their lack of knowledge about the present. In Chapter Nine we explore their orientation towards the future.

9 Hopes for the future

Introduction

When the present study started in 1981, the concept of 'possible selves' had not entered the literature in those terms, but we were interested in the linked concept of the future orientation of the children in West and East Belfast, Dublin and London. As the study and theoretical perspectives developed it became clear that attitudes towards the future probably depended to a large extent on the kinds of possible selves generated in the different groups through their differing experiences. We also were interested in seeing whether there would be any change over the period of the study when many developments had been taking place in Northern Ireland which were likely to affect self-concept, personal identity and attitudes towards the future.

Thinking about the future preoccupies everyone at some stage or another and can help focus behaviour. The kind of future people see for themselves will probably ultimately influence the direction in which their society moves to some extent, even if they do not directly relate their own goals to those of the community. A negative view or a view which is based on a perception of low personal control and low self-esteem may inhibit constructive action; a positive view or a view based on a perception of high personal control and self-efficacy is more likely to lead to constructive behaviour. Future orientation will be affected by a child's experience of violence (Garbarino, 1995), though the impact will depend on the ideological climte created by significant adults in the child's immediate environment.

The extent to which a person is inclined to think and plan ahead is part of his or her self-concept in that it relates to the perception of a 'possible self' (Markus and Nurius, 1986, Oyserman and Markus, 1990, Curry, Trew, Turner and Hunter, 1994). The 'possible self' is linked to the dynamic properties of the self-concept and is derived from a pool of possible selves which has its origins in the individual's particular sociocultural and historical context and from the models, images and symbols provided by the media and by the individual's immediate social experience. Although we see by means of the 'possible self' how inventive and constructive the self can be, we must recognize also that the 'possible self' is socially determined and constrained to a considerable extent (Elder, Hagell, Rudkin and Conger, 1992, Stryker, 1984) and that the ecological context provides a system of support for particular identities, a means of organizing experience, ensuring predictability and stabilizing self-esteem (Deaux, 1991).

As already noted, early adolescence is an important time for the task of establishing a concept of self-identity which will include subjective ideas about one's present and also about one's future self. One may assume that the way adolescents anticipate and evaluate their future influences their life planning, decision making and behaviour (Trommsdorff, 1986). Possible selves are seen as motivational resources that provide individuals with some control over their own behaviour; as such they are conceived of as the self-relevant internal structures that embody and give rise to generalized feelings of self-efficacy (Bandura, 1986), effectance (White, 1959), competence (Harter, 1993) and control (Burger, 1985).

This 'future orientation' develops in relation to other personality variables in early adolescence and is partly determined by processes of cognitive development and partly influenced by external social learning conditions. Adolescents who are, for example, required to take personal responsibility for their behaviour will have opportunities to structure means-ends relationships, to cope with frustrating situations, to restructure goals and make realistic judgements about their own competence, the responsiveness of the environment and the interaction between both in the future. This will assist them in developing a positive self-concept, a related positive future orientation and realistic life planning (Trommsdorff, 1983). As a result of the socio-cognitive experiences of the individual, the working self concept will sometimes be dominated by conceptions of negative possibility and sometimes by positive possibilities. The idea of diminished agency may be linked to the existence of negative possible selves that give vivid cognitive form to an individual's fears and insecurities, and do not contain strategies or self-scripts for how to escape them (Oyserman and Markus, 1990).

Change in the self-concept

Research on self-concept change has shown on the one hand impressive stability and continuity, but on the other considerable malleability. Explanations for this apparent inconsistency have recently centred on the 'possible self' as that element of the self-concept which allows an opening for change (Markus and Nurius, 1986). It has been proposed that possible selves, because they are not anchored in the environment, comprise the self-knowledge that is the most vulnerable and responsive to changes in the environment; they are the first elements of the self-concept to absorb and reveal such changes and they are particularly sensitive to those situations which communicate new or inconsistent information about the self. Existing data suggest that self-concept change occurs primarily and perhaps only in response to major changes in role or situational demands; the self is seen as consistent in its motives and conservative in its strategies, yet ultimately responsive to environmental contingencies (Banaji and Prentice, 1994).

If we see the individual as functioning and developing as an integrated whole and if we conceptualize behaviour in terms of an organized system involving the interaction of social and individual processes (Magnusson and Törestad, 1993), it would seem reasonable to expect that the working self-concept would be modified as a result of a serious challenge to a prevailing self-conception. This could have been happening in Northern Ireland over the past 25 years, given the events outlined in Chapter Two. Possible selves may thus be the instruments of the intense temporary changes in self-evaluation that seem critical in everyday functioning; they may also be the mechanisms of the more long-term enduring changes in self-concept that seem intuitively inevitable but are not evident in studies of self-concept over the life course (Markus and Nurius, 1986). In terms of the relationship of self-concept to identity, change in the characteristics of self concept associated with an identity would not necessarily mean a change in the category of identity to which the individual claims allegiance (in the present instance Northern Ireland Protestant or Northern Ireland Catholic), but rather a change in the meanings associated with that identity (Deaux, 1991).

Trommsdorff (1986) proposes that a number of factors will come into play before future orientation is transformed into life planning and points out that many of the relevant factors are not necessarily stable person variables, but are context dependent. While systematic studies have as yet to be carried out, it can be hypothesized that these factors include judgements of environmental conditions in the present and in the future, heuristic competence in problem solving, readiness to tolerate frustrations and to delay gratification, the relevance of goals and flexibility in restructuring goals. Life-course models of development (Elder, Hagell, Rudkin and Conger, 1992, Elder, 1995) support Trommsdorff's research findings that the developmental conditions influencing the generation of a person's future orientation will include the impact of situational demands, the level of cognitive maturation, the impact of social learning and motivational and cognitive factors related to social roles. There have been changes in a number of these factors in Northern Ireland in recent times.

Influences on future orientation

In relation to situational demands, studies with economically disadvantaged groups have shown that their future orientation is more directed to events and available rewards in the near future as compared to the more extended future orientation of more privileged adolescents and this may be interpreted as a realistic appraisal of, and way of coping with, the given social setting. Spenner and Featherman (1979) while stating that certainty regarding future goals may develop into late adolescence, say there is little strong evidence to suggest that such ideas change drastically over that period. Trommsdorff (1986) reports a study which found striking similarities between adolescents and adults sharing the same social (educational and occupational) background, suggesting a stability of future orientation across generations where environmental conditions remain constant. In the present study it will be interesting to see whether the four groups of children, at two timepoints, of similar socio-economic backgrounds, with slight variations in detail as we have seen above, vary in their future orientation and whether this can be seen as a function of background factors other than the strictly socio-economic.

In relation to cognitive maturation, the age range of the children in our sample was selected so that it was likely that they would be at a similar stage in the development of formal operational intelligence. This enables the child to anticipate future events and to think in terms of future consequences. With maturation, they increase their perspective into the future, become more realistic and learn to take into account specific causes of future events.

The impact of social learning is mediated by motivational and cognitive factors related to social roles, but differences in cognitive ability and intelligence do not necessarily always explain differences in some aspects of future orientation - e.g. whether the time span is more extended or less extended (Bouffard, 1981, Trommsdorff, Lamm and Schmidt, 1978). On the other hand poor school achievement and lower levels of cognitive ability have been found to be correlates of negative thoughts about the future (Sarigiani, Wilson, Petersen and Vicaray, 1990) as distinct from having an extended versus a short-term view. And any or all of these factors can influence self-esteem and low self-esteem tends to characterize children with lower occupational goals, when cognitive ability is controlled (Chiu, 1990, Nurius, 1991).

Results from the Shell study (Jugendwerk der Deutschen Shell, 1982) showed that individuals low in belief of their personal control of the social environment also had less extended expectations about the future and were more pessimistic about political, social, environmental and economic aspects of the future. The relevance of child-rearing practices for the development of the self-concept has been referred to previously, but in relation to future orientation, it has been found that adolescents who perceived their parents as loving and supporting had a more trusting, hopeful and positive future orientation, believed in more personal control in their future and were more willing to delay gratification (Trommsdorff, Lamm and Schmidt, 1978).

It has been suggested that the more social settings require the testing of one's competence and allow for the awareness of one's abilities and options, and require and reinforce personal responsibility and independence, the more one's future orientation focuses on the belief in personal control. And conversely, the less social settings allow for success and social acceptance, the more pessimistic one's future orientation (Trommsdorff, 1986). When anticipating primarily negative outcomes, it seems less worthwhile to undertake investments, to tolerate frustrations or to pursue far-reaching goals. The reasoning seems to be that since it does not matter anyhow what one does, one might as well look for self-fulfillment in the very near future and in some cases at least, this means choosing activities which are socially disapproved of and which have negative consequences for the distant future. The range of possible selves is obviously relevant here and Oyserman and Markus (1990) who examined the relationship of the balance between feared and expected possible selves with delinquency found that the most delinquent youth had considerably less balance between their expected and feared selves than officially nondelinquent youths.

Future orientation and possible selves for Belfast Dublin and London children

We asked if the children in West and East Belfast, Dublin and London would have:

- more extended or less extended views of the future, involving more delayed or more immediate gratification,
- more simplistic or more complex views of the future, involving just themselves or other people too,
- more generative or less generative views of themselves in relation to the future, involving more or less investment in themselves

and
- whether there were changes over time.

It was also of interest to determine whether their future orientation was associated with any of the aspects of self-concept discussed in earlier chapters - social intelligence through declarative knowledge, self-efficacy through commitment, their sense of autonomy / independence, their experience of outreach, their awareness of their role in society.

The questions

The specific questions asked related to:

i) The aims of education - if these were seen either as a means of getting employment or alternatively as a means of self-development, this was interpreted as having a more extended view of the future since education was regarded in a positive light; within these categories, the instant-job-related responses were seen as lower on the scale, and the self-development, qualifications responses were seen as higher on the scale;

ii) The children's wishes - if these were altruistic or generally non-materialistic or reflected ideas of societal action and socially responsible behaviour, they were interpreted as presenting a more complex view of the future; if they were materialistic and self-centred in focus they were interpreted as being more simplistic;

iii) Their aspirations - these contributed in terms of what they told us about the children having a more versus a less extended view of the future; if they hoped for employment which involved further training, they were classified as having a more extended view and if the jobs they wanted did not require post-school education and training, they were regarded as having a less extended view;

iv) Their definitions of happy people - these were seen as part of a more complex view of life if they involved interaction with others and a less complex view if they were self centred or materialistic.

v) a composite score of 'generativity' made up of responses to the questions about wishes, aspirations and happy people.

Aims of education

The subjects' views on the aims of education and the school system were elicited by means of two items: They were asked to complete these statements:

•School is supposed to help us in life because it......
    (name three things)
•It's worth trying to do well at school because......
    (name three things)

It was decided to focus on two categories of responses: the first category was for those responses which put employment first (categorized as the less extended view of the future) and the second was for those which put self-development, qualifications, third level education or related outcomes as the main reason for doing well and/or the way in which school could help them in life (categorized as the more extended view of the future). Both of these kinds of responses could be seen as indicating a positive attitude towards education - they could both be said to endorse the usefulness of it.

We first determined whether the groups differed overall in the percentages who gave either of these responses and then looked at the percentages who gave the different types of response. Some children gave other responses which could not be categorized under either of the headings just outlined, such as 'to please my parents/ teachers'; 'to stay out of trouble'.

Wishes

Sometimes wishes can be associated with an individual's psychological and social problems. Does this differ for 12 year-olds in different places? For example would children in Belfast be sensitive to issues related to the 'Troubles' in Northern Ireland in making their wishes?

The children were asked to complete the following statement:

•*If I had a wish I would wish that..............*

The statement on wishes was intended to elicit the first spontaneous wish that came into respondents' heads. Taking the first response has been found by previous researchers to be a valid and reliable approach to people's real feelings.

Categorizing wishes

There has been very little research reported on the categorizing of wishes made by normally functioning children. A study in Nigeria (Maduwesi, 1982) for example, found that children aged between 7 and 13 most commonly wished for material possessions. While Chiu and Nevius, (1989) differentiated four nominal categories of wishes in a comparison study of Mexican-American and Anglo- American children - materialistic, altruistic, personal and goal oriented and these classifications have been used by other researchers, it was thought necessary to expand the categories in order to cover the range of wishes in the present study.

Two basic categories of wish and subcategories within them were identified:

A. Non-materialistic
    i)   Global altruistic - 'peace in the world,' 'no famine in Africa',
    ii) Family altruistic - 'that my father could get a job', 'that we could have a car', 'that my mother would get better'
    iii) Self-development - 'that I could do well in exams', 'be a good person'.
    iv) Northern Ireland-related wishes - 'peace in Northern Ireland'.

B. Materialistic

> v) 'Goods' and possessions - 'a motor bike', 'lots of money', 'more wishes'
> vi) School-related wishes - 'school would blow up'; 'no school', 'leave school'

Aspirations

In relation to aspirations, we asked whether similar proportions of 12 year-olds from similar socio-economic backgrounds but different locations, as in our sample, would want to have jobs which provided instant gratification in the way of a wage, but little prospect of development in the future; or would similar proportions look for jobs that required training and would constitute an investment in themselves. Such ambitions will reflect their view of their possible selves and their potential. The children were asked to complete these statements:

> *•I would like most of all when I grow up to be a......................*
> *•But if that is not possible I wouldn't mind being a ....*

The statement asking about what respondents most wanted to be when they grew up was intended to elicit the ideal career or occupation, if nothing prevented it happening. The other statement was intended to bring realism into the matter by encouraging the respondents to recognize that there might be problems in achieving their ambitions and asking them to have another option which might be considered. Aspirations and ambitions were categorized as:

A) *Requiring training*: Professional/managerial, skilled non-manual, skilled manual

B) *Not requiring formal training*: Sports/popstars, unskilled manual, other (oil millionaire, security forces/IRA,)

Happiness defined

How do people define happiness? This too could make a difference to their plans for the future and to the decisions they make about options in education and beyond. We asked further whether it was related to the kinds of wishes and aspirations they had - did it reflect the same value system and range of possible selves? Was this the case for children in the different locations? Did they have similar kinds of possible selves? And did these as expressed in wishes and aspirations change over time - for example over the past eleven years? Had they changed to the same extent in Belfast London and Dublin?

The children were asked to complete the following statement:

> *•Happy people are people who...*

Responses were evaluated in terms of whether they were, broadly speaking simplistic, self-centred, materialistic or more developmental, complex, non-materialistic, involving other people.

Generative and non-generative views of the future

On the basis of the responses given to the four items on wishes, aspirations and happy people, two composite variables were derived:

i) 'Generative' responses seemed to involve, in Kotre's terms (1984), the 'desire to invest one's substance in forms of life and work that will outlive the self'. The responses grouped under this heading included those which were non-materialistic in orientation - non-materialistic wishes, aspirations involving self-development and definitions of happy people involving service to others and self-development. In other words they could be said to reflect a more extended and complex view of the future.

ii) 'Non-generative' responses were more short-term focused, more egocentric, more simplistic. The answers which made up this composite variable were more materialistic in nature - materialistic type wishes, unskilled jobs and materialistic definitions of happiness.

It was hypothesized that underlying these different kinds of future orientation were different sets of possible selves which had been socially determined and it was of interest to establish whether the percentages in each location giving these responses remained stable over a period when considerable social change was happening and a reassessment of group identities was being encouraged.

Results are given first for each variable individually and then for the composite variable.

Views about the aims of education

Less extended view - school as a means to a job

There were significant differences by group at both time points (figure 9.1). The London children had the lowest percentage of those oriented towards seeing school as a means to employment and the Dublin children had the highest percentage at both timepoints. The percentage giving this response decreased in every location over time, but least of all in the East Belfast group, suggesting that they were still somewhat more inclined to take a short-term view of education than the other groups. Higher percentages of girls than of boys overall were employment-oriented at both timepoints (35 per cent boys 29 per cent girls in 1981; 26 per cent girls, 21 per cent boys in 1992). Situational effects are clearly important - like the impact of a particular teacher in a particular school at a particular time, or the employment opportunities for school-leavers.

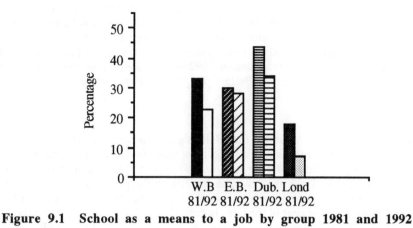

Figure 9.1   School as a means to a job by group 1981 and 1992

ii) Education as a means of self-development / obtaining qualifications

The Dublin children followed by the West Belfast children had higher scores on this variable at both time points, and could be seen as having a more positive view of education than the other groups. The percentages giving this response did not change substantially between 1981 and 1992 (Figure 9.2).

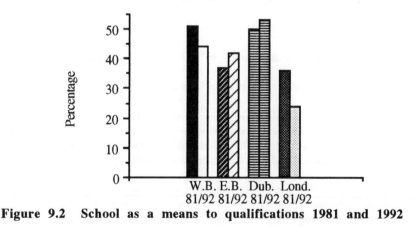

Figure 9.2   School as a means to qualifications 1981 and 1992

This attitude towards education would seem to be fairly enduring in a community and not to be as susceptible to change as the 'school as a means to a job' attitude which had fewer responses everywhere in 1992 than in 1981. The West and East Belfast children had been further apart in 1981, when more West than East Belfast children gave this response, as had been the case also for the 'school as a means to a job' response, but in 1992, very similar percentages from both locations had this more extended view of the purposes of education. The increase in the percentage of

East Belfast children having this more positive attitude should be noted. They seemed to be becoming more congruent in their attitudes with the children of West Belfast on this issue. The London children's scores were lowest at both time points and also decreased by the greatest amount - reflecting perhaps the more transient nature of their neighbourhoods as noted earlier. A slightly higher percentage of the Dublin children gave this response in 1992 than in 1981; this meant that about 10% more of them than of either Belfast group had this view of education in 1992.

Girls and boys

More girls than boys in West and East Belfast gave this response whereas in Dublin and London the percentages of girls and boys were similar at both time points. In 1981, a higher percentage of girls in West Belfast than in East Belfast felt this way about school, but in 1992, there was an increase in the percentage of East Belfast girls giving this response, bringing them up to the same level as the girls in West Belfast. Around 32 per cent of the boys in both East and West Belfast saw school as a means to self-development. The differences between girls and boys in Belfast are interesting and one's first reaction might be to think that it was a school-induced finding. But it is not so straightforward as that as may be seen from the comparison between the London and Dublin children where similar percentages of girls and boys within each location seemed interested in self development. While the schools in Dublin were coeducational, those in London were single sex and separate. In Belfast they were all single sex and separate in 1981, but in 1992, all the East Belfast boys and some of the girls came from coeducational schools, while one group of girls was attending a single sex school. The girls in Belfast were more positive about education than the boys, whether they had a shorter-term or a more extended view of the future.

Relationships between attitudes to school and other variables

i) The less extended view of the future (school as a means to a job)

'Goods' The better-off children did not necessarily have a less extended view than the less well off in this sample of not very advantaged children. Relationships between the amount of money obtained as pocket money and this view or between amount of money earned and this view were not statistically significant either.

Parental salience For most of the children, there would appear to have been no relationship between salience of mother and this less extended view of the future, but in 1981 salience of mother was significantly negatively related to this attitude for the girls in East Belfast and not for the other groups. Those with high mother salience in that location were less likely to have even the less extended view of the future as expressed by seeing school simply as a means to a job, and therefore to have a less positive view of education. Salience of father was fairly low everywhere, so any apparent 'relationships' should be treated with caution but it appeared to be significantly positively associated with the job-related school attitude for the West Belfast girls in 1981 and for the London children, especially the girls in 1992 and therefore with a positive view of education. In terms of locations overall, it was significant only for London in 1992. Salience of both parents was positively correlated with this kind of attitude in 1992 and significantly so for the London children, particularly the boys.

Independence   The more independent 12 year-olds in every location were more likely to have the less extended view of the future and a more positive view of education and the less independent children were not so likely to have this point of view particularly in 1981. In 1992, the two variables were becoming more dissociated, and the relationship was less strong in all locations.

Commitment and choice   Perhaps the most interesting variable in this group was the 'Commitment' variable which was significantly correlated overall for the WB and EB (1981) groups and for the London group in 1992. Children who contributed to the household by doing jobs etc. around the house (and probably earned some money by doing so, although as we have seen, money *per se* was not a factor), were more likely to see school as a means to a job and to have a more positive view of education than were children who gave less help. The variable 'Choice' was not related to this attitude for any group at either time point.

School as a means towards qualifications

"Goods'   Relationships between 'Goods' and the attitude towards school which saw it as a means of gaining qualifications, thus expressing a more extended view of the future, varied across locations and by time point. There were differences especially between the children in Belfast both East and West, and those in Dublin and London.

There was no significant relationship for the Belfast children at either time point - level of standard of living was not statistically related to this attitude towards school for them. But there was a significant positive relationship between the 'Goods' variables and the 'school as qualifications' attitude for the Dublin children in 1981 - the higher the score on 'Goods', the more likely they were to see school as a means to qualifications. By 1992 this had changed to a negative relationship - the lower the score on 'Goods', the more likely to see school as a means to qualifications which appears to show a shift in attitudes, but could also show how situational variations over time can be important determinants of responses.

For the London children there was no relationship in 1981, but a positive one in 1992 - with higher scores on 'Goods' related to the likelihood of seeing school as a means towards qualifications and a more positive view of education

The amount of money received as pocket money or earned was not generally associated with this attitude to school.

Parental salience   The salience of both parents was significantly correlated with this kind of attitude in London, at both time points, and in West Belfast, in 1992 only, to a higher level than in the other locations. Salience of Dad was important for London children at both timepoints, but especially for girls there in 1981. Salience of Mum was positively correlated for London girls in 1992. But data reported earlier showed that the salience of both mother and father was lower in London than elsewhere. The relationship finding should therefore be treated with caution.

Independence   The question here was whether experience of autonomy would be related to the attitude which saw school as a means towards getting qualifications, a more extended view of the future and a positive view of education. There was a significant relationship for the West Belfast, and Dublin children in 1981, both girls and boys, and for the London children only in 1992. There was no relationship between these variables for the East Belfast group at either time point and this too is interesting as it is one of the elements on which they differ from the West Belfast children and may reflect a different set of family values underlying the development of attitudes.

Summary

Their hopes from education are one indication of how children see the future. More of the Dublin children seemed to have a more positive view at both time points; there was a slight increase in the percentages of East Belfast children with positive feelings and a slight decrease in the West Belfast children who saw it this way in 1992 compared to 1981. Emler (1993) suggests that the way in which young people adapt to formal education is central to their relations with normal society generally. Young people who experience failure at school and have a less positive attitude towards education are likely to begin to reject formal education and the formal authority it represents. In the present instance we do not know whether the subjects in this study were experiencing failure at school but fewer of the Belfast and London children than of the Dublin children appeared to have positive attitudes towards education. This could mean eventually a turning away from the institutions of society, a lack of 'engagement', such as was reflected by the findings in Chapter Eight for the East Belfast and London children in particular..

Aims of school

- More Dublin children gave positive responses and the lowest percentage seeing school as mainly as a means to getting a job or mainly as a means towards qualifications came from London at both time points.
- More girls than boys saw school as a means to a job in every location (less extended view).
- Similar percentages of girls and boys in Dublin and London saw school as a means towards qualifications - the more extended view.
- More girls than boys in Belfast saw school as a means to qualifications.

Job-related attitude (less extended view) and other variables

- This was significantly related to lifestyle variables (material possessions) for London children, but not for the Belfast or Dublin groups.
- It was not related to amount of money as pocket money received or money earned.
- Salience of both parents was significantly correlated with the job-related attitude in 1992 for the London children, particularly the boys.
- Involvement with Mum and Dad separately was differentially related by sex and by location and time.

- The job-related attitude was significantly related to Independence variables for Belfast and Dublin children in 1981 and for the London children in particular in 1992.
- It was positively and significantly related to the variable Commitment for both boys and girls, but differentially over time - for Belfast in 1981 and London 1992.

School as a means for qualifications (more extended view) and other variables

- For the London children there was no relationship in 1981 between 'Goods' variables and the view of school as a means towards qualifications, but there was a positive one in 1992 - with higher scores on 'Goods' related to the likelihood of seeing school as a means towards qualifications.
- It was related for Dublin children - negatively in 1981, positively in 1992, but not for the Belfast children at either time point.
- The amount of money received as pocket money or earned money was not generally associated with this attitude to school.
- It was significantly correlated with parental salience (both parents) for London boys.
- Salience of mother was positively correlated for London girls in 1992.
- Dad was important for the London children overall in 1992, but for no other group.
- It was related to the Independence variables for the West Belfast and Dublin children in 1981, both girls and boys, and for the London children only in 1992.
- It was not related to Independence variables for the East Belfast children at either time point.

Findings on wishes 1981

Wishes by location

As may be seen in Figure 9.3, children in all four locations made wishes in all the categories. There were some interesting differences between the groups in the percentages making the different kinds of wish.

Non-materialistic wishes

A higher percentage of the Dublin children (51 per cent) than of any other group made non-materialistic-type wishes (43 per cent London; 37 per cent West Belfast; 16 per cent East Belfast), and could therefore be said to have a more complex view of the future, less bounded by the need for instant gratification. We wondered whether there was any particular subcategory of wishes which might distinguish between the groups and which might suggest why the overall score of the East Belfast children was so much lower than that of the other groups.

While the percentages making wishes related to family matters were fairly steady across locations, there were interesting findings for some of the other categories which differentiated between the East Belfast children and the others and seemed to

203

indicate a more self-centred, less extended, less complex view on the part of the East Belfast children than of the other groups and a more materialistic, short-term view of the future in general on the part of the Belfast children, both East and West.

Within the non- materialistic category, more of the Dublin children (17 per cent) and the West Belfast children (16 per cent) made wishes about global peace issues than did the children of East Belfast (8 per cent) or London (5 per cent). This was not balanced by a greater preoccupation on the part of the Belfast children, East or West, with peace in Northern Ireland - perhaps they were closing their eyes to the realities of what was going on around them just as we saw in an earlier chapter with regard to their attitude to current affairs. Or it could be due to the 'distancing' effect (Cairns and Wilson, 1989). Very few (N=2) respondents mentioned Northern Ireland.

Even more significantly perhaps, the Belfast children appeared to be less concerned about their own potential and how they might invest in themselves for their own future. Dublin and London children were twice as likely to make self-development wishes as the Belfast children. And within the Belfast groups there were differences between West and East Belfast in 1981 with more West Belfast children making this kind of wish. But was this due to differences between girls and boys?

Girls and boys

A higher percentage of girls overall (45 per cent) than of boys (31 per cent) made wishes in the non-materialistic categories, but the trend was not the same in every location. The figures for self-development type wishes were interesting especially for the Belfast children. In West Belfast similar percentages of boys and girls (about 12 per cent) made this kind of wish in 1981 and again in 1992. In East Belfast, no girls at all made this kind of wish in 1981 and only 2 per cent of the boys. When we compare this to the 29 per cent of girls in Dublin and London and the 19 per cent of boys in those places who made that kind of wish it seems to suggest a different set of values and expectations and a different set of 'possible selves' in the East Belfast children from those held by the children in all the other locations at that time.

Materialistic wishes

A higher percentage of the East Belfast children than of the others made materialistic-type wishes (73 per cent), again suggesting a different set of 'possible selves', needing more instant gratification and having a more self-centred, simplistic attitude. There were greater differences between boys and girls in East Belfast however on this type of wish than in the other locations in 1981. Considerably more boys than girls made materialistic wishes in East Belfast and while more boys than girls also did so in Dublin and London the differences were not so great. But in West Belfast, by contrast with East Belfast in 1981 the percentages of girls and boys giving this response were similar showing a more congruent set of values between boys and girls.

Similar percentages in every location had wishful feelings about abolishing school or homework or some other aspect of the educational system. While the percentages were not large enough to be a cause for concern (7–12 per cent), and while the fact that the questionnaire was administered in the context of the school classroom may have influenced the responses to some extent, it is perhaps worth noting that this was the first thing that came into some pupils' minds when asked to make a wish. The finding does indicate however that the problem was similar in each of the locations - none of the groups felt any more strongly than any other about this, so the crisis with authority, insofar as it existed, was no worse in Belfast than in Dublin or London.

Any changes in 1992?

Figure 9.3 shows the findings for both 1981 and 1992. The East Belfast children still showed different tendencies from the others although there was a slight leveling up of the percentages making each type of wish. The East Belfast and London children again tended to make fewer non-materialistic wishes than the West Belfast (44 per cent) and Dublin (41 per cent) children. If this reflects their possible selves it would certainly account for them having different priorities and a different set of values and contribute to difficulties for adults in having dialogue.

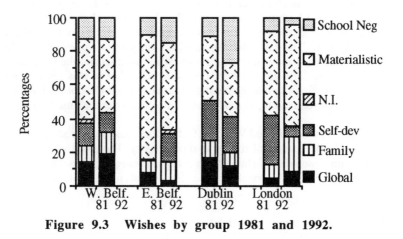

Figure 9.3   Wishes by group 1981 and 1992.

Looking at the non-materialistic wishes in more detail, slightly more of the West Belfast (19 per cent) than of the Dublin (12 per cent) East Belfast (3 per cent) or London (9 per cent) children again made wishes related to global issues. For self-development wishes, the West Belfast and Dublin children remained at around the same percentages, showing consistency in their views about themselves and reflecting a willingness in their communities to take a longer term positive view and invest in the future. The East Belfast children, of whom the lowest percentage of any group had made self-development wishes in 1981 showed an increase in that category in 1992, perhaps an indication of a more positive view than they had had in 1981. The sharp decrease for the London children, may reflect the economic downturn there, but it is interesting that the economic downturn was not having the same psychological effect for the Belfast children, although as we have seen there were some signs of it in the standards of living data for 1992. There was also a big increase in wishes related to family for the London group, so perhaps they were also having more problems in that area, but for the others that category remained stable over the eleven years.

London children this time had the highest percentage of materialistic wishes (60 per cent) which would link in with greater felt economic hardship, though, as intimated above, this is unlikely to have been the only factor underlying this finding, followed by East Belfast (53 per cent) - who were not the most disadvantaged - and then by West Belfast (43 per cent) and Dublin (32 per cent).

Trends over time and summary

Global issues The West Belfast and Dublin children made more wishes in this area than the other groups at both timepoints; they seemed to be less ego-centric, or even less ethnocentric than the other groups and to have a more complex view of the future and perhaps also they had access to a greater range of possible selves.

Family issues These were of equal concern to children in all locations and the degree of concern overall changed very little, except in London where it increased.

Self-development The Dublin children were steadily ahead in the percentage giving this kind of wish at both time points; the West Belfast children were also steady at both time points - about 8 per cent fewer of them than of the Dublin children gave this kind of wish. The East Belfast and London groups appeared to reflect an instability, with the former increasing interest in this area and the latter showing a massive decrease. The groups were not like each other in this respect, with the Dublin and West Belfast children having a more extended view of the future and the East Belfast children tending to move in that direction over the time period.

Materialistic The Dublin and West Belfast children had similar slight (5 per cent) decreases in the percentage of wishes in this category. The East Belfast and London children again seemed less stable with a big decrease (20 per cent) for the East Belfast children and a substantial increase (10 per cent) for the London children.

Summary of findings on wishes

There were some differences between groups in the patterning of their wishes and the differences remained over time. The differences could be interpreted as expressing contrasting views about their own futures. The Dublin and West Belfast children had more extended views, were less inclined to wish for instant gratification, more inclined to give wishes indicating a willingness to invest in the future, to take into account more complex issues like the requirements of other people and society. They seemed more geared towards societal action. This more positive attitude contrasted with the views of the East Belfast children who seemed to express a more negative view of the future particularly in 1981, but indicated movement in a positive direction in 1992.

Ideal aspirations and ambitions

Differences by location

There were differences between locations. In 1981 (Figure 9.4), more Dublin (54 per cent) and London (65 per cent) children set their sights higher than the Belfast children and hoped for jobs in the professional-managerial category. The East Belfast group appeared to have least confidence in its self-efficacy and to be most disadvantaged in that they were the least ambitious in hoping for jobs requiring further training of any kind. Their possible selves appeared to be more limited than those of the other groups. The West Belfast children appeared to be possibly the most realistic - more of them than of any other group opted for skilled jobs (other than the managerial/professional category) requiring further training. This may be an indication of greater self-confidence than was found for the East Belfast children, and such realism has also been found to be linked to the acceptance of higher levels of personal responsibility and positive self-concepts. Apart from the differences in the skilled manual category, the percentages of East and West Belfast children were similar in every category except sports/popstars (more EB) in 1981.

Girls had higher aspirations than boys in both West and East Belfast in 1981 by contrast with Dublin where the reverse was the case and London where similar percentages of boys and girls aspired to jobs requiring further training.

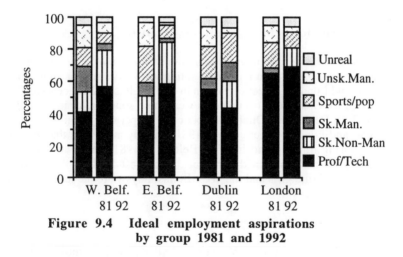

Figure 9.4   Ideal employment aspirations by group 1981 and 1992

1992   Changes and differences by location

There were very slight differences between locations again in 1992. There was a trend in all the groups for more children to want jobs with training, but the change was more dramatic in some locations than in others - for example in East Belfast - and this would tie in with the increased interest in self-development shown by the children there as found in the 'Wishes' item and the more positive view of education as found in the 'Education' item in 1992. It would seem to reflect a more positive view of the future showing perhaps greater confidence and more interest in investing in it. Girls were still ahead of boys in every location except London in aspiring to jobs requiring further training

The profiles for West and East Belfast were much more similar in 1992 than they had been in 1981 with similar percentages hoping for professional/managerial careers, and similar percentages for skilled non-manual and manual jobs. This suggests a gradual coming together of possible selves and a closer understanding of what the future might mean between the communities.

The Dublin and London children had very different profiles. London again had a far higher percentage of children with aspirations in the professional/managerial level than the other locations and fewer skilled non-manual or manual aspirants and Dublin had the lowest percentage aspiring to professional/managerial status and more skilled manual than the other groups - again a realistic attitude which could be linked to a more positive self-concept. There was an increase everywhere to a similar level in the percentages hoping for skilled non-manual work.

Trends over time

There was an increase generally in aspirations expressing a more extended and more complex view of the future, which we are characterizing as a more positive view, but this was most striking in East Belfast, where the possible selves seemed in 1992 to be more constructive than in 1981.

Realistic employment aspirations: realistic

In response to the second item on aspirations (*'But if that's not possible I wouldn't mind being a....'*), jobs that required training were more sought after in Dublin (74 per cent) and London (69 per cent) than in West Belfast (62 per cent) or East Belfast (53 per cent). Glamorous occupations were more sought after in more determined style in East Belfast and Dublin (13 per cent; 14 per cent) than in West Belfast (5 per cent) and London (7 per cent) in 1981. Slightly more girls than boys opted for jobs requiring training and in West Belfast in 1981 there was a big difference between girls and boys in this respect. The West Belfast girls were the most ambitious of all the girls and the West Belfast boys were the least ambitious of all the boys in 1981.

Trends over time and summary

'Realistic' responses in 1992 showed a similar pattern to those of the idealistic wishes in 1992. More children everywhere hoped for jobs requiring training - high status jobs; their hopes for the future were more complex and more extended than in 1981. The percentages expecting unskilled manual jobs fell everywhere but were still highest for West Belfast boys in 1992 (13 per cent), while more East Belfast boys than anyone else hoped for glamorous careers as pop stars or sports stars (18 per cent). There were huge increases in particular for the girls in East Belfast in the percentages hoping for jobs requiring training and this brought them up to the same level as the West Belfast girls who also had an increased percentage in this category. The East Belfast boys had been more ambitious than the West Belfast boys in

1981, but in 1992, while both groups had increased percentages in this category, they were on a level for ambition.

Summary The findings from both items - the ideal occupation and the more realistic occupational aspiration - showed similar trends. There was a growing recognition of the need for training for jobs; there was a residual group everywhere who wanted to be sports or pop stars; the percentages opting for unskilled jobs decreased enormously over the period. Future orientation as expressed through their aspirations became more extended and more complex for all the groups over time, but the increase was most striking for the East Belfast children. The Belfast groups became more like each other over time than they were like the Dublin or London children.

Happy people

Responses to the statement about happy people were categorized, following the model used for the wishes as follows:

A. *Non-materialistic, other-centred, complex*
    i) Service to others
    ii) Personal achievement
B. *Materialistic and simplistic*
        iii). Materialistic - owning possessions
        iv). Circular
        v). Silly.

A slightly higher percentage of Dublin children gave responses of a materialistic nature, but the percentages overall ranged from 8–12 per cent so there was not a great deal of difference between the groups in their preferred definitions. A slightly lower percentage of East Belfast children gave responses in this category but it was not statistically significant at either time point.

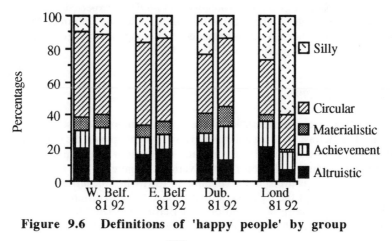

Figure 9.6 Definitions of 'happy people' by group

It seemed however that the percentages of children giving definitions within the broad categories of non-materialistic versus non-materialistic showed a slight increase for everyone over time and were quite similar across locations, except for the London children.

Slightly more boys than girls defined happiness in materialistic terms at both time points. More girls in Dublin and London than in Belfast saw happiness in terms of service to others or self-development / achievement in both 1981 and 1992.

Future orientation: 'generative' and 'non-generative' types

The rankings on the four items about wishes, aspirations and definitions of happy people were combined to give scores on 'generativity' and 'non-generativity'.

Differences in generativity by location 1981

All things being equal you would expect degrees of future orientation to be fairly equally distributed, just as IQ is fairly evenly distributed, since generally in every society you get a reasonably balanced mixture of people and orientations. But in the special circumstances of Northern Ireland, we wondered if this would be the case in 1981 and whether there would have been any changes in 1992.

In 1981 more of the Dublin and London children seemed to view the future in generative terms than the Belfast children, and in particular the East Belfast children. The percentages scoring three or more were 37 per cent (Dublin) and 47 per cent (London), but 32 per cent in West Belfast and 22 per cent in East Belfast. The mean score was higher in London and Dublin than in Belfast.

Overall significantly more of the girls than of the boys scored more than three points, but within locations there were only slight differences between the sexes in 1981. The main differences were by location (Figure 9.7).

Non-generative scores in 1981

What about the non-generative category? As might be expected, the East and West Belfast children had higher scores than the London or Dublin children and this suggested a more negative, less extended, less complex view, geared more towards instant than delayed gratification (Figure 9.8).

Findings in 1992

In 1992, there were considerable changes. All the groups increased their generativity scores. The Belfast children appeared to have caught up with the others and in 1992, there were no statistically significant differences between locations in the percentages having high scores on this variable (Figure 9.7).

This presents a contrast to the situation in 1981 when the differences were marked and the attitudes of the Belfast children seemed to be so different from those of the others. In 1992, more of the children in Belfast and Dublin were closer in their orientation towards the future than had been the case in 1981. In addition, more of those of West and East Belfast were closer than had been the case in 1981. The shift towards a higher percentage of East Belfast children having a more extended, more complex attitude was remarkable. The shifts in West Belfast (upwards), London (upwards) and Dublin (downwards) were of a lesser order. But was it due to differing degrees of movement in girls and boys?

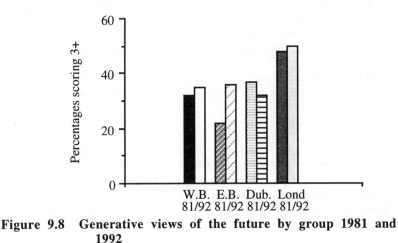

Figure 9.8   Generative views of the future by group 1981 and 1992

Girls and boys

In looking at the findings in a little more detail it would seem that the shift was largely brought about by changes in the orientation of the girls in every location. Interestingly the boys in East Belfast were the only group of boys to increase their generativity score substantially over the period. That increase brought them level with the West Belfast boys, (about 39 per cent scoring 3 or more) but it was still the case that there was a big gap between them and the girls of whom 72 per cent in West Belfast and 55 per cent in East Belfast scored 3 or more on generativity. And they were still scoring on a slightly lower level than the boys in Dublin and London.

Trends over time

The findings on generativity which combined those from the items on wishes, aspirations and happy people thus showed change over time in the future orientation and 'possible selves' of the subjects, especially for the East Belfast children. The implications of this change and possible causes will be explored in the Chapter Ten.

Summary

• Children in all locations made wishes in all the defined categories.

- A higher percentage of Dublin children than of children from elsewhere made non-materialistic type wishes in 1981 and also in 1992 when the West Belfast children had similar percentages.
- In 1981 Dublin and London children were twice as likely to make self-development wishes as the Belfast children.
- In 1992, the percentages in Dublin and West Belfast had not changed; but more children in East Belfast made this kind of wish and fewer in London.
- There was an increase in the percentage of materialistic wishes for the London and West Belfast boys only.
- West Belfast and Dublin children were more likely to make wishes concerning global issues.
- Family issues were of equal concern in all locations at both time points.
- There were differences between the groups in relation to materialistic wishes.

Aspirations and ambitions

- There was a tendency in all locations for more children to hope for jobs which required training in 1992 than in 1981.
- Girls were more ambitious than boys.
- Differences between locations were slight.
- 'Realistic' responses showed a similar pattern to that of the idealistic ambitions.

Happy People

- Around 30 per cent of boys and girls defined happy people as those who gave service to others or aimed for personal achievement.
- This percentage was stable over time.
- The percentages giving materialistic definitions were similar across locations and hardly changed over the period.

Non-materialistic orientation vs. materialistic orientation

- More of the Dublin and London children seemed to view the future in non-materialistic terms than the Belfast children in 1981, but the Belfast children had increased their scores in 1992 and scores for all four locations were similar.
- Materialistic and non-materialistic orientations were negatively correlated at a statistically significant level for all groups at all times.

Trends over time

Dublin children gave more responses indicating a positive attitude towards the usefulness of education than did the Belfast or London children and this was interpreted as showing a more constructive, more extended and more complex attitude towards the future. There appeared to be an increase in the percentages of children taking a positive view over time. More children in each location gave responses in 1992 than in 1981 relating school to either job or qualifications outcomes, except for the London children who showed least concern at both timepoints and whose mean score was lower on both counts in 1992 than in 1981. Slightly more children at each time point described education in terms of a means towards qualifications than as a means to a job and this percentage increased for some groups over the period of the study.

Some differences, particularly in the relationships between the school-related variables and variables described in earlier chapters, were found between the London children on the one hand and the Belfast and Dublin children on the other; and between the East Belfast children on the one hand and the Dublin and West Belfast children on the other, giving support to the view that there are some differences between the family and socio-environmental contexts operating in these locations which are influencing the attitudes of the children and which could matter in terms of their orientations towards the future and their views of their possible selves..

Findings on 'Generativity' showed that the Belfast children and in particular the East Belfast children has less extended, less complex and more negative views of the future in 1981 than the other groups, suggesting a different set of 'possible selves'. In 1992, however, the percentage in East Belfast scoring high on 'generativity' had greatly increased and was similar to the percentage in West Belfast.

If these findings on orientation towards the future are a reflection of adult attitudes, it is not surprising that there was no meeting of minds either between the West and East Belfast communities, or between the Belfast communities and the London and Dublin groups in 1981. The change in attitudes and values by 1992, particularly in the East Belfast groups would certainly give one cause to hope that some progress might be possible since it would seem that in 1992 the percentages of respondents who had more congruent sets of attitudes towards the future were closer than in 1981. If this reflects progress in the thinking of the communities in general, the outlook for progress must be more hopeful.

Is there an explanation for these changes? Can they be linked to other underlying trends or to other findings in the present study? Could they be part of a wider movement, reflected also in variables discussed in earlier chapters and related to wider issues in society as a whole? This possibility will be explored in Chapter Ten.

10 Conclusions: Changing times: challenges to identity?

Introduction

Could the changing times in Northern Ireland have provided a challenge to people's self-concept and personal identity and was this reflected in our findings for 12 year-olds?

In defining identity at the beginning of this study, we took a broader view of the concept than is usually adopted by researchers in Northern Ireland. Taking for granted the 'reference group orientation' or 'national identity' aspect - which has been the focus of many studies - we focused on a number of other elements underlying personal identity and the self concept. These were elements which we considered important for an understanding of people's motivation to undertake action. They included aspects of declarative knowledge which form part of social intelligence, attitudes towards education and future orientation. These were seen as underlying the ability of people to make plans, to communicate effectively, and to interact constructively on an equal basis with people of different traditions, all of which would influence the range of 'possible selves' available to them. We asked whether people in Belfast differed from those in Dublin and London in these respects and whether Catholics differed from Protestants in Belfast along those lines. We tried to determine whether there were differences in socialization experiences which might explain any differences between the groups. We presented evidence from previous research which supported the notion that in the attitudes and values of 12-year-olds we would find a reflection of the attitudes and values of the adults in their society, a reflection of their identity. We asked whether these elements were stable or whether over time, with changes in society, there was a possibility of change, not in their identity *per se* but in the meaning of their identity for them.

In this chapter we look first at the socialization experiences of our groups of 12-year-olds in 1981 and 1992 and relate those of the Belfast children to the background of events in Northern Ireland at those times. We look at their experiences within the family setting - the findings about their standard of living, their leisure activities, the extent to which their parents were salient in their lives individually and jointly, and the degree of independence/autonomy they enjoyed. We then look at the peripheral ecology of their lives - at what we found out about their extra-familial experiences - their contacts with other adults through jobs for money, club

214

attendance and travel. From these and the literature we can make cautious assumptions about their respective likely levels of self-confidence, self-efficacy and self-esteem and those of the communities in which they live.

We then moved on to investigate factors which may underlie their level of declarative knowledge and contribute to their social intelligence - their access to newspapers, television and radio and whether they showed interest in any particular type of news item. The findings on these are discussed in relation to background events before we summarize the results from our questions on their actual level of declarative knowledge, in the form of current affairs and sports. This too will have contributed to their levels of self-efficacy, self confidence and self-esteem.

Their orientation towards the future, the expression of the range of possible selves which they had developed, was explored through questions on their views about education and items which encouraged them to express wishes and ambitions. From these it was possible to deduce whether their view of the future was short-term or extended, simplistic or complex, ego-centred or other-oriented and what kinds of 'possible selves' they envisaged for themselves. The literature in this area has found associations between differing views of the future and measures of self-esteem and self-efficacy and we cautiously extrapolate from those findings to our sample. Since our study was conducted within a life-course framework and covered two timepoints in a period of great structural change in Northern Ireland, we were able to explore the possibility that changes in attitude expressed through the future orientation of the children might be linked to changes in that society in the late 80s.

Everyday family life for 12 year-olds in Belfast Dublin and London in 1981 and 1992

Standards of living

In setting up this study efforts had been made to select schools in Belfast, Dublin and London in areas of comparable socio-economic level. Northern Ireland is known to be disadvantaged economically in relation to the rest of the UK and it was felt important that this particular factor should, if possible, be controlled for in looking at the issues of interest. Frequently the socio-economic factor is seen as an explanatory, if not a confounding factor for any outcomes being investigated and we wished to look beyond that kind of explanation for any possible findings of difference between our groups. As it turned out, our Belfast samples appeared to be slightly better off materially in some respects than our groups in Dublin and London at both time points. Basic household amenities such as a telephone, books, a child's bicycle and a car were more plentiful for the East Belfast (Protestant) group than for the other groups in this study in 1981. The West Belfast (Catholic) group were the next best endowed and the London and Dublin children came lower down the scale. In 1992, the West Belfast children had caught up with the East Belfast children and the Dublin children were at a similar level to them too. Ownership of these goods was less for the 1992 London sample than for the 1981 sample.

These findings reflect the situation in the communities in Belfast from which the samples were drawn. The Continuous Household Survey (PPRU, 1985, 1993) shows that in 1983-84, with the exception of the three most commonly owned

215

items - a television, a refrigerator and a washing machine - Catholics were less likely to own each of the items on the list presented of consumer durables; these included a telephone, central heating, car or van, freezer and dishwasher. In the 1988-91 survey however, it was found that the gap was narrowing between Catholics and Protestants for all items. As we saw in Chapter Two, the economic recession had been biting hard in Britain in the late 80s, and this is reflected in the findings for our London sample; but Northern Ireland had been spared some of the worst financial cuts because of the already disadvantaged state of the economy and because of the feeling that investment in improved social conditions could be constructive in the search for an end to the conflict. The economic position of the Republic of Ireland was improving steadily throughout the 80s and this too is reflected in our findings. Information from the London schools which participated in this study confirm the picture obtained from the data of a decline in living standards in the populations served by them. The number of free school dinners, for example, issued to 12 year-olds, increased by 77 per cent in the girls' school and 63 per cent in the boys' school between 1981 and 1992.

Ready money

The mean amount of pocket money was slightly but not significantly higher in East Belfast in 1981 and more of the East Belfast children received higher amounts of pocket money than the children in the other groups. In 1992, the East Belfast children got the lowest mean amount of pocket money (though again this was not statistically significant), but more of them than of the West Belfast children were still getting higher amounts. This too can be associated with trends in society. Income levels for Catholics in Northern Ireland tend to be lower than for Protestants. Catholics experience higher levels of unemployment, and they tend to be employed in less skilled occupations; in addition their households are larger, on average, which means that the income has to stretch over more people. Figures reported by Melaugh (1995) from the Continuous Household Survey for the periods 1986-87 and 1988-91, which are close to the 'windows' of this study, show that total gross household income by religion was higher for Protestants than for Catholics, but that the gap was narrowing. This is reflected in our findings and they may also be seen as reflecting the higher incidence of job losses suffered by Protestants in the late 80s and early 90s through the smaller increase in the mean amount of pocket money available to the children. At the same time, the enhanced levels of money available to some of the children in East Belfast may be seen as an indication of more materialistic attitudes and values which was supported by the responses to other items in the questionnaire and which constituted one area of difference between them and the other groups.

Opportunities for 12 year-olds to earn money by doing jobs for money were similar in the areas of Dublin and Belfast in which the study took place at both timepoints. There was a trend in 1981 for slightly fewer opportunities to be availed of by the East Belfast children, but they had caught up with the others in 1992. A much lower percentage in London had done jobs for money. The mean amount of money earned per job was highest in Dublin, with East Belfast next in 1981 and 1992. The London children had the same level of mean earnings in 1992 as the East Belfast children and the West Belfast children had the lowest amount. All groups had increased their mean earnings per job over time.

Cultural differences could explain the lower percentage of London children having jobs - the ethnic composition of the participating schools in 1981 was about 40 per cent non-Caucasian in the girls' school and 55 per cent in the boys' school. This had increased in both schools in 1992 (55 per cent in the girls' school; 65 per cent in the boys' school). Different attitudes towards child development (as found in different ethnic groups by Goodnow, 1986) could explain why fewer London children did jobs for money. Or perhaps there were simply fewer opportunities in the areas where they lived. It looked however, as though the girls in London were holding their own - as many of them had earned money from jobs in 1992 as in 1981; whereas opportunities for boys actually declined. The Dublin children had more opportunities to work for people outside the home and this was probably the reason for their enhanced earnings. And it is interesting that the East Belfast children earned so much, although not so many of them were actually working. The West Belfast children had the lowest earnings, although their job opportunities were nearly as good as those of the Dublin children.

Working for other people, whatever about the kind of money earned, would have had implications for the development of autonomy, self-efficacy, self-confidence and self-esteem and it looks as though the London children were least well off in this respect and the Dublin and West Belfast children might have had a better start, with the support of their parents, while the East Belfast children were slightly behind in 1981, but had caught up in 1992.

Leisure activities

We found more differences between girls and boys than between the locations overall when we looked at how they spent their free time and the kinds of books and television programmes they enjoyed. The 'Troubles' in Belfast did not seem to be a constraint and all the children had similar opportunities for social interaction with their peers. Trends over time were similar in all locations, though they were different for girls and boys. Homework or quiet activities, seeing friends and watching television were important for all in the afternoons and evenings, but boys were more involved in sports activities and this involvement increased in 1992 for both girls and boys. On Saturdays, girls everywhere liked to go into town and look at the shops or be with friends and this increased over time. Boys did this too, but many more of them than of the girls took part in sports activities. Sports participation by girls increased slightly over the period. Visiting relations as an activity decreased over the time period and church-going on Sundays was mentioned by high percentages everywhere in 1981 but not at all in 1992. This should not necessarily be interpreted as meaning that none of them went to church, but rather that it was not a salient aspect of Sundays for them. A decline in church attendance has been noted by other researchers in all the locations of this study.

Books and television preferences showed slight differences between locations in 1981 and these had largely leveled out by 1992. Differences were greater between girls and boys and these remained stable. Girls read slightly more popular fiction than boys and in 1992 more teenage romance; boys read more comics than girls in 1981 and more non-fiction. In television viewing, children's television programmes were viewed by more 12 year-olds in 1981 than in 1992. Soap operas were more popular especially with girls in 1992; boys watched more sport and this increased in

217

1992. The patterns of reading and viewing preferences converged for the different locations over the time period, though the differences by sex remained stable.

The findings here suggested that the children in the sample had fairly similar experiences as far as leisure time activities were concerned and that they were becoming more alike over time. This could have implications for the development of personal identity at the different timepoints of the study.

Parental salience/child autonomy.

Parental salience for the children was investigated by looking at eleven situations within the home where children and parents would be expected to interact and asking the children to say who took the lead in these situations. The situations were classified as nurturing or controlling and the data made it possible to establish whether Mum, Dad, both parents jointly, or the child in question took responsibility. Nurture/support and control have been found to be very important for the development of the self-concept and in the context of the Northern Ireland 'Troubles' it was of interest to establish whether levels of nurturance and control were different there. If so we could have part of an explanation for the resilience of the children.

Nurturance and control

We found that there were differences on nurturance between the sexes by location in 1981. Girls in Belfast and London were similarly high on nurturance; the Dublin girls had less. Boys in Belfast were favoured more than boys in London and Dublin. In 1992, levels of nurturance had fallen everywhere, but girls in Belfast and London were still higher than girls in Dublin and boys in Belfast and also in London this time were higher than boys in Dublin. This suggests that the children in Belfast were in fact getting more support especially in 1981, than the children in London and Dublin. We do not know whether this was also the case before the 'Troubles' or whether it developed in response to the situation, but it is possible that it made a difference to the feelings of security of the children and contributed to their resilience. The lower level of nurturance in 1992 may reflect the lessening of the violence as well as the general trend, obvious from the groups in Dublin and London, towards less interaction between parents and children in these situations.

Controlling behaviours were exemplified as decision-making about television-viewing, radio listening, giving pocket money and driving the car. We found that parents in West Belfast and Dublin were more controlling than parents in East Belfast and London in 1981 especially with regard to television viewing. In 1992 however, there were substantial changes which affected Dublin and, to a greater degree, West Belfast where the percentage of children who could decide on their own television viewing increased to the same level as in East Belfast. The same differences did not obtain for radio listening. The findings on television viewing provides another example of a leveling out of differences between the groups over time.

Sources of pocket money changed over time in all locations, perhaps a reflection of changing family structures. They were different in 1981, with more children in London getting money from Mum only, and children in Belfast and Dublin being

218

more likely to get it from Dad. In 1992, the position in London had not changed, but the percentages being given money by Mum only increased in Belfast and Dublin and those being given it by Dad only decreased. This could mean increased father absence, or increased father unemployment, or it could result from more mothers being in employment and having some extra money to dole out. The percentage everywhere receiving money from both parents increased over the time period. This could mean more broken homes, with both parents contributing separately, or it could mean more homes where both parents were employed and both were contributing.

Salience of parents

The increasing independence of women is seen also in the data on driving the family car. Although fathers were most likely to drive it in each of our four locations in 1981, the percentages who said that Dad alone drove the family car decreased over time, as did the percentages saying that Mum alone drove. In 1992 a more common reply was that both parents drove the family car. This does not tell us about family structures however, as parents living together might have driven the same car and parents living separately might have had a car each. The trends were similar in all locations, except that Dublin had the highest percentage of homes where both parents drove in 1981 and again in 1992.

In terms of the salience of parents individually, Mum was more salient in Belfast, both West and East, than in London or Dublin, at both timepoints. The salience rating decreased everywhere in 1992 though it remained higher in East Belfast than elsewhere. Dad was much less salient than Mum everywhere and the differences between locations were not so striking as for Mum. Salience of Dad decreased slightly everywhere except in West Belfast and the East Belfast ratings were similar to West Belfast in 1992, having been higher in 1981.

Parents were most salient in West Belfast and Dublin in 1981 - measured by the number of responses citing both Mum and Dad as being responsible for particular actions - and joint parental salience increased everywhere in 1992 except in London where it fell. Even taking into account the finding that joint parental salience was lower than that for either parent individually this could be seen as suggesting that more of the children in the samples from Belfast and Dublin than in London were living in intact family situations, with both parents available for nurturance and control. Although this would undoubtedly have an influence on their self-concept and range of 'possible selves' we do not, unfortunately, have accurate data on the actual family situations of the children and are not in a position to estimate whether or not it was important in the context of the issues being investigated in this study.

The Dublin children were highest on Independence and Choice at both timepoints and the other three groups had similar ratings. These increased everywhere between 1981 and 1992, but least of all in London.

Implications for self-concept

The findings in this section suggest that Belfast children were more protected and that mothers were more salient there than for the children elsewhere, especially in 1981. This should have resulted in higher levels of self-esteem and a more stable self-concept for them than for the children in Dublin and London and could have contributed to their resilience. It could also result in more conformity, a reduced awareness of personal responsibility and hence lower levels of self-efficacy and self confidence. And the effects of high nurturance may have been moderated by what we found about controlling behaviours. The West Belfast and Dublin children were more tightly controlled than the others. High levels of control have been found to be linked to high self-esteem in Protestant males but to low self-esteem in Catholic males. These findings suggest that both of Belfast groups could have had low self-esteem because of the different régimes of control. The loosening of control for the Catholics in West Belfast and Dublin in 1992, may have resulted in higher self-esteem for them at that point, but this could have been countered by the lesser degree of nurturance which might have been countered in turn by the greater degree of independence and choice. It would seem that we must look at factors other than parental control and nurturance to get clues about the state of their self-concept and possible causes for change.

Reaching out

Opportunities to develop self-efficacy, self-confidence and self esteem through experience of social situations away from the family were explored through items assessing the survival skills of the subjects, the kinds of commitment opportunities they had and the extent to which they availed of them and also the extent to which they interacted with people outside the family through doing jobs for money, attending clubs and going on holiday.

Survival skills

Survival skills measured included using a public telephone and a telephone book, pouring tea and peeling potatoes, and traveling alone in a bus or taxi. Composite scores showed no differences between groups or over timepoints, but when the items were looked at separately, there was a difference on one item which could be significant. The West Belfast and Dublin children had had more experience of traveling alone in a bus or taxi than the East Belfast and London children. This could have been due to the fact that more of the sample families in London and East Belfast than in Dublin and West Belfast were car-owners and perhaps they transported their children themselves rather than allowing them to travel alone. It was a little surprising to find how much more independently mobile the West Belfast children were than the East Belfast children, even in 1981 when there were a lot of street disturbances. This finding could be interpreted as suggesting different attitudes on the part of the West and East Belfast parents. The former were perhaps more inclined to let life go on, encouraging the children to continue normal activities, giving them the opportunity to develop autonomous coping skills and take responsibility for their actions, while the latter appeared to be more protective, perhaps kept their children at home more and did not let them have the same freedom to begin to get involved in socially responsible actions and to develop an internal locus of control.

In 1981, Dublin children scored highest on the composite variable 'Commitment' and the London and Belfast children had similar scores. Girls everywhere did more household chores than boys, but both girls and boys did less in 1992. Analysis of individual items showed that the East Belfast children had less experience of household chores and of shopping for the family than the West Belfast children, though more of them had pets that they cared for. This finding could also be a reflection of greater determination on the part of the West Belfast families to carry on life as usual and encourage the children to undertake chores such as shopping which ultimately would increase their autonomy. This could mean a higher level of self-esteem for the West Belfast children, in that more of them had access to a greater variety of social situations. There were changes over time and in 1992, the East Belfast children were second highest to the West Belfast children on this variable, suggesting that they were being given more opportunities then than in 1981 to have experiences which would increase their self-efficacy and self-confidence. Both of these groups showed less of a decrease than the others in the scores on Commitment and this could be a reflection of tighter family control.

East Belfast children had the highest membership of clubs in 1981 and 1992, but they were not the most frequent attenders. More of the West Belfast children attended more frequently in 1981 and again in 1992 although attendances declined for all four groups. Basic travel opportunities without the family were similar for West and East Belfast children in 1981, but when factors such as age, length of time away, destination and number of times away were taken into account the East Belfast children were less advantaged than any of the other groups in 1981. This indicates again a different attitude on the part of the East Belfast parents, a more protective one perhaps, which could have the effect of making the children feel more secure, but could also inhibit the development of self-efficacy skills and the self-confidence and self-esteem that would go with that. It could also have the effect of encouraging conformity to parental values and discouraging independent thought. In 1992 however, there had been changes which resulted in fewer opportunities for everyone, but there seemed to be also changes in the attitudes of the parents which meant that the East Belfast children had similar scores on this variable to the West Belfast children and were having similar opportunities to spend time away from home.

The findings in this section suggest differences between the East and West Belfast parents in 1981 in their attitudes towards allowing their children to reach out to the community beyond the family. The East Belfast parents appeared to be more protective and restricting in 1981, but they had relaxed a little in 1992; they were encouraging more commitment from the children and allowing them to take advantage of more travel opportunities, to be more self-directed, so that in 1992 there were fewer differences between them and the West Belfast sample.

Access to information

Over 95 percent of the children in all the groups said that they looked at a newspaper regularly in 1981 and this decreased slightly in all locations in 1992. But still over 93 per cent of the children everywhere read newspapers regularly except in

London where there was a bigger decline. In 1981, over 70 per cent in all groups claimed to have a newspaper within the past 24 hours; this had fallen to under 50 percent everywhere except Dublin in 1992. The majority of children tended to read newspapers produced in their own location. Both West and East Belfast children read papers produced for the 'other side' but there was a slight tendency for more West than East Belfast children to do so; British tabloids were read by more children in all four places in 1992 than in 1981 and the London children read little else.

Even higher percentages watched television news regularly and had looked at the news on television within the past 24 hours. Although there was a decrease of about 10 percent in that number in 1992, it was still higher than those who had looked at a newspaper within that time. Between 69 per cent and 91 per cent of the children listened to the news on the radio regularly in 1981 and this too declined everywhere, but to a lesser extent in Dublin, in 1992. Belfast children were more avid readers and watchers of news than the children in Dublin and London at both timepoints, though their preoccupation declined in line with the decrease in interest in the other locations over the period of the study. Dublin children were more stable in their level of interest than any of the other groups.

Items of interest in the media

When asked to recall an item they had read in the paper or seen on the television news, Belfast children were more likely than the others to respond with an item of current affairs. especially in 1981. More of them recalled such items from television news than from the newspaper. Within the category of current affairs the Belfast children were more likely than the other children to respond with a specific item of local salience from newspapers. Dublin and London children appeared to have more general interests. Locally relevant items from television news were recalled first by children from all locations, but more of the Belfast children did so in 1981. In 1992, the picture was somewhat different. Fewer children everywhere mentioned current affairs items as what they recalled from newspapers and the decrease was especially striking in both East and West Belfast. In addition fewer of the items recalled by the Belfast children from newspapers or television were related to local NI issues. This could be a reflection of the quieter times in the early 90s compared to the early 80s. But they, especially the East Belfast children, did not appear to have developed interests in broader issues to the same extent as the Dublin and London children, although there had been a slight increase in the non-local newspapers read by them.

Implications for self-concept

The dominance of local issues for the Belfast children and their almost exclusive preoccupation with them is understandable, given the situation in Northern Ireland and the coverage by local media. When they are compared to the children in Dublin and London, it is clear that, especially in 1981, fewer of the Belfast children were taking an interest in events beyond their immediate environment. This finding could be partly due to the selection of events presented in the local newspapers and on television, although other factors, at home and in school as well as in the community, could determine the kinds of news items which attracted their attention. It is possible that because of the local situation they were being restricted in the kinds of declarative knowledge to which they were being exposed by the media; because of this their cognitive processing skills were not being given the same opportunities to develop as was happening for the children in Dublin and London. Lack of familiarity in dealing with different kinds of information would make them less sure of themselves, less self-confident, and this would have implications for their self-concept and for their effectiveness in communicating positively with others. This may have been a problem especially for the East Belfast sample, who relied more on television than on newspapers for their information for although television may give a broader exposure, as found in this study, the resulting knowledge base is shallower than that obtained from newspapers (Robinson and Davis, 1990).

Knowledge of current affairs

Declarative knowledge is seen as an important component of social intelligence - a fundamental part of identity as defined by Cantor and Kihlstrom (1987). This means knowledge about other people and social situations, which helps individuals make sense of social events. In the present study this was operationalized as knowledge of current affairs, the score awarded to participants on the basis of their responses to 10 general knowledge questions about political matters and 10 general knowledge questions about sport.

The results showed that the groups were stable with regard to their positions in relation to each other over time. The Belfast and London children scored lower than the Dublin children at both time points for both political matters and sports questions. Most interesting was the finding that the East Belfast children had consistently lower scores than the children from West Belfast and that they were more similar to the London children than to the other groups in both 1981 and 1992. Level of knowledge was not enhanced even where questions were locally relevant. This seems to be telling us something about different frames of mind, different attitudes towards acquiring this kind of knowledge which differentiate between the children in East Belfast and London on the one hand and those in West Belfast and Dublin on the other. The implications of the lower scores for the individuals concerned could include lower self-esteem, a feeling of less self-efficacy, of uncertainty about basic facts, a difficulty in acquiring more information since the base-line is so low and in planning strategies since the knowledge base is so poor. This would inevitably result in weaknesses in communication skills and problems in relating effectively with people who have different levels of knowledge especially if the 'other side' are better informed. This in turn feeds into the cycle of low self-esteem eventually leading to discouragement.

Can we find an explanation for the lower level of declarative knowledge in the East Belfast and London children in any of the other variables on which they differed from the Dublin and West Belfast children?

Socio-economic variables and declarative knowledge

We asked first whether the better-off children were less, or more, knowledgeable about current affairs than the less well-off. The better-off might have the time and energy, or feel that it was good to become involved for status reasons, or on the other hand, they might feel that there was no need for them to become involved, they were doing alright. The less well-off might not have the time or energy to become interested, but on the other hand they might feel that it would be in their interest to become knowledgeable.

It will be recalled that the East Belfast children were the best off and the Dublin children were the worst off when household possessions only were taken into account; their mean scores on 'Goods' alone in 1981 would seem to have been inversely related to their scores on declarative knowledge. If that were the main underlying explanation, it should have remained constant, but that was not the case. The London children were worst off in 1992 and the West Belfast children had caught up with the East Belfast children. If household possessions were inversely related to declarative knowledge you would have expected the London children to have the highest scores in 1992 and the West Belfast children to be similar to the East Belfast children whereas the scores on declarative knowledge remained in the same rank order as in 1981.

The Dublin and Belfast children were not significantly different on 'Goods Plus' - when money entered into it as well. If this variable were related to the outcome we would expect similar scores from them on declarative knowledge, but the Dublin children were ahead. And when correlations were calculated it turned out that there was no significant relationship for individuals in the groups between high scores on for the various categories of 'Goods' - household possessions, possessions plus money, possessions plus amount gained and acquired - and high scores on current affairs. Interest in acquiring general knowledge was not directly linked, as measured by correlational procedures with socio-economic status as measured in this study.

Salience of parents / autonomy

Dad Salience of Dad appeared to have some relevance for level of declarative knowledge. Dad was more salient for the East Belfast and London children in 1981 and their level of declarative knowledge was lower than that for the children in West Belfast and Dublin. This might suggest that a more dominant Dad was actually off-putting for these children in terms of the development of their social intelligence. The only significant correlation was, however, for the West Belfast children for whom Dad had not been so salient, suggesting a positive relationship between involvement of father and general knowledge scores in that group. The correlation was not significant however in 1992, even though salience of Dad was similar then in West Belfast to what it had been in 1981. And there were no significant relationships in the other locations where salience of Dad had decreased..

Mum The salience of mum was not related to declarative knowledge for any group at either time point.

Parents Salience of parents jointly was highest in West Belfast and Dublin in 1981 and also in 1992. It looks as though children in Dublin and West Belfast found their parents as a couple more salient than the children in East Belfast and London; in real terms, the implications were that this may have meant more interactions involving both parents together perhaps including conversation about issues of the day, a feeling of being more comfortable with such issues and eventually higher levels of declarative knowledge. The correlations with declarative knowledge were positive but not significant and appeared to be stable and as such might be worth further investigation. However, the 'scores' for parental salience were low in all groups, lower than for Dad, and this too should be borne in mind.

Independence The groups retained their ranked positions on 'Independence' between 1981 and 1992 while all registered an increase. The Dublin children were consistently highest and in 1981 the Belfast and London children had similar scores; in 1992 however, the East and West Belfast children were still quite close, while the London children had dropped behind. This would suggest that independence/autonomy might be related to declarative knowledge, but this proposition works only for the Dublin and London children, and not for the Belfast children. If more independence is associated with greater declarative knowledge, we would expect the West Belfast children to be scoring higher than the East Belfast children on the independence scale and this was not the case. In fact when correlations were calculated, there were no significant relationships for any group between declarative knowledge and independence. But there could be some other mediating variables which depend on autonomy/independence and then directly influence declarative knowledge. Or, it is possible that although on an individual level independence/autonomy did not correlate with declarative knowledge, there was a general climate which went with the greater autonomy in Dublin and West Belfast and which encouraged the acquisition of knowledge in these areas.

Reaching out and declarative knowledge

It might be thought that contact with other people would be a good way of increasing declarative knowledge, but on the other hand it may be a case of the blind leading the blind even further astray. It did not look as though membership of clubs and attendance were important either way - the Belfast children had the highest levels of membership and attendance, and London children had the lowest. As far as travel was concerned, the London children had the highest mean composite score and more of them also had higher scores on travel. The East Belfast children seemed a little more disadvantaged on this variable than the West Belfast children, especially in 1981, but the Dublin children had lower scores still. It could be that it was important for the Belfast children, but not for the Dublin children or London children - lower scores on travel did not mean that the Dublin children had lower scores on declarative knowledge, nor did higher scores on travel mean that the London children had higher scores on declarative knowledge.

Access to information and level of declarative knowledge

If *access to information* were all that counted we might expect the Belfast groups to be equal to one another and to have higher scores than the Dublin and London children, since they had scored higher on 'News' in 1981. But, although 'News' was significantly related to current affairs scores for all groups except the London children at one timepoint or the other, the fact that the Belfast children had higher scores did not appear to ensure that their actual knowledge base would also be good.

Interest in current affairs - scored on the basis of the kinds of items remembered from both television and newspapers - was highest in Belfast in 1981 and again in

1992. East and West Belfast were close at both timepoints. One possible contributory factor to the higher scores of the Dublin and West Belfast children for current affairs could lie in the finding, already mentioned, that more of the West Belfast and Dublin children than of those from East Belfast and London gleaned their current affairs awareness from newspapers; in addition where the Dublin and West Belfast children were able to name specific items, more of the East Belfast and London children claimed to have read 'headlines'. The overall decline in scores could be linked to the increase in tabloid newspaper reading among all groups.

The most promising explanations from the data on socialization for their higher scores on declarative knowledge and hence putative higher self-confidence and self-esteem and ease in communicating in areas requiring declarative knowledge seem to be the greater use of newspapers by the Dublin and West Belfast children, and their greater interest in non-local events on television than the other two groups, and also perhaps the broader experiences of travel compared to the East Belfast children. Although the findings from the other socialization data would seem to lead us to expect that the East Belfast children would be at least as high in self-esteem as the others, and possibly higher - they were better off at the basic material level, they were more likely to be members of clubs - it is possible that the kind of self-esteem engendered by these factors was not sufficient to cover for their lack of social intelligence and so they would end up at a disadvantage. It could also be suggested that the kind of self-esteem and self-confidence needed for negotiations of the kind which have been attempted for the past 25 years would need to have a firm basis in declarative knowledge. Lack of this could go some way towards explaining the slow progress.

As noted earlier, however, family interactions do not take place in a vacuum, but are firmly embedded in a societal context. Might there be factors from within the wider spectrum of societal functioning which might explain the lower scores of the East Belfast children on declarative knowledge and hence, social intelligence ?

Explanations from social structures

One possibility is the remoteness of the political system for the children in Northern Ireland - but in that case the West Belfast children should have had equal scores with the East Belfast children and we would not have to explain why the West Belfast children had higher scores. Another possibility is psychological and arises from the socio-ecological background - the kinds of events outlined in Chapter Two. Not having had the responsibility of making decisions which would be questioned and which would have real meaning, even during the Stormont régime - when, for example, their financial needs were met with little questioning - some of the unionists (Protestants), as represented here by the children in East Belfast, may somehow lack the tradition and experience in their folk-memory of fact-gathering and dispassionate weighing-up of information - they never saw the need to do that. Neither did they feel the need to know the facts about how government functioned or details of related organizations as they felt secure in their membership of the United Kingdom and indeed had invested so much emotional energy in that membership.

Perhaps it is an example of the perception of an external locus of control for the community influencing attitudes and practices within the family. The counterpart in socialization practices may perhaps be seen in the findings of this study that the

East Belfast parents were slightly more protective of their children and appeared to give them fewer opportunities to develop responsibility for their own actions - an internal locus of control - even in small ways, like traveling alone by bus or taxi, doing shopping and housework for the family and going on holiday without the family, especially in 1981. This reliance on an external locus of control would eventually promote distrust in politics, as may be reflected in the scores of the East Belfast children on declarative knowledge. The West Belfast population, although also ruled from London, historically did not accept it or perceive it as a locus of control to the same extent, hence in their socialization practices the greater encouragement of activities promoting an internal locus of control and their greater independence in seeking out and retaining information of the kind asked for here.

The knowledge level of the East Belfast children in current affairs could also reflect an attitude of disinterest in politics on the part of the adults in their environment who may have been disillusioned by the events leading up to and following the prorogation of Stormont and perhaps had a feeling of powerlessness which resulted in them switching off from information and discussion in the area of politics. They lack proper representation, they have little or no control over decisions or policies, there is little accountability; so they are metaphorically washing their hands of it. This explanation would also fit the case of the London children, mostly the children of immigrants who do not feel part of the system and probably wish to return eventually to their own countries, so have no interest in learning about the system in Britain. The relative remoteness of the political system for the London children compared to the Dublin children parallels that of the Belfast children, and might also explain their scores, but is not sufficient to explain the higher scores of the West Belfast children .

But the fact that the lower scores in declarative knowledge found for the children extended even to sport, suggests that it is not simply items of political interest, but everyday knowledge in general that is affected by this not-wanting-to-know attitude. Intelligence would not seem to be a factor (Gattigin, 1980), and as we saw above, socio-economic measures do not appear to be related to this finding either. It could therefore be a sign of opting out of the system, a desire not to become involved; by not wanting to find out, and therefore not knowing about the political scene, they are indicating that they are not interested in developing themselves politically. Perhaps there is a fear of the responsibility involved and how it might change them. It could be proposed that they are subconsciously keeping themselves aloof from possible solutions by simply not finding out the basics.

The higher scores of the West Belfast and Dublin children on the other hand, both girls and boys, could be due to a subconscious awareness on their part, or even the influence of a conscious awareness in the adults around them that they need to know the system if they are going to be effective members of it. History has shown them that it can be to their advantage to be proactive and that it is possible to make progress if you become knowledgeable and actively involved. Having had to struggle for longer than the Protestants in Northern Ireland, the Catholics, as the underdogs, probably got to know and understand the system better. We saw earlier also that more of the West Belfast children tended to read a wider variety of newspapers than the children in East Belfast. This would give them access to different kinds of information and different perspectives. It is also possible - though we do not have supporting data - that there may be more talk about current events in the West Belfast homes and perhaps the schools in our sample than in those of East Belfast.

Attitudes towards education

We found that the Dublin children had a more positive view of education at each timepoint - more of them saw it as a means to employment, more of them saw it as a means to self-development than the Belfast children or the London children. There was a difference then between the groups in their general attitude towards education. There was not much difference between the percentages in East and West Belfast at either time point, though the tendency was for more of the West Belfast children to have those attitudes in 1981. In 1992 the percentages everywhere who saw school as a means to employment had fallen. They fell less in East Belfast than elsewhere.

There was a difference between the Belfast children and the Dublin children (and the London children scored lower each time than the Belfast children) in their view of what education was all about, and there were two kinds of differences between the West and East Belfast children. The West Belfast children had a generally more positive attitude towards education, but the East Belfast children continued to see it as a means towards employment, suggesting a less extended view of the future with a desire for more instant gratification, when this tendency had declined everywhere else.

Attitudes towards education related to other variables

Socio-economic measures   The attitude which saw school as a means to employment did not seem to be related at a significant level to socio-economic status as measured by goods or goods plus money in the present study for the Belfast and Dublin children at either time point. Being better or worse off materially did not appear to be associated with attitude to school either positively or negatively for them. But for the London children there was a positive and significant relationship in 1992. This suggests that socio-economic level has an effect only in conjunction with other socio-cultural variables and this is shown also when we look at the relationship between the attitude which saw schools as a means towards self-development through qualifications and 'Goods'. These were significantly correlated for the Dublin children in 1981 and 1992 and for the London children in 1992 - the better off children were more likely to want qualifications. But there was no relationship for the Belfast children - seeing school as a means towards qualifications was not related to material possessions for either group of them at either timepoint.

Salience of parents   The findings did not really give us a consistent pattern of the importance of parental salience for attitudes towards education for any group except that it did not appear to be directly related for the Dublin children, was fairly strongly related for the London children and irregularly related for the Belfast children (for example salience of Mum was negatively related to a positive view of education for East Belfast girls).

Degree of independence/autonomy was positively related to seeing school as a means to a job in 1981 for all groups and to a lesser extent for all groups except London in 1992. This variable was significantly related to seeing school as a means towards self-development for the West Belfast and Dublin children in 1981 and for the London children only in 1992. It was not related for the East Belfast children - there was no significant relationship for them between independence/autonomy and wanting qualifications, although there was a relationship between independence and seeing school as a means to a job for them. This appears to indicate a different attitude towards the future for them.

More of the East Belfast children saw education mainly as a means to a job - which would lead to possession of material goods perhaps in the shorter term than if they waited to get further qualifications - and they were fairly consistent in this attitude. Maybe they needed this as security more than the children in the other locations who were more likely to be willing to wait a while, invest in themselves, develop their potential. In addition, there was a greater decrease in the percentages of children in the other locations who viewed education in this way in 1992 - as if they were beginning to see, realistically, that school would not perhaps lead to the kinds of jobs they wanted, or to the kind of life they wanted and something more would be necessary.

The attitude of the East Belfast children changed less and may reflect their social history - school did get you a job in the old days, it was what you expected, often by means of a network. School did not lead directly to a job to the same extent in Dublin or in West Belfast but in O'Connor's words 'Catholic schools have traditionally been the community's agent of upward mobility' (1993, p. 318); Catholics had to think a bit more about how best to prepare themselves to improve their position; it was not a case of finding a job straight after school, they had to try harder and the attitudes of the children in the sample probably reflect this. So while the Catholics in West Belfast were dependent also on the British economy, like the Protestants in East Belfast, their place in the local society shaped their attitudes, towards the uses of education for example, in quite different ways and this could have implications for their joint future.

The Dublin children would seem to reflect the attitudes of the West Belfast children to an even stronger degree. Looking at the societal background we could propose that their history of coping with independence as an Irish state had shown the need for education and for self-development and the value of qualifications. It also shows more willingness to assume responsibility for the future by investing in further qualifications rather than looking for instant rewards through a job directly on leaving school. And it will be remembered that this was not related to lack of material possessions - the East Belfast children were better off at the basic level, but there were no differences between the Dublin and Belfast children when money variables came into it; so it wasn't as if the Dublin children in this sample were worse off and therefore had greater ambitions. There was in fact a positive correlation for them however as noted above between 'Goods Plus' and seeing school as a means towards qualifications; and this was not the case for either Belfast group.

Salience of school could also have been a factor. In the present study we could get some estimation of how school impinged on their lives generally and whether it was a compartmentalized factor through the ways in which they spent their leisure time - how much time was spent on homework - and the extent to which they involved parents in school activities, specifically homework. Would the Belfast, London and Dublin children differ along these lines?

As we saw in Chapter Four, school and its obligations seemed to loom larger in the lives of the Dublin children than of the children elsewhere. Although 'Homework' was the first ranked activity in the afternoons and evenings in all locations, the percentages who mentioned it were far higher in Dublin than in either part of Belfast or London and they were higher for boys in West Belfast than in East Belfast in 1981 and for both girls and boys in West Belfast than in East Belfast in 1992. This would mean that school was more a part of their lives for the Dublin children and the West Belfast children and seen as fairly central, taking up a lot of time. This could have been a contributing factor to their attitudes towards its usefulness.

As far as getting help was concerned, the West Belfast children appeared to consult both parents more than the other groups, and the East Belfast children consulted Dad (who was not very salient in other respects) more than the others, especially in 1992 (maybe more Dads were around then, due to unemployment). This suggests that the ethos in the West Belfast families as a whole was more geared towards an interest in education, than it was for those in East Belfast, where Dad was perhaps more dominant. Both parents in West Belfast were more involved in keeping up with what the children were doing at school and this may have contributed to the more positive attitudes of the children.

The Dublin children also had higher levels of joint parental salience than the East Belfast and London children, but in their case there were no significant statistical correlations between parental salience and attitudes towards education, so their greater interest in school, as a group, would not appear to have been directly associated with that factor. Here again, the wider societal ethos may have been important. Within the Northern Ireland context, parental salience was perhaps more important for these attitudes than it was in Dublin where there were possibly other factors influencing attitudes of this kind to a greater extent than in Belfast. The East Belfast children had less joint parental interest, and perhaps the ethos of their working class community inclined them to be less aware of the benefits that education could bring, since traditionally it had been possible to find employment within the trades and industries without much stress on educational qualifications. The greater parental interest and involvement and motivation for upwards mobility could explain the greater achievement orientation found in other studies for Catholic children and the findings in the present study of a more positive attitude towards school for the West Belfast children.

The findings on declarative knowledge/social intelligence and on attitudes towards education show that the East Belfast and London children scored lower on these variables at both time points than the Dublin or West Belfast children. This suggests that the East Belfast and London children may have less self-esteem and less self-confidence; it could explain why the East Belfast and West Belfast communities have problems communicating. An additional complicating factor is that the Catholics have traditionally seen themselves as having less self-esteem, being 'second-class citizens' (O'Connor, 1993 p. 349), and feeling inferior (O'Connor, 1993, p. 176) and have been perceived by others also as having less self-esteem and and this can be justified as arising from the established facts that they are more disadvantaged than the Protestants within Northern Ireland (Jardine 1995, Melaugh, 1995).

The findings from this study on social intelligence and attitudes towards education suggest that the Catholics in West Belfast may have more basic self-esteem and self-confidence than the Protestants in East Belfast and this will contribute to their self-concept and personal identity. Similar impressions are reported by O'Connor (1993) who is careful to chart and to emphasize the complexity of Catholics' feelings along a number of dimensions. The reluctance of Protestants to come to terms with the present situation (O'Connor, 1993, P. 194) and to engage themselves in the question of identity (O'Connor, 1993, p. 370, Dunlop, 1995, Kinahan, 1995) provide additional illustrations of a lower level of self-confidence and could, it may be suggested, be based on the dependency syndrome with lack of experience of autonomy and reliance on an external locus of control as part of the background.

However, we must ask now to what extent these findings reflect individuals' general orientation towards the future. This is what really matters, as the future of their society depends on it. We must look therefore at their commitment to societal action, to socially responsible behaviour, to investment in the future as distinct from the present and determine whether future orientation is as stable across time in the groups in East and West Belfast, Dublin and London as the findings on social intelligence and attitudes towards education appeared to be, or whether there is hope of change.

Orientation towards the future

The composite variables 'generativity' and 'non-generativity' assembled from responses to items about wishes, aspirations and a definition of 'happy people' showed firstly that in 1981 the London and Dublin children scored higher than the Belfast children, and West Belfast children scored higher than East Belfast children on generativity, or a willingness to invest in the future. The situation was reversed, as might be expected, for non-generativity, or a more materialistic view. The highest scorers here came from East Belfast, followed by West Belfast, then Dublin and London on an equal level. This supports the idea previously expressed of a more short-term, less confident view of the future, but one based more on materialistic values, a legacy of the dependency syndrome and of economic disadvantage again, for the Belfast children in 1981. But the finding that it showed to a greater extent in the East Belfast children is interesting. They were not, as a community, so economically disadvantaged as the West Belfast people - why should they be so materialistic, so self-centered? Whatever the explanation, with such differing perspectives on the future, it is not surprising that dialogue about it is difficult. Can we find an explanation from their socialization experiences?

Socio-economic measures and future orientation

The East Belfast children were the best off in terms of 'Goods' and the Dublin children were the worst off. You might therefore expect the East Belfast children to be less materialistic (because they already had the goods) and the West Belfast and Dublin children to be more materialistic in their outlook towards the future (because they did not have the goods). But other factors obviously come into the equation for that was not what was found, but rather something approaching the reverse. The pattern of correlations also showed that it was not a simple relationship. The West Belfast children were lower than the East Belfast children on the variable 'Goods' and slightly higher than but very close to the Dublin children. In 1981 'Goods' variables were negatively related to generativity for West Belfast children - the more goods they had the more materialistic they were and the less generative their future orientation. For the Dublin children, on the other hand, there was a positive relationship between 'Goods' and generativity - the more goods they had the more generative they were. And they were in fact slightly worse off on 'Goods' than the West Belfast children. The relationship between 'Goods' and associated variables and generativity was not significant for the East Belfast or London children. There would seem to be more to it than simple possession of goods.

Parental salience and autonomy: relationship to generativity

These measures might be expected to show some relationship with future orientation. The Dublin children had been highest on Autonomy measures in 1981, followed by East Belfast, then London and then West Belfast. The ranked order of the group mean scores on independence did not correspond to the rank order for generativity and in fact the correlation with Independence/autonomy was significant in 1981 only for the West Belfast children who, in 1981, had scored the lowest on independence. The more independent the child the more likely he or she was to have a generative orientation. There was for the most part, no statistical relationship between parental salience variables - Dad, Mum or Parents - and future orientation for any of the groups. The one exception was the finding of a negative relationship between salience of Dad and generativity for the Dublin children. This provides a parallel to the finding for East Belfast and London children of a negative relationship between salience of Dad and declarative knowledge and for the East Belfast girls of a negative relationship between salience of Mum and attitude towards education. These may all have been chance associations and perhaps an artefact of the sample.

Experiences outside the family offering opportunities for commitment and outreach might be expected to be related to generativity. The Dublin children were highest on Commitment in 1981, West and East Belfast followed in that order, quite close together and London was lowest. The association might seem to be apparent for all except the London groups, but in fact correlations were not significant for any of them. The same was true for the variable 'Travels', where the ranked order of the mean group scores had been London, then West Belfast then East Belfast and Dublin.

Access to information and generativity

As noted in Chapter Seven, the Belfast children were the group most interested in news in 1981, with London least interested - a rank order which was the reverse of their generativity scores. However the news of which the Belfast children were aware was predominantly local and while the correlations were not significant between 'News' and generativity, it seems likely that their interests were somewhat restricted and that this would have impinged on their orientation towards the future.

It may be relevant also that the Dublin and London children were more interested in non-local events than the Belfast children in 1981 and this may have had the effect of broadening their horizons also in terms of their plans for the future and their possible elves.

A generative attitude towards the future might be expected to have its counterparts in attitudes towards self-development *per se* in terms of what was hoped for from school. But here again we find differences between the Belfast children and the others. They seem to have compartmentalized their lives, separating out different areas and there was no significant relationship for them between the attitudes towards school and future orientation. The Dublin children however had a correlation in the predicted direction - seeing school as a means for self-development was significantly related for them with having a generative view of the future. For the London children there was a negative correlation between seeing school as a means to a job and generativity scores - also as might be predicted.

Among these variables which related to daily life and might have been important for future orientation, it looks as though there was little consistency across locations. It is likely that we will have to look beyond the microsystem of the family and its daily life to the mesosystem of the community beyond the family for ideas about what may have been influencing the future orientation of the children.

Societal structures and generativity

Looking at the socio-historical situation, a possible explanation for the findings of lower scores on generativity for the Belfast children, especially the East Belfast children and higher scores for the Dublin and London children in 1981 may be advanced along the same lines as has been already suggested for the findings on social intelligence and attitudes towards education. A basic feeling of insecurity and distrust among the East Belfast community about their situation may have resulted in their being unable and unwilling to think very far ahead, to invest in something they could not see; their economic situation in 1981 meant that their basic need to look after themselves and their material requirements was paramount at that time. The finding that so few of the boys and none of the girls in the East Belfast sample in 1981 made a wish which could be seen as related to their own self-development epitomises this feeling. They had a less extended, more ego-centred, less complex view of the future and their possible selves.

The West Belfast children may not have felt quite the same way; they had a more generative view, they were more used to dealing with economic hardship, they had more confidence in themselves and in their future even at that time, just after the hunger-strikes. From the pont of view of the community, some reforms had been put in place though they were slow to take effect and much remained to be done. They could see, however, that change was possible. They were more ready to think of others, to invest in their own self-development. This suggests greater self-confidence, greater self esteem, a greater feeling of being in control or self-directed of being able to plan ahead, and a willingness to engage in socially responsible behaviour through a knowledge of how the system works than on the part of the children in East Belfast. When O'Connor did her survey in 1992, she recorded a flexibility and openness (p. 42) in her Catholic interviewees in relation to their political future, and the feeling that they had a part to play (O'Connor, p. 176). From the present study, if we accept that the attitudes of the children reflect those of

233

the community, we can say that it looks as though the movement towards this position was well under way in 1981 in the West Belfast community and as though there was a picture of despair and stagnation among those in East Belfast at that time.

Orientation towards the future in 1992

In 1992, however we find a changed picture with regard to East Belfast - an increase in mean scores for generativity and a decrease for non-generativity or materialistic scores, which brought them to a similar level as the West Belfast children on both of these variables. The scores of East and West Belfast caught up with Dublin at this point, although the London children were still ahead (non-significantly). The movement in East Belfast contrasts with the relatively stable scores found for the other locations on this variable. A change in community attitude has been noted by other sources also (Bew, Gibbon and Patterson, 1995) and by surveys such as the 'person-in-the-street' opinion poll following the Framework document in February 1995 which found a much higher degree of support for it among unionists than had been found for any previous document which tried to point a way towards settling the issues of government of Northern Ireland. The question is how has this happened? What forces were working in the background to bring about this fundamental change of orientation on the part of the community of East Belfast as reflected in its children by 1992? Were there changes in socialization practices which could have contributed to it and which would have affected the children in East Belfast more than those in the other locations? Were there changes in the wider societal structures which might have contributed?

Socialization and future orientation variables

As far as socio-economic variables were concerned we have seen how the West Belfast children caught up with the East Belfast children, with the Dublin and London children still behind in 1992. The increase in living standards might explain changes in the orientation of the West Belfast children, but there was in fact little change in this regard for those of East Belfast, so the argument that changes in living standards will help promote a more generative attitude towards the future does not work here for the East Belfast children. In addition, the London children had a low score on 'Goods' at both time points and yet their scores on generativity were highest.

There were increases in the Independence/Autonomy areas for children in all four locations, especially in West and East Belfast. This might be seen as related to the increases in generativity scores.....but the London children had the lowest scores of all on independence/autonomy and still maintained their position at the top for generativity in 1992.

The scores on Travels may have been a factor, in that the East Belfast children's composite mean score increased whereas for all other groups it decreased. This might have been one contributory factor in their increased score on generativity - the expansion in horizons brought about by travel may have helped. On the other hand, changes in the other 'Reaching Out' variables were in a downward direction for all four groups and the Belfast and Dublin groups were on a level in 1992. It does not seem likely that this made any difference to their generativity scores.

The increased interest registered by the West Belfast children in nonlocal current events in 1992 could have been a factor in their increased scores on generativity, but this did not apply to the same extent, if at all, to the children in East Belfast. The Dublin and London children still maintained their lead on this item and there was a significant correlation for the Dublin children between generativity and access to news variables, but not for any of the others. There were no other statistically significant associations.

Changes on the family socialization variables were dramatic in some instances, but while they may have had an effect on the children's future orientation, this was not very specific or direct and other factors obviously also entered the equation. This is clearly illustrated by the fact that different practices occurred in different places and yet the outcomes were similar; and that similar practices occurred in other places and resulted in different outcomes.

It is necessary to look beyond the family at the wider society and assess whether changes there could have been creating a climate for changes of attitude which could have percolated into smaller units

Changes in society 1981-92 and future orientation

We have already noted (Chapter Two) changes in societal structures, in the delivery of services, in the financing of education, in the enforcement of anti-discrimination, in the housing programmes which affected people in Northern Ireland in the period after 1969. O'Connor (1993, p. 157) suggests that Catholics were becoming reconciled to direct rule by the 1990s although they had profound reservations about the justice system and police and army responses to terrorism (Committee on the Administration of Justice, 1995).

The greater participation in the civil administration and the economy by Catholics has also helped what O'Connor (1993, p. 331) terms their 'growing political and economic confidence'. This change was probably under way from the early 1970s and is reflected in the answers by 12 year-olds in 1981 which showed that their orientation towards the future was more generative and showed more willingness to invest, than the orientation shown by the Protestant children in East Belfast.

But were there comparable changes in the period 1981-1992 which might have helped the people in East Belfast to take a broader, more long-term view, to feel more secure with ambiguity and uncertainty and feel more confident in their future? Their responses in 1981 on all three outcome variables - social intelligence, attitude to education and future orientation seemed to indicate a rather closed, narrow view of things, an unwillingness to consider other options. The findings on other variables supported this - their reluctance to move outside local happenings and take an interest in non-local events; their lower scores on 'Travel', their restricted independence/autonomy - although in some of these, they were no lower than at least one of the other groups.

In 1992, it was different; children were allowed more independence; they were similar to the Dublin and West Belfast children in a number of other respects, and their responses seemed to indicate a more constructive view of what might be possible in the future.

Economic and political factors and future orientation?

The economic situation was not much better. In 1992, Northern Ireland was still relying very heavily on British subsidization and unemployment was still much higher for Catholic males than for Protestants, many of whom had found work in the security 'industry' when manufacturing jobs dried up. And yet, Catholics seemed as generative and optimistic as Protestants, at this time. If the economic situation was reflected in the children's attitudes towards the future, it would seem that on the Protestant side it was not quite so depressing as in 1981. But there could have been other factors too.

Politically the Anglo-Irish Agreement had introduced a new dimension greatly resented by many Protestants in 1985 and bitterly opposed by all the means at their disposal, including physical, verbal and psychological, for a number of years. The British Government had stood firm in refusing to make any changes and protest rallies, marches and demonstrations had been kept in line by the RUC much to the amazement of both Protestants and Catholics. There were beginning signs of flexibility within the IRA/Sinn Fein bloc known only to those 'in the know' (Bew, Gibbon and Patterson, 1995, p. 222). Events following the signing of the Anglo-Irish Agreement also led to the weakening of the (extremist loyalist) Democratic Unionist Party and at the same time, in 1991-92, there was an increase in killings by loyalist (Protestant) paramilitaries.This may have led to a realization among the grassroots of 'ordinary' unionists that the 'old ways' were not going to get them very far and that they were only resulting in still more horror and bloodshed. In line with this possibility there was the beginning of movement among the Official Unionists as noted by Bew Gibbon and Patterson (p. 219) who detected increasing evidence of a 'new-found Official Unionist flexibility'.

While this flexibility has as yet to prove itself publicly among the leaders of the Unionist parties, it is understandable, up to a point, that they should be trying every trick in the book so as not to lose status with the negotiators and their opponents and so as not to lose face with their supporters. At grass-roots level however, there have been indications of a greater willingness to consider options previously deemed impossible even to raise.

Social organization developments and future orientation

It would seem that a broadening of attitudes may have come about gradually during the 1980's - perhaps towards the end of the decade. The period had seen changes in many of the procedures 'ordinary' people need to go through in their daily lives in coping with civil administration and changes in the bodies doing the administration. They had had to adapt to different routines, deal with different officials, assimilate new information and act on it to an extent unheard of during the previous six decades. Catholics had gone through this phase in the early 1970s in Belfast when there was a massive displacement of population. O'Connor (1993) gives figures of between 30,000 and 60,000 people (8,180 families of whom 80 per cent were Catholic), forced to flee their homes between August 1969 and February 1973). They had set up structures themselves in their own areas to deal with the needs of the people; they had had to adjust to a changing situation, cope with ambiguity; they had to engage with the state in organizing the redistribution of resources, and eventually, with the reforms, some, at least, were able to take on responsibilities and a share of power. In doing this, they were basically challenging their own underlying folk belief that such occurrences were impossible within the Northern Ireland state. They had been dealing with this ambiguity in their situation.

Now in the 1980s the reforms and the new situation began to impinge on the Protestants and they had to begin to come to terms with many novelties. But they did not have the means of having their voices heard on issues which concerned them at local level. They had not had the tradition of organizing themselves into groups in order to press for action although as pointed out in Chapter Two, community groups had been a feature of Northern Ireland life since the 50s. At that time, the most common types of group were credit unions and similar self-help organizations, often spearheaded by the Catholic church in Catholic areas, where perhaps disadvantage and need were more easily identified than in Protestant areas. Poverty was more often and more easily hidden in Protestant East Belfast than in Catholic West Belfast. The unwillingness to acknowledge the existence of the problem - because that would have signified disloyalty to the state - meant a reluctance and psychological unwillingness to organize action to deal with it.

Oliver (1990) says it has been the experience of community workers that action can be stimulated with relative ease in Catholic areas. He attributes this to the historical experience of solidarity in adversity, folk memories of famine, collective response to problems and the Catholic church's sense of community. It had been a different story in Protestant areas. The traditional emphasis on the individual as opposed to the collective, the variety of Protestant sects, the greater conservativism of Protestants which means that they are less likely to be willing to take on social or economic issues, their lack of tradition in challenging the wisdom of government all are quoted to explain the slowness of the development of community action in Protestant areas such as East Belfast compared to West Belfast (see also Dunlop, 1995).

But by the end of the 1980s perhaps there was a growing awareness that action was necessary among the Protestant community; in addition, some Protestant areas were within the areas of social need, targeted by the programme of that name and this together with the activities of the Community Relations Commission appears to have stimulated the development of local community groups in Protestant areas and people very slowly began to participate in them to a greater extent than previously. Figures published in the 1989-90 *Index of Community Groups in Northern Ireland* (NICVA, 1989) list 32 such groups in (mostly Protestant) East Belfast and 51 in (mostly Catholic) West Belfast (excluding the Protestant Shankill). One could hypothesize that the outcome of participation in groups at local level could have included those experiences already referred to in Chapter Two:

- the formation of networks sometimes crossing the sectarian divide,
- increases in declarative knowledge - information about matters affecting their lives,
- increases in procedural knowledge - how things work, including committees, meetings, delegations and protests,
- increases in organizational skills,
- increases in self-confidence and self-esteem,
- enhanced ability to cope with stress.

A first step according to Wilson and Tyrrell (1995) was possibly learning to deal with members of their own community who would not have had much practice with the notion of groups and discussions and challenges to the status quo. They had to come to terms with different procedures accepted as 'normal' for discussion and decision-making but which differed for different groups coming from different spaces. It would seem likely that their ways of processing information have been changed gradually as they tried to integrate new knowledge which was obviously beneficial to them; they will have developed different ways of thinking and perhaps become more flexible, more able to deal with ambiguity and to realize that the normal rules don't always apply.

The increased participation in these groups by working class Protestants which became evident during the 1980s in Belfast may have added to their self-confidence as a community and helped restore their faith in a future. Unfortunately figures are not yet available (Oliver, 1995) which would tell us the participation rates for men and women respectively, but the general perception seems to be that there are more women than men involved. The process was not without its difficulties psychologically. As Oliver (1990) points out, being seen to challenge the state to which they are proclaiming political loyalty makes a mockery of that very loyalty. This kind of ambiguity has to be dealt with when the individual decides to take up a more proactive stance than previously. We do not have firm data on the participation rate of members of the families in our sample in such groups, but we suggest that such participation was likely and that it would provide part of an explanation for changes in attitude. It could also underlie the relaxation of more authoritarian family systems which was evident in our Belfast samples.

Social policy and support for cultural traditions

A further challenge to the identity of the Protestants with which they have been dealing has been provided by the new official recognition, which is slowly emerging, of the legitimacy of different cultural traditions. Accustomed to feeling that only their own traditions were appropriately typical of Northern Ireland, the Protestants are now being told from official sources not only that other traditions should be seen as having equal rights and in many cases a longer history, but that they should be seen also as part of their own heritage. This is difficult to accept psychologically as these different cultural traditions had previously been used as one of the comforting markers to distinguish the 'out-group' from the 'in-group'. And now they are being asked to accept not only that they should be seen as equally legitimate manifestations of Northern Ireland culture, but that they should see them as contributing to their own cultural identity. Psychologically this is a challenge, a challenge to reinterpret the meaning of their own identity and the reaction could well be seen in the responses to the current events questions in the present study - they are switching off from this aspect at the moment. As already noted, Protestants have been found to have greater difficulty in deciding on their political reference group than Catholics in Northern Ireland. This also could be linked to lower self-esteem and self-confidence (Marcia, 1990).

A further ingredient which may have been contributory has been the movement towards developing mutual understanding which has been taking place through schools and local community groups as well as groups involved in conciliation, spearheaded by organizations such as the Irish Association and Co-operation North.

With only an estimated 7% of people in Northern Ireland currently living in 'integrated' communities and most people living with a majority of 'their own kind', it is difficult to see how mutual understanding could possibly develop without programmes such as these. The take-up of official financial grants for such activities has been such that it looks as though some inkling of the thought processes behind them must be making some kind of tiny impression on people in general. The reaction to such initiatives may well be a negative one for some at the early stages and many especially among the middle classes have signaled their disapproval of the way things are going and their reluctance and unwillingness to broaden their interpretation of the meaning of their identity in these ways by encouraging their children to attend universities 'on the mainland'. Research has shown (Cairns, 1983, Williamson, Reid, Cormack and Osborne, 1982) that these young people once graduated tend not to return and a tendency is now becoming apparent for parents to follow their children out of Northern Ireland when they retire. But it is possible that, as people realize that they may actually benefit from the development of contacts with the 'other side' and as they gain more basic declarative knowledge about them this position will ease.

Conclusions

Changing times have brought challenges to identity for the Protestants at a later stage than for the Catholics in Northern Ireland. History has shown that changes in the meaning of one's identity are possible and that people's attitudes and values feed into societal processes as well as the other way round. The findings in the present study suggest that among young people, there have been changes in their orientation towards themselves and towards the future in a positive direction, especially among the Protestants, over the past eleven years. It is likely that they are reflecting the attitudes of the adults around them, and if there is some convergence of opinion about the kind of future people want, there must be hope for the peace process.

Theorists tell us that this aspect of the self-concept - ideas of 'possible selves' linked to orientations towards the future - is the first to show the effects of challenges from the social environment and to be modified in accordance with information judged to be ultimately beneficial for the self, using cognitive processes acquired through social experiences. The findings here appear to fit this formulation. Future orientation and ideas about possible selves will influence motivation and decisions about the acquisition of declarative knowledge, about attitudes towards education and participation in societal action. Changes in these areas would be expected to come later. Following this reasoning, a future study along the same lines as the present one should show changes for Protestants from the 1981 baseline in these areas also.

The differences between girls and boys are worth noting. In the present study it was seen that the increase in scores for East and West Belfast is largely accounted for by changes in the girls' scores. There was less movement among the boys and this may indicate an issue and a group where positive action to promote changes in attitude would be appropriate. The more positive attitude of the girls towards the future is complicated by their lack of basic knowledge and therefore probably lower self-esteem; steps should be taken to address this and to ensure that they have an equal voice in the peace process. It would seem also that particular efforts should be made to target boys whose attitudes towards the future seem less generative than those of the girls in this study. It seems ironic that the negotiations currently in progress (1995) are being conducted almost entirely from a male perspective. This very fact may explain the painful slowness and difficulty of the process.

It would seem in general that, in addition to educative measures for girls and boys, the way forward must lie along the path of raising awareness about the need to help people in Northern Ireland and especially those who are not Roman Catholic to feel secure with developing their identities so that they will encompass elements which are new for them and to encourage them to perceive these new elements as enriching. Only then will they feel able to acquire knowledge without feeling threatened by it, feel able to take responsibility for investing in themselves, gain the self-esteem and self-confidence to be able to dialogue effectively and hence bring the peace process forward.

Questionnaire

SECOND   EXPERIMENTAL   VERSION

Name:_____

Date:_____

Age:_____Date of Birth:_____

School:_____

Class:_____
                                  ____

1. Pretend this is a postcard: address it to yourself.

```
┌─────────────────────────────────┐
│                                 │
│                                 │
│                                 │
│                                 │
│                                 │
│                                 │
└─────────────────────────────────┘
```

2. Have you written any letters to friends or relatives during the last six
   months or so?   (Circle your answer)
   No
   Yes
   - To whom did you write?
    Why did you write?

3. Have you ever written to someone you did not know well - like entering a
   competition, answering an advertisement, asking for information ?
   No
   Yes
   - To whom did you write?
   - Why did you write?

4. Do you ever look at a newspaper?
   No
   Yes
   - On weekdays?
           No
           Yes
             - When did you last look at a daily paper?
                                                   Today
                                                   Yesterday
                                                   A few days ago
                                                   Last week

        - Name one paper you have seen lately
        - Mention something you read in it
        - What else did you look at in it?

5.   Do you ever see the News on television?
        No
        Yes
        - When did you last see a news programme on television?
                                        Today
                                        Yesterday
                                        A few days ago
                                        Can't remember
        Mention something you saw on the news lately

6.   Can you choose what you want to watch on television yourself?
        Yes
        No
        - Who decides what you can watch?
        - Name the three programmes which you have enjoyed most during the
        past week
        1.
        2.
        3.

7.   Do you ever hear the news on the radio?
        No
        Yes
        - When did you last hear the news on the radio?
                                This morning
                                Yesterday
                                A few days ago
                                Last week

8.   Do you ever listen to other programmes on the radio?
        No
        Yes
        - What have you listened to during the past week?
        1.
        2.
        3.

        - Who turns the radio on and off in your house mostly?

9.   Have you got a telephone in your house?
        No
        Yes
        - Have you ever rung anyone up on it by yourself?
                                        No
                                        Yes

10. Have you ever used a public telephone to make a telephone call by yourself?
Yes
No

11. Have you ever used the phone book to find a number?
Yes
No

12. Do you ever read books outside school?
No
Yes
- Do you belong to a library
No
Yes
- Have you got any books of your own?
No
Yes
- Name three books you have read in the last month.
1.
2.
3.

13. Do you ever read comics or magazines?
No
Yes
- Name one you have read lately
- When did you read it?
Yesterday
During the past week
During the past month.

SECTION   B
(each section was on a new page in the original version)

1.   What team won the last Cup Final?

2.   What internationally famous sporting event takes place every four years?

3.   Name two well-known boxers.
1.
2.

4.   Who won the last All-Ireland Final in hurling or Gaelic Football?

5.   What sport is played for the Davis Cup?

6.   Name a famous athlete and say what he or she is famous for.

7.   What kind of sporting event takes place at the White City?

8.   Name two famous snooker players.

                        1.

                        2.

9.   What is meant by the term 'freestyle'?

10.   Give the name of a famous horse race that takes place every year.

SECTION C

1.   Who is the President of the United States?

2.   What do the letters E.E.C. stand for?

3.   Who is the Prime Minister of the United Kingdom?

4.   Name any three political parties

       1.

       2.

       3.

5.   Who is the Secretary of State for Northern Ireland?

6.   What do the letters M.P. stand for?

7.   Who is the Russian Prime Minister?

8.   What do the letters U.N.O. stand for?

9.   At what age can you vote?

10.   Who is the Prime Minister of the Republic of Ireland?

SECTION D

1.   <u>Do you belong to any club or organization for young people?</u>

       No

       Yes

       - Which one?

       - How often do you go each week altogether?

                            Once

                            Twice

                            More than twice

- What do you like doing there?

1.

2.

3.

2. <u>What did you do yesterday afternoon after school?</u>

- What did you do the day before that in the afternoon?

- What else do you sometimes do after school?

3. <u>What did you do yesterday after your evening meal?</u>

-What did you do in the evening the day before yesterday?

- What else do you sometimes do in the evenings?

4. <u>What games and activities do you enjoy outside school hours?</u>
(tick any you have enjoyed during the last month)

<u>Group A</u>

Athletics	Gymnastics
Badminton	Riding
Bowling	Swimming
Boxing	Table-tennis
Dancing	Tennis

<u>Do you play for a club?</u>   Yes   No

<u>Group B</u>

Basketball/Netball
Football
Handball
Hockey/Camogie

<u>Do you play for a team?</u>   Yes   No

<u>Group C</u>

Art	Handicrafts
Birdwatching	Knitting
Chess	Model-making
Cooking	Music lessons
Drama/Speech	Night classes
Reading	Sewing/embroidery

Anything else? Please name it

5.   <u>What do you usually do on Saturdays?</u>

6.   <u>What do you usually do on Sundays?</u>

7.   <u>Have you ever been away without your family?</u>
        No
        Yes

        -How many times?

        -Where have you been to without the family?

        - How long were you away the last time without the family?

        - What age were you then?

8.   <u>Do you ever travel on a bus or taxi on your own or with your friends?</u>

        <u>(apart from a school bus)</u>

        - How much is the fare?

        - Where did you last go on a bus or taxi?

        - Where else do you usually go on a bus or taxi by yourself or with
          friends?

9.   <u>Do you ride a bicycle?</u>
        No
        Yes
        - Have you got one of your own?

                                        Yes
                                        No
                                        - Whose bike do you ride?

10.   Has your family got a car at the moment?
        No
        Yes
        - Who drives it usually?

        - Have you been in it within the past month?
        No
        Yes
        - Where did you go to?

        - Have you been out in it within the past week?
        No
        Yes

SECTION   E

1.   When you are washing your hair who helps you?

2.   If you have a bath who runs the water?

3.   Who decides when you are going to have a bath?

4.   Does anyone call you in the mornings?

5.   Are your clothes left ready for you?

6.   Who usually switches off the light when you are in bed?

SECTION   F

1.   Do you ever go shopping for your mother?
        No
        Yes
        - What did you buy the last time you went shopping?

        - When was that?
                        Yesterday
                        During the past week
                        More than a week ago

        - How many shops do you usually go to?
                        One
                        Two or three
                        More than three
        - How often do you go shopping?
                        Every day
                        At least twice a week
                        Once a week or less

2. <u>Does anyone give you pocket money?</u>
No
Yes
- Who gives it to you?

- About how much do you get each week altogether?

3. <u>Have you ever done a job to earn money?</u>
No
Yes
- What did you do?

- How much did you earn?

4. <u>What do you spend your money on?</u>

sweets	books magazines
cokes/drinks	youth club
crisps	space invaders
comics	clothes
charity	records

<u>Please say what else</u>

- Where do you usually spend your money?

Local shops
City shops
Youth Club
Community Centre

5. <u>Do you save any of your money?</u>
Yes
No

6. <u>Does your family have any animals or pets?</u>
No
Yes
(circle whatever you have)

dog/dogs	*budgie*
cat/cats	*parrot*
pigeons	*hamster*
goldfish	*gerbil*
Tropical fish	*canary*

Other - please name

- Do you help look after it or them?

No

Yes

- What did you do the last time you had to do something for it?

2. <u>Do you ever pour tea for yourself or for others</u>

No

Yes

 - every day?

 - now and again ?

3. <u>Can you peel apples or potatoes?</u>

No

Yes

4. <u>Do you ever do any of these jobs at home?</u>

(tick any you have done during the past week)

Laying the table	making the bed
clearing the table	getting in coal or fuel
washing up	polishing shoes
shopping	

•Other jobs around the house - what?

<u>Have you ever done any of these jobs?</u>

(Tick any you have ever done)

cleaning car	cleaning own room
cleaning and oiling	weeding in garden
bicycle	fixing plug onto flex
helping prepare dinner	planting seeds
making tea	mending puncture
washing socks or other	fixing shelves
clothes	cutting grass or hedges
minding small children	lighting fire
painting doors or windows	

<u>Any other jobs you have done around the house</u>

SECTION H

1. What I enjoy most <u>outside </u>school is..........(name three activities)

  1.

  2.

  3.

2. What I enjoy most <u>in</u> school is...............(name three activities)
   1.
   2.
   3.

3. School would be better if..................(name three things)
   1.
   2.
   3.

4. School is supposed to help us in life because it .....(name three things)
   1.
   2.
   3.

5. It's worth trying to do well at school because it......(name three things)
   1.
   2.
   3.

6. If I get stuck with my homework I...

7. If I had a wish I would wish that...

8. I would like most of all to be a...

9. But if that is not possible I wouldn't mind being a.........................

10. Happy people are people who..

THANK YOU FOR COMPLETING THIS QUESTIONNAIRE

References

Abbott, M. and Frazer, H. (1985) (eds.), *Women and Community Work in Northern Ireland*, Farset Cooperative Press, Belfast.

Abramson, P. (1977), *The political socialization of black Americans*, Free Press, New York.

Abramson, P. (1983), *Political Attitudes in America*, Freeman, San Francisco.

Adamson, I. (1974), *Cruthin: The Ancient Kindred*, Nosdama Books, Newtownards, Co. Down, N. Ireland.

Adamson, I. (1981), *The Identity of Ulster*, The author, Belfast.

Adelson, J. (1980) (ed.), *Handbook of Adolescent Psychology*, John Wiley and Sons, New York.

Adelson, J. (1986), *Inventing Adolescence: The Political Psychology of Everyday Schooling*, Transaction Books, New Brunswick, U.S.A.

Alva, S. A. (1985), 'The political acculturation of Mexican American adolescents', *Hispanic Journal of Behavioral Sciences*, 7 (4), pp. 345-364.

Amuchie, F. A. (1982), 'Age and sex differences among adolescent participants in recreational activities'. *International Review of Sport Sociology*, 17, pp. 79-84.

Arthur, A. (1974), *Attitude Change and "Neuroticism" among Northern Irish Children Participating in Joint-Faith holidays'*, MSc Thesis, Queen's University, Belfast.

Astin, A., Green, K. and Korn, W. (1987), *The American Freshman: Twenty-Year Trends, 1966-1985*, Graduate School of Education, University of California, Los Angeles.

Avery, P. (1989), 'Adolescent political tolerance: findings from the research and implications for educators', *High School Journal*, 72 (4), pp. 168-174.

Bachman, J. G. and van Duinen, E. (1971), *Youth Look at National Problems*, Institute for Social Research, Ann Arbor, Michigan.

Baltes, P. B. and Schaie, K. W. (1973) (eds.), *Life-Span Developmental Psychology,: Personality and Socialization*, Academic Press, New York.

Banaji, M.R. and Prentice, D. A. (1994), 'The self in social contexts', *Annual Review of Psychology*, 45, pp. 297-332.

Bandura, A. (1977), 'Self-efficacy: toward a unifying theory of behavioral change', *Psychological Review*, 84 (2), pp. 191-215.

Bandura, A. (1986), *Social Foundations of Thought and Action: A Social Cognitive Theory*, Prentice-Hall, Englewood Cliffs, New Jersey.

Bandura, A. (1990), 'Social Cognitive Theory of Mass Communication', in Groebel, J. and Winterhoff, P. (eds.), *Empirische Medienpsychologie*, Psychologie Verlags Union, Munich.

Bandura, A. (1993), 'Perceived self-efficacy in cognitive development and functioning', *Educational Psychologist*, 28, pp. 117-148.

Bandura, A. (1995) (ed.), *Self-efficacy in Changing Societies*, Cambridge University Press, Cambridge.

Bardon, J. (1992), *A History of Ulster*, Blackstaff Press, Belfast.

Barritt, D.P. and Carter, C.F. (1962), *The Northern Ireland Problem*, (2nd ed. 1972), Oxford University Press, Oxford.

Beattie, G. (1979), 'The "Troubles" in Northern Ireland', *Bulletin of the British Psychological Society*, 32 (June), pp. 249-52.

Belfrage, S. (1987), *The Crack: a Belfast Year*, André Deutsch, London.

Beloff, H. (1980), 'A Place Not So Far Apart: Conclusions of an Outsider', in Harbison, J. and Harbison, J. (eds.), *A Society under Stress: Children and Young People in Northern Ireland*, Open Books, London, pp. 167-176.

Bengston, V. L. and Laufer, R. S. (1974) (eds.), 'Youth, generations and social change', *Journal of Social Issues*, 30 (1 and 2).

Berger, P. L. (1977), *Facing Up to Modernity*, Harmondsworth, Penguin.

Bew, P., Gibbon, P. and Patterson, H. (1995), *Northern Ireland 1921-1994: Political Forces and Social Classes*, Serif, London.

Bill, J. (1977), 'Effects of varying structure and method on the validity of self-report measures', *Research Intelligence*, 3, pp. 19-21.

Blackman, T., Evason, E., Melaugh, M. and Woods, R. (1989), 'Housing and health: a case study of two areas in west Belfast', *Journal of Social Policy*, 18, 1, pp. 1-26.

Blease, M. (1983), 'Maladjusted School Children in a Belfast Centre', in Harbison, J. (ed.), *Children of the Troubles: Children in Northern Ireland*, Stranmillis College Learning Resources Unit, Belfast, pp. 21-32.

Blos, P. (1979), *The Adolescent Passage: Developmental Issues*, International Universities Press, New York.

Blumler, J. (1974), 'Does mass political ignorance matter?' *Teaching Politics*, 3, pp. 59-65.

Bouffard, L. (1981), *La Perspective Future chez les Africaines*, Unpublished manuscript, Collège de Sherbrooke, Québec.

Bowman, D. and Shivers, L. (1984), *'More than the "Troubles" '*, New Society Publishers, Philadelphia.

Breakwell, G. (1986), *Coping with Threatened Identities*, Methuen, London.

Breakwell, G. M., Fife-Schaw, C. and Devereux, J. (1989), 'Political activity and political attitudes in teenagers: is there any correspondence? a research note', *Political Psychology*, 10 (4), pp. 745-755.

Breslin, A. (1982), 'Tolerance and moral reasoning among adolescents in Ireland', *Journal of Moral Education*, 11 (2), pp. 112-127.

Bronfenbrenner, U, (1986), 'Ecology of the family as a context for human development: research perspectives', *Developmental Psychology*, 22 (6), pp. 723-742.

Bronfenbrenner, U. (1977a), 'Toward an experimental ecology of human development', *American Psychologist,* 32, pp. 513-531.

Bronfenbrenner, U. (1977b), 'Lewinian space and ecological substance', *Journal of Social Issues,* 33, pp. 199-213.

Bronfenbrenner, U. (1979), *The Ecology of Human Development,* Harvard University Press, Cambridge, Mass.

Brown R. and Wade, G. (1987), 'Superordinate goals and intergroup behaviour: the effect of role ambiguity and status on intergroup attitudes and task performance', *European Journal of Social Psychology,* 17, pp. 131-142.

Bruce, S. (1986), *God Save Ulster! The Religion and Politics of Paisleyism,* Clarendon Press, Oxford.

Buckland, P. (1981), *A History of Northern Ireland,* Gill and Macmillan, Dublin.

Buckley, A. D. (1988), 'Collecting Ulster's Culture: Are there *really* Two Traditions?' in Gailey, A. (ed.), *The Use of Tradition:,* essays presented to G.B. Thompson, Ulster Folk and Transport Museum, Cultra Co. Down, N. Ireland, pp. 49-60.

Burger, J. M. (1985), 'Desire for control and achievement-related behaviors', *Journal of Perronality and Social Psychology,* 48, pp. 1520-1533.

Burton, F. (1978), *The Politics of Legitimacy: Struggles in a Belfast Community,* Routledge and Kegan Paul, London.

Cairns, E, (1989), 'Social Identity and Intergroup Conflict: A Developmental Perspective', in Harbison, J. (ed.), *Growing Up in Northern Ireland,* Stranmilllis College Learning Resources Unit, Belfast.

Cairns, E. (1980), 'The Development of Ethnic Discrimination in Children in Northern Ireland', in Harbison, J. and Harbison, J. (eds.), *A Society under Stress: Children and Young People in Northern Ireland,* Open Books, Wells, Somerset, pp 116-127.

Cairns, E. (1982), 'Intergroup Conflict in Northern Ireland' in Tajfel, H. (ed.), *Social Identity and Intergroup Relations,* Cambridge University Press, Cambridge.

Cairns, E. (1983), 'The political socialization of tomorrow's parents', in Harbison, J. and Harbison, J. (eds.), *A Society under Stress: Children and Young People in Northern Ireland,* Open Books, Wells, Somerset.

Cairns, E. (1983), *Children's Perceptions of Normative and Prescriptive Interpersonal Aggression in High and Low Areas of Violence in Northern Ireland,* Unpublished paper, University of Ulster, Coleraine.

Cairns, E. (1987), *Caught in Crossfire: Children and the Northern Ireland Conflict,* Appletree Press, Belfast, p. 65.

Cairns, E. (1994), 'Understanding conflict and promoting peace in Ireland: psychology's contribution', in *The Irish Psyche, Special Issue of the Irish Journal of Psychology,* 15 (2-3), pp. 480-493.

Cairns, E. and Cairns, T. (1995), Children and Conflict: A Psychological Perspective, in S. Dunn (ed.), *Facets of the Conflict in Northern Ireland,* St Martin's Press/Macmillan, London.

Cairns, E. and Conlin, L. (1985), *Children's Moral Reasoning and the Northern Irish Violence,* Unpublished paper, University of Ulster, Coleraine.

Cairns, E. and Toner, I. J. (1993), 'Children and Political Violence in Northern Ireland: From Riots to Reconciliation', in Leavitt, L.A. and Fox, N.A. (eds.),

The Psychological Effects of War and Violence on Children, Lawrence Erlbaum, Hillsdale, New Jersey.

Cairns, E. and Wilson, R. (1985), 'Psychiatric aspects of violence in Northern Ireland', *Stress Medicine*, 1 (3), pp. 193-202.

Cairns, E. and Wilson, R. (1989a), 'Mental health aspects of political violence in Northern Ireland', *International Journal of Mental Health*, 18 (1), pp. 38-56.

Cairns, E. and Wilson, R. (1989b), 'Coping with political violence', *Social Science and Medicine*, 28 (6), 621-624.

Cairns, E., Dunn, S. and Giles, M. (1993), 'Surveys of Integrated Education in Northern Ireland: A Review', in Osborne, R., Cormack, R. and Gallagher, A. (eds.), *After the Reforms: Education and Policy in Northern Ireland*, Avebury, Aldershot.

Cairns, E., Dunn, S., Morgan, V. and McClenaghan, C. (1992), *The Impact of Integrated Schools in Northern Ireland on Cultural Values and Social Identity*, Final Report to the Economic and Social Research Council, UK.

Cairns, E., Wilson, R., Trew, K. and Gallagher T. (1995), 'Psychology's contribution to understanding conflict in Northern Ireland', *Peace and Conflict: Jurnal of Peace Psychology*, 7 (2), pp. 131-148.

Cairns, R.B. and Cairns, B.D. (1994), *Lifelines and Risks: Pathways of Youth in our Time*, Cambridge University Press, Cambridge.

Canning, D., Moore, B. and Rhodes, J. (1987), 'Economic growth in Northern Ireland: problems and prospects', in Teague, P. (ed.), *Beyond the Rhetoric: Politics, the Economy and Social Policy in Northern Ireland*, Lawrence and Wishart, London, pp. 211-235.

Cantor, N. and Kihlstrom, J. F. (1987), *Personality and Social Intelligence*, Prentice-Hall, Englewood Cliffs, N.J.

Carrington, B., Chivers, T. and Williams, T. (1987), 'Gender, leisure, sport: a case study of young people of South Asian descent', *Leisure Studies*, 6, pp. 265-270.

Chaffee, S. and Yang, S. (1990), 'Communication and Political Socialization', in Ichilov, O. (ed.), *Political Socialization, Citizenship and Democracy*, Teachers College Press, New York.

Chaffee, S. H. (1977), 'Mass Communication in Political Socialization', in Renshon, S. A. (ed.) *Handbook of Political Socialization: Theory and Research*, Free Press, New York.

Chaffee, S. S., Ward, L. S. and Tipton, L. P. (1970), 'Mass communication and political socialization', *Journalism Quarterly*, 47, pp. 647-659.

Chaffee, S.H. and Schleuder, J. (1986), 'Measurement and effects of attention to media', *Human Communication Research*, 13 (1), pp. 76-107.

Chaffee, S.H., McLeod, J. M. and Wackman, D. B. (1973), 'Family Communication Patterns and Adolescent Political Participation', in Dennis, J. (ed.), *Socialization in Politics*, John Wiley, New York.

Cheek, J. M. (1989), 'Identity Orientation and Self-Interpretation' in Buss, D. M. and Cantor, N. (eds.), *Personality Psychology: Recent Trends and Emerging Directions*, Springer-Verlag, New York.

Chiu, L-H. (1990), 'The relationship of career goals and self-esteem among adolescents', *Adolescence*, 25, pp. 593-597.

Chiu, P. and Nevius, J. (1989), 'Wishes of young middle-class Mexican-American and Anglo-American children: perception of personal preferences', *Perceptual and Motor Skills*, 68 (3, pt.1), p. 914.

Clausen, J. A. (1993), *American Lives*, Free Press, New York.

Cohler, B. J. (1987), 'Adversity, Resiliency and the Study of Lives', in Anthony, E. J. and Cohler, B. J. (eds.), *The Invulnerable Child*, Guilford Press, New York, pp. 363-504.

Colley, A. (1984), 'Sex roles and explanations of leisure behavior', *Leisure Studies*, 3, pp. 335-341.

Collins, W.A. (1990), 'Parent-Child Relationships in the Transition to Adolescence: Continuity and Change in Interaction, Affect and Cognition', in Montemayor, P.R., Adams, G. R.and Gullotta, T. P. (eds.), *From Childhood To Adolescence: A Transitional Period?* Sage, New York, pp. 85-106.

Committee on the Administration of Justice (1995), *It's Part of Life Here: The Security Forces And Harassment In Northern Ireland*, Committee on the Administration of Justice, Belfast.

Comstock, G., Chaffee, S., Katzman, N., McCombs, M. and Roberts, D. F. (1978), *Television and Human Behavior*, Columbia University Press, New York.

Conger, R. D., Ge, X., Elder, G. H. Jr., Lorenz, F. O. and Simons, R. L. (1994), 'Economic stress, coercive family process and developmental problems of adolescents', *Child Development*, 65, pp. 541-561.

Conroy, J. (1988), *War as a Way of Life: A Belfast Diary*, Heinemann, London.

Corken, J. P. (1989), *The Development of the Teaching of Irish History In Northern Ireland in its Institutional and Political Context*, MA Thesis, Queen's University, Belfast.

Csikszentmihalyi, M. and Larson, R. (1984), *Being Adolescent*, Basic Books, New York.

Curry, C., Trew, K., Turner, I. and Hunter, J. (1994), 'The effect of life domains on girls' possible selves', *Adolescence*, 29 (113), pp. 133-150.

Damon, W. (1989), *Child Development Today and Tomorrow*, Jossey-Bass, New York.

Darby, J. (1986), *Intimidation and the Control of Conflict in Northern Ireland*, Gill and Macmillan, Dublin.

Darby, J. (1995), 'Conflict in Northern Ireland: a Background Essay', in Dunn, S. (ed.), *Facets of the Conflict in Northern Ireland*, St. Martin's Press/Macmillan, London.

Darby, J. and Dunn, S. (1987), 'Segregated Schools: The Research Evidence', in Osborne, R. D. and Cormack, R. J. (eds.), *Religion, Occupations and Employment 1971-1981*, Fair Employment Agency, Research Paper No. 11, Belfast.

Darby, J., Murray, D., Batts, D., Dunn, S., Farren, S., and Harris, J., (1977), *Education and Community in Northern Ireland: Schools Apart?* New University of Ulster, Coleraine, Co. Londonderry.

Deane, E. (1981), 'Community Work in the 70s', in Frazer, H. (ed.), *Community Work in a Divided Society*, Farset Press, Belfast.

Deaux, K. (1991), 'Social Identities: Thoughts on Structure and Change', in Curtis, R. C. (ed.), *The Relational Self: Theoretical Convergences in Psychoanalysis and Social Psychology*, Guilford Press, New York.

Dennis, J. (1986), 'Preadult learrning of political independence: media and family communication effects', *Communication Research*, 13 (3), pp. 401-433.

Dickson, B. (1995) 'Criminal Justice and Emergency Laws, in Dunn, S. (ed.) *Facets of the Conflict in Northern Ireland*, Macmillan/St Martin's Press, London.

Doob, L. W. and Foltz, W. J. (1973), 'The Belfast workshop: an application of group techniques to a destructive conflict', *Journal of Conflict Resolution*, 17 (3), pp. 489-512.

Douglas, J. N. H. and Boal, F. W. (1982), 'The Northern Ireland Problem' in Boal, F. W. and Douglas, J. N. H. (eds.), *Integration and Division: Geographical Perspectives on the Northern Ireland Problem*, Academic Press, London.

Dunlop, J. (1995), *A Precarious Belonging: Presbyterians and the Conflict in Ireland*, Blackstaff Press, Belfast.

Dunn, S. (ed.), *Facets of the Conflict in Northern Ireland*, St. Martin's Press/Macmillan, London.

Dusek, J. B. and Flaherty, J. F. (1981), *The Development of the Self-Concept during the Adolescent Years*, Monographs of the Society for Research in Child Development, 46, pp. 1-61.

Eder, D. (1985), 'The cycle of popularity: interpersonal relations among female adolescents', *Sociology of Education*, 58, pp. 154-165.

Elder, G. H. Jr. (1974), *Children of the Great Depression: Social Change in Life Experience*, University of Chicage Press, Chicago, (Midway Reprint 1984).

Elder, G. H. Jr. (1994), 'Time, human agency and social change: perspectives on the life course', *Social Psychology Quarterly*, 57 (1), pp. 4-15.

Elder, G. H. Jr. (1995), 'The Life Course Paradigm: Social Change and Individual Development', in Moen, P., Elder, G. H. Jr. and Lüscher, K. (eds.), *Examining Lives in Context: Perspectives on the Ecology of Human Development* , APA Press, Washington D.C.

Elder, G. H. Jr., Hagell, A., Rudkin, L. and Conger, R.D. (1992), 'Looking Forward in Troubled Times: The Influence of Social Context on Adolescent Plans and Orientations', in Silbereisen, R. K. and Todt, E. (eds.), *Adolescence in Context: The Interplay of Family, School, Peers and Work in Adjustment*, Springer, New York.

Elder, G. H. Jr., Modell, J. and Parke, R. D. (1994), *Children in Time and Place: Developmental and Historical Insights*, Cambridge University Press, Cambridge.

Elkind, D. (1967), 'Egocentrism in Adolescence', *Child Development*, 38, pp. 1025-1034.

Elkind, D. and Bowen, R. (1979), 'Imaginary audience behavior in children and adolescents', *Developmental Psychology*, 15, pp. 38-44.

Emler, N. (1993), 'The Young Person's Relationship to the Institutional Order', in Jackson, S. and Rodriguez-Tomé, H. (eds.), *Adolescence and its Social Worlds*, Lawrence Erlbaum, Hillsdale, N.J.

Engstrom, L. M. (1974), 'Physical activities during leisure', *International Review of Sport Sociology*, pp. 83-102.

Entwisle, D. R. (1993), 'Schools and the Adolescent', in Feldman, S. S. and Elliott, G. R. (eds), *At the Threshold: The Developing Adolescent*, Harvard University Press, Cambridge, Mass.

Erickson, E. H. (1968), 'Identity and Identity Diffusion', in Gordon, C. and Gordon, K.G. (eds.), *The Self in Social Interaction*, Wiley, New York.

Erickson, E.H. (1959), 'Identity and the life-cycle', *Psychological Issues,* Monograph 1, International Universities Press, New York.

Essen, J. and Ghodsian, M. (1977), 'Sixteen-year-olds in households in receipt of supplementary benefit and family income supplement', in *Supplementary Benefits Commission Annual Report,* HMSO, London.

Essen, J. and Wedge, P. (1982), *Continuities in Social Disadvantage,* Heinemann, London.

Evason, E. (1985), *On the Edge: A Study of Poverty and Long-Term Unemployment,* Child Poverty Action Group, London.

Fairleigh, J. (1975), 'Personality and Social Factors in Religious Prejudice', in *Sectarianism - Roads to Reconciliation:, Proceedings of the 22nd Annual Summer School of the Social Study Conference,* St. Augustine's College, Dungarvan, Co. Waterford, Ireland, Three Candles, Dublin.

Feather, N. T. (1980), 'Values in Adolescence', in Adelson, J. (1980) (ed.), *Handbook of Adolescent Psychology,* New York, John Wiley and Sons, pp. 247-294.

Fee, F. (1980), 'Responses to a Behavioural Questionnaire of a Group of Belfast Children', in Harbison, J. and Harbison, J. (eds.), *A Society under Stress: Children and Young people in Northern Ireland,* Open Books, Wells, Somerset.

Fee, F. (1983). 'Educational Change in Belfast Schoolchildren 1975-1981', in Harbison, J. (ed.), *Children of the Troubles: Children in Northern Ireland,* Stranmillis College Learning Resources Unit, Belfast.

Feldman, S. S. and Elliott, G. R. (1990), *At the Threshold: The Developing Adolescent,* Harvard University Press, Cambridge, Mass.

Fennell, D, (1989), *The Revision of Irish Nationalism,* Open Air, Dublin.

Fields, R. M. (1973), *A Society on the Run: A Psychology of Northern Ireland,* Penguin, Middlesex.

Fields, R.M. (1977), *Society under Siege: a Psychology of Northern Ireland,* Temple University Press, Philadelphia, Pa.

Fife-Schaw, C. and Breakwell, G. (1990), 'Predicting the intention not to vote in late teenage: a UK study of 17- and 18-year-olds', *Political Psychology,* 11 (4), pp. 739-755.

Fine, G. A., Mortimer, J. T. and Roberts, D. F. (1993), 'Leisure, Work and the Mass Media', in Feldman, S. S. and Elliott, G. R. *At the Threshold: The Developing Adolescent,* Harvard University Press, Harvard, Mass.

Flackes, W. D. and Elliott, S. (1994), *Northern Ireland: A Political Directory, 1968-1993,* 4th ed., Blackstaff Press, Belfast.

Flegle, M. J. M. (1972), *The Use of Leisure Time by High School Students in the Suburbs of Detroit, Michigan,* PhD Dissertation, University of Michigan.

Florian, V. and Har-Even, D. (1984), 'Cultural patterns in the choice of leisure time activity frameworks', *Journal of Leisure Research,* 16, pp. 330-337.

Fraser, M. (1973), *Children in Conflict,* Secker and Warburg, London.

Frazer, H. (1981), Speech given at I.V.S Workshop, Glencree, reported in Frazer, H. (ed.) *Community Work in a Divided Society,* Farset Press, Belfast.

Furnham, A. and Gunter, B, (1987), 'Young people's political knowledge', *Educational Studies,* 13 (1), pp. 91-104.

Furstenberg, F. F. (1993), 'Coming of Age in a Changing Family System', in Feldman, S. S. and Elliott, G. R. (eds), *At the Threshold: The Developing Adolescent,* Harvard University Press, Cambridge, Mass.

Gafikin, F. and Morrissey, M. (1987), 'Poverty and Politics in Northern Ireland'. In Teague, P. (ed.), *Beyond The Rhetoric: The Economy and Social Policy in Northern Ireland,* Lawrence and Wishart, London.

Gallagher, A. M. (1991), *Employment, Unemployment and Religion in Northern Ireland: The Majority Minority Review No. 2,* Centre for the Study of Conflict, University of Ulster, Coleraine, Co. Londonderry.

Gallagher, A. M. (1992), 'Education in a divided society', *The Psychologist,* 5, pp. 353-356.

Gallagher, A. M. (1995), 'The approach of Government: Community Relations and Equity' in Dunn, S. (ed.), *Facets of the Conflict in Northern Ireland,* St Martin's Press/Macmillan, London,

Gallagher, E. and Worall, E. (1982), *Christians in Ulster 1968-80,* Oxford University Press, Oxford.

Gallatin, J. (1980), 'Political Thinking in Adolescence' in Adelson, J. (ed.), *Handbook of Adolescent Psychology,* John Wiley and Sons, New York, pp. 344-382.

Garbarino, J. (1995), *The Role of Identity in Children's Violence,* paper presented at Biennial Meeting of the Society for Research in Child Development, Indianapolis, March 30 - April 3rd 1995.

Garmezy, N. (1985), 'Stress Resistant Children: The Search for Protective Factors', in Stevenson, J. E. (ed.), Recent Research in Developmental Psychopathology, *Journal of Child Psychology and Psychiatry,* Book Supplement No. 4, Pergamon, Oxford, pp. 213-233.

Garramone, G. and Atkin, C. (1986), 'Mass communication and political socialization: specifying the effects', *Public Opinion Quarterly,* 50 (1), pp. 76-86.

Garton, A. F. and Pratt, C. (1987), 'Participation and interest in leisure activities by adolescent school children', *Journal of Adolescence,* 10, pp. 341-351.

Glass, J., Bengston, V. L. and Dunham, C. C. (1986), 'Attitude similarity in three-generation families: socialization, status inheritance or reciprocal influence?', *American Sociological Review,* 51 (5), pp. 685-698.

Glassie, H. (1982), *Passing the Time: Folklore and History of an Ulster Community,* O'Brien Press, Dublin.

Goldberg, D. (1978), *Manual of the General Health Questionnaire,* NFER/Nelson, Windsor, England.

Goldstein, E. (1979), *An Exploration of the Relationships between the Leisure Attitudes and Leisure Activities of an Adolescent Group,* PhD Dissertation, Columbia University Teachers College.

Goode, W. J. (1982), 'Why Men Resist', in Skolnick, A. S. and Skolnick, J. H. (eds.), *Family in Transition,* Little Brown, Boston, pp. 201-218.

Goodnow, J. and Collins, W. A. (1990), *Development according to Parents,* Lawrence Erlbaum, New York.

Goodnow, J. J. (1986), 'Cultural conditions and individual behaviours: conceptual and methodological links', *Australian Journal of Psychology,* 38 (3), pp. 231-244.

Gough, B., Robinson, S., Kremer, J. and Mitchell, R. (1992), 'The social psychology of intergroup conflict: an appraisal of Northern Ireland research', *Canadian Psychology,* 33 (3), pp. 645-650.

Gras, F. (1976), 'Problems of the social structure of children and young people participating in youth spartakiads', *International Review of Sport Sociology*, 11, pp. 47-52.

Greenberg, M., Siegel, J. and Leitch, C. (1983), 'The nature and importance of attachment relationships to parents and peers during adolescence', *Journal of Youth and Adolescence*, 12, pp. 373-386.

Greer, J. E. (1980), 'The persistence of religion: a study of adolescents in Northern Ireland', *Character Potential*, 9, pp. 139-149.

Greer, J. E. (1985), Viewing "the other side" in Northern Ireland; openness and attitudes to religion among Catholic and Protestant adolescents', *Journal for the Scientific Study of Religion*, 24 (3), pp. 275-92.

Grotevant, H. D. and Cooper, C. R. (1986), 'Individuation in family relationships: a perspective on individual differences in the development of identity and role-taking skills in adolescence, *Human Development*, 29, pp. 82-100.

Guelke, A. (1995), 'Paramilitaries, Republicans and Loyalists', in Dunn, S. (ed.) *Facets of the Conflict in Northern Ireland*, St Martin's Press/ Macmillan, London, pp. 114-130.

Hadden, W. A., Rutherford, W. H. and Merrett, J. D. (1978), 'The injuries of terrorist bombing: a study of 1532 consecutive patients', *The British Journal of Surgery*, 65, p. 525.

Hall, G. S. (1904), *Adolescence: Its Psychology and its Relations to Anthropology, Sex, Crime and Education*, Appleton, New York.

Hall, M. (1986), *Ulster: the Hidden History*, Pretani, Belfast.

Harbison, J. (1983) (ed.), *Children of the Troubles: Children in Northern Ireland*, Stranmillis College Learning Resources Unit , Belfast:

Harbison, J. (1989a), *Growing Up in Northern Ireland*, Stranmillis College Learning Resources Unit, Belfast.

Harbison, J. (1989b), 'The Social and Economic Context of Growing Up in Northern Ireland', In Harbison, J. (ed.). *Growing Up in Northern Ireland*, Stranmillis College Learning Resources Unit, Belfast, pp. 1-11.

Harbison, J. and Harbison, J. (1980) (eds.), *A Society under Stress: Children and Young People in Northern Ireland*, Open Books, Wells, Somerset,

Harevan, T. K. (1982), *Family Time and Industrial Time*, Cambridge University Press, New York.

Harter, S. (1993), 'Self and Identity Development' in Feldman, S. S. and Elliott, G. R. *At the Threshold: The Developing Adolescent*, Harvard University Press, Harvard, Mass.

Havighurst, R. J. (1948), *Developmental Tasks and Education*, Plenum Press, New York.

Havighurst, R. J. (1972), *Developmental Tasks and Education*, Davis McKay, New York.

Heskin, K. (1980), 'Children and Young People in Northern Ireland: A Research Review', in Harbison, J. and Harbison, J. (eds.), *A Society under Stress: Children and Young People in Northern Ireland*, Open Books, Wells, Somerset, pp. 8-21.

Hetherington, E. M., Lerner, R. M. and Perlmutter, M. (1988), *Child Development in Lifespan Perspective*, Lawrence Erlbaum, Hillsdale N.J.

Hettema, P. J. (1989) (ed.), *Personality and Environment: Assessment of Human Adaptation*, John Wiley and Sons, New York.

260

Hill, J. P. (1983), 'Early adolescence: a research agenda', *Journal of Early Adolescence*, 3 (1-2), pp. 1-21.

Himmelweit, H. and Swift, B. (1971), *Social and Personality Factors in the Development of Adult Attitudes towards Self and Society*, SSRC, London.

Hosin, A. and Cairns, E. (1984), 'The impact of conflict on children's ideas about their country', *Journal of Social Psychology*, 118, 2, pp. 161-8.

Houston, J. E., Crozier, W. R. and Walker, P. (1990), 'The assessment of ethnic sensitivity among Northern Ireland schoolchildren', *British Journal of Developmental Psychology*, 8, pp. 419-422.

Howe, L. (1989a), 'Unemployment: "Doing the Double" and Labour Markets in Belfast', In Curtin, C. and Wilson, T. M. (eds.), *Ireland from Below: Social Change and Local Communities*, Galway University Press, Galway.

Howe, L. (1989b), '"Doing the Double" or Doing Without: The Social and Economic Context of Working 'On the Side' in Northern Ireland', in Jenkins, R. (ed.), *Northern Ireland: Studies in Social and Economic Life*, Aldershot, Avebury, in association with the Economic and Social Research Council.

Hume, J. (1964), letter to the Irish Times quoted in Bardon, J. (1992) *A History of Ulster*, Blackstaff Press, Belfast, p. 649.

Hurrelmann, K. (1988), *Social Structure and Personality Development: The Individual as a Productive Processor of Reality*, Cambridge University Press, Cambridge.

Hurrelmann, K. and Engel, U. (1989), *The Social World of Adolescents: International Perspectives*, de Gruyter, New York.

Ianni, F. (1989), *Search for Structure: A Report on American Youth Today*, Macmillan, New York.

International Youth Bridge (1985), *Young Ideas in Northern Ireland: Christian Belief and Life Style among Young Adults in Northern Ireland*, City of Belfast YMCA, Belfast.

Irwin, C. (1993), 'The integrated aspiration', *Fortnight*, 315, pp. 24-25.

Jackson, S. and Rodriguez-Tomé, H. (1993) (eds.), *Adolescence and its Social Worlds*, Lawrence Erlbaum, Hillsdale, N.J.

Jackson-Beeck, M. and Chaffee, S. H. (1975), *Family Communication, Mass Communication and Differential Political Socialization*, paper presented at the International Communication Association Meeting, Chicago, April 1975.

Jahoda, G. and Harrison, S. (1975), 'Belfast children: some effects of a conflict environment', *Irish Journal of Psychology*, 3 (1), pp. 1-19.

Jankowski, M. S. (1986), *City Bound: Urban Life and Political Attitudes among Chicano Youth*, University of New Mexico Press, Albuquerque.

Jardine, E. (1995), *Growing through conflict: the impact of 25 years of violence on young people growing up in Northern Ireland*, paper presented to the Conference of the International Association of Juvenile and Family Court Magistrates, Belfast, April.

Jenkins, R. (1982), *Hightown Rules: Growing Up in a Belfast estate*, Routledge and Kegan Paul, London.

Jenkins, R. (1983), *Lads, Citizens and Ordinary Kids: Working-Class Lifestyles in Belfast*, Routledge and Kegan Paul, London.

Jennings, M. and Niemi, R. (1971), 'The division of political labour between fathers and mothers', *American Political Science Review*, 65, pp. 64-82.

JEPI (1965), Junior Eysenck Personality Inventory, S. B. G. Eysenck, University of London Press, London

John, P. (1993), *Local Government in Northern Ireland,* York, Joseph Rowntree Foundation.

Jugendwerk der Deutschen Shell (1982) (ed.), *Jugend '81. Lebensentwürfe - Alltagskulturen-Zukunftsbilder,* Leske and Budrich, Oplaen.

Kaplan, L. (1984), *Adolescence: The Farewell to Childhood,* Simon and Schuster, New York.

Kelly, K. (1985), 'Women's Information Days'. In Abbott, M. and Frazer, H. (eds.),*Women and Community Work in Northern Ireland,* Farset Cooperative Press, Belfast,

Kennedy, D. (1988), *The Widening Gulf: Northern Attitudes to the Independent Irish State, 1919-49,* Blackstaff, Belfast.

Kestenbaum, G. I. and Weinstein, L. (1983), 'Personality, psychopathology and developmental issues in male adolescent video game use', *Journal of the American Academy of Child Psychiatry,* 24, pp. 329-337.

Kinahan, T. (1995), *Where Do We Go From Here? Protestants and the Future of Northern Ireland,* Columba Press, Dublin.

Kirchler, E., Palmomari, A. and Pombeni, M.L. (1993), 'Developmental Tasks and Adolescents' Relationships with their Peers and their Family', in Jackson, S. and Rodriguez-Tomé, H. (eds.), *Adolescence and its Social Worlds,* Lawrence Erlbaum, Hillsdale, N.J.

Knox, C. and Hughes, J. (1995), 'Local Goverment and Community Relations', in Dunn, S. (ed.), *Facets of the Conflict in Northern Ireland,* St. Martin's Press/Macmillan, London, pp.43-60.

Kobak, R. and Sceery, A. (1988), 'Attachment in late adolescence: working models, affect regulation and representations of self and others', *Child Development,* 59, pp. 135-146.

Kobasa, S. C. O. and Puccetti, M. C. (1983), 'Personality and social resources in stress resistance', *Journal of Personality and Social Psychology,* 45 (4), pp. 839-850.

Kohn, M. L. and Slomczynski, K. M. (1990), *Social Structures and Self-Direction,* Basil Blackwell, Oxford.

Kotre, J. (1984), *Outlining the Self: Generativity and the Interpretation of Lives,* Johns Hopkins University Press, Baltimore, MD.

Kraus, S. and Davis, D. (1976), *The Effects of Mass Communication on Political Behavior,* Pennsylvania State University Press, Pennsylvania Park, Pa.

Kremer, J., Barry, R. and McNally, A. (1986), 'The misdirected letteer and the quasi-questionnaire: unobtrusive measures of prejudice in Northern Ireland', *Journal of Applied Social Psychology,* 16 (4), pp. 303-9.

Kreppner, K. and Lerner, R.M. (1989), *Family Systems and Life-Span Development Issues and Perspectives,* Lawrence Erlbaum, Hillsdale, N.J.

Krosnik, J. A. and Alwin, D. F. (1989), 'Aging and susceptibility to attitude change', *Journal of Personality and Social Psychology,* 57 (3), pp. 416-425.

Lamare, J. (1974), 'Language Environment and Political Socialization of Mexican-American Children', in Niemi, R. (ed.), *The Politics of our Future Citizens,* Jossey-Bass, San Francisco, pp. 63-72.

Larsen, S. S. (1982), 'The Two Sides of the House: Identity and Social Organization in Kilbroney, Northern Ireland', in Cohen, A. P. (ed.), *Belonging:*

Identity and Social Organization in British Rural Cultures, Manchester University Press, Manchester.

Lerner, R.M. (1989), 'Individual Development and the Family System'. In Kreppner, K. and Lerner, R.M.(eds.), *Family Systems and Life-Span Development*, Lawrence Erlbaum, New York.

Lewin, K. (1948), *Resolving Social Conflicts: Selected Papers on Group Dynamics,* Harper, New York.

Lewin, K. (1951), *Field Theory in Social Science,* Harper, New York.

Liebes, T., Katz, E. and Ribak, R. (1991), 'Ideological reproduction', *Political Behavior,* 13 (3), pp.237-252.

Livesley, W. J. and Bromley, D. M. (1973), *Person Perception in Childhood and Adolescence,* Wiley, New York.

Livingstone, S. and Morison, J. (1995), *An Audit of Democracy in Northern Ireland,* with *Fortnight,* 337, Fortnight Educational Trust, Belfast,

Lorenc, L. and Branthwaite, A. (1986), 'Evaluations of political violence by English and Northern Ireland schoolchildren', *British Journal of Social Psychology,* 25 (4), pp. 349-352.

Lösel, F. and Bliesener, T. (1994), 'Some high-risk adolescents do not develop conduct problems: a study of protective factors', *International Journal of Behavioral Development,* 17 (4), pp. 753-777.

Loughrey, G. C., Bell, P., Kee, M., Roddy, R. J. and Curran, P. S. (1988), 'Post-traumatic stress disorder and civil violence in Northern Ireland, *British Journal of Psychiatry,* 153, pp. 554-560.

Lunzer, E.A. (1966), *The Manchester Scales of Social Adaptation,* National Foundation for Educational Research, Slough, Bucks.

Luthar, S. S. and Zigler, E. (1991), 'Vulnerability and competence: a review of research on resilience in childhood', *American Journal of Orthopsychiatry,* 61, pp. 6-22

Lyons, H. A. (1974), 'Terrorist bombing and psychological sequelae, *Journal of the Irish M edical Association,* 67, p. 15.

MacFarlane, G. (1989), 'Dimensions of Protestantism: The Working of Protestant Identity in a Northeren Irish Village', in Curtin, C. and Wilson, T. M. (eds.), *Ireland from Below: Social Change and Local Communities,* Galway University Press, Galway Ireland.

Maduewesi, E. (1982), 'Nigerian elementary children's interests and concerns', *Alberta Journal of Educational Research,* 28 (3), pp. 204-211.

Magnusson, D. (1981) (ed.), *Toward a Psychology of Situations: An Interactional Perspective.* Lawrence Erlbaum, New Jersey.

Magnusson, D. and Törestad, B. (1993), 'A holistic view of personality: a model revisited', *Annual Review of Psychology,* 44, pp. 427-452.

Manning, P. K. and Campbell, B. (1973), 'Pinball as game, fad, synedoche', *Youth and Society,* 4, pp. 333-358.

Marcia, J. E. (1967), 'Ego identity status: relationship to change in self-esteem, "general maladjustment " and authoritarianism', *Journal of Personality,* 35, pp. 118-133.

Marcia, J. E. (1980), 'Identity in Adolescence' in Adelson, J. (ed.), *Handbook of Adolescent Psychology,* Wiley, New York, pp. 159-187.

Markus, H and Nurius, P, (1986), 'Possible selves', *American Psychologist,* 41, pp. 954-969.

Markus, H. and Kitayama, S. (1991), 'Culture and the self: implications for cognition, emotion and motivation', *Psychological Review*, 98 (2), pp. 224-253.

Masten, A. S. (1989), 'Resilience in Development: Implications of the Study of Successful Adaptation for Developmental Psychopathology', in Cicchetti, D. (ed.), *The Emergence of a Discipline: Rochester Symposium on Developmental Psychopathology, Vol. 1*, Lawrence Erlbaum, Hillsdale, New Jersey, pp. 261-294.

Masten, A. S., Best, K. M. and Garmezy, N. (1990), 'Resilience and development; contributions from the study of children who overcame diversity', *Development and Psychopathology*, 2, pp. 425-444.

McAuley, R., and Troy, M. (1983), 'The impact of urban conflict and violence on children referred to a child psychiatry clinic', in Harbison, J. (ed.),*Children of the Troubles: Children in Northern Ireland*, Stranmillis College Learning Resources Unit, Belfast, pp. 33-43

McCartney, C. (1993), 'A council of hope', *Fortnight*, 313, pp. 34-35.

McClenaghan, C., Cairns, E., Dunn, S. and Morgan, V. (1992), *Views of Northern Ireland Secondary Schoolchildren: Intergroup Differences*, paper presented at Annual Conference, Northern Ireland Branch, British Psychological Society, Virginia, Co. Cavan, April 1992.

McDowell, J. (1993), 'Bitter pills', *Fortnight*, 314, p. 10.

McGrath, A. and Wilson, R. (1985), *Factors which Influence the Prevalence and Variation of Psychological Problems in Children in Northern Ireland*, paper presented to the Annual Conference of the Developmental Section of the British Psychological Society, Belfast.

McGuire, W. J. (1986), 'The Myth of Massive Media Impact: Savings and Salvages', in Comstock, G. A. (ed.), *Public Communication and Behavior, Vol 1*, Academic Press, Orlando, Fla.

McKernan, J. (1980), 'Pupil Values as Indicators of Intergroup Differences', in Harbison, J. and Harbison, J., (eds.), *A Society under Stress: Children and Young People in Northern Ireland*, Open Books, Wells, Somerset, pp, 128-140.

McRobbie, A. and Garber, J. (1976), 'Girls and Subculture', in Hall, S. and Jefferson, T. (eds.), *Resistance Through Ritual*, Hutchinson, London, pp. 202-222.

McWhirter, L. (1981), *The Influence of Contact on the Development of Interpersonal Awareness in Northern Ireland Children*, paper presented at British Psychological Society Development Section Conference, Manchester, 1981.

McWhirter, L. (1983a), *How Troubled are the Children in Northern Ireland Compared to Children Living outside Northern Ireland?* paper presented to the Annual Conference Psychological Society of Ireland, Athlone.

McWhirter, L. (1983b), 'Looking Back And Looking Forward: An Inside Perspective', in Harbison, J. (ed.), *Children of the Troubles: Children in Northern Ireland*, Stranmillis College Learning Resources Unit, Belfast. pp. 127-157.

McWhirter, L. (1984), *Is Getting Caught in a Riot More Stressful than Seeing a Scary Film or Moving to a New School?* Paper presented at the Annual Conference, Northern Ireland Branch, British Psychological Society, Portballintrae, Co. Antrim.

Melaugh, M. (1995), 'Majority-Minority Differentials: Unemployment, Housing and Health', in Dunn, S, (ed.), *Facets of the Conflict in Northern Ireland*, St. Martin's Press/Macmillan, London.

Miller, P.H. (1989), 'Theories of Adolescence' in Worell, J. and Danner, F. (eds.), *The Adolescent As Decision-Maker*, Academic Press, New York.

Minns, D. R. and Williams, C. B. (1989), 'Agent influence on political learning: an experimental study', *Social Science Journal*, 26 (2), pp. 173-188.

Modell, J. (1989), *Into One's Own: From Youth to Adulthood in the United States 1920-1975*, University of California Press, Berkeley.

Modell, J. and Goodman, M. (1993), 'Historical Perspectives', in Feldman, S. S. and Elliott, G. R. (eds.), *At the Threshold: The Developing Adolescent*, Harvard University Press, Cambridge, Mass.

Modell, J. and Siegler, R. S. (1994), 'Child Development and Human Diversity', in Elder, G. H. Jr., Modell, J. and Parke, R. D.(eds.), *Children in Time and Place: Developmental and Historical Insights*, Cambridge University Press, Cambridge.

Moen, P., Dempster-McClain, D. and Williams, R. M. Jr. (1992), 'Successful aging: a life-course perspective on women's multiple roles and health', *American Journal of Sociology*, 97, pp. 1612-1638.

Moffat, C. (1992), 'Seats ceded', *Fortnight*, 312, p. 11.

Montemayor, R., and Flannery, D.J. (1990), 'Making the Transition from Childhood to Early Adolescence'. In Montemayor, R., Adams, G. R. & Gullotta, T. P. (eds.), *From Childhood to Adolescence*, Sage, New York, pp. 291-301.

Moxon-Brown, E. (1983), *Nation, Class and Creed in Northern Ireland*, Gower, Aldershot.

Murphy, D. (1978), *A Place Apart*, John Murray, London.

Murray, D. (1985), *Worlds Apart: Segregated Schools in Northern Ireland*, Appletree Press, Belfast.

Murray, D. (1995), 'Culture, Religion and Violence', in Dunn, S. (ed.), *Facets of the Conflict in Northern Ireland*, St Martin's Press/Macmillan, London,

Neisser, U. (1988), 'Five kinds of self-knowledge', *Philosophical Psychology*, 1, pp. 35-59.

Nelson, S. (1984), *Ulster's Unionist Defenders: Protestant Political Paramilitary and Community Groups and the Northern Ireland Conflict*, Appletree Press, Belfast.

New Ireland Forum (1984), *Report of Proceedings 1983-84*, Stationery Office, Dublin.

Ng, D. and June, L. (1985), 'Electronic leisure and youth: Kitchener arcade video game players', *Society and Leisure*, 8, pp. 537-548.

NICRC (Northern Ireland Community Relations Council) (1993), *A Guide to Peace and Reconciliation Groups*, NICRC, Belfast.

NICVA (Northern Ireland Council for Voluntary Action) (1989), *Index of Community Groups in Northern Ireland*, NICVA, Belfast.

Nurius, P. (1991), 'Possible Selves and Social Suport: Social Cognitive Resources for Coping and Striving', in Howard, J. A. and Callero, P. (eds.), *The Self-Society Dynamic: Cognition Emotion and Action*, Cambridge, Cambridge University Press.

O'Callaghan, M. (1989), 'The catholic school in the context of change', in *The Catholic Teacher in the Catholic School: Conference Report,* Council for Catholic Maintained Schools, Holywood, Co. Down, N.I.

O'Connor, F. (1993), *In Search of a State: Catholics in Northern Ireland,* Blackstaff Press, Belfast, Northern Ireland.

O'Donnell, E. E. (1977), *Northern Irish Stereotypes,* College of Industrial Relations, Dublin.

O'Kane, D. and Cairns, E. (1988), 'The development of conservatism in Northern Ireland: a cross-cultural comparison', *Journal of Social Psychology,* 128 (1), pp. 49-53.

O'Malley, P. (1983), *The Uncivil Wars: Ireland Today,* Blackstaff: Belfast.

Oerter, R. (1985), 'Developmental Tasks through the Life-Span: A New Approach to an Old Concept'. In Featherman, D. L. and Lerner, R. M. (eds.), *Life-Span Development and Behaviour, Vol. 7,* Academic Press, New York.

Ogbu, J. (1987), 'Variability in responses to schooling: Nonimmigrants vs Immigrants', in Spindler, G. and Spindler, L. (eds.), *Interpretive Ethnography of Education,* Lawrence Erlbaum, Hillsdale, New Jersey.

Olbrich, E. (1990), 'Coping and Development', in Bosma, H.A. and Jackson, A.E. (eds.), *Coping and Self-Concept in Adolescence,* Springer-Verlag, Heidelberg.

Oliver, Q. (1995), Director, Northern Ireland Council for Voluntary Action, personal communication.

Orbell, S., Trew, K. and McWhirter, L. (1990), 'Mental illness in Northern Ireland: a comparision with Scotland and England', *Social Psychiatry and Psychiatric Epidemiology,* 25, pp. 165-169.

Osborne, R. D. and Cormack, R. J. (1989), 'Gender And Religion as Issues in Education, Training and Entry to Work', in Harbison, J. (ed.), *Growing Up in Northern Ireland,* Stranmillis College Learning Resources Unit, Belfast, pp. 42-65.

Owen, D. and Dennis, J. (1987), 'Preadult development of political tolerance', *Political Psychology,* 8 (4), pp. 547-561.

Oyserman, D. and Markus, H. (1990), 'Possible sselves and delinquency', *Journal of Personality and Social Psychology,* 59 (1), pp. 112-125.

Palley, C. (1972), 'The Evolution, Disintegration and Possible Reconstruction of the Northern Ireland Constitution' (Repr. from the *Anglo-American Law Review,)* Barry Rose, London in association with the Institute of Irish Studies, Queen's University, Belfast.

Parham, T. and Helms, J. (1985a), 'Attitudes of racial identity and self-esteem of Black students: an exploratory investigation', *Journal of College Student Personnel,* 26, pp. 143-147.

Parham, T. and Helms, J. (1985b), 'Relation of racial identity attitudes to self-actualization and affective states of Black students', *Journal of Counselling Psychology,* 32, pp. 431- 440.

Parker, T. (1993), *May the Lord in His Mercy Be Kind to Belfast.,* Cape, London.

Pearl, D., Bouthilet, L. and Lazar, J. (1982), *Television and Behaviour, Vol. 2: Ten Years of Scientific Progress and Implications for the Eighties,* US Dept. of Health and Human Services Technical Reviews, Rockville, Md.

Phinney, J. (1989), 'Stages of ethnic identity in minority group adolescents', *Journal of Youth and Adolescence,* 9, pp. 34-49.

Phinney, J. (1990), 'Ethnic identity in adolescents and adults: a review of research', *Psychological Bulletin,* 108 (3), pp. 499-514.

Phinney, J. and Alipuria, L. (1990). 'Ethnic identity in older adolescents from four ethnic groups', *Journal of Adolescence,* 13, pp. 171-183.

Piaget, J. (1947), *The Psychology of Intelligence,* Harcourt Brace, New York.

Pinner, F.A. (1965), 'Parental overprotection and political distrust', *The Annals of the American Academy of Political and Social Science,* 361, pp. 59-70.

Pollak, A. (1993) (ed.), *A Citizen's Inquiry: the Opsahl Report on Northern Ireland,* Lilliput Press and Initiative '92, Dublin.

Poole, M. A. (1983), 'The Demography of Violence', in Darby, J. (ed.), *Northern Ireland: The Background to the Violence,* Appletree, Belfast.

Poole, M. E. (1983), *Youth: Expectations and Transitions,* Routledge and Kegan Paul, Melbourne.

Powers, S. I., Hauser, S. T., Schwartz, J. M., Noam, G. G. and Jacobson, A. M. (1983), 'Adolescent Ego Development and Family Interaction: a Structural Developmental Perspective', in Grotevant, H. D. and Cooper, C. R. (eds.), *Adolescent Development in the Family,* Jossey-Bass, San Francisco.

PPRU (Policy, Planning and Research Unit) (1985), *Continuous Household Survey - Religion, No. 2/85,* Dept. of Finance and Personnel, Belfast.

PPRU (Policy, Planning and Research Unit) (1993), *Continuous Household Survey - Religion, 1988-1990,No. 1/93,* Dept. of Finance and Personnel, Belfast.

Quicke, J. (1991), 'Social background, identity and emergent political consciousness in the sixth form', *Cambridge Journal of Education,* 21 (1), pp. 5-18.

Raven, J. and Whelan, C. T. (1983), *Political Culture in Ireland: The Views of Two Generations,* I.P.P., Dublin.

Rea, D. (1982) (ed.), *Political Cooperation in Divided Societies: A Series of Papers Relevant to the Conflict in Northern Ireland,* Gill and MacMillan, Dublin.

Renshon, S. A. (1974), *Psychological Needs And Political Behavior,* Free Press, New York.

Renshon, S. A. (1975), 'The Role of Personality Development in Political Socialization', in Schwartz, D. W. and Schwartz, S. K. (eds.), *New Directions in Political Socialization,* Free Press, New York.

Rice, K. (1990), 'Attachment in adolescence', *Journal of Youth and Adolescence,* 19, pp. 511-538.

Roberts, D. F. and Maccoby, N. (1984), 'Effects of Mass Communication', in Lindzey, G. and Aronson, E. (eds.), *Handbook of Social Psychology, Vol 2,* 3rd ed. Addison-Wesley, Reading, Mass., pp. 539-598.

Robinson, A. (1971), 'Education and sectarian conflict in Northern Ireland', *The New Era,* 52 (1), pp.384-88.

Robinson, J. P. and Davis, D.K. (1990), 'Television news and the informed public: an information-processing approach', *Journal of Communication,* 40 (3), pp. 106-119.

Rogers, E. M. (1969), 'Motivations Values and Attitudes Of Subsistence Farmers: Toward a Subculture Of Peasantry', in Warton, E. (ed.), *Subsistence Agriculture and Economic Development,* Aldine Publishing Co., Chicago.

Rolston, B. (1981), 'Sectarianism and Community Politics', in Frazer, H. (ed.), *Community Work in a Divided Society,* Farset Press, Belfast.

Rolston, B. and Tomlinson, M. (1988), *Unemployment in West Belfast: the Obair Report*, Beyond the Pale Publications, Belfast.

Rose, R. (1971), *Governing without Consensus: an Irish Perspective*, Faber and Faber, London.

Rosenberg, M. (1965), *Society and the Adolescent Self-Image*, Princeton University Press, Princeton, New Jersey.

Rowlands, B. (1985), 'St. Peter's Centre: an experiment in women's education in West Belfast', in Abbott, M. and Frazer, H. (eds.), *Women and Community Work in Northern Ireland*, Farset Press, Belfast,

Runyan, W. McK. (1988), *Psychology and Historical Interpretation*, Oxford University Press, New York.

Russell, J. (1974), 'Sources of conflict', *Northern Teacher*, 11 (3), pp. 3-11.

Rutter, M. (1985), 'Resilience in the face of adversity: protective factors and resistance to psychiatric disorder', *British Journal of Psychiatry*, 147, pp. 598-611.

Rutter, M. (1990), 'Psychological Resilience and Protective Mechanisms', in Rolf, J., Masten, A. S., Cicchetti, D., Nuechterlein, K. H. and Weintraub, S. (eds.), *Risk and Protective Factors in the Development of Psychopathology*, Cambridge University Press, Cambridge, pp. 181-204.

Rutter, M., Cox, A., Tupling, C., Berger, M. and Yule, Q. (1975), 'Attainment and adjustment in two geographic areas: 1. The prevalence of psychiatric disorder', *British Journal of Psychiatry*, 126, pp. 520-533.

SACHR (Standing Advisory Commission on Human Rights) (1987), *Religious and Political Discrimination and Equality of Opportunity in Northern Ireland: Report on Fair Employment*, HMSO, Cm. 237, London:

Salters, J. (1970), *Attitudes Towards Society in Protestant and Roman Catholic Schoolchildren*, MEd Thesis, Queen's University Belfast.

Sarigiani, P. A., Wilson, J. L., Petersen, A. C. and Vicary, J. R. (1990), 'Self-image and educational plans of adolescents from two contrasting communities', *Journal of Early Adolescence*, 10, pp. 37-55.

Schwartz, S. K. (1975), 'Patterns of Cynicism: Differential Political Socialization among Adolescents', in Schwartz, D. W. and Schwartz, S. K. (eds.) *New Directions in Political Socialization*, Free Press, New York.

Schweder, R. A. and Sullivan, M. A. (1993), 'Cultural psychology: who needs it?' *Annual Review of Psychology*, 44, pp. 497-523.

Seiffke-Krenke, L. (1992), *Stress, Coping and Relationships*, Lawrence Erlbaum, Hillsdale, New Jersey.

Seiffke-Krenke, L. and Shulman, S. (1990), 'Coping styles in adolescence: a cross-cultural study', *International Journal of Cross-Cultural Psychology*, 21, pp. 351-377.

Selman, R. L. (1980), *The Growth of Interpersonal Understanding: Developmental and Clinical Analyses*, Academic Press, New York.

Sidanius, J., Ekehammar, B. and Brewer, R. (1986), 'The political socialization determinants of higher order socio-political space: a Swedish example', *Journal of Social Psychology*, 126 (1), pp. 7-22.

Sigel, R. and Hoskin, M. (1981), *The Political Involvement of Adolescents*, Rutgers University Press, New Brunswick, New Jersey.

Sigel, R. S. (1975), 'Psychological antecedents and political involvement: the utility of the concept of locus-of-control', *Social Science Quarterly*, 39, pp. 315-322.

Sigel, R. S. and Hoskin, M. B. (1977), 'Affect for government and its relation to policy output among adolescents', *American Journal of Political Science*, 21, pp. 111-134.

Silbereisen, R. K., Eyferth, K. and Rudinger, G. (1986), *Development as Action in Context: Problem Behaviour and Normal Youth Development*, Springer-Verlag, Berlin.

Silbereisen, R. K., Noack, P. and Eyferth, K. (1986), 'Place for Development: Adolescents, Leisure Settings and Developmental Tasks', in Silbereisen, R. K., Eyferth, K. and Rudinger, G. (eds.), *Development as Action in Context: Problem Behaviour and Normal Youth Development*, Springer-Verlag, Berlin.

Simmons, R. G., and Blyth, D. A. (1987), *Moving into Adolescence: The Impact of Pubertal Change and School Context*, Aldine de Gruyter, New York.

Singleton, D. (1985), 'Housing and planning policy in Northern Ireland: problems of implementation in a divided community', *Policy and Politics*, 13 (3), pp. 305-326.

Smith, A. (1995), 'Education and the Conflict', in Dunn, S. (ed.), *Facets of the Conflict in Northern Ireland*, St Martin's Press/Macmillan, London.

Smith, D. J. (1987), *Equality and Inequality in Northern Ireland, Part 3: Perceptions and Views*, Policy Studies Institute, London.

Smith, T.E. (1983), 'Parental Influence: a review of the evidence of influence and a theoretical model of the parental inflluence process', *Research in the Sociology of Education and Socialization*, 4, pp. 13-45.

Spenner, K. I. and Featherman, D. L. (1979), 'Achievement ambitions', *Annual Review of Sociology*, 4, pp. 373-420.

Stacey, B. (1978), *Political Socialization in Western Society*, Arnold, London.

Steinberg, L. (1993), 'Autonomy, Conflict and Harmony in the Family Relationship', in Feldman, S. S. and Elliott, G. R. (eds.), *At the Threshold: The Developing Adolescent*, Harvard University Press, Cambridge, Mass.

Steinkopf, K. (1973), 'Family communication patterns and anticipatory socialization', *Journalism Quarterly*, 50, pp. 24-30.

Stewart, A. T. Q. (1977), *The Narrow Ground: Aspects of Ulster, 1609-1969*, Faber and Faber, London.

Stone, V. and Chaffee, S. H. (1970), 'Family communication patterns and source-message orientation', *Journalism Quarterly*, 47, pp. 239-246.

Stryker, S. (1984), *Identity Theory: Developments and Extensions*, in Symposium on Self and Social Structure: Conference on Self and Identity at British Psychological Society, Cardiff, Wales.

Tajfel, H. and Turner, J. (1979), 'An Integrative Theory of Intergroup Conflict', in Austin, W.G. and Worchel, S. (eds.), *The Social Psychology of Intergroup Relations*, Wadsworth, Belmont, California.

Tallman, I., Marotz-Baden, R. and Pindas, P. (1983), *Adolescent Socialization in Cross-Cultural Perspective: Planning for Social Change*, Academic Press, New York.

Taylor, R. L. (1988), 'Social scientific research on the 'Troubles' in Northern Ireland: the problem of objectivity', *Economic and Social Review*, 19 (2), pp. 123-145.

Teague, P. (1987) (ed.), *Beyond the Rhetoric. Politics, The Economy and Social Policy in Northern Ireland*, Lawrence and Wishart, London:

Thomas, D. L., Gecas, V., Weigert, A. and Rooney, E. (1974), *Family Socialization and the Adolescent: Determinants of Self-Concept, Conformity, Religiosity and Counterculture Values*, Lexington Books, New York.

Toner, I. J. (1994),'Children of "the Troubles" in Northern Ireland: perspectives and intervention', *International Journal of Behavioral Development*, 17 (4), pp. 629-647.

Torney-Purta, J. (1985), *Predictors of Global Awareness and Global Concern among Secondary School Students*, Mershon Center, Ohio State University, Columbus, Ohio, ERIC 271364.

Torney-Purta, J. (1989), 'Political cognition and its restructuring in young people', *Human Development*, 32, pp. 14-23.

Torney-Purta, J. (1993), 'Youth in Relation to Social Institutions', in Feldman, S. S. and Elliott, G. R. (eds), *At the Threshold: The Developing Adolescent*, Harvard University Press, Cambridge, Mass.

Townshend, C. (1988) (ed.), *Consensus in Ireland: Approaches and Recessions*, Clarendon Press, Oxford.

Trew, K. (1980), *Sectarianism in Northern Ireland: A Research Perspective*, Paper presented at the British Psychological Society, Social Psychology Section Annual Conference, Canterbury, September, 1980.

Trew, K. (1981), *Social Identity and Group Membership*, paper presented to Northern Ireland Branch, British Psychological Society, Rosapenna, Donegal.

Trew, K. (1986), 'Catholic-Protestant Conflict in Northern Ireland', in Hewstone, M. and Brown, R. (eds.), *Contact and Conflict in Intergroup Encounters*, Blackwell, Oxford, pp. 93-106.

Trew, K. (1989), 'Evaluating the Impact of Contact Schemes for Catholic and Protestant Children', in Harbison, J. (ed.), *Children of the Troubles: Children of Northern Ireland*, Stranmillis College Learning Resources Unit, Belfast.

Trew, K. (1992), 'Social psychological research on the conflict', *The Psychologist*, 5, pp. 342-344.

Trew, K. (1994), 'What it means to be Irish from a Northern perspective', *Irish Journal of Psychology*, vol. 15 (2 &3), pp. 288-299.

Trew, K. and Kilpatrick, R. (1984), *The Daily Life of the Unemployed*, Queen's University, Belfast, .

Trew, K., Mcwhirter, L., Maguire, A. and Hinds, J. (1985), *Irish children's summer program in Greensboro (NC): Evaluation 1984-85*. Unpublished paper, Queen's University, Belfast.

Trommsdorff, G. (1983), 'Future orientation and socialization', *International Journal of Psychology*, 18, pp. 381-406.

Trommsdorff, G. (1986), 'Future Time Orientation and its Relevance for Development as Action', in Silbereisen, R. K., Eyferth, K. and Rudinger, G. (eds.), *Development as Action in Context: Problem Behaviour and Normal Youth Development*, Springer-Verlag, Berlin.

Trommsdorff, G., Lamm, H. and Schmidt, R. W (1978), 'A longitudinal study of adolescents' future orientation (time perspective)', *Journal of Youth and Adolescence*, 8, pp. 131-147.

Turner, J. C. (1988), 'Personality in society: social psychology's contribution to sociology', *Social Psychology Quarterly*, 51, pp. 1-10.

Turner, J. C. and Oakes, P. J. (1989), 'Self-categorization theory and Social Influence', in Paulus, P. B. (ed.), *The Psychology of Group Influence*, Lawrence Erlbaum, Hillsdale, New Jersey, pp. 233-275.

Valsiner, J. (1987), *Culture and the Development of Children's Action*, Wiley, New York.

van der Linden, F. J. (1988), 'Adolescent Lifeworld and Youth Research: A Plea for an Ecopsychological Approach', in Meeus, W., Hazekamp, J. L. and te Poel, Y. (eds.), *European Contributions to Youth Research*, Free University Press, Amsterdam.

van Hasselt, V. B. and Hersen, M. (1987), *Handbook of Adolescent Psychology*, Pergamon, New York.

Vannan, E. J. (1989), 'Community Differences in Vulnerability to Stress', in Harbison, J. (ed.), *Growing Up in Northern Ireland*, Stranmillis College Learning Resources Unit, Belfast, pp. 107-115.

Werner, E. E. (1985), 'Stress and Protective Factors in Children's Lives', in Nicol, A. R. (ed.), *Longitudinal Studies in Child Psychology and Psychiatry*, John Wiley, Chichester, pp. 335-355.

Werner, E. E. (1989), 'Vulnerability and Resilience: A Longitudinal Perspective', in Bambring, M., Lösel, F. and Skowronek, H. (eds.), *Children at Risk: Assessment, Longitudinal Research and Intervention*, De Gruyter, New York, pp. 157-172.

White, R, (1959), 'Motivation reconsidered: the concept of competence', *Psychological Review*, 66, pp. 297-333.

Whyte, Jean (1983a), 'Control and supervision of urban 12 year olds within and outside Northern Ireland', *Irish Journal of Psychology*, 6 (1), pp. 37-45.

Whyte, Jean (1983b), 'Everyday Life for 11 and 12 Year-Olds in a Troubled Area of Belfast: Do "the Troubles" Intrude?' In Harbison J. (ed.), *Children of the Troubles: Children in Northern Ireland*, Stranmillis College Learning Resources Unit, Belfast, pp. 98-108

Whyte, Jean (1983c), 'Educational Enrichment with Deprived Children: The Long-Term Consequences', in Harbison, J. (ed.), *Children of the Troubles*, Stranmillis College Learning Resources Unit, Belfast, N. I. pp. 59-73.

Whyte, Jean (1984), *The Leisure Pursuits Of Young People In Northern Ireland*, paper presented at International Conference of the International Association of Educational and Vocational Guidance, Dublin.

Whyte, Jean (1986), 'The usefulness of literacy for 11 and 12 year olds'. *Proceedings of the 8th Annual Conference, Reading Association of Ireland*, Dublin, pp. 30-38.

Whyte, Jean (1989a), 'The views of the consumer in education', *Irish Educational Studies*, 7 (1), 221-231.

Whyte, Jean (1989b), 'The Long-Term Consequences of a Pre-School Language Intevention Programme', in Harbison, J. (ed.), *Growing Up in Northern Ireland*, Stranmillis College Resources Unit, Belfast. pp.

Whyte, Jean (1992a), *Do we always Wish upon a Star? A Longitudinal and Cross-Cultural Study of Wishes in Preadolescents and Adolescents*, paper presented at 7th Australian Developmental Conference, Brisbane. Qld., July.

Whyte, Jean (1992b), 'Disadvantage and unemployment: a longitudinal study of psychosocial variables', *Irish Journal of Psychology*, 13 (2), pp. 193-209.

Whyte, Jean (1993a), *Have Things Changed? The Social Context of 12 Year Olds in Belfast, London and Dublin in 1981 and 1992*, paper presented at the ACIS Conference, Villanova Pa., April.

Whyte, Jean (1993b), 'Longitudinal correlates and outcomes of initial reading progress for a sample of Belfast boys', *European Journal of Psychology of Education*, 8 (3), pp. 325-340.

Whyte, Jean and Montgomery, P. (1984), *Encounters with Violence and Anxiety Levels in a Sample of Belfast Boys*, paper presented at Annual Conference, Northern Ireland Branch, British Psychological Society, Portballintrae, Co. Antrim.

Whyte, Jean. (1988), *Born to Conform? the Child in Northern Ireland'*, paper presented at the Annual Conference, Northern Ireland Branch, British Psychological Society, Belleek, Co. Fermanagh.

Whyte, John (1990), *Interpreting Northern Ireland*, Oxford University Press, Oxford.

Wichert, S. (1991), *Northern Ireland since 1945*, Longman, London and New York.

Williamson, A., Reid, N., Cormack, N. and Osborne, R. (1982), 'The characteristics of Ulster's students', *Times Higher Educational Supplement*, 8, pp. 10-11.

Willis, P. and Cairns, E. (1986), *Attitudes towards Voting among Young People in Northern Ireland*, Unpublished paper, University of Ulster, Coleraine.

Wilson, J. D. and Tyrrell, J. (1995), 'Institutions for Conciliation and Mediation', in Dunn, S. (ed.), *Facets of the Conflict in Northern Ireland*, St Martin's Press/MacMillan, London.

Wilson, R. and Cairns, E. (1994), 'Psychological consequences of the Remembrance Sunday explosion in Enniskillen: a community survey', manuscript submitted for publication.

Winkley, L. (1982), 'The implications of children's wishes: a research note', *Journal of Child Psychology and Psychiatry and Allied Disciplines*, 23 (4), pp. 477-483.

Worell, J. and Danner, F. (1989) (eds.), *The Adolescent as Decision-Maker*, Academic Press, New York.

Wright, F. (1987), *Northern Ireland: A Comparative Analysis*, Gill and MacMillan, Dublin.

Wulff, H. (1988), *Twenty Girls: Growing Up, Ethnicity and Excitement in a South London Microculture*, Stockholm Studies in Social Anthropology, Stockholm.

Yankelovich, D. (1973), *The Changing Values on Campus*, Washington Square Press, New York.

Yankelovich, D. (1974), *The New Morality: A Profile of American Youth in the 70s*, McGraw Hill, New York.

Zellman, G. L. and Sears, D.O. (1971), 'Childhood origins of tolerance for dissent', *Journal of Social Issues*, 27, pp. 109-136.

Index

Abbott, M. 38, 48
ability level of participants
11
Abramson, P. 169, 173
access to information 12,
20, 23, 24, 145, 221
and generativity 232
and level of declarative
knowledge 225
acculturation 16, 175
Act of Union 31
Adamson, I. 31
Adelson, J. 22, 29
adolescence 12, 14, 16, 18,
19, 20, 27, 194
Adolescent values and society
27
and parents 19
African-Americans 16
afternoon activities, boys 77
girls 76
alcohol 67, 75
Alienation from institutions
of state 39
Alipuria, L. 26
All-Ireland Final 186
Alva, S. 175
Alwin, D. F. 26
ambiguity 27, 49, 117, 236,
238
Amuchie, F. 72
Anglo-Irish Agreement 42,
43, 44, 162, 236

reactions from both sides
43
Anglo-Irish Inter-
Governmental Council 42
Arthur, A. 15, 136
Asia 136
aspirations 12, 18, 195
categorizing 197
changes 207
realistic 208
Astin, A. 169
Atkin, C. 144, 169
Atkins, Humphrey 41, 42
attachment 101
attitude transmission across
generations 170
attitudes to authority 23
attitudes towards education
20, 202, 216, 230
Australia 72
autonomy 12, 14, 24, 102,
108, 117, 217, 224, 229
of Stormont government
32
Avery, P. 23

B Specials 35
babysitting 125, 133
Bachman, J. G. 27
Baltes, P. 3
Banaji, M. R. 14, 16, 192
Bandura, A. 18, 21, 86, 144,
192

Bardon, J. 9, 30, 32, 33, 34, 35, 37, 39, 40, 42, 43, 47
Barritt, D. P. 5
Barry, R. 15
Batts, D. 5
Beattie, G. 15
behaviour problems 100, 117
Belfrage, S. 15, 40
Belgian adolescents 24
Bell, P. 7
Beloff, H. 28
Bengston, V. L. 20, 170
Berger, P. L. 7 25
Best, K. M. 130
Bew, P. 9, 30, 33, 43, 236, 236
bicycle 54, 55, 215
Bill, J. 11
biological basis for differences 15
Blackman, T. 40
Blease, M. 7
Bliesener, T. 129
Bloody Sunday 36
Blos, P. 20, 100
Blumler, J. 168
Blyth, D. A. 29, 118
Boal, F. W. 25
books 23, 54, 55, 84, 215, 217
   kinds of books read 84, 86
Bored 75
Bouffard, L. 194
Bouthilet, L. 86
Bowen, R. 21
Bowman, D. 49
boxing 186, 189
Bradford, Rev. Robert 37
Branthwaite, A. 15
Breakwell, G. 26, 168, 170
Breslin, A. 101

Brewer, R. 170
British Army 35, 54
British Labour Party 33
British Prime Minister 177
Bromley, D. M. 8, 26
Bronfenbrenner, U. 2, 10, 21
Brown, R. 26
Bruce, S. 25
Buckland, P. 32
Buckley, A. D. 15
Burger, J. M. 192
Burton, F. 15, 40
café job 131, 132
Cairns, B. D. 50
Cairns, E. 1, 3, 4, 5, 6, 7, 9, 15, 16, 36, 37, 100, 101, 117, 171, 174, 239
Cairns, R. B. 50
Cairns, T. 1, 194
Caledon 34, 47
Campaign for Democracy in Ulster 33
Campaign for Social Justice 33
Campbell, B. 72
Canada 136
Canning, D. 40
Cantor, N. 18, 23, 144, 223
car 55, 121, 124, 215, 219
   drivers 109
   washing 131
Carrington, B. 72
Carter, C. F. 5
cartoons 87
Catholic schools 5
Catholics 2, 4, 5, 9, 10, 31, 32, 33, 34, 35, 37, 40, 41, 45, 49, 101, 111, 172, 174

274

178, 216, 230,
236, 237, 239;
centre-periphery
progression 171
Chaffee, S. 23,
144, 169, 173
change 10, 47, 49,
213
in education 33-
49
and future
orientation 235;
Cheek, J. 16
children's television
programmes 86
children's reactions to
violence 1, 9
Chiu, L-H. 193
Chiu, P. 194
Chivers, T. 72
Choice 19, 101,
201, 219
and other
variables 114;
Church 75, 81, 83,
217
cigarettes 67
city travel by bus or
taxi 124
civic responsibility
24
Claudy 36
civil rights
movement 32,
33, 34, 35, 38
Clausen J. A. 3
cleanliness 104
clinical groups 7
clothes 67
clubs 75, 76
frequency of
attendance 134,
135
membership
123, 134
Co-operation North
237
cognitive capacity
171

cognitive
competence 160
processing 27
development through
participation in groups
48, 49
restructuring 26
skills 20
transformations
and behaviour
145
Cohler, B. J. 129
Colley, A. 72
Collins, W. A. 22,
100
comics 84
commitment 19,
102, 120,
120,130, 201,
221
and independence
and choice 142
composite
variable 131
and socio-
economic level
142
Committee on the
Administration of
Justice 45, 235
common bonds 15
Community
Relations
Commission 47,
237
community
development 9,
46, 47, 117 236
benefits to
individuals 48
community groups
237
community relations
holidays 49
composite variables
12
computers 83
Comstock, G. 144
conflict research 4

conformity 128,
145, 221
Conger, R. D. 118,
191, 193
Conlin, L. 101
Conroy, J. 40
Constitutional
Convention 41
contextual
framework 101
Continuous
Household
Survey 215, 216
control 110, 128,
192, 218, 220
cooking 92, 96
Cooper, C. R. 100
coping behaviour 19, 129
Corken, J. P. 5
Cormack, R. J. 5,
239
Cox, A. 7
crime 100, 154,
160
cross-community
33
friendships 6
Crozier, W. R. 6
Csikszentmihalyi,
M. 72
cues used for social
categorization 15
Cultural Traditions
238
cultural background
186
differences 116,
217
diversity of self
4
heritage 45
identity 173, 186
psychology 14;
Cup Final 184
Curran, P.S. 7
current affairs 145,
168
items recalled from
television news 162

items recalled from
newspapers 153
curriculum 5
Curry, C. 191

Damon, W. 3
Danner, F. 118
Darby, J. 5,31, 40
Davis, D. K. 143, 163, 168,
Davis, D. 144
dependency syndrome 231
Deane, E. 47
deaths 156, 160
due to 'Troubles' 37, 42
Deaux, K. 7, 16, 17, 192,
193
decision-making 47, 168
in families 102
by parents 108
participation in 38
declarative knowledge 9, 12,
18, 23, 48, 72, 144, 145,
152, 168, 171, 214, 215,
223, 226, 227, 230, 237,
239
delinquency 194
Democratic Unionist Party
(DUP) 178, 182, 236
Dempster-McClain, D. 3
Dennis, J. 22, 145, 168
Derry Unemployed Action
Committee, 47
Derry, 31, 36, 37
developmental tasks 17, 18
Devereux, J. 172
difference between girls and
boys, 'Goods' 56
housework 127
knowledge of politics 183
independence 113
job opportunities 58
afternoon activities 76
attitudes towards education
200
clubs 134
'Commitment' 130 '
expenditure 67
generativity' 211

items from television
news 163
jobs earning money 132
newspaper reading 148,
165
perceptions of control 108
sources of pocket money
109
sports questions 186
sports, games, leisure
activities 88;
television preferences 86
value systems 101
wishes 202
interest in current events
159
jobmoney 64
pocket money 61
differences between
communities 14-15, 31
different traditions 9, 214
disadvantage 45, 171, 231
discrimination 32, 33, 38
disengagement 20
district councils 38, 44, 45
divorce 99
domestic violence 53
Doob, L. W. 15, 148
double-minority model 25
Douglas, J. N. H. 25
Dungannon 33
Dunham, C. C. 170
Dunlop, J. 15, 227
Dunn, S. 5, 6, 30, 101
DUP see Democratic
Unionist Party
Dusek, J. B. 8, 26

earnings 50
Easter Rising 31, 34
economic background 4, 7,
38, 39, 50, 121, 205, 216
deprivation 32, 47
differences between
Catholics and
Protestants 40
ecopsychological
approach 21
ecumenism 15

Eder, D. 72
Education Act 34
Education for Mutual
Understanding 5
education 1, 9, 29, 31, 38,
45, 195, 198
and individual development
118
more extended view 199
segregated 3
short term view 198
educational level of family
170
EEC 179, 183
Ekehammar, B. 170
Elder, G. H. Jr. 2, 3, 52,
118, 191, 193
Elkind, D. 21
Elliott, G. R. 37,
Elliott, S. 118
Emler, N. 29, 118
emotional disengagement 19
employment 7, 25, 32, 40,
45, 196, 198
Engel, U. 27, 29, 117, 118
England 7, 15, 136
English children 7
Engstrom, L. M. 72
Enniskillen 44
Entwistle, D. R. 119
environment 3, 6, 8, 9, 14,
18, 20, 21, 26, 99, 118,
127, 161, 192
effects on development, 2
Erickson, E. H. 14, 20
ethnic attitudes 16
ethnic composition
of participants
217
ethnic identity 4, 6,
15, 17, 26
Europe 137,
European Cup 185,
186
Evason, E. 40, 53
evening activities,
boys 79
girls 78
expenditure 12, 54, 67

experiences of 'Troubles' 7, 36, 37

Eyferth, K. 3, 22, 52

failure at school 202

Fair Employment
    Commission 39
    legislation 41

Fairleigh, J. 15

Familism 24

family 3, 7, 14, 19, 22, 23, 24, 29, 54, 99, 118, 144, 171
    as primary source of socialization 22
    car 55
    within society 23

Farren, S. 5

fathers 105, 106, 108, 110

Feather, N. T. 22, 26

Featherman, D. L. 193

Fee, F. 3, 7

Feldman, S. S. 117

female athlete 189

Fennell, D. 15

Fields, R. 25, 101

Fife-Schaw, C. 168, 170

Fine, G. A. 72, 84, 86, 131

Fitt, Gerry 33

FitzGerald, Garrett 42

Flackes, W. D. 37

Flaherty, J. F. 8, 26

Flannery, D. J. 3, 99

Flegle, M. J. M. 72

Florian, V. 72

Foltz, W. J. 15, 148

Football Association 185

Fortnight 30, 35

Framework document 234

Fraser, M. 15, 99

Frazer, H. 38, 47, 48

free school dinners 56, 216

free time activities 8, 72ff

friends 75, 76, 81, 217

funding for schools 5

Furnham, A. 169

Furstenberg, F. F. 99

future orientation 6, 9, 12, 20, 23, 26, 28, 191, 193, 214, 236, 241 influences on 193

GAA (Gaelic Athletic Association) 186

Gafikin, F. 47

Gallagher A.M., 1, 4, 6, 16, 37, 44, 49, 100

Gallatin, J. 169

games 88

Garber, J. 72

gardening 131

Garmezy, N. 129

Garramone, G. 144, 169

Garton, A. F. 72

Ge, X. 118

Gecas, V. 29, 101, 107, 111

General Health Questionnaire 7

generational conflict 20

generativity 195, 213, 231, 233
    responses 200
    by location 210

Gibbon, P. 9, 30, 33, 43, 232, 234

Gibralter 44

Giles, M. 6

Glass, J. 172

Glassie, H. 15

global issues 206

Goldberg, D. 7

Goldstein, E. 72

Goode, W. J. 100

Goodman, M. 19

Goodnow, J. J. 3, 18, 22, 147, 219

'Goods Plus' 55, 66, 224

Goods, 54, 56, 200, 201, 224

Gough, B. 6

Government of Ireland Act 31

Gras, F. 72

Green, K. 169

Greenberg, M. 100

Greer, J. E. 15, 101, 148

Grotevant, H. D. 100

group identity 16, 24, 164, 172, 177

Guelke, A. 35
Gunter, B. 169

Hadden, W. A. 7
Hagell, A. 191, 193
Hall, G. S. 19,
Hall, M. 31
happy people 195, 209
Har-Even, D. 72
Harbison, Jeremy 7
Harbison, Joan 7, 32
Harevan, T. K. 3
Harris, J. 5
Harrison, S. 15
Harter, S. 16, 192
Haughey, Charles 42
Hauser, S. T. 100
Havighurst, R. J. 18
Heath, Edward 36
Helms, J. 26
Hersen, M. 3
Heskin, K. 9
Hetherington, E. M. 118
Hettema, P. J. 8, 145
hierarchical framework 101
Hill, J. P. 29, 102
Himmelweit, H. 169
Hinds, J. 136
historical time and individual
    development 118
hobbies 72
home rule 31
Homeless Citizens' League
    33, 47
homelessness due to
    'Troubles' 35
homework 75, 76, 77, 83,
    106, 128, 217
horse race 187;
Hosin, A. 174
Hoskin, M. 27, 172
household amenities 51, 215
Housework 75, 76, 78, 80,
    83, 120, 125, 127, 131
    differences by location
    125
housing 32, 33, 35, 38, 53
Houston, J. E. 6
Howe, L. 53

Hughes, J. 45
Hume, John 32
hunger strikes 38, 42, 48
Hunter, J. 191
Hurrelmann, K. 9, 14, 22,
    27, 29, 117, 118

Ianni, F. 172
identification with parents 23
identity 1, 2, 3, 4, 6, 10, 12,
    14, 15, 16, 20, 22, 25,
    26, 27, 29, 45, 56, 101,
    144, 145, 168, 214, 238
    definition 17
    meaning of 193
    stability and change 26
impressionable years
    hypothesis 26
income 12, 41, 54, 216
increasing persistence
    hypothesis 26
independence 19, 24, 102,
    105, 110, 113, 116, 117,
    120, 127, 194, 201, 202,
    219, 224, 229, 231
    of women 104, 110, 219
Index of Community Groups
    in Northern Ireland 237
Initiative '92 46
integrated communities 239
integrated education 4, 5,
    117,
interest in current affairs
    152, 225
    in education 230
    in local politics 171
International Youth Bridge
    171, 174
international 154, 160, 163,
    164, 179, 182, 188
internment 35
intimidation 31, 35
IRA 34, 35, 37, 42, 236
Iraq 174
Irish Association
    237
Irish dimension 41
Irish family 100
Irish general election 161

Irish Government 42, 43
Irwin, C. 6
Israeli 72

Jackskon-Beeck, M. 23
Jackson, S. 18, 22, 29
Jacobson, A. M. 100
Jahoda, G. 15
Jankowski, M. S. 173
Jardine, E. 50, 99, 100
Jenkins, R. 15, 40
Jennings, M. 169
JEPI 7
job for money 51, 55, 57,
  63, 131, 213, 216
job losses 216
jobmoney 63, 129
John, P. 38
joint parental authority 108
  ecisions 108
  salience 230
Jordan 176
Jugendwerk der Deutschen
  Shell 194
June, L. 72

Kaplan, L. 100
Katz, E. 23
Katzman, N. 144
Kee, R. 7
Kelly, K. 48
Kennedy, D. 25
Kestenbaum,G. I. 72
Kihlstrom, J. F. 18, 23,
  144 223
Kilpatrick, R. 53
Kinahan, T. 15
Kirchler, E 18
knowledge about public
  affairs 144, 180
Knox, C. 45
Kobak, R. 100
Kobasa, S. C. O. 9
Kohn, M. L. 25, 29
Korn, W. 171
Kraus, S. 145
Kremer, J. 6, 15
Kreppner, K. 3
Krosnik, J. A. 26

Lagan College 6
Lamare, J. 170
Lamm, H. 194
Larsen, S. S. 15
Larson, R. 72
Laufer, R. S. 20
Lazar, J. 86
leisure 12, 20, 72ff, 88, 217
Leitch, C. 100
Lemass, Seán 33, 34
Lerner, R. M. 3, 99, 117
Lewin, K. 21
Liebes, T. 23
life course, model 2, 3, 4,
  193
Livesley, W. J 8, 26
Livingstone 9, 31, 38, 41,
  44, 46, 48, 100, 171
local context 172, 184, 186,
  187, 222,
local government 32; reform,
  38
local politics, interest by NI
  young people 174
locus of control 24, 139,
  173, 226, 231
Lorenc, L. 15
Lorenz, F. O. 118
Lösel, F. M. 129
Loughrey, G. C. 7
Lunzer, E. A. 188
Luthar, S. S. 129
Lyons, H. A. 7

Maccoby, N. 144
MacFarlane, G. 27
magazines 84, 144
Magnusson, D. 3, 14, 52,
  192
Maguire, A. 136
Major, John 181, 183
Making Belfast Work 44
Manchester 7
  Scales of Social
  Adaptation 188
Manning, P. K. 72
Marcia, J. E. 17, 19, 26, 28
Margaret Mead 20

Markus, H. 17, 191, 192, 193, 194
Marotz-Baden, R. 18, 23, 24, 27, 117
Masten, A. S. 128
materialistic 206, 210
  attitudes 216
  outlook, 56
McAuley, R. 7
McClenaghan, C. 6, 101
McCluskey, Conn and Patricia 33
McCombs, M. 146
McDowell, J. 45
McGrath, A. 7, 37
McGuire, W. J., 145
McKernan, J. 101
McLeod, J. M. 23
McNally, A. 15
McRobbie, A. 72
McWhirter L., 2, 7, 29, 52, 99, 100, 117, 136
media 70, 86, 144, 168, 187, 191
  and tolerant values 145
  influence on political knowledge 169
Melaugh, M. 35, 40, 216
mental health 1, 4, 7
Merrett, J. D. 7
Miller, P. H. 18
Milltown cemetery 44
Minneapolis 101
Minns, D. R. 170
minority 16, 25, 31, 45
Mitchell, R. 6
Modell, J. 3, 19, 52, 118
Moen, P. 3
Moffat, C. 5
Mohammed Ali 186
money earned 50, 51, 216
  how spent 51
Montemayor, R. 3, 99
Montgomery, P. 7
Moore, B. 40
moral development 101
Morgan,V. 6, 101
Morison, J. 9, 31, 38, 41, 44, 46, 48, 100, 171

Morrissey, M. 47
Mortimer, J. T. 72, 84, 86, 131
mothers 104, 105, 106, 108, 110
Moxon-Browne, E. 25
Murphy, D. 15
Murray, D. 5, 31
music 72

nationalist 31, 32, 41, 44, 178, 179
negative possible selves 192
  self-concept 26
Neisser, U. 17
Nelson, S. 15
networks 48, 237
neurotic 7
New Ireland Forum 15, 42, 46
Newe, Gerard 33
newspapers 23, 144ff, 160, 164, 168, 221
Ng, D. 72
NI Secretary of State 177
NICRC (Northern Ireland Community Relations Council) 49
NICVA (Northern Ireland Council for Voluntary Action) 48, 237
Niemi, R. 169
Nigeria 72
Noack, P. 52
Noam, G. G. 100
non-generative responses 198, 210, 231
non-materialistic wishes 205; orientation 24
non-materialistic 210
North American children 7
Northern Ireland Housing Executive 38
Northern Ireland Labour Party 32
Northern Ireland 3, 4, 6, 7, 10, 15, 25, 27, 30, 31, 32, 34, 37, 38, 39, 41, 42, 46, 47, 50, 52, 53,

100, 101, 136, 145, 164,
170, 173, 174, 196, 204,
214
Nurius, P. 17, 191, 192,
193, 194
nurturance 106, 218

O'Callaghan M., 7
O'Connor, F. 15, 35, 81,
83, 229, 230, 235, 236
O'Donnell, E. E. 15
O'Kane, D. 15
O'Malley,P. 25
O'Neill, Captain Terence 33,
34, 38
Oakes, P. J. 16
Oerter, R. 18
Official Unionist 182, 236
Olbrich, E. 19
Oliver, Q. 48, 237, 238
Olympic Games 188, 189
open-mindedness 5
opposition in Stormont 32
Opsahl Commission 6
Opsahl, Torkvel 46
Orbell, S. 7
Osborne, R. D. 5, 239
outreach 12, 119
Owen, D. 22, 145
Oyserman, D. 191, 192, 194

PAFT (Policy Appraisal and
Fair Treatment guidelines)
44
Palley, C. 25
Palomari, A. 18
paper round 131
paramilitaries 34, 233, 236
parent-child resemblances 22
parental attitudes, 170
control, effects for
females, males,
Protestants, Catholics
101; employment 11
occupations 53
political ideology 170
political interests, 169

salience 12, 24, 100, 102,
111, 112, 117, 127, 200,
201, 218, 232
support 101, 10
effects for females,
males, Protestants,
Catholics 101
parenting styles 100
parents as drivers 110
parents 14, 20, 22, 29, 53,
72, 83, 106, 109, 118,
120, 124, 218, 230
joint salience 219
reproducing ideologies 23
Parham, T. 26
Parke, R. D. 3, 52, 118
Parker, T. 40
Patterson, H. 9, 30, 33, 43,
234,
Pearl, D. 86
peers 14, 25, 72, 170
People's Democracy 34
Perlmutter, M. 118
personal control 191, 194
personal hygiene 103
personal identity 8, 9, 12,
14, 16, 18, 25, 30, 38,
45, 49, 72, 99, 101, 118,
191, 214, 231
personal reponsibility 220
personality development 3, 9
personality differences 15
pet care 121
ownership 128
Petersen, A. C. 194
Phinney, J. 16, 17, 26
physical maturation 18
Piaget, J . 21
Pindas, P. 18, 23, 24, 27,
117
Pinner, F. A. 24
pocket money 51, 55, 59,
60, 61,130, 109, 216;
218,
police 35, 38
political activity 15, 168,
172, 174, 227
attitudes and susceptibility
to change, 26

awareness 169, 170
change 9, 27, 41
conflict 7
cynicism 175
developments 49, 223,
227
distrust 24
inefficacy 175
information 24, 145, 169,
170, 173
influence of parents and
peers 169
knowledge 172
learning in children 26
orientation 173
parties 177, 178, 180,
182, 183
socialization 24, 169, 173
politics scores 176
Pollak, A. 46
Pombeni, M. L. 18
Poole, M. E. 72
Poole, M.A. 25
positive future orientation
194
positive self-concept 26
possible selves 4, 9, 12, 17,
23, 25, 26, 100, 119, 191,
194, 198, 205, 213, 214,
215,
pouring and peeling 124
power-sharing executive 41,
43, 45
Powers, S. I. 100
PPRU (Policy, Planning and
Research Unit, Belfast)
215
Pratt, C. 72
preferential employment
policies 40
prejudice 5, 15
Prentice, D. A. 14, 16, 192
President of Russia 179 182
President of USA 179 181
Prime Minister 177, 181
Prior, James 41
problems between
communities 6

procedural knowledge 12, 18,
23, 48, 72, 144, 237
prorogation of Stormont 36
protectiveness 24, 117, 119,
124, 139, 173, 219, 221,
227
factors 9, 129
Protestant 2, 4, 5, 9, 10, 30,
32, 33, 34, 35, 40, 42,
43, 45, 49, 101, 111, 172,
178, 216, 236, 237, 239,
psychiatric morbidity 7
psychoanalytic 20, 100
psychological development 8
research in NI 29
psychological reactions to the
'Troubles' 3, 7, 117
psychosocial theory 20
psychoticism 7
public expenditure 44
Puccetti, M. C. 9

qualifications 199, 201, 213,
229
quangoes (quasi auntonomous
non-governmental
organizations) 31, 38
questionnaire 2, 11, 30, 37,
53, 73, 102, 165, 174,
186, 188
Questions 11, 24, 53, 54,
73, 74
access to newspapers 146
access to radio news 146
access to television news
146
aims of education 195
analysis 12
club membership and
attendance 122
control 104
household chores 121
ideal and realistic
aspirations 197
nurturance/support 103
on current affairs 174
on sport 175
pet care 121
urban survival 119

what recalled from newspaper 153 wishes 196
happy people 197
jobs done to earn money 123
away without the family 123
Quicke, J., 22

radio 23, 108, 144, 168, 222
how many listened to news 150
recency of listening 150
Raven, J. 168
Rea, D. 15
reading 73, 74, 83
reappraisal by Catholics 33
by Protestants 33
reconciliation 1, 39, 46, 49, 238
Records/tapes 67
Rees, Merlyn 41
Reference group orientation 15, 16, 26, 214;
reforms 33, 34, 36, 38
Reid, N. 239
relaxation 117, 238
religious instruction 5
Renshon, S. A. 24
Republic of Ireland 15, 25, 30, 31, 33, 34, 53, 101, 136, 170, 171, 173 174, 178, 182
republicans 35, 35, 37, 42, 43
research problems 28, 52
resilience 2, 8, 9, 99, 101, 106, 117, 129, 220
responsibility 32, 46, 101, 104, 105, 113, 116, 145, 192, 194, 207, 227, 229
Rhodes, J. 40
Ribak, R. 23
Rice, K. 20
riot 31, 35, 42, 75
Roberts, D. F. 72, 84, 86, 131, 144

Robinson, J. P. 5, 6, 144, 163, 164, 169, 223
Roddy, R. J. 7
Rodriguez-Tomé, H. 18, 22, 29
Rogers, E. M. 24
Rolston, B. 38, 40, 47, 53
Rooney, E. 29, 101, 107, 111
Rose, R. 5, 15
Rosenberg, M. 173
Rowlands, B. 48
Royal Irish Rangers 54
RTE 186
RUC (Royal Ulster Constabulary) 35, 42, 54, 235
Rudinger, G. 3, 22
Rudkin, L. 191, 193
Runyan, W. McK. 3, 19
Russell, J. 15
Rutherford, W. H. 7
Rutter, M. 7, 129

SACHR (Standing Advisory Commission on Human Rights) 44, 53
salience, composite measure 102
of father 111
of local current affairs items 153
of local events on television news 156
of mother 111
of parents 20, 111, 219, 224, 228
of school 227ff
of television 164
Salters, J. 15
Sarigiani, P. A. 194
Saturday activities 80
savings 55, 65
scaffolding 14, 16
Sceery, A. 100
Schaie, K. W. 3
Schleuder, J. 144
Schmidt,R. W. 194

schools 4, 5, 25;
    in the study 11
Schwartz, J. M. 100, 173
Schweder, R. A. 14
Scotland 7, 136
SDLP (Social Democratic and
    Labour Party) 42, 178,
    182
Sears, D. O. 24
sectarian 35, 47, 48, 237
segregation 49
    in housing 6, 238
    education 3, 4, 6, 49
Seiffke-Krenke, L. 19
self-centred values 169
self-concept 1, 2, 3, 4, 5, 6,
    8, 12, 14, 16, 17, 18, 21,
    26, 29, 38, 49, 56, 72,
    119, 130, 144, 191, 207,
    214, 219, 222, 231
    definition 17
    stability and change 16,
    192
self-confidence 16, 19, 48
self-development 196, 204,
    205, 206, 210, 229
self-direction 25
self-efficacy 8, 17, 18, 19,
    108, 117, 119, 128, 131,
    138, 145, 171, 173, 191,
    192, 215, 220
self-esteem 17, 19, 24, 26,
    48, 50, 72, 101, 107, 110,
    117, 118, 131, 139, 145,
    191, 192, 194, 215, 217,
    219, 226, 230, 237
    and interest in public
    affairs, 173
Selman, R. L. 21
Shivers, L. 49
shop job 131, 132
shopping 75, 120, 128, 131
Shulman, S. 19
Sidanius, J. 170
Siegel, J. 100
Sigel, R. 27, 174
Silbereisen, R. K. 3, 22, 52
Simmons, R. G. 29, 118
Simons, R. L. 118

Singleton,D. 25
Sinn Fein 37, 41, 42, 43,
    178, 182, 236
Slomczynski, K. M. 25, 29
slot machine 72
Smith, A. 5
Smith, D. J. 37
Smith, T. E. 22, 29
smoking 75
snooker players 187
Soap operas 86, 88
Social Democratic and Labour
    Party (SDLP) 41
social activity and cognitive
    processes 21
social address model 2
social categorization 6, 16
social comparison 6
social conditions 7, 21, 40,
    100, 216
social distance 15
social identity theory 1, 6
social identity 6, 25, 26, 99
social injustice 7
social institutions 23
social intelligence 9, 12, 18,
    23, 24, 28, 144, 214, 215
    223
social issues and adolescents
    168
social learning 193
    theories 20, 23
social policy 38, 44
    and support for cultural
    traditions 238
    changes 45
social structures 3, 4, 18,
    25, 26, 27, 46, 117, 226
socialization 2, 3, 8, 9, 10,
    19, 21, 22, 23, 30, 100,
    102, 170, 214, 226
    and future orientation 234
societal structures 7, 8, 9,
    10, 14, 21, 27, 29, 38,
    49, 235
    and generativity 233
socio-cultural theories 20

socio-economic level 10, 120, 127, 170, 215, 227, 228, 234
and future orientation 231
and declarative knowledge 223
and 'Autonomy' 114
socio-historical influences on political knowledge 170
Spenner, K. I. 193
sports 72, 75, 77, 80, 81, 88, 169, 172, 184, 188, 217, 223, 227
Stacey, B. 170
standard of living 12, 51, 56
Steinberg, L. 100
Steinkopf, K. 23
stereotyping 5, 95
Stewart, A. T. Q. 15, 25
Stone, V. 23
storm and stress 18, 19
Stormont 31, 32, 33, 34, 35, 38, 227
stress 1, 48, 130, 227
Stryker, S. 191
student activism 20
subvention 40
Sullivan, M. A. 14
Sunday activities 81
survival, composite variable 123
and socio-economic level 139
skills 19, 220
Sweden 72
Swedish high school students 170
Swift, B. 169

tabloids 160
Tajfel, H. 6
Tallman, I. 18, 23, 24, 27, 117
Targeting Social Need 44
Taoiseach (Prime Minister of Republic of Ireland) 177, 178
Taylor, R. L. 52
teachers 172

Teague, P. 40
team sport 88
teenage romance 85
telephone directory 123
telephone 55, 215
using a public telephone 121
television 23, 72, 73, 74, 75, 76, 79, 81, 86, 108, 144, 163, 164, 168, 217, 222
how many watched News 148
leveling effects of 88
recency of watching news 149
items recalled 155
girls' and boys' preferred programmes 86
Thatcher, Margaret 42, 177, 181, 183
Thomas, D. L. 29, 101, 107, 111
Tipton, L. P. 145
tolerance 15, 22, 24, 27
Tomlinson M., 40, 53
Toner, I. 9, 36, 136
Törestad, B. 14, 192
Torney-Purta J, 26, 145, 168, 169, 171, 183
Townshend, C. 15
traditions 5
recognition of 44
training 207, 208
travel 19, 123, 125, 129, 131, 135ff
composite variable 138
relationship with other variables 141
Trew, K. 1, 4, 5, 6, 7, 15, 16, 37, 53, 99, 100, 136, 172, 191
triple-minority situation 25
Trommsdorff, G. 192, 193, 194
'Troubles' 1, 7, 25, 30, 34, 37, 52, 73, 76, 101, 106, 118, 129, 160, 164, 196, 218

related violence 1981 and
1992 37
variation by intensity,
quality, location 36
Troy, M. 7
Tupling, C. 7
Turner I. F. 191
Turner, J. C. 3, 16
Turner, J. 3
Tyrrell, J. 49, 238

Ulster Defence Regiment 54
Ulster Volunteer Force 34,
35
Ulster Workers Council. 41
Ulster Workers' Strike 43
unemployment 39, 40, 50,
53, 216, 219, 230
Unionist MPs 43
unionists 31, 32, 35, 41, 43,
178
United Kingdom (UK) 22,
25, 31, 32, 40, 50, 53,
164, 171, 173
United States (USA) 8, 33,
72, 84, 136, 168, 169,
173
UNO 179, 183
urban survival 119

Valsiner, J. 21
value systems 25, 26, 101,
117, 140, 168, 169
Van Hasselt,V. B. 3
van der Linden, F. J. 18, 117
van Duinen, E. 27
Vannan, E. J. 100
Vicary, J. R. 194
Vietnam War 27
violence 1, 3, 7, 8, 29, 35,
36, 37, 49, 191
effects not so negative as
feared 7
variations in intensity,
quality and location 9
direct effects 3
Visiting relations 75, 81,
83, 217
voting 168, 177, 182

by young people, 169

Wackman, D.B. 23
Wade, G. 26
Wales 135
Walker, P. 6
Ward, L. S. 145
Watergate 27
Weigert, A. 29, 101, 195,
11
Weinstein, L. 72
Werner, E. E. 129
Westminster 31, 32, 35, 38,
41, 42, 46, 171
Whelan, C. T. 168
White, R. 192
Whitelaw, William 36, 41
Whyte, John 15, 30, 31, 35,
40, 172
Whyte, Jean 2, 7, 53, 174,
188
Wichert, S. 9, 30, 32, 35,
40, 42
Williams, T. 3, 72, 170
Williamson, A. 239
Willis, P. 171
Wilson, R. 1, 3, 4, 6, 7, 9,
16, 37, 49, 100, 194, 238
wishes 196ff
women 46, 50
employment, 40
Woods, R. 40
Worall, E. 49
Worell, J. 118
World Cup 184, 186, 188
Wright, F. 33
Wulff, H. 72

Yang, S. 144, 169
Yankelovich, D. 27
Youth Club 67, 133
Yule, Q. 7

Zellman, G. L. 24
Zigler, E. 128